D1562976

Crusading in the Fifteenth Century

Crusading in the Fifteenth Century
Message and Impact

Edited by

Norman Housley

First published 2004 by
PALGRAVE MACMILLAN
Houndmills, Basingstoke, Hampshire RG21 6XS and
175 Fifth Avenue, New York, N.Y. 10010
Companies and representatives throughout the world.

PALGRAVE MACMILLAN is the global academic imprint of the Palgrave Macmillan division of St. Martin's Press, LLC and of Palgrave Macmillan Ltd. Macmillan® is a registered trademark in the United States, United Kingdom and other countries. Palgrave is a registered trademark in the European Union and other countries.

ISBN 1–4039–0283–6 hardback

This book is printed on paper suitable for recycling and made from fully managed and sustained forest sources.

A catalogue record for this book is available from the British Library.

Library of Congress Cataloging-in-Publication Data
    Crusading in the fifteenth century: message and impact / edited by Norman Housley.
        p. cm.
    Includes bibliographical references and index.
    ISBN 1–4039–0283–6
        1. Crusades – Later, 13th, 14th, and 15th centuries. 2. Europe – Social conditions – 15th century. 3. Europe – History – 15th century. I. Housley, Norman.

D172.C83 2004
940.2'1—dc22   2004048577

10 9 8 7 6 5 4 3 2 1
13 12 11 10 09 08 07 06 05 04

Printed and bound in Great Britain by
Antony Rowe Ltd, Chippenham and Eastbourne.

Contents

List of Illustrations

Notes on the Contributors

János M. Bak is Professor of Medieval Studies at the Central European University of Budapest and has published extensively on the social and legal history of Hungary and its neighbours.

Nancy Bisaha teaches at Vassar College. She is the author of a book and several articles on humanism and crusade: *Creating East and West: Renaissance Humanists and the Ottoman Turks* (University of Pennsylvania Press, 2004); 'Pope Pius II's Letter to Sultan Mehmed II: A Reexamination', *Crusades* 1 (2002); and 'Petrarch's Vision of the Muslim and Byzantine East', *Speculum* 76 (2001).

John Edwards is Senior Research Fellow in Spanish at the University of Oxford. He has published extensively on Spain and on the Jews in the Middle Ages, in particular *Christian Córdoba. The City and its Region in the Late Middle Ages* (Cambridge, 1982); *The Jews in Christian Europe, 1400–1700* (London, 1988); *The Jews in Western Europe, 1400–1600* (Manchester, 1994); *Religion and Society in Spain, c. 1492* (Aldershot, 1996); *The Spanish Inquisition* (2nd edition Stroud, 2003); and *The Spain of the Catholic Monarchs, 1474–1520* (Oxford, 2000).

Johannes Helmrath is Professor of Medieval History at The Humboldt University in Berlin. He is author of *Das Basler Konzil 1431–1449* (Cologne: Böhlau, 1987), and of several articles about conciliar and parliamentary history, the humanist Aeneas Silvius Piccolomini, and European humanism. He is preparing a book on Piccolomini and oratory at the German *Reichstage*.

Norman Housley is Professor of History at the University of Leicester. He has written several books on the history of the later crusades, in particular *The Later Crusades, 1274–1580: From Lyons to Alcazar* (Oxford, 1992); *Documents on the Later Crusades, 1274–1580* (Basingstoke, 1996); *Crusading and Warfare in Medieval and Renaissance Europe* (Aldershot, 2001); and *Religious Warfare in Europe, 1400–1536* (Oxford, 2002).

Margaret Meserve teaches at the University of Notre Dame. She has published several articles on the historical and political writing of humanists on the Islamic East. She is translating the *Commentaries* of Pope Pius II for the I Tatti Renaissance Library (vol. 1 appeared in

2003), and writing a book on the historiography of Islam in the Renaissance.

Natalia Nowakowska has recently completed a doctoral thesis on Cardinal Fryderyk Jagiellon, Prince of Poland (1468–1503) at Lincoln College, University of Oxford.

Jacques Paviot is Professor of Medieval History at Université de Paris XII – Val de Marne. He is author of *La Politique navale des ducs de Bourgogne, 1384–1482* (Lille, 1995), and *Portugal et Bourgogne au XVe siècle* (Lisbon-Paris 1995). He organized and published the international colloquium *Nicopolis 1396–1996* (Dijon, *Annales de Bourgogne*, 1997). His most recent book is *Les Ducs de Bourgogne, la croisade et l'Orient (fin XIVe s.– Xve s.)* (Paris, 2003).

Claudius Sieber-Lehmann teaches medieval history at the University of Basel. His dissertation was published as *Spätmittelalterlicher Nationalismus. Die Burgunderkriege am Oberrhein und in der Eidgenossenschaft*, Veröffentlichungen des Max-Planck-Instituts für Geschichte Nr. 116 (Göttingen 1995).

Nicolas Vatin is Director of Research at the CNRS (Paris), and Director of Studies at the École Pratique des Hautes Études (IVe Section). A specialist in Ottoman history, he has published, among other studies, *L'Ordre de Saint-Jean-de-Jérusalem, l'Empire ottoman et la Méditerranée orientale entre les deux sièges de Rhodes (1480–1522)* (Louvain-Paris, 1995); *Sultan Djem. Un prince ottoman dans l'Europe du XVe siècle d'après deux sources contemporaines* (Ankara, 1997); *Rhodes et l'ordre de Saint-Jean-de-Jérusalem* (Paris, 2000); and *Les Ottomans et l'Occident (XVe s.–XVIe s.)* (Istanbul, 2001).

Preface

I am grateful to Luciana O'Flaherty for accepting the proposal for this collection of essays, and for showing patience in the face of delays. The essays by Johannes Helmrath, Jacques Paviot, Claudius Sieber-Lehmann and Nicolas Vatin were translated by myself, and I apologize to the authors for any inaccuracies or infelicities that resulted.

Norman Housley
Leicester, June 2004

1
Introduction

Norman Housley

Crusading in the fifteenth century

In August 1463 the Cardinal-legate John Bessarion issued detailed instructions 'to the preachers appointed by him to preach the cross in the illustrious city of Venice and its lordship'.[1] Bessarion began by outlining the framework for the preaching campaign that he envisaged. He divided the Venetian lands into zones and allocated them to his preachers. They could conscript other clerics to assist them and had the authority to remit 100 days' enjoined penance to people who came to hear them preach the crusade. They were to preach on all feast-days and other occasions as they saw fit, and they were to exhort their audiences to take the cross to fight personally, to send substitutes or donate money or items that could later be sold. Helpfully, for both his preachers and for us, the cardinal sketched out the themes he intended his appointees to use. These revolved around the cross as 'the most potent symbol of our salvation' and the justice and sanctity of the struggle against the Turks. 'Those who up to this point have lived badly, involving themselves in murders, thefts, rapes, arson and all manner of crimes' were now being offered the chance to redeem themselves and earn eternal life.

Bessarion went further. He provided the wording of the prayer that was to be said when the cross, made of red silk or cloth, was pinned with a needle to the breast of the *crucesignandus*, who would later sew it firmly into place. He outlined the formula of the absolution and the wording of the letter that the *crucesignatus* was to receive conferring on him the plenary indulgence, including the variants that were to be used in the case of substitutes and their sponsors. He set out guidelines relating to groups of religious who clubbed together to send fighters, and he called for collection chests to be set up and for weekly masses to be said on behalf of the crusade. Domestic opposition also received his attention: anybody who impeded the crusade preaching was to be excommunicated, and absolution was to be denied to those who defrauded funds collected for the crusade, transported arms to the Turks or their allies, or placed obstacles in the path of crusaders seeking to fulfil their vows. And Bessarion was realistic enough to allow his preachers to draw five ducats a month as a subsistence allowance from the money that they collected.

Bessarion's instructions of 1463 are a remarkable synthesis of the old and the new. Certain themes, such as the fall of Constantinople and the threat that the Turks posed to home and hearth, were relative newcomers to crusading rhetoric. 'The Turk, not content [with what he has], is making eager preparations to subjugate the entire world, starting with Italy.' Other themes, like the atrocities committed by the Turks, their destruction of relics and their taunting of Christians, the call for vengeance, the imperative to defend fellow Christians in the East, the potency of the cross and the summons to repentance, were as old as Urban II's preaching at Clermont in 1095. And here, in a nutshell, is the paradox that confronts the serious student of crusading in the fifteenth century. Faced with documents like this one, nobody could seriously deny that the crusade was still being preached with vigour in the mid-fifteenth century and that Catholics had as much opportunity to earn redemption through penitential combat as their forefathers had for three centuries before them. It is true that the cardinal's text forms one thread in a very large tapestry: the last big attempt to organize a broad-based *passagium* against the Turks, to which its author, Pope Pius II, devoted an unusual amount of his time and energy. But if it was a particularly impressive enterprise, it was far from unique. Crusading, in other words, was an important feature of the period; it formed a part of people's lives. Yet a case can also be made for the viewpoint that this crusading did not cut deep into contemporary affairs, that it was reactive, formulaic and lacked popular resonance. According to this view, it was reactive because, without the threat posed to Catholic Christianity by the Turks, it is possible that there would have been no crusading at all. Bessarion's appeal to self-interest makes this clear: 'If we are unmoved by love for religion and calamity [in the East], let us be moved by our country, our homes, our children, our family, and our wives.' It was formulaic because the essential features of crusade preaching and of taking the cross had long since been clarified and made subject to the centralized direction of the Church. The chain of command, from Pius II down to those clerics who were dragooned into service by Bessarion's appointees, is apparent. As for lack of resonance at grass roots level, Pius II's own lament in his *Commentaries* constitutes powerful testimony to it. People no longer believed what was said by those in authority in the Church; 'like insolvent tradesmen we are without credit'.[2]

It is thus possible to adopt very different positions on crusading in the fifteenth century: that the volume of surviving evidence forces us to take it seriously as an expression of religious life that possessed numerous political and cultural ramifications, or that it was a stale and sterile response to the new Islamic threat. In the past historians have taken up both positions as well as others lying somewhere in between.[3] In many cases their approach has derived from their own perspective on these events. Steven Runciman's well-known *A History of the Crusades* makes a good starting point. The brief Runciman set himself was to tell the story of the Latin settlements in the Holy Land and of the series of great expeditions (*passagia*) that established them and helped defend them against their Islamic neighbours. From that point of view it made methodological sense to end in 1291, which also provided a satisfying grand finale in terms of narrative structure. But Runciman was by training and sympathy a Byzantinist. He viewed the crusades to the Holy Land, and the states which they set up in Syria and Palestine, essentially as intrusions into a region which remained alien to the western Europeans involved, and he believed that their impact on the history of Byzantium was disastrous. The Fourth Crusade and the Latin conquest of Constantinople weakened the Byzantine Empire irreparably and laid the basis for the fall of the capital to the Ottoman Turks in 1453. For Runciman it was the latter date that gave true closure to his story, so he wrote an epilogue, entitled 'The Last Crusades', that dealt not just with projects to recover the Holy Land after 1291, but also with western attempts to defend Constantinople. Nor could he resist continuing past 1453 to include the crusade ambitions of Pope Pius II. Indeed, there was a narrative logic in doing so, for Pius's inability to rekindle the enthusiasm aroused by Pope Urban II at Clermont, and his death at Ancona in August 1464 while awaiting the arrival of an army which did not exist, formed conclusions which were as convincing as the Mamluk conquest of Acre in 1291. In a sense, therefore, Runciman's account has two conclusions, one bringing to a close the epic of Latin Christendom's occupation of the holy places, and the second approaching the crusades from the broader viewpoint of relations between Western and Eastern Christianity. Both were sombre perspectives, telling a tale of prejudice, misunderstandings and disasters, but the second had more tragic dimensions because of the opportunities that were lost and the many lives that were ruined as a result.[4]

Runciman's view was that from the imperial palaces of Constantinople. A rather different perspective was held by those whose native lands were subjugated and in some cases occupied by the Turks. They had a deep sense of the historical significance of events that played such a large part in shaping the histories of their countries, in some cases right up to the wars of liberation in the late nineteenth and early twentieth centuries. One of the most intriguing collections of sources for fifteenth-century crusading is Nicolae Iorga's *Notes et extraits pour servir à l'histoire des croisades au XV siècle*, published in six series between 1899 and 1916. The *Notes et extraits* is a remarkable series illustrating both the strengths and the weaknesses of its editor. It consists of hundreds of documents about the Turkish advance in the Balkans and attempts to resist it, transcribed in dozens of libraries and archives scattered across Europe in the years before the First World War by a man whose stamina has surely never been surpassed in the historical profession. In his preface to series four, Iorga wrote with nostalgia of his 'projet de jeunesse',

> une histoire de l'idée de la croisade après les dernières expéditions dirigées contre la Syrie ou l'Égypte du Soudan, c'est-à-dire des projets formés à partir du XV-e siècle et des combats portés au nom du même idéal qui avait inspiré jadis Godefroy de Bouillon, mais contre des ennemis nouveaux, les Turcs établis en Europe pour fonder et dominer une Byzance musulmane.[5]

Reading the *Notes et extraits* in the light of Iorga's formidably learned early study, *Philippe de Mézières (1327–1405) et la croisade au XIVe siècle* (Paris, 1896), it is hard not to regret the diversion of efforts which occurred. Iorga was a polymath and an exceptionally gifted scholar. He was capable of dictating a 350-page history of his native land in 28 hours and he maintained a scarcely credible pace of work: in a single year, 1928, he wrote 46 books, gave 370 lectures and attended 64 conferences.[6] Yet it may be misguided to regret such a lost work. Iorga's central concern was the history of Romania and of the succession of powers that had occupied it. What drove him to collect and publish his texts on the crusades was his burning nationalism, and his determination to fill the distressing lacunae that existed in Romanian history and made it vulnerable to the territorial claims of its more powerful neighbours. This nationalism, coupled with his strong sense of public duty, led him to invest his energies in numerous other projects, scholarly, literary, educational and journalistic; above all, he pursued a career in politics, which did not suit his temperament and ended with his assassination by the Romanian fascists in 1940. His sheer speed of production, moreover, bore a price in terms of care and accuracy. It is characteristic that the later volumes of the *Notes et extraits* carry no editorial system or apparatus: the impression they give is that Iorga was keen to rush as many documents into print as quickly as possible. His later scholarly works were criticized for their errors.[7]

It is not hard to imagine how a multi-volume *Histoire des croisades au XVe siècle* written by Nicolae Iorga would have read. Although he was fascinated by the Ottoman Empire and wrote a highly praised history of it,[8] his underlying belief in the national principle caused him to view the Ottoman conquests as a retrograde step in the development of the Balkan peoples. In particular, it was the historic mission of Romania to act as western Europe's *antemurale*. It was a land where the best elements of Latin, Germanic and Slavic influences coexisted, and the Romanians could only achieve their full potential if these elements were held in balance. In the same way, extraneous influences, be they Muslim or Jewish, were detrimental to the flowering of the national character and must be resisted. When it was associated with the heroic resistance of the Balkan peoples, the crusade was regarded as by definition a good thing, 'les nobles efforts faits, à l'époque de la Renaissance triomphante, par l'Europe chrétienne pour s'opposer à l'envahissement des "barbares" asiatiques'.[9] Attempts to organize it merited praise, contemporary sceptics were dismissed as misguided and ultimate failure was a cause for regret. It would be harsh to censure a scholar of Iorga's generation too heavily for holding to value judgements such as these: explicitly or implicitly they have characterized a good deal of the more recent scholarship. In 1979 a Turkish delegate at a NATO meeting held in Fort St Angelo, the great Maltese fortress of the Knights of St John, commented, 'I believe I am the first Turk that has penetrated this far'.[10] Such jocularity was a breakthrough of sorts: it is hard to imagine it being expressed even a generation previously.

A residual anti-Turkish sentiment can be detected even in the work of the scholar who has come closer than anybody else to providing a full account of the crusading response to the Turkish advance, the American Kenneth M. Setton. In his monumental four-volume *The Papacy and the Levant (1204–1571)* (1976–84) Setton set himself the task of describing the papacy's relations with the East from the Fourth Crusade to the battle of Lepanto in 1571. Of necessity this entailed a detailed treatment of all crusading projects directed towards the East, though they were woven in with accounts of papal negotiations with Byzantium and the Christian Churches in the East. On the other hand, the emergence of the Ottoman threat in the fifteenth century, coupled with the papal resort to crusade as a means of resisting it, meant that Setton's second volume, which deals with the period 1402–1503, is to all intents and purposes an account of papal crusading activity during these years. Setton's scholarly interests, and to a large extent his sympathies, were divided between Rome and Venice, with whose archives he was very familiar.[11] This was beneficial because while he gave full attention to the efforts made by the popes to regenerate crusading activity, he accorded equal weight to the host of commercial and political factors which in the case of Venice above all (though far from uniquely) stood in the way of these efforts succeeding. In the breadth of his scholarly concerns, his massive learning and his close familiarity with archival documents, Setton sometimes reminds one of Iorga, but by focusing on his planned study over a long period of time, and deploying meticulous scholarly techniques, he was able to deliver the detailed study of crusading activity which had eluded the Romanian.

That said, volume II of *The Papacy and the Levant* is not a definitive account of anti-Ottoman crusading activity. There are several reasons for this. One is that, as I have already mentioned, Setton was unable to be completely objective in his treatment of the Turks. This is not to say that he displayed prejudice, rather that he was content to convey the stereotyped and demonic portrayal of the Turks that he encountered in his sources, instead of trying to probe the underlying values and views of the world that created and sustained such images. This reflected Setton's most serious scholarly failing, his lack of interest in analysis as a tool of historical study. The condemnation of 'l'histoire événementielle' which occurred in the 1960s and 1970s, the veneration for structured analysis as the only credible explanatory mechanism available to the professional historian, and the eventual reinstatement of narrative as a respectable approach, were trends which bypassed Setton altogether. Throughout his career he preferred the narrative mode, the alternative being a style of essay which reads less like intellectual engagement than a leisurely stroll in the company of a learned and urbane guide.[12] For all its remarkable qualities *The Papacy and the Levant* is best approached not as a work of history but as a mediated form of source collection; it is rich in quotations from and references to original documents, but its author rarely used them to recreate why things happened as they did. Moreover, despite his remark that the historian 'opens up the approach to the hovels of the poor as well as to the palaces of the great',[13] Setton was fascinated by court and governmental records, the sources of the elite, above all those of the papacy and Venice. This meant that when examining crusading projects he rarely followed the trail beyond the issuing of bulls decreeing preaching and the collection of funds. His love for a good story led him to describe what happened at 'ground floor level' in the case of great events such as the fall of Constantinople in 1453, the relief of Belgrade in 1456 and the defence of Rhodes in 1480. But he showed little interest in the 'middle ground' of crusade preaching and recruitment, together with its essential backcloth, the place which crusading held in contemporary culture. This means that the view that we acquire of crusading from *The Papacy and the Levant* is partial and selective; it resembles the picture of contemporary life that would result from reading only *The Financial Times* or *The Economist*.

Kenneth Setton's other major contribution to the subject came in his editing of the multi-volume *History of the Crusades* (second edition 1969–90). We might expect that this, the most ambitious post-war collaborative treatment of the crusades, would offer the analysis that *The Papacy and the Levant* fails to deliver. Such hopes are bolstered by the fact that the crusades which occurred after 1291 are given a good deal of attention, with the whole of volume III dedicated to the fourteenth and fifteenth centuries and further chapters on this period appearing in volume VI. Unfortunately, the chapters on crusading in the fifteenth century are not strong. It is perhaps inevitable that in a collaborative work, no central argument emerges relating to the place which crusading held in fifteenth-century society. But even the descriptions of military activity, whether it was conducted by crusading forces or by the Knights of St John, exist without more than a cursory consideration of the role which was played by religious values and beliefs in the mobilization of men and the raising of money.

To date, then, fifteenth-century crusading has not been accorded a comprehensive and in-depth study, despite attracting the attention of scholars of the calibre of Nicolae Iorga and Kenneth Setton. On the other hand, it has generated an encouraging number of studies addressing specific aspects or episodes in the struggle to hold back the Turks by crusading means. If these studies do not fully address the central issue of vitality or decline, they do provide a scaffolding of scholarship which makes that issue easier to approach with confidence. The work of Setton and others on the papacy as the initiating authority has, for example, been complemented by a broad range of published studies on the role played by the dukes of Burgundy and their court. In these works, moreover, the continuing appeal of crusading and its roots in court and chivalric culture have received the attention they require, because the Burgundian response to the Ottoman advance and the resulting papal exhortations to take action was obviously much more than a simple defence mechanism.[14]

In accounts of Burgundian interest in crusading against the Turks the emphasis often placed on copying the deeds of ancestors and Christian heroes from the past has the effect of pointing to an essential continuity in ideals and attitudes. Much the same can be said of Portuguese crusading enthusiasm in the age of Henry 'the Navigator'.[15] But an important strand in the most recent research has demonstrated the impact on crusading goals and rhetoric of the new humanist values. A large group of scholars, including Nancy Bisaha, Robert Black, James Hankins, Johannes Helmrath and Margaret Meserve, have explored the symbiosis of the New Learning with crusading which was achieved by Italian humanists like Benedetto Accolti, Francesco Filelfo and, most notably, Aeneas Silvius Piccolomini (Pope Pius II).[16] It is becoming apparent that the coexistence of old and new ideas within crusading in this period is an important consideration in achieving a balance between the positive and negative views on the subject outlined above, because it is only when we have a full view of what crusading actually meant to contemporaries that we can gauge their receptivity to it.

Another area of research characterized by impressive recent output is the early history of the Ottoman Turks. Thanks to the scholarship of men like Franz Babinger, Kenneth Setton's generation was far from being ill-informed on the enemy faced by crusading enthusiasts, but more recently scholars such as Daniel Goffman, Colin Imber and Cemal Kafadar have analysed afresh both the sultanate's fourteenth-century origins and the nature of its drive to conquest once it had recovered from Timur the Lame's devastating onslaught.[17] This is highly relevant to the crusading response to that drive. Our overall view of the military viability of the West's reaction is obviously shaped in part by our evaluation of its Turkish adversary. This applies in particular to certain key events, such as the relief of Belgrade in 1456 and the defence of Rhodes in 1480, our reading of which hinges on our knowledge of the Turkish military system and the efficiency with which it was put to work in specific campaigns. And the comparative quiescence of the Balkan peoples in the face of Turkish conquest becomes easier to comprehend once such easily demonized features of the Ottoman system as the *devşirme* (the round-up of promising Christian children for enlistment in the sultan's service) are properly understood. It is possible that the shrill denunciation of the Turks which we encounter in the writings of

Bessarion and Pius II derived from the unpalatable fact that Turkish conquest was actually not that painful an experience. This may be deduced from the way in which the rule of some Christian princes came to be unfavourably contrasted with that of the sultan. The extent of contemporaries' knowledge of the Turks is a problematic issue, but clearly the more we know about the nature of the sultanate and the goals of its ruling cadres, the more confident we can feel in assessing the public response in the West which, it is increasingly clear, was both subject to change and more nuanced than one might expect.[18]

Message and impact

The twofold agenda of this collection of essays can best be illustrated by returning to the Bessarion text of 1463. First, there are clear gains to be made from focusing on what the message of crusading consisted of in the fifteenth-century context. This is partly because of the entry of new themes, values and language into the discourse of crusade. It is also because the message differed in accordance with both circumstances and audience. In our 1463 text, for example, Bessarion made great play of the fall of Constantinople ten years previously, and of the fact that Venice was now at war with the sultan.

> The rulers of Venice have taken up arms against the Turks, and must persevere until the death of the last enemy, and others should be encouraged by their example, since through heaven's favour they are the most powerful and worthy of all Christians. Also, their lands are nearer to the Turks.

In other words, a person moved to take the cross, above all in the lands subject to Venice, could expect encouragement and perhaps assistance from the state in fulfilling their vow. More generally, the message that reached Hungary was couched in terms of that kingdom's *antemurale* function, a role to which the Knights of St John also made repeated claim in their fund-raising techniques.

In the Iberian lands the message varied even more. The crusade for which Bessarion hoped to recruit in 1463 was preached in Castile, where it aroused an amount of interest which disconcerted the king, and the papal curia repeatedly hoped to enlist the services of the king of Aragon/Naples and his fleet against the Ottoman Turks. But in Iberia the *cruzada* normally meant the war against the Moorish emirate of Granada. In Castile the historic duty of reconquest (*Reconquista*) was taken seriously by the kings and their critics, while their neighbours in Portugal let no opportunity slip to climb aboard the crusading bandwagon by claiming equivalent rights and privileges for the warfare they were conducting or sponsoring in Morocco, West Africa and the Atlantic Islands.[19] The message of Iberian crusading both resembled and differed from that of the anti-Turkish conflict. From a just war perspective, the Castilian *Reconquista* could be likened to the defensive struggle in the East. Portuguese expansion, on the other hand, was couched in somewhat different terms, those of expanding the limits of the Christian faith through the encouragement of conversion.

These variations in the crusading message can be monitored with relative ease though the study of such evidence as papal bulls of crusade and instructions like those issued by Bessarion. But the message was not communicated in this way only. To begin with, the words on the page give us at best a shadow of what was experienced by people who attended crusade sermons, which always contained an element of improvization and at their most elaborate were carefully orchestrated in a way which came close to modern multi-media events.[20] The 'spin' put on the message in such circumstances by gifted preachers who were skilled at 'reading' the reactions of their audiences, and made immediate adjustments to their material in response to them, can only be guessed at. In addition, the crusading message was communicated through secular means, above all to audiences within a chivalric milieu. One of the most famous occasions on which an attempt was made to recruit crusaders in this period was Duke Philip the Good's 'Feast of the Pheasant' in 1454, in which banqueting, play-acting, spectacle and display played central roles in summoning the duke's nobles to take arms against the Turks.[21]

Having said that, the message usually remains easier to gauge and describe than its reception. It is clear that a straightforward measurement of impact in terms of people taking the cross or making financial contributions towards crusading is not possible. Let us take the example of Germany. Here much of the responsibility for taking action lay with the imperial estates, without whose financial support military activity was all but impossible to organize. Study of the *Reichtage* reveals a response that was complicated by issues of constitutional reform, regional rivalries, the perennial jockeying for imperial and papal favour, and a consciousness of other threats to the empire, notably the Hussites to the east and Burgundy to the west. In the end, the German estates did fail to rise to the occasion, for which Hungary and some of the Austrian lands paid a heavy price. But to label their response as one of apathy or irresponsibility, though at times it is tempting and certainly reflects the disappointment felt by some contemporaries, including Bessarion, is too glib a judgement. It also fails to take into account the fact that if a military response to the Ottoman advance was not forthcoming, the repeated discussion of the Turkish threat made the *imago turci* one of the most familiar and multifaceted aspects of the empire's religious, political and cultural life from the mid-fifteenth to the mid-sixteenth century. We have to consider the possibility that the deepest impact of the crusade lay not, as in the twelfth and thirteenth centuries, in the raising and despatch of large armies of armed pilgrims, but in the way the preaching, rhetoric and liturgy of the crusade moulded a rapidly changing European society.[22] Too often the assumption has been made that in instances when military consequences were few, the message simply bounced off a soil which had ceased to be receptive to it: in fact, it could have entered the soil and borne quite different fruit.

Sometimes, in any case, the soil did prove fruitful in the way that was hoped for. The preaching of the *cruzada* in Iberia, in particular Castile, is the clearest example. In his *Historia de la Bula de la cruzada en España* (1958) Jose Goñi Gaztambide carefully catalogued the numerous occasions when the *cruzada* was preached in Spain, and its financial returns for the monarchies of Castile and Portugal could clearly be substantial. The crusading message was carefully orchestrated by royal government, and it accorded with periodic waves of eschatology and messianic conviction as well as with chivalric urges. In Iberia, more than anywhere else, the popularity of crusading can scarcely be doubted. Because of the assumption that the *cruzada* meant nothing but the sale of indulgences and the conviction that this was at heart a corrupt practice which undermined devotion, there has been a tendency to view the *cruzada* as discreditable. Certainly, the way it was preached aroused disquiet, yet its close association with the final act of the *Reconquista*, the conquest of Granada, can hardly be questioned, and the broad popularity of this war is not in doubt.

In this respect the problem becomes the very different response that the crusading message achieved in Hungary and Poland. These were territories, especially Hungary, where the threat posed by the Turks was obvious. Here, to use Bessarion's language, country, homes, children, family and wives were at stake; even more than in Castile and Portugal, one would expect the call to arms to have succeeded. But in practice the response was highly problematic. Large-scale armies of crusaders were raised by preaching in Hungary in 1456 and 1514, but on both occasions they were armies of peasants, and in 1514 their crusade mutated into a social revolt. The paralysis of the Hungarian ruling elite is remark-able, and even more than in the case of the German estates, the question must be posed whether this paralysis was political, structural, cultural or some combination of these. The comparison with Poland helps. Once the threat posed by the Teutonic Knights' *Ordensstaat* had been ended with the peace of Thorn in 1466, Poland was in a position to respond more effectively to the Ottoman threat. Its failure to respond to papal promptings seems to have been due to several interlocking causes: the population at large was suspicious of the motives and intentions of the ruling elites in both Church and State, while those elites harboured the hope that the Carpathians provided a sufficient barrier to Ottoman incursions on any large scale (a geographical *antemurale*, in fact), and that the riches of the Danubian plain would prove to be a more seductive prospect.

Whichever geographical area we take and social or political level we inspect, the impact of the crusading message was complex, but remained important. The rulers of Poland and Hungary, and the Knights of St John at Rhodes, welcomed and nurtured the *antemurale* ideology, as the kings of Castile did that of *Reconquista*, not only because it might attract external or release internal resources, but because it flattered their self-image. To view them as coldly and methodically 'milking' the advantages of crusade is almost certainly misguided. The crusade was a part of their present world as well as their heritage from the past and, in the eastern lands, the Turks were advancing. In the case of their subjects, crusading was associated with fraud and disappointment, but it also belonged to their beliefs, and the spiritual benefits conferred by crusade were part of a sacramental system in which they vested their hopes of salvation. It is too easy to dismiss crusading as part of a world which was vanishing as all the regions of Europe moved towards the 'new world' of Reformation, consolidated military structures, and the practice of *Realpolitik*. Such changes were slow and piecemeal, and they incorporated parts of the 'old' world rather than rudely discarding them. This applies to the military and political aspects of crusading, but above all to its place in the religious thinking of contemporaries. Like other features of late medieval religion, the place of crusading becomes harder to assess the more we question the exact nature of the break-up of Catholic unity in the early sixteenth century.

2
Italian Humanists and the Problem of the Crusade

Margaret Meserve

Historians of the Renaissance often refer to the Turkish 'problem' as one of the defining issues in the diplomatic and political landscape of fifteenth-century Europe.[1] Between 1300 and 1450, thanks to strong central leadership, an aggressive policy of military expansion and a good measure of geopolitical luck, the Ottoman Turkish state grew from a minor provincial emirate to a formidable world power. With independent Christian despotates in the Balkans eclipsed, Italian trading colonies in the eastern Mediterranean reduced and, in 1453, Constantinople captured and the Byzantine Empire overthrown, the Ottomans posed a serious challenge to the Renaissance political economy.

For most fifteenth-century commentators, however, the urgency of the Turkish problem derived not so much from the fact of Turkish aggression itself, as from Christian Europe's embarrassing failure to contain it. Writing from the imperial chancery in 1454, just after the fall of Constantinople, Aeneas Silvius Piccolomini decried the continuing passivity of the European states in the face of the Turkish threat. A wary self-interest seemed to have paralysed the best intentions of every prince and republican government. No one wanted to be the first to commit men and resources to a new crusade; no one wanted to leave his own borders exposed, his own lands and treasure at risk, to fight a battle that might well benefit a rival power. In Aeneas's view, moreover, the petty infighting of the Italian city-states and dynastic squabbles among the northern princes were signs of a deeper crisis in European character. Commercial self-interest and political cynicism had together corrupted all sense of common good:

> Do you see how men act, and what our princes do? Do you see the sink of greed, sloth, and gluttony that lies open before us? ... Do you

think that an army of Turks can be defeated by men of such character?[2]

The problem was endemic; moreover – and this was a crucial point for Aeneas – it had started at the top. Christendom's failures in the East were the direct result of a failure of authority at home in the West:

> What grounds are there for hope? Christendom has no head whom all will obey – neither the pope nor the emperor receives his due. There is no respect, nor obedience: we think of pope and emperor alike as figureheads, rulers in name alone. Every city has its own prince; there are as many lords as there are households. How do you persuade the crowns of Christendom to take up arms together?[3]

The crusade, as an ideal, a rallying cry, seemed to have lost its power, because the institutions most closely associated with it were themselves in deep decline. In Aeneas's letters from the 1450s, as in much contemporary political and intellectual discourse, the failure of the crusade came to stand in vivid synecdoche for the host of problems confronting contemporary Christendom: from the eclipse of imperial and papal authority by new dynastic states and the near-constant warfare that had accompanied their emergence, to the disaffection of large numbers of believers, the eruption of popular heresy and the recurring threat of schism in the Church. What Europeans had to address, then, and what crusade propagandists exhorted them to address, was not just the Turkish problem, but the problem of the crusade. In their minds, the solution to that problem, however it might be devised, was closely bound to the resolution of the larger spectrum of troubles confronting Christian Europe.

With the popes absent in Avignon and mercenary warfare practically endemic throughout the peninsula, Italy had suffered the ill-effects of the late medieval crisis of authority more than most. It was in this confused and troubled context that the Italian humanists had emerged as an intellectual and political class. As scholars, civil servants, diplomats, educators, lawyers and churchmen, the humanists drew their inspiration not only from the literary remnants of antiquity but also from its political traditions, cleaving to the ancient ideal of the *vita activa*, of applying their intellectual gifts to the service of the state. With their keen sense of history and rhetoric, law and the mechanics of power, humanists like Aeneas Silvius applied themselves to the resolution of Italy's troubles and the institution of long-term political and ecclesiastical reform. As shrewd propagandists and loyal servants of the states that employed them, however, the humanists also contributed much to the interim scramble for power.

In short, the same political and social developments that created the problem of the crusade in the fifteenth century (namely, the failure of any European power, including the papacy, to mount an effective military response to Islamic aggression and, more generally, the crisis of legitimate authority that lay behind that failure), also produced the class of humanist scholars, advisers, orators and propagandists who so consistently decried it. In this essay I shall argue that the fortunes of the humanists and the problem of the crusade were closely linked at a number of levels. The humanists recognized the problem early on. They were among the first to chart its contours. But they did more than just define the terms of the debate over Islamic aggression in fifteenth-century Europe; they also co-opted the problem to serve their own agendas, both public and private.

In arguing for a crusade, Renaissance humanists embraced the ostensible project of championing Christendom against the forces of Islam while, at the same time, pursuing a variety of more specific, often personal goals. These included institutional reform in Europe; the legitimation of particular political claims; and (more indirectly) the advancement of their own cultural interests and careers. Accordingly, in the vast corpus of humanist crusade rhetoric, comprised of private and public letters, orations, diplomatic briefs, scholarly treatises, crusade histories, strategic plans and a host of literary and poetic treatments, humanist authors alternate between expressions of genuine concern, shrewd political manœuvring and self-conscious displays of erudition and expertise. The crusade for which the humanists so ardently campaigned never materialized – at least, not in the form they had imagined nor on the scale they would have liked. But through their advocacy, the humanists developed methods of analysis, argumentation and self-presentation which would exercise a profound influence on European political and historical scholarship – and, equally important, on attitudes toward the *value* of these kinds of knowledge – long after the Ottoman threat had receded from European view.

Crusade as a project of reform

Though Italian humanists were typically engaged in the business of government, often working to advance the interests of their employers over the competing claims of rival powers, most remained sensitive to the larger problems that contemporary Europe faced. Many were in fact deeply concerned with the question of reform. To them, the rise of energetic new Muslim empires in the East, the decline of Byzantine power and the plight of Eastern Christians under Muslim rule were not isolated problems. They seemed, rather, intimately connected to the contemporary crisis in the West, external symptoms of a disease that had taken root in the heart of Christendom.

In looking to the East, humanists at the close of the fourteenth century focused attention, at first, on the rising tide of the Ottoman Turks. The short-lived but spectacular incursions of Timur around the turn of the century also occasioned humanist comment, but the astonishing revival of Ottoman power after Timur's death, culminating in 1453 with the Turkish conquest of Constantinople itself, came quickly to dominate humanist discussions of the problem of the crusade. Early humanists tended to view the new Islamic empires in a remarkably abstract way. Whether identified with the Turks or the Tartars (as the followers of Timur were styled), the Islamic threat was of interest to these observers primarily as an index of Europe's own political health. The Christian body politic had been weakened to the point of real vulnerability to external attack. Now there appeared on the scene a formidable series of Islamic aggressors poised to exploit that very weakness. How could a continent mired in violence and contention mount an effective resistance?

The Florentine chancellor and famed humanist scholar Coluccio Salutati (1331–1406) was among the first humanists to discuss the Ottoman Turks at any length and in precisely such self-critical terms. He voiced his thoughts in a letter of 1397 to Jobst of Luxemburg, the margrave of Moravia, a powerful figure in northern politics who would soon stake a contentious claim to the imperial throne. At the time of Salutati's letter, he was closely involved in negotiations to resolve the Great Schism and return the papacy to Rome. In calling the margrave's attention to the threat posed to Europe by the Turks, Salutati was not really trying to raise the alarm or call for a new crusade; rather, he was using the Turkish menace as a rhetorical ploy, invoking it dramatically to underscore the need for Jobst and his fellow northern princes to sort out their political quarrels and resolve the schism in the Church.

In the letter, Salutati presents the margrave with an idealized estimate of Turkish energy and resolve, clearly intended to shame him out of his own inaction. According to Salutati, the Turks train from boyhood in the arts of war. They spend their days hunting and in military drill. They live on dry bread or game or herbs of the field; they endure extremes of cold and heat and foul weather without complaint; they sleep on the bare earth. In short, what other men find intolerable, they not only endure but enjoy.[4] Salutati marvels at the Spartan simplicity of Turkish life, the strict military discipline of the ranks and their profound obedience to the sultan's will. 'We Christians,' he says by contrast, 'are mired in debauchery and sloth; we aim at only indulgence and gluttony.'[5] Standards are slipping, morals are weak and, worst of all, without a legitimate pope, Christendom itself lies leaderless and in disorder. 'Shall we wait until this dispute escalates (alas!) into war? Or until the Turks in their boldness ... advance against Christians and attack them? It will be too late to seek a resolution [to the schism] then.'[6]

For Salutati, as for his most likely ancient models, Tacitus and Pompeius Trogus, the harsh discipline and endurance of the barbarians, as he imagined them, serve as a provocative example to his compatriots: *they*, despite being uncivilized, have achieved a virtuous life; how shameful that we, with all our cultural advantages, should fail.[7] At heart, his letter is a call for reform at home, not a campaign abroad. Certainly, a useful by-product of reform would be a new imperviousness to Turkish attacks, perhaps even new momentum for an offensive campaign against them; but there can be no doubt that Salutati's real interest lay in strengthening the moral fibre of Christendom and thus resolving its domestic troubles.

In the early 1430s, the Milanese humanist Andrea Biglia (c. 1395–1435) undertook another, much more ambitious, estimate of the Islamic threat to Christendom, with a similar view to criticizing contemporary Europe's inability to contain it.[8] In quintessentially humanist fashion, Biglia believed the best explanation for the current, sorry state of affairs in both Europe and the East could be found in an examination of its ancient roots. His sprawling, twelve-book *Commentaries on the Decline of Christendom in the East* document the course of Christian–Islamic conflict from the time of the first campaigns of Muhammad, through the all-too-brief successes of the early crusades, to the recent incursions of Timur. Biglia also traces each development in Eastern history back to a particular political or ecclesiastical failure in the Christian West. Biglia was the first humanist to undertake a systematic study of Islamic history and politics. His work set the pattern for almost all later humanist discussions of the character of the Muslim enemy and the potential benefits of a new crusade. The text remains unedited and has never received much critical attention, in part, it would seem, because his focus on the Ilkhanids as the chief troublemakers in the region became so quickly outdated.[9] It repays a close examination.

By the 1430s, when Biglia was writing, the schism that Salutati decried had been resolved; but even after Martin V's return to Rome in 1420 the fortunes of the papacy remained precarious. In 1431, the cantankerous Eugenius IV found himself taken to account by a new generation of conciliarists at Basel, whose calls for reform threatened to reopen the schism in the Church. The situation was further complicated by the uncertain state of imperial politics: Sigismund, the newly elected king of the Romans, vacillated weakly between support for the northern conciliarists and his own desire to receive the imperial crown from the hands of the pope in Rome. Biglia, professor of moral philosophy in the University of Siena, observed at first-hand Sigismund's arrival in Tuscany in the summer of 1432 on his way to his coronation. The humanist was persuaded, for a short while at least, that the emperor-elect meant to forge a resolution between council and pope. He seems even to have imagined, like Dante a century before him, that the northern prince's progress south was the first step towards the reassertion of imperial power in Italy.

Fired with enthusiasm, Biglia set to work on his *Commentaries*, which he completed in the spring of 1433. The work presents a formidable array of obscure information on the history of medieval Asia together with a complicated (possibly over-subtle) argument to demonstrate the relevance of that history to the contemporary situation in the West. In Biglia's view, the origins of Islam could be traced to the late-antique split between the empire and the papacy: now, eight centuries later, Islam could only be defeated by an imperial–papal *rapprochement*. Relying on slightly outdated sources, Biglia identified the 'Tartar' armies of Timur (d. 1405) and his Ilkhanid successors, whom Biglia imagined were the direct heirs of Genghis Khan, as the Islamic aggressor threatening contemporary Christendom. In Biglia's scheme, the calamitous depredations of the Tartars not only reflected the divided nature of the Christian polity but were in fact the direct result of the medieval decline of the two once great Roman institutions; accordingly, the Tartar menace must be remedied by a programme of *renovatio* for both Church and State.

Though not a civil servant like Salutati, Biglia was deeply concerned with current affairs. Educated in humanism, and a prominent university professor, he was one of a new generation of public intellectuals who sought to comment on the political issues of their day without necessarily taking an active part in their prosecution.[10] A prolific correspondent and a tireless scholar, he had taught at the universities of Bologna, Florence and Siena, was proficient in Greek and possibly Hebrew, and in his short life produced more than 60 works, including translations of

Aristotle, a *Milanese History* in nine books, and several short treatises on contemporary religious and political issues.[11] He was renowned as much for his eloquent secular oratory as for his preaching; in both, he firmly averred the centrality of the Roman Church to European affairs, both spiritual and political. He was a critic of popular religious movements and a staunch advocate of reform.

As an historian, Biglia embraced the traditional, medieval view of Rome as a universal political empire whose historic destiny had been fulfilled by the birth of Christ. But he approached this model of universal history with an innovative, humanist slant. In his view, the spread of Christianity through the empire had strengthened, but in no way replaced, the secular virtues of Roman civilization. These included admirable degrees of political autonomy, moral goodness and intellectual culture, traits which Biglia considered together under the potent rubric of *humanitas*. But the fruitful union of classical culture and Christian faith – that abiding humanist ideal – was fated not to last: almost as soon as he adopted Christianity, the Emperor Constantine had abandoned Rome for a new capital in the East. It was from this fatal rupture, Biglia believed, that almost all Europe's subsequent troubles, including the rise of Islam, arose. With the seat of empire removed from the seat of the Church, both institutions had been fundamentally debased.[12] The Christian faith grew susceptible to heresy and the political structures of empire became increasingly frail. Thereafter, Western and Eastern Romans each lacked one of the elements necessary for spiritual and political health. Constantine thus opened the way for both barbarians *and* heretics, whether in the guise of Germans, Goths, Huns or Arabs, to encroach.[13]

In investigating the origins of Islam Biglia, unlike most medieval crusade historians, placed little emphasis on the machinations or cunning of Muhammad, nor even on the credulity of the Christians whom he, in the usual formulation, had 'seduced' to his cause.[14] In Biglia's view, responsibility for the spread of Islam lay neither with the Prophet nor with his willing converts, but rather with Rome itself: Islam was an aberration, the ugly outward sign of internal corruption which the Church and Empire had together allowed to erupt. Had Constantine stayed in Rome, the empire and its subjects would have been able to withstand any challenge. As it was, the Byzantine emperor Heraclius (on whose watch Islam emerged) reigned in a place from where neither the West nor the East could be ruled, neither Italy nor Asia could be saved.

Biglia saw the rise of Islam as a complex phenomenon, part religious heresy, part political rebellion. Its success was the mirror image of

Rome's failure. The unruly Arabs, 'enemies of the empire and the faith', rebelled against Byzantine rule, rejecting 'both the imperial yoke and religion'. They had managed to unite their heretical creed with independent political power (the very thing Rome had failed to do) with the result that as Rome declined, 'the strength of their faith and their power grew alike throughout the world'.[15] The effects of Islam on the old Roman East were thus twofold: as unbelief spread through formerly Christian lands, the rich culture of classical civilization also declined: 'The Machometan superstition rendered people so senseless that they seemed to have entirely rejected *humanitas*. All memory of the ancients ... perished, so that not even a trace of the virtue once known [in Asia] survived.'[16] In short, Biglia held that the vitality of a religion was inextricably linked to the political authority of the state that adopted it, as was the cultural character of the people who offered their obedience to both. All rose and fell together. The implications for the current crisis in Italy were clear.

The subsequent history of the East revealed a tale of continuing decline, according to Biglia, despite a brief period of recovery around the turn of the millennium. Then, a series of valiant Frankish lords had pushed back the barbarian Arab hordes, first in Muslim Spain, then in the Holy Land itself, culminating in the conquest of Jerusalem in 1099. But this brief moment of glory was not to last. Among the crusaders in the Latin kingdom, moral corruption and greed quickly set in. Their dereliction of civic duty led rapidly to the loss of the holy city itself. Not long after, the Tartars appeared on the eastern horizon, bringing new waves of chaos and devastation in their wake. A worse scourge even than the Arabs, the savage Tartars brought fitting punishment for a world that had betrayed its ancient heritage twice. Biglia radically condensed the history of the Mongol invaders and their successor states in western Asia, making Genghis Khan and Timur appear quite close in both time and political character. Now, as Biglia surveyed the contemporary situation in the East, he saw barbarian hordes swarming and civilization once again in peril. The West must respond with unity, concord and a new commitment to *humanitas*, which could be achieved only by the reunification of papal and imperial power. If Constantine's fateful partition could be undone, Christian Europe would regain a measure of internal fortitude it had not enjoyed since the end of Antiquity.

It is no coincidence that Biglia ends his work with a description of Sigismund's coronation in Rome.[17] And yet he did not dedicate his work to the emperor or to the pope. Instead Biglia addressed each of its twelve books to a different public figure – prominent cardinals, chancellors, *condottieri*, all involved in some way with either the Council of Basel or the current Italian stalemate over Florence's war on Lucca – in other words, to those European politicians who, in his opinion, could contribute most to the resolution of conflict either within the Church or in Italy.[18] Biglia did not write as a partisan of any one faction in the various contemporary disputes he tried to address through his work: rather, he was (like Salutati, in this context at least) an idealist, who raised the issue of the Islamic threat as a way to spur all parties involved towards reconciliation, the first step towards meaningful reform. Biglia believed that Sigismund needed to reassert his authority in Italy and that Italy needed to receive him – but Sigismund, too, must respect the See of Rome. Only then would the forces of Asiatic disorder and barbarism retreat before the one, true Christian Empire; only then would Europe and Asia *both* be restored to the glories of their ancient past.

Biglia died of the plague in 1435, only a few years after completing his *Commentaries*. It is impossible to say how he would have viewed the sudden resurgence of Ottoman power and the almost total eclipse of Timur's Ilkhanid successors in western Asia during the middle decades of the fifteenth century. As the political landscape in the East was transformed, his warnings about the Tartar threat grew increasingly irrelevant. But, particulars aside, Biglia's innovative approach to the question of the age-old conflict between Christianity and Islam was quickly adopted as a humanist norm. His basic premises – that Islamic imperialism was a political and cultural, as well as a religious threat to Christian Europe; that the solution to the problem lay in a similarly multifaceted reform of European political, cultural and spiritual life; and that a proper understanding of all the issues involved could only be derived from an examination of their historical origins (the sort of treatment only a trained humanist historian could provide) – these assumptions would continue to underpin humanist debates on the problem of the crusade throughout the Renaissance period.

From reform to restoration: the crusade and the Quattrocento papacy

A decade after Biglia's death, the humanist Flavio Biondo (1392–1463) took up the theme of Islamic–Christian conflict and its significance for both universal history and present-day affairs. Like Biglia, Biondo traced the problems of the contemporary East back to various episodes of imperial maladministration in the late antique and early medieval past. But several factors distinguish Biondo's account of the problem from

Biglia's: Biondo saw the Turks, not the 'Tartars', as Europe's main cause for concern; he viewed them as a far more urgent and concrete threat to European interests in the East and at home. Not least, Biondo aligned his assessment of the problem and its likely resolution much more closely to the interests of one political power (that of the papacy) than either Biglia or Salutati had done.

Biondo was only slightly younger than Biglia, but his career followed a quite different trajectory, typical of the next generation of Italian humanists. While Biglia took orders and found employment within the university, Biondo cut his own path through the chanceries of various Italian states, working as a secretary, speechwriter and diplomat first in the service of Venice and then, from the pontificate of Eugenius IV until his death in 1463, at the Roman Curia.[19] His researches clearly bear the mark of his Roman allegiance. Though Biglia examined the Eastern question within a larger and generally disinterested discourse of reform, Biondo's interest in the problem was more politically motivated, as were his conclusions.

Biondo first worked out a model for understanding the role of Islam in history in the *Decades*, his groundbreaking survey of the fall of the Roman Empire and the medieval history of Italy, begun sometime in the late 1430s and published by about 1444.[20] Biondo opens the second decade of the work with an account of the papal crisis of 755, during which the Lombard Aistulf besieged Rome and forced Pope Stephen II to flee north to the court of Pepin, king of the Franks. For Biondo this was an important milestone in the decline of the ancient Empire, with grave implications for the future of Italy.[21] The pope's flight should have been a matter of great concern to the Byzantine emperor Constantine V, Biondo argues; above all, it provided an opportunity to reassert imperial authority in Italy. Instead, like his namesake Constantine the Great, the hapless Constantine V neglected his responsibilities to the peninsula and allowed both the Lombards and Franks to exercise power unchecked. At precisely this moment, Constantine saw new troubles erupt on his eastern frontier:

> While Rome and Italy were agitated and distressed by such great losses and dangers, Constantine took no steps to alleviate the problem, although this was a change in fortunes which was hardly of advantage to himself. And afterwards this emperor had a second such change of luck, because it was at this time that the Turks first invaded Asia, molesting the Alans, then the Colchians and Armenians, and thereafter the peoples of Asia Minor and finally the Persians and

Saracens, seizing land and slaughtering great numbers of people whom they found there or who dared to gather [in opposition].[22]

At this fateful moment of imperial dereliction, the Turks first appeared on the horizons of Europe; seven centuries later, the secular rulers of Europe continued to fail the popes; and the Turks had yet to be repelled.

Biondo held that the eighth-century rift between imperial Constantinople and papal Rome marked the final collapse of the ancient empire.[23] And yet, unlike Biglia, Biondo imagined that these incidents had not damaged the Roman See nearly as much as they had the imperial throne. In his view, the mantle of imperial authority in the West had passed relatively intact to the popes. A firm believer in the Donation of Constantine, Biondo saw Christendom as the modern embodiment of the old Roman *imperium*, now with the pope, rather than the emperor, at its head.

As Biondo surveyed the medieval history of the Islamic world, he looked here, too, for continuities with the ancient past. Specifically, he sought to integrate the Turks into a larger narrative of ancient Roman struggles against an Eastern imperial foe. In Biondo's view, the primary locus of power in the medieval East had remained, as in Antiquity, in Persia. By overthrowing the Sassanian dynasty, the Saracen Arabs had assumed Persia's role as the chief political rival of Rome; when the Turks appeared on the scene in the eighth century – significantly, at a moment when the imperial authority was at a distinctly low ebb – they too adopted the anti-Roman stance of the Parthian Empire.

The duty of the popes, then, was nothing less than to defend the old imperial frontiers of Rome against aggression from the East. Biondo's secular, political interpretation of the issue achieved its fullest articulation later in the *Decades*, in his account of the Council of Clermont and his rendition of Urban II's famous sermon launching the First Crusade. The words he puts in the pope's mouth here proclaim the expedition against the Saracens and Turks as a campaign of imperial Roman as well as Christian *recuperatio*.[24] Although the liberation of Jerusalem is an important goal, Biondo's Urban declares that the crusade is also necessary to re-establish throughout the East the imperial authority of ancient Rome, to which the papacy is the rightful heir. In recent years, Urban explains, the Saracens and Turks have emerged from Persia to occupy not just the Holy Land but 'all those lands which once were subject to the Roman Empire, and afterwards to the Roman pope'.[25] Though Byzantium used to defend Europe from such incursions, the Eastern empire has weakened to the point where not only the Mediterranean lands, but even the countries of eastern Europe lie in danger. The idea that the Seljuks posed a threat to Hungary, Poland, Bohemia, and even Germany is perhaps the most obvious example of Biondo's reading contemporary concerns back into the eleventh-century past.[26] Therefore, in the absence of any effective imperial authority, the Roman pope must take up the task of defending and restoring Christendom, an entity which was once, and should still be, coterminous with the boundaries of the ancient Empire, against an enemy who attacks not only the Christian religion, but also the political integrity of Rome.[27]

In developing a secular, political interpretation for the significance of Islam in Western history, Biondo follows Salutati and Biglia to a certain extent. But the earlier authors had proposed solving the problem of Turkish aggression through the institution of general reforms and a renewed commitment from all the Christian parties to the debate – neither the pope, nor the emperor, nor the new dynastic states were excused from complicity in the crisis. Biondo, by contrast, uses his interpretation of medieval Christian–Islamic conflicts in the East to show how all the major powers of Christendom had failed in their duty, with the exception of the papacy. In his view, only the popes had retained power and authority through the chaotic Middle Ages; they alone now bore the mantle of imperial authority; they alone carried the banner of war against Islam. They had no reason to reform; rather, it was the rest of Europe that needed to consider changing its ways. The French, the Germans, the Italian states, the emperor, all must declare their obedience to the pope and fall in behind the standard of the crusade. The success of the crusade hung on the renewal of papal supremacy.

Such an interpretation was clearly useful for Biondo's then employer, Pope Eugenius IV. Indeed, after the failure of a northern crusading attempt (led by Burgundy and Poland) at Varna in 1444 and the catastrophe of Constantinople nine years later, as the Turkish menace grew to be one of the most pressing issues on the contemporary scene, the inefficiency of the European response fed a growing conviction not only in Rome, but elsewhere as well, that only Rome could solve the worsening problem of the crusade. Not long after he vented his frustration at the paralysis of the European states in 1454,[28] and having witnessed the meagre results of Frederick III's cynical and prevaricating Turkish policy, Aeneas Silvius left imperial service altogether. He transferred his allegiance and energies to the Curia and, simultaneously, to the cause of promoting a papal crusade. The sincerity of Aeneas's commitment to the cause has sometimes been called into doubt. It could be seen as a cynical ploy, as the former conciliarist leapt adroitly to the defence of a quintessentially papal project. But disappointment with Frederick's vacillation at the diets of 1454–55 may well have driven Aeneas to seek advancement in the Church under the militant Calixtus III (1455–58). As the inaction of the secular princes repeatedly showed, no one in Europe but the pope seemed to possess the moral authority and strength of purpose to confront the Turkish problem.[29]

Over the course of the 1450s, the crusade came increasingly to be seen as a peculiarly Roman venture. At his own election to the papal throne as Pius II, in 1458, Aeneas embraced the crusade as a personal project, resolving at the moment of his coronation 'to stake not just the city and the patrimony of Peter, but his own health, indeed his very life'[30] against the onslaught of the Turks. But he had no illusions about the fact that the crusade would also be a useful theme to invoke in the pursuit of his domestic agenda, to reassert papal authority in Italy, for example, and to restore the city of Rome to its ancient splendour.[31] Accordingly, Biondo, as one of Pius's most trusted secretaries, deftly updated his arguments for the imperial Roman character of the papacy (which he had first developed in the *Decades*) to the current climate of enthusiasm for a papal crusade. In both the preface and the conclusion to his antiquarian treatise *Roma triumphans*, which he completed while attending the Congress of Mantua in 1459 in the pope's train,[32] Biondo heralded Pius as a long-awaited renovator of ancient Roman institutions, mores and values. Pius must see his project of Roman restoration through, Biondo urged, for only thus could Italy, indeed, all of Europe, regain the strength it had enjoyed under ancient Roman rule and be in a position, at last, to triumph over the Turks.[33]

Knowing the enemy: the origin of the Turks

The fall of Constantinople also threw the problem of the enemy's identity into sharper relief. No longer an abstract threat, the real and growing spectre of Turkish aggression now transcended the moralizing speculation of earlier humanist accounts. In written works from 1454 on, Aeneas and the close circle of humanist friends and clients who shared his enthusiasm for the crusade sought to secure support for the venture by delving further into the question of the origins and ethnic character of the Turks. Their historical researches shifted the debate away from the earlier humanist discourse of self-criticism and reproach towards a more external focus on the enemy himself. Now, instead of showing how the Islamic threat was a problem of Europe's making, history was used to demonstrate the perennially dangerous character of the

Turks themselves and the irrational aggression with which they had pitted themselves (as in antiquity, so now) against the forces of a blameless civilization.

The humanists' efforts in this vein resulted in what I would term a less critical understanding of the historical roots of the problem of the crusade. Though Biglia and Biondo often treated the Muslims as little more than ciphers in their historical schemata for the decline of classical civilization, they had none the less managed to expand and redefine traditional interpretations of the conflict between Christianity and Islam. Going beyond (though never completely eschewing) the issue of religious difference, Biglia and Biondo had sought to explain the problem of the crusade with reference to such diverse factors as the political fall-out from the imperial move to Constantinople, the peculiar strains of medieval Mediterranean society, and the secular cultural character of individual nations, Christian and infidel alike. After 1453, the humanists' insistence on the barbarity of the Turks lent a different colour to the debate, one that, while appearing to perpetuate the secular focus and source-critical standards of early humanist historiography, in fact owed far more to the traditional canons of medieval Christian polemic against Islam.

In the immediate aftermath of Constantinople's fall, most humanist commentators had stressed the barbarity of the Ottoman Turks over all other factors. In late 1453, the Byzantine émigré scholar and diplomat Cardinal Bessarion described Constantinople's capture in just such terms:

> A city which only recently was blessed with such an emperor, so many distinguished men, so many famous and ancient families and such an abundance of resources – the capital of all Greece, the splendour and glory of the East, the nursery of the most noble learning, the repository of all that is good – has been captured, stripped, plundered and pillaged by the most inhuman barbarians, the most savage enemies of the Christian faith, the most ferocious wild beasts.[34]

The Milanese humanist Francesco Filelfo also stressed the contrast between Western civilization and Turkish barbarity. Turkish expansion should be considered a moral affront to the civilized nations of the West, he wrote, for:

> The baser the men who inflict it, the more debasing is the indignity – if, indeed, the Turks should be called men at all, and not some kind

of completely unrestrained and savage beasts, since they have nothing of humanity in themselves beyond a human form, and even that is deformed and depraved on account of the disgusting filthiness of their shameful habits.[35]

Starting from these assumptions, humanists in the 1450s undertook further to underscore the barbarity of the Turks by developing an historical narrative of identity that placed them firmly beyond the pale of all civilizations, ancient or modern. Thus developed the minor industry of humanist writing *de origine Turcorum*, a scholarly enterprise intended to prove their barbarous pedigree and inborn barbarian character.[36]

The question of the origin of the Turks was not an easy one to answer: Turks are not mentioned in classical literature, nor do they appear in the Bible. What humanists concerned with the problem did was to search, instead, through late antique, Byzantine and medieval Latin texts for references to *Tourkoi* or *Turci* that might shed light on their origins and early activities. A number of sources could have helped them reconstruct the story fairly accurately (William of Tyre, for example, and the Byzantine chroniclers Skylitzes and Kedrenos all trace the history of the Seljuk Turks back to their rise to power in eleventh-century Persia); but the humanists chose to tell a different tale, one which located the primordial Turks in Scythia and fixed their early history in an established pattern of barbarous behavior, in between the ancient raids of the Scythians and Huns and the more recent depredations of the Mongol hordes. It was a narrative of identity which, not coincidentally, associated the Turks with some of the darkest locations on the medieval map.

Biondo himself had laid the groundwork for the story in the *Decades*; after introducing the Turks into history in his account of the depredations of Aistulf, he commented on their ethnic identity: the Turks, he wrote, could be identified as Scythians, descended from the wild tribes whom St Jerome had said were locked up by Alexander the Great in the Caucasus mountains, behind the Caspian Gates.[37] Around the same time, Filelfo had proposed a similar identification: he traced the Ottomans back to a Scythian tribe whom the Byzantine *Suda* recorded as engaging in violent raids around the northern shores of the Black Sea.[38] In 1454, Aeneas Silvius, relying on a late-antique cosmography by the geographer 'Ethicus', also stressed the barbarous ancestry and character of the Turks; they were, he wrote, 'a nation of Scythians, originating in the heart of Barbary, beyond the Black Sea and the Pyrrichean Mountains toward the northern Ocean, an unclean and disgusting race, fornicators indulging in every kind of depravity.'[39] This was a claim he was to repeat almost compulsively in his crusade letters and orations over the next decade, adding further evidence from other medieval sources (including a reference by the twelfth-century chronicler Otto of Freising to Turks erupting from the Caspian Gates during the reign of Pepin, king of the Franks) which stressed the barbarity, treachery and violence of the Turkish race. In 1456, Aeneas also commissioned the Byzantine émigré scholar Niccolò Sagundino to produce a more detailed account of Turkish origins, which Aeneas later incorporated verbatim into his own works on the subject.[40] Sagundino, writing to order, also identified the Turks as ancient Scythians and, in an elaborate pastiche of ancient ethnographic commonplaces on the behaviour of nomads, claimed the culture of the present-day Ottomans was still unmistakably Scythian, characterized by violence, restless wandering and phenomenal skills in archery and the training of horses. In 1459, Filelfo, in his oration to the pope on behalf of Francesco Sforza at the Congress of Mantua, described the course of the Scythian Turks' invasions south from the Caspian Gates into the civilized world:

> Who on earth is unaware that the Turks were the fugitive slaves of the Scythians, shepherds who burst out of the confines of the vast and forbidding Mount Caucasus ... and descended into Persia and Media in order to pillage, settling nowhere in particular, but dwelling instead in barren wastes and wild forest lairs?[41]

Around this time, Nicola Loschi also dedicated a poem to Pius in which he lamented that a 'Caspian race' should threaten the West and that Christian authority should be challenged by Mehmed II, a lowly 'Scythian boy'.[42]

Underpinning all these claims of Scythian ancestry was the humanists' insistence on the permanent influence of origins. As the papacy drew power and prestige from its institutional roots in imperial Rome, so the Ottoman Empire should be regarded with fear and contempt on the grounds of its degraded Scythian pedigree. The stain of barbarity was indelible, as Aeneas himself explained:

> And [the Turks] still have the scent of their original barbarity about them, even though, having lived in a milder climate and on gentler soil for many years, they now seem a little civilized. But the change of environment has not scrubbed away all their savagery. They still eat [unclean foods]; they are slaves to lust, addicted to cruelty, and they despise literature and the arts.[43]

Moreover, by portraying the Turks not only as enemies of the faith but also as barbarian opponents of Western civilization, humanists in Pius's circle could suggest that the popes, by contrast, stood for all that was good: champions of culture and political order as well as the one true faith.

And yet, as I have argued elsewhere, the humanist identification of the Turks as Scythians rested on the shakiest historical grounds.[44] Many of the sources they used were corrupt or fantastic, and they knew it. Aeneas's main source for their Scythian origins, the apparently ancient cosmographer 'Ethicus', is in fact an idiosyncratic medieval geographical compendium which draws heavily on the apocalyptic *Revelations* of ps.-Methodius. The entry on the Turks in the original text explicitly identifies them with Gog and Magog and other unclean nations whom biblical prophecy had said would burst out of Alexander's Gates in the Caucasus at the start of Armageddon. It also attributes to them a host of spectacularly unpleasant and possibly supernatural habits, details which Aeneas edited out of his own account in order to make his source look like an apparently credible work of ancient ethnography. The Byzantine and medieval Latin chronicles Filelfo and Biondo used, meanwhile, offer enthusiastic and positive descriptions of various Turkish tribes in the Caucasus who had served as valuable allies of Byzantium in their wars against the Arabs in the seventh and eighth centuries AD. Only by quoting these sources selectively and out of context could the humanists produce a portrait of the Turks as savage invaders, 'bursting through' the Caspian Gates in a suggestively catastrophic manner. And Sagundino's apparently eyewitness ethnographic excursus on the 'nomadic' Scythian Turks, meanwhile, echoes the famous description by Ammianus Marcellinus of the fourth-century Huns with suspicious fidelity.

Humanist scholars of Turkish origins engaged in the creative and purposeful manipulation of their sources, quoting them out of context or deliberately distorting them in order to present the historical Turks (and by extension, their modern descendants) in the worst possible light. Their accounts of the origins of the Turks can hardly be considered examples of the kind of critical, objective inquiry which the Italian humanists themselves claimed as one of their greatest achievements. Yet it was the appearance of just this sort of informed, critical empiricism which Aeneas and the humanists in his circle strove to cultivate. They investigated the origins of the Turks in a way that seemed historically credible and beyond methodological reproach, with a wealth of detail and authoritative citations, while all the while darkly hinting at the true, apocalyptic significance of their existence.

Humanist crusade propagandists never lost sight of the fundamentally religious nature of the crusade nor the religious identity of the enemy it sought to defeat. Indeed, as the project of a new crusade became more closely identified with the political agenda of the restoration papacy, it grew all the more imperative to assert the religious nature of the conflict, one in which only the Vicar of Christ could prevail. The crusade propaganda produced in the pontificate of Pius II is remarkable for its fusion of secular and religious themes. Pius's own rhetoric became, not surprisingly, increasingly charged with religious fervour over time. While his letters and speeches immediately after the fall of Constantinople stressed Turkish depredations against the newly revived glories of classical Greek culture, in his oration at the Congress of Mantua he dwelled on the bloodthirsty rapacity of the infidels as they slavered after Christian blood. Now the cry was not just to avenge Constantinople, 'the Athens of the modern age', but rather all of Asia Minor, nursery of the Christian faith, where the apostles had walked and where the Gospel was first embraced by gentiles. Turkish aggression was, moreover, part of a larger move on the part of infidels everywhere, including Moors in Africa and pagan tribes in Scandinavia, to encircle and destroy Christendom.[45] Whether framed in the language of history or geography, the pope's arguments essentially turned on the point that blasphemous infidels were besmirching the moral and cultural purity of Christendom, and that it was the duty of Christians everywhere to follow his call to its defence.

In short, despite the classical veneer they gave to their accounts of the Scythian character of the Turks, what the humanists in Pius's circle perpetuated in their discussion of the Turkish foe was nothing other than a medieval Christian image of barbarity. The unclean nations were pouring down from the north, blazing a trail for Satan. In recent years, a number of critics have interpreted the humanist idea of a Scythian origin for the Turks as evidence of precisely the opposite mentality.[46] In their view, humanist crusade propagandists faithfully revived a classical model of barbarism while rejecting the medieval image of the 'infidel' Turk as an enemy of Christ and the Church; the rise of the Ottoman Empire came to be seen as the latest phase in an ancient and perpetual contest between West and East, civilized Europe and barbarous Asia – a trope of cultural antithesis dating back as far as Herodotus.[47] Where medieval crusade propaganda viewed Islam as inspired by irrational hatred of the Christian religion and quite possibly unleashed by a vengeful Christian God, the humanists put forward an altogether more rational and secular assessment of the situation, as one of age-old political tension between two world empires divided by political and cultural incompatibility.

I would argue, however, that the humanists' portrayal of the 'Scythian' Turks owed little in its particulars to classical precedents. Even as they revived literary common places from classical ethnographical writing about barbarians (and as they tinkered with their medieval sources to make them sound more historically credible, more like classical historical texts than they actually were), the spirit of their ethnographic descriptions is hardly classical at all. Ancient writers from Herodotus to Tacitus had observed barbarian habits, history and society with a detached and neutral curiosity which derived, ultimately, from a sense of cultural confidence and political and military security. This was a view that writers of mid-fifteenth century Europe could not have begun to understand, much less emulate. In contemplating the origins and rise of the conquerors of Constantinople, their reactions come much closer to the sense of fear and doubt that fourth- and fifth-century Romans, both pagan and Christian, expressed in the face of the encroaching Huns and Goths: the Turks were a monstrous, inhuman scourge sent by God against a sinful civilization. The humanists' idea of what it meant to be 'Scythian' owed very little to classical notions of the primitive.

Renaissance politics and the problem of the crusade

It took a devastating failure – or rather, a series of failures – to prise humanist thinking loose from these traditional models. Pius's efforts to will a crusade into existence had ended in disaster: the debacle at Ancona in 1464 starkly demonstrated the impotence of papal crusade policy as a whole and, in particular, the strategies of his own crusading rhetoric. When, six years later, Ottoman forces stormed the Venetian colony of Negroponte, reducing one of the most important remaining Christian outposts in the eastern Mediterranean, the surviving humanists of Pius's generation reacted to the catastrophe with bitter resignation.

For the first time in his life, words failed Francesco Filelfo – otherwise renowned as the century's most prolific crusade propagandist. Responding to a request for comment from a friend in Rome, Filelfo wrote that he had nothing left to say on the problem of the crusade. The European powers had ignored every warning so far; why should this time be different?[48] Cardinal Bessarion, too, claimed to have lost his voice in the wake of the tragedy, but soon after the events of July 1470 he did turn

pen to paper. He composed a remarkable collection of letters and orations (prose essays, certainly never delivered publicly) which he circulated among various friends and highly placed confidants in both Rome
and Venice. Interspersing clear-eyed realism with withering scorn,
Bessarion's orations offer, on the one hand, a radical reappraisal of
the nature of the Turkish threat unlike anything Pius or his humanist
circle had devised in the previous two decades and, on the other, a harsh
assessment of Europe's complicity in the crisis which brought back the
debate nearly full-circle to the self-critical calls for European reform
Salutati had issued some 70 years before.[49]

Having witnessed the failure of Pius's 1464 crusade, Bessarion was
painfully aware of how jealously the Italian states guarded their interests and how reluctant they were to confront the Turkish threat.
Exhortations to reform had had no effect, nor had oratorical demon-
strations of their Scythian barbarity. Much of Bessarion's text was given
over to decrying the imperviousness of contemporary governments to
all previous forms of crusade propaganda:

> Who will stop [the sultan] in the course of such great victories? ...
> Who will stand in his way ... the Italians? The enemy looms over
> them, brandishes and threatens slaughter, massacre, slavery, and
> exile. But they demur; they pay no attention; they cannot be made
> to acknowledge how close the peril is.[50]

Worse still, he suspected, their neglect of the problem was deliberate.
Scornfully, Bessarion imagined the Italian states responding to news of
Venice's recent misfortune:

> What does it have to do with us? Let Venice take care of it. It's right
> that they should handle it – in fact it will be quite useful for the rest
> of us, if matters get even worse for them. Then we can live in peace
> and security. The weaker Venice gets, the more we can relax ...[51]

Keenly aware of the political cynicism that had hobbled the crusade
movement over the previous decades and, perhaps even more important, freed from the obligation to curry anyone's favour, the elderly cardinal took an independent and original approach to the question of the
Turkish threat. In his first oration, he focuses on the state of the Turkish
empire, the tactics and intentions of the sultan, the pressures under
which he operates, and the practical question of whether Christian
Europe is prepared to repel his attack. In Bessarion's view, it is not.

In the second oration he presents a realistic appeal for peace and concord among the Christian princes, without which any defence of Europe is impossible.

Bessarion had been an ardent advocate for a new crusade since the time of his arrival at the Council of Florence in 1438. He had devoted much of his career in the Roman Church to the project, writing, preaching and leading high-level embassies around Europe in search of material support for a papal expedition to the East. In his earlier writings on the Turkish problem, he employed a range of standard rhetorical tropes, from the traditional barbs of medieval religious polemic to more current humanist claims of Turkish violence and barbarity.[52] He uses the image of a Turk 'thirsting for Christian blood' in the 1470 *Orations* as well;[53] but very soon in this work, Bessarion switches to a more reasoned approach.

He starts by offering his own account of the origins of the Turks. Unlike previous humanist writers, his intention here is not to trace the roots of their inborn moral depravity nor to contrast their barbarian origins with the splendours of the Christian East. Rather, Bessarion reconstructs Turkish history in order to establish the political character of the Turks, specifically, their longstanding policy of military expansion.[54] That their domain was once far-off Scythia is not proof of their uncivilized nature but rather of an ancient propensity (and talent) for conquest. Upon emerging from their Hyperborean *patria* and invading Asia Minor, Bessarion says, the Turks were able to overcome the Greeks in fierce battles and soon annexed the Asian half of the Byzantine Empire. Internal squabbling likewise could not retard their progress. According to Bessarion, the seven major Turkish tribes had divided their Anatolian conquests among them; but the Ottomans, the lowliest of the seven, wasted no time in expanding out from their allotted territory of Cilicia, to the detriment of their Turkish neighbours and kin. Once the Byzantine pretender John Cantacuzenus invited them into Europe (hoping for their help in obtaining the disputed imperial succession), they took full advantage of their host, broke their treaties, and changed their nomadic ways in favor of cultivation. They were now set on an unstoppable course of conquest north and west into Europe.

Not all of this is strictly true, as Bessarion may well have known. Contemporary Byzantine chronicles accurately report how the Turks annexed Asia Minor not in major battles but rather when the Greeks, distracted by the Latin occupation of Constantinople (1204–61), had withdrawn their troops from Anatolia; how the seven Turkish families dividing Anatolia allotted the Ottomans Bithynia, in north-west Asia Minor, not Cilicia in the south-east; and how the Ottomans then roamed the poorly guarded Byzantine hinterland for decades before making their move across into Europe.[55] But these versions ill-suited Bessarion's purpose. In his account, the Turks defeated the Greeks in great battles, and the Ottomans moved west, steadily and inexorably, from the furthest corner of Asia Minor to the shores of Europe itself.

The inaccuracy of Bessarion's account recalls the historical manipulations made by Pius II and the scholars in his employ. But Bessarion, by emphasizing the Turks' recent political and military manœuvrings rather than their remote origins and primitive habits, aimed at a more rational explanation of their current policies towards the West, one that was intended to appeal to the hard-headed political instincts of contemporary European governments rather than to their religious convictions or their concern for the monuments of classical culture. Bessarion transformed the usual device of vilifying the enemy's moral character into a believable portrait of his political temperament, illuminating precisely those aspects of Turkish state policy which Europeans should most fear. Moreover, by emphasizing how unsuccessfully the Greeks had handled this enemy, Bessarion also stressed for his contemporary audience the dangers of trying to coexist or negotiate with the Turks.

To prove that the defence of the West was not only just in theory but also necessary – now – in practice, Bessarion also had to show both that the Turks were capable of moving further west and that they intended to do so. Previously, crusade rhetoricians had argued this point by stressing, again, the innate violence of the Turkish character in general or by dwelling on the formidably aggressive personality of the sultan in particular. Pius and his colleagues had argued that Mehmed II was fascinated by, and believed he could rival, the achievements of Alexander the Great. Warlike and restive by nature, he thought night and day of nothing but the destruction of Christendom and the conquest of the world.[56] Bessarion too claims that Mehmed hopes to surpass the conquests of Alexander[57] as he 'rages against us with all his soul and all his mind, day and night'.[58]

But this strategy could only go so far. Portraying the sultan as a mad general, drunk on power and driven by irrational hatred for the West, could not prove that a Turkish invasion was actually imminent. Bessarion thus introduces a second explanation for his actions, less sensational but more plausible: the sultan's designs on the West are determined by political pressures beyond his control. Again Bessarion seems to address the pragmatic, sceptical princes of Europe on their own terms, invoking the classical rhetorical considerations of security and honour – from the point of view of the Turks, not Europe. Invading the West would obviously increase Mehmed's security, Bessarion says. The last 130 years of Turkish growth have been impressive indeed, but the sultan now faces the daunting task of conserving those conquests. 'He sees no safer route to accomplishing this than by increasing his power through foreign campaigns.'[59] Hatred of Christendom has little role to play in this scenario:

> Surely he knows that it is a law of nature that nothing stays in the same place, but everything is driven by constant, various, and new impulses. But if he has a great empire, and if that empire must, by the law of the universe, change in some way, surely it must decrease unless it is increased? Do not think the Turk strives and desires to increase his empire; but certainly he hopes to conserve it. Yet he cannot conserve it unless he increases it. For whatever does not advance, recedes; whatever does not rise up, falls down; whatever does not grow, falls to ruin. Confirmed in this belief, he daily increases his massive army. He invades foreign lands so as not to lose his own.[60]

This massive army, moreover, is a standing militia, paid whether Mehmed is at peace or war; therefore he must keep it fighting and bringing home plunder.[61]

Bessarion also examines the advantages to Mehmed's honour which an invasion of the West will bring. As a typical prince, the sultan naturally desires fame and glory, and since there is no place more glorious than Italy, he craves a conquest there.[62] But why should he want fame and glory in the first place? Bessarion explains:

> There are not a few Asian tribes who hate him and threaten him to his peril, whom he knows will work openly against his authority should he either put down his arms or let his army's reputation be mocked or scorned. And thus he loads his army with praise, so he can make it terrifying to his Asian enemies ... He is despised by his family; his allies hate him; his household does not love him. At the slightest provocation they all could be driven to slaughter and kill him. Since he knows this well, he has decided to undertake, wage and win foreign wars, lest he be beset with domestic and civil unrest.[63]

The sultan's intentions, expressed this way, would have sounded quite familiar to his European counterparts.

Having shown in his first essay that a Turkish threat was imminent and had to be repelled, Bessarion turns in the second to a discussion of the conditions necessary for mounting a response. No successful campaign can be launched against the Turks, he says, unless the nations of Europe are at peace. The European body politic is sick, weak and at war against itself; if it can heal itself through peace, however, no external threat will defeat it. This marks the start of a long, philosophical meditation on the subject of political concord.[64] As he draws various stock analogies between political concord and a healthy body, a happy family, or a well-run ship, Bessarion introduces a secondary theme: not only does concord enable a community to function properly, but discord, by contrast, leaves it open to external attack. The Turks had not captured Greece by themselves: 'It is nothing but discord which has destroyed wretched Greece; nothing but civil war has laid waste that part of the world.'[65] Concord requires peace between allies and forbids any one party to negotiate with the enemy. Turning to more ancient history, Bessarion reminds his readers why Philip of Macedon overcame Greece: not only because Athens, Thebes and Sparta had ceased to cooperate with one another, but also because various cities began to call on Philip to help them fight their neighbours.[66] In his first oration Bessarion made much of the fact that the Cantacuzenus pretender had invited Mehmed's ancestors into Europe to serve his own designs; his examples here are likewise intended to warn those Western states hoping to make a separate peace with the sultan.

Bessarion had no truck with contemporary initiatives to explore coexisting with or even converting the Turks. Although his friend Nicholas of Cusa devoted much thought to a theory of a universal concord which would transcend the barriers of different religions (an idea dating back as far, perhaps, as Raymond Lull), Bessarion maintained the hard-line view of the Turk as an intractable enemy.[67] While there can be no doubt that his faith supported him in this view, Bessarion's acute appraisal of the enemy's military impulses convinced him that negotiation with the Turks was more than simply impious; from a political perspective, it was also dangerously irresponsible.

In his orations Bessarion brought the two principal themes of the Renaissance humanist debate over the problem of the crusade together into a single argument: a corrupt and complicit Europe, assailed by an implacable Eastern foe. In articulating these themes in combination, he also managed to transform them. Although Salutati and Biglia had discussed the political background to the rise of Islam and called for political reforms in Europe in order to contain its further spread, ultimately each remained wedded to a highly moralized view of the problem of the crusade. Europe had sinned – in their eyes, the dereliction of political responsibilities, decline of civic virtues and loss of classical culture that together characterized the Middle Ages in Europe had been grave offences against the principles of *humanitas*. As a result, Europe would be punished by the spectre of barbarian aggression until it could repent and reform itself, at which point the problem would go away. Bessarion's call for concord and unity in Europe touched on many of the same points, but in essence he appealed to the self-interest of the European states, not their moral compass. Contemporary princes should tackle the problem of Islam as a means of achieving stability and security at home, and not vice versa. Likewise, though Aeneas Silvius and the humanists in his circle tried to portray the Turks as culturally barbaric and historically aggressive nomads, and therefore a threat to the political economy of Western civilization, in fact their polemical portraits of the Scythian Turks disguised a traditional image of the bloodthirsty infidel only thinly. Their historical and ethnographical researches 'proved' that the Turks were, in fact, demonic agents of chaos and terror, whom only the Vicar of Christ could deflect.

But appeals for a crusade on moral or spiritual grounds, however well cloaked in the current, humanist vocabulary of historical causation, necessity, or security, elicited little response in the tense fray of real Renaissance politics. As an alternative, Bessarion tried to address the princes of Europe on their own terms, presenting them with a Turkish state and sultan whose motivations they would recognize, sympathize with and therefore, as he hoped, understand well enough to fear. And yet, having compiled perhaps the fifteenth century's most convincing set of arguments in favour of an expedition against the Turks, in the end Bessarion's work served only to compound the already intransigent problem of the crusade. By shifting his focus onto the character of the present-day Ottoman state, away from decades of fevered speculation into the nature of their past, Bessarion gave voice to a secret most Renaissance governments already knew exceedingly well: the Ottoman Turks were just like them. Possessed of a sophisticated political apparatus, confronted with relentless domestic economic and social pressures, and exercising a shrewd foreign policy, the circumstances in which the Turks had to work hardly differed from those attendant on any contemporary European state. Bessarion tried to give the Christian princes of Europe good reasons to fear the sultan. But those same reasons, when drawn to their logical conclusions, pointed the way not to war but towards a precarious balance of power. If the Turks were simply a naturally aggressive nation, given to occasional bouts of territorial expansion, then it would not be so difficult to address their needs rationally, by searching out opportunities for cooperation and collaboration with them, even diplomatic *rapprochement* – precisely the mode of interaction that would increasingly define relations between the European states and the Ottoman Empire over the course of the sixteenth century.

3
Pope Pius II and the Crusade

Nancy Bisaha

On 13 August 1464, Pope Pius II (Aeneas Silvius Piccolomini) received communion and addressed his cardinals for the last time, exhorting them to carry on with the work he had begun. 'Woe unto you, woe unto you, if you desert God's work,' he warned, before dying in his sleep a few hours later.[1] On the surface Pius's death was like that of many popes before and after him. But the circumstances were neither peaceful nor ordinary: he died not in one of the papal residences, but far from home at the port of Ancona whence he had intended to embark upon the crusade he had summoned and organized. It seemed a strange, unexpected end for a man who had spent most of his life as a humanist, poet and bureaucrat. Known for his clear-headed political insights and wry humour, Aeneas was never a soldier, nor was he a theologian or saintly figure. He enjoyed a long career as a valued secretary and diplomat who travelled across Europe with or on behalf of his superiors. Refusing to take holy orders for many years, he entered the Church only after he had reached middle age, sired two illegitimate children and written some provocative love poetry and prose. Added to all of this, he was old and very ill when he took up his final journey. Why, when so many other popes were content to summon a crusade, did Pius feel compelled to participate in one? This essay will attempt to explain what personal factors led him to Ancona as well as the religious and political currents that helped point him down that path. Pius's death at Ancona may always seem bizarre, colourful and, to some, uncharacteristically noble for the age, but it can teach us a good deal about fifteenth-century Europe and Pius's life.[2]

It may well be argued that Pius's decision to accompany his crusade was the natural, if extreme, culmination of a lifelong obsession with holy war and a hatred for the Ottoman Turks.[3] He had called attention to the Turkish threat as early as 1436 at the Council of Basel.[4] Aeneas also repeatedly lobbied for crusade in letters before and especially after the fall of Constantinople on 29 May 1453. He urged Popes Nicholas V and Calixtus III and Emperor Frederick III among others to organize or lead a crusade to the East. As pope, one of his first official acts was to organize a European-wide conference at Mantua with the sole purpose of orchestrating a large-scale crusade. If he could find a way to bring divided Europeans together, he believed, and put a large enough army in the field, the Turks could be crushed or at the very least halted. When all his hard work did not succeed in making the crusade a reality, he sought to initiate the process by going (or at least threatening to go) himself.

But was it a natural progression or did Aeneas's views of the Turks and crusade change over time, especially after his election to the papacy? A good place to begin answering this question is a consideration of a few works written before he became pope. Responses to the fall of Constantinople offer examples of some of his most passionate rhetoric. At this point, Aeneas was bishop of Trieste and Siena, but still serving as secretary to Frederick III. Deeply disturbed by the conquest of the Byzantine capital, Aeneas wrote letters to Nicholas V and Nicholas of Cusa in which he expresses righteous indignation at the abuses of fellow Christians and their shrines, and calls for action in defence of the Christian faith and Europe. Equal space, however, is given to the siege's impact on learning and culture. Repeating tales to the pope of the destruction of countless books in the siege, Aeneas laments the event as 'a second death of Homer and Plato'.[5] He goes on at great length in his letter to Cusanus about these losses. What sort of men, he wonders, would attack learning? Xerxes and Darius 'waged war on men, not letters', and the ancient Romans held Greek learning in high regard despite their conquest of the land. But under the Turks, he asserts, Greek learning is sure to perish.[6] For Aeneas, as for many other humanists, tales of the Turks' brutal sack of so rich a city, particularly its libraries, conjured up parallels of the fifth-century sacking of Rome and the subsequent 'Dark Ages'.[7]

As with most humanists, the fall of Constantinople greatly increased Aeneas's interest in and commitment to crusade.[8] He did not have to wait long to put his eloquence to work in this cause. Over the next two years he was charged by Frederick III to deliver orations on his behalf at the diets of Regensburg (Ratisbon), Frankfurt and Wiener Neustadt, where crusade plans were discussed. His orations from Regensburg and Frankfurt were circulated, and one of them was printed.[9] Here Aeneas speaks more specifically of recent losses and areas that are on the brink of succumbing to the Turks as well as the desperate need for Christians to unite against them. Still, Aeneas uses the same blend of themes, lamenting both the losses to Christians and their faith as well as to Western culture. Constantinople was a venerable city, a pillar of the Roman Empire and a seat of distinguished learning. While some had argued that the Turks were descended from the Trojans and therefore had a right to reclaim their ancient patrimony, Aeneas dismisses this notion summarily: 'The Turks are truly not, as many judge, of Asian origin, which they call Trojan; the Romans, who are of Trojan origin, did not hate literature.' The savage Scythians, he argues, were the true ancestors of the Turks.[10] Aware that his tirade against the destruction of learning might be lost on the warriors in his audience, Aeneas asserts that soldiers should be moved by the Turkish threat to literature since heroes require this vehicle to immortalize their deeds.[11] As such, he plays to his audience's desire for both heavenly rewards and earthly glory.

These works reveal Aeneas's concern about the Turkish advance to have been multifaceted. He worried about the consequences for his faith, as seen in his lengthy appeal to his audience about how much weightier their debt was to Christ, who suffered, died for and redeemed them, than to the princes, relatives and friends for whom they readily fought. He also speaks to the security of Christendom and Europe, particularly Hungary and Dalmatia. But the most original and passionate part of the oration is where Aeneas speaks as a humanist, painting an anguished portrait of the Turks as agents of cultural destruction. He seems able to comprehend their opposition to Europe and even the faith, but is almost mystified as to why they would endanger letters. His only answer is that they are barbarians, and as such pose a threat to Europe not seen since the dawn of the dreaded 'Middle Ages'.

Pius's eloquence and political experience, not to mention his passionate support of crusade, caught the attention of Nicholas V's successor, Calixtus III (1455–8).[12] Aeneas became a cardinal in 1456 and was elected pope in 1458. Having taken holy orders only twelve years earlier, it was a stunning and rapid rise to the top of the ecclesiastical hierarchy. What Aeneas had lacked in wealth or familial power, he made up in talent and diplomatic skill. Cardinals and the rulers they represented viewed him as sensible and agreeable; his ardent and public support of crusade also helped his candidacy. Calixtus's vigorous support of the war against the Turks helped bring about Christian victories at Belgrade, Mytilene and Lemnos.[13] Aeneas, with his unrivalled knowledge of

European politics and his diplomatic finesse, seemed the right man to keep the crusade momentum going. But would his position as pope change Aeneas fundamentally as well as his approach to the Turks? The name he chose upon election sends a mixed message. Pope Pius I (c. 142–c. 155) had been a staunch defender of orthodoxy against heretics like Marcion. Perhaps Aeneas wanted to imitate his defence of the faith. Another, more likely, influence on his name choice was Virgil, who frequently referred to the main character of his epic work as 'pius Aeneas'.[14] As his name choice provides no clear answers, let us look to his actions regarding crusade.

Pius's initial efforts to launch a crusade fell right in step with his former life as a statesman and orator. Rather than publish a crusading bull and leave the haggling to his legates, Pius announced a European-wide congress whose only goal was the planning of a large-scale crusade – a congress over which he would preside.[15] As he told his cardinals, his intent was to 'ask advice of those whose aid he needed'.[16] Initially, then, Pius was willing to share planning and control of the crusade with others; he saw it as a multinational task requiring much planning, tact and patience. Patience was required in abundance at Mantua. The congress was due to open on 1 June 1459, but few delegates had arrived by that date. In his opening oration Pius chided rulers and governments for delaying sending delegates or for sending undistinguished representatives who lacked the authority to make decisions or promises: 'Christians are not so concerned about religion as we believed. We fixed the day for the Congress very far ahead. No one can say the time was too short; no one can plead the difficulties of travel. We who are old and ill have defied the Apennines and winter.'[17] It was beginning to dawn on the pope how little respect his directives had commanded. Still, Pius opted to wait at Mantua, hectoring rulers and governments to send ambassadors at once. Against the wishes of his cardinals, he waited almost four months for delegates to arrive.[18]

By the autumn, more representatives had finally arrived. Italians made the best showing, encouraged in no small part by the personal appearance and seeming commitment of Duke Francesco Sforza of Milan.[19] Although non-Italian support was still wanting, with the notable exception of Philip of Burgundy, Pius was sufficiently contented with the attendance and attitude of the present delegates to proceed with planning his crusade. He launched these proceedings with another oration, which was circulated widely and later printed.[20]

Although Pius's goals at Mantua were in many ways similar to those at the imperial diets of 1454–5, his oration is different in several ways.

Unlike the earlier speech, the Mantua oration contains almost no references to the Turks as barbaric threats to learning and Western culture. Nor does he go into detail about the ancient Scythians, the Turks' supposed ancestors. Where he does discuss the classical past, he invokes heroic Greco-Roman models of warfare and honour.[21] Pius's focus, it seems, has shifted to religious matters. He describes how Christendom is increasingly hemmed in by the forces of Islam, who conquered Jerusalem and now threaten to overrun Europe. The atrocities at Constantinople are also listed, as well as the Turks' continuing destruction of churches and blasphemy against Christ. Pius even discusses the origins of Islam in great detail, discrediting it as a sect of pleasure and violence founded by a charlatan, in sharp contrast to the righteousness and purity of Christianity. Another religious theme is the power of prayer. Here Pius cites the biblical examples of Moses and Judith among others, as well as the more recent, miraculous victory of Christian forces at Belgrade. The army defending the Balkan city had the charismatic leadership of the preacher Giovanni da Capistrano and general John Hunyadi, but it was heavily outnumbered by the Turks and comprised largely of peasants. 'They conquered the Turks none the less,' Pius declares, 'fighting the enemy not so much with steel as with faith.'[22]

Crusade rhetoric also appears throughout the oration in echoes of Urban II's sermon at Clermont (1095), which spawned the First Crusade – despite the many differences between Pius's congress and the Council of Clermont.[23] Like Urban, Pius laments the desecration of the Holy Land and the loss of Christian lives in the East while the faithful fight each other in Europe. He urges his audience in traditional crusade rhetoric, to 'brandish weapons not among yourselves but to defend the Church, religion, and the Christian faith from the incursions of barbarians and infidels'.[24] His description of atrocities at Constantinople also recalls the strong language of Urban's sermon: temples are polluted, relics abused, priests killed and women raped. Still bolder connections to the First Crusade are found in his references to participants in that historic campaign:

Oh if Godfrey, Baldwin, Eustace, Hugh the Great, Bohemond, Tancred and other great men were here who once penetrated Turkish battle lines and recovered Jerusalem by force, they would not allow us to speak at such length, but rising up, as in the presence of Urban II our predecessor, they would cry out passionately, 'God wills it [Deus vult]!'

This speech is not the first time Pius referred to the First Crusade, but this is the first time it occupies so central a position in a crusading oration, replacing his cherished humanist themes of culture versus barbarism.

Why the shift? To state the obvious, in 1454–5 Aeneas spoke as bishop and secretary; in 1459 he spoke as the highest authority in the Church and all of Christendom. In 1454–5 he called for crusade under the leadership of the emperor; in 1459 he called for a cooperation of Christians under the mantle of the papacy. And yet, despite the changes in Pius's life, the audiences he addressed were quite similar – delegates representing the interests of governments, all being asked to commit to the common cause of crusade. Perhaps he was trying to convince his audience that he was every bit the crusading pope and leader Christendom needed at this time of crisis and not a lightweight poet as many still suspected or feared. If this was the case, his oration was a deliberate effort to veil his identity as humanist and rise to the stature of crusading pope at Mantua. The attempt to inhabit this new role, however, seems a little awkward; he repeats arguments already stated by himself and others at the expense of more original material.[25] Despite his claims that this three-hour speech held the audience transfixed, this piece is probably not among his best.[26]

As we will see, Pius did not give up his interests in classical and secular culture once he became pope, but his papal orations, bulls and letters on the Turks do exhibit a preference for religious and traditional crusade rhetoric. Impassioned tirades about losses to learning whilst preaching defence of the faith would be likely to send the wrong signal. Besides, he had tried moving audiences a few years previously with arguments about culture, learning and even heroic glory, but saw no long-term results once the cheers and compliments had subsided. His decision to speak in the mode of Urban seems calculated to rekindle some of the spirit of 1095. None the less, Pius does not appear to have been so naïve as to think he would receive the same wholehearted response. Immediately after invoking the 'Deus vult!' of the first crusaders, he commented on the appalling contrast between Clermont and Mantua: 'You quietly await the end of our oration and do not seem to be moved by our exhortations.'[27]

The Congress of Mantua ended in January of 1460. Although Pius received many pledges of ships, money, men at arms and the collection of tithes, it was clear that these promises were shaky at best. Years of experience had taught him how to recognize evasion and lack of resolve. His decision to publish the papal bull *Execrabilis* that same month was a desperate effort to keep governments firm to their promises, at least regarding the collection of tithes in their territories.[28] With this move and others, Pius has been criticized for turning his back on his old allegiance to conciliarism; he has also been charged with using crusade as a thinly veiled bid for power.[29] But this seems unlikely given his more democratic approach going into Mantua. Most scholars agree today that his desire for greater unity within Christendom, especially against the Turks, was unwavering, despite his seemingly opposing efforts to accomplish that unity.[30] For all the frustration that gave rise to the bull, it reflects his faith in the authority of the papal office to coerce Christians even if his personal charisma failed to move them.

Following the Congress of Mantua, peninsular upheaval consumed Pius, leaving him little hope for crusade until these issues were resolved.[31] Still, he continued to write avidly on all subjects, as seen in his famous *Commentaries*. A mix of history, autobiography, social commentary, poetry, even epic, they reflect Pius's creativity, his intellectual restlessness and his eclecticism.[32] In between his third-person narration of his deeds as pope, he provides long digressions on the history of countries and cities, frank character sketches of individuals, lush descriptions of the Italian countryside and even amateur archaeological explorations. Yet for all the broadness, candour and wit of the *Commentaries*, most passages on the Turkish advance in the *Commentaries* are markedly restrained. They are neither as frequent nor as long as one might expect given his statement that 'Among all the purposes he had at heart none was dearer than that of rousing the Turks and declaring war against them'.[33] In fact, the Turks are rarely mentioned between early 1460 and 1463. One might read his long silence and inactivity as a lack of commitment on his part, but it seems rather to have sprung from his belief that a small crusade was not worth launching and a large one required the cooperation of, or at least peace between, Italians. No one was more aware of this inactivity than Pius himself, as he admitted to his cardinals, while confessing the near despair such stagnation caused him.[34]

When Pius does focus on the subject of the Turks in the *Commentaries*, his language is noticeably more subdued than in orations. He generally refers to them simply as 'Turks', 'the Turkish race' or, on occasion, 'enemies of the cross'. There is little notion of the Turks as barbarians, poised to demolish Western civilization. If we take these passages at face value as simple accounts of Pius's mood and actions, they show his attitude towards the Turks to have been strikingly sober; he appears cool and tactical, even political, in the face of a potentially emotional issue. The more likely possibility is that Pius intentionally avoided discussing the Turks as barbarian threats to culture here as part of his programme to present himself as a worthy religious leader of crusade. While the *Commentaries'* structure is chronological and unpolished in places, the work is no mere diary; it is a well-crafted composition intended to celebrate and defend Pius's papacy. As such, he generally appears in a favourable, if not perfect, light.[35] Rhetorical flights of fancy might only serve to distract the reader and create a sense of frenzy instead of the control he sought to project.

If papal orations, letters and his *Commentaries* did not offer Pius an arena to express his views on the Turkish advance in humanistic terms, he found a congenial outlet for such musings in his historical writing, specifically the *Asia*, which was part of a longer projected and partially completed work, the *Cosmographia*.[36] In the *Asia*, he discusses threats and losses to the faith, but spends much time examining the Turks from a secular, cultural standpoint. The result has been hailed as surprisingly 'modern', in contrast to contemporary chronicles that continued to cite apocalyptic thought and myth.[37] The history of the Turks was a subject that had interested Pius for many years; he had often referred to their supposed ancient Scythian origins in order to add polemical fire to his letters and orations. In the *Asia* he set about to expand on these foundations. Citing such authorities as Jordanes and a certain 'Aethicus' he describes the Scythians as 'a fierce and ignominious people, fornicators engaging in all kinds of sexual perversions and frequenters of brothels, who ate detestable things: the flesh of mares, wolves, vultures, and, what is even more horrifying, aborted human fetuses'.[38] Pius's emphasis on Scythian barbarity is worth noting since he believed their Turkish descendants had evolved very little over the centuries and were, in fact, destined to perpetuate similar savage patterns of behaviour.[39]

Continuing on the theme of origins, when Pius arrives at the history of the Ottoman line, he underscores the obscurity of Osman's birth. The history of Islam also, as would be expected, receives a similarly bleak and hostile portrayal as a sham religion that encourages indulgence of the flesh, while opposing learning.[40] Pius's aim, then, is to establish the Ottomans as illegitimate and lowly in every way, from their family's origins to the religion they espouse. They have ruined the once flourishing Christian territory of Asia Minor by driving it into barbarism. It is worth noting, however, that Pius's view of modern Asia is not completely negative; beyond the Turks and Muslims of Western Asia lay nations that possess more promising qualities. If the Turkish obstacle could be removed, they might yet be brought to Christ.[41] The *Asia*, in short, can be seen as a continuation of Pius's humanistic thought on the Turks and Islam. These pronouncements reflect a more secular appraisal, albeit one that is stamped by a strong sense of cultural chauvinism.

Pius's focus returns to religion in his perplexing letter to Mehmed II, where he invites the sultan to convert to Christianity in exchange for papal legitimation and support. Many have taken this letter at face value and view it as a brief but shining moment when Pius's attitude towards the Turks and crusade softened. I have argued at length elsewhere why this letter should not be regarded as a genuine effort to convert Mehmed II.[42] Instead it was intended for a Christian audience, most likely for propagandistic purposes. The bulk of the letter is devoted to a polemical treatment of Islam and a defence of Christian tenets. As in his papal crusade orations, the theological content is very conventional. Pius's faith was strong, but he avoided taking part in debates and held to the letter of doctrine as explained by Church fathers.[43] Repeating religious themes seen in his other works, Pius was trying to remind Christians of the rich tradition they stood to lose as well as the evils that would be forced upon them under the religion of the Turks. There are some forceful moments of humanistic praise of Europe for its superiority in warfare and learning, but the majority of the letter seems an attempt to position Pius as a religious authority. In this respect, the letter to Mehmed falls in line with most of Pius's works written as pope on crusade.

What seems to be the case so far is that Pius divided his rhetoric and interests almost schizophrenically regarding the Turks once he became pope. He took very seriously the moments when he spoke *ex cathedra* on crusade and attempted to bring an air of gravity and authority to his words – apparently, he did not trust humanist rhetoric on culture and history to do this for him. This might make Pius seem very calculated in how he approached crusade: he donned the cap of a devout crusade pope when it suited him, but occasionally found more appropriate venues to vent his humanistic outrage against the Turks. Might this mean that the papacy did not bring about a personal change in Pius so much as a shift in his carefully constructed public façade? Was his plan to go on crusade a public relations stunt meant to bolster his authority as spiritual leader of the war? A less cynical explanation of the schizophrenic quality of his writing is that he was deeply engaged in a struggle between his new religious position and his old secular loves, at least in regard to crusade. His elevation to the papacy may well have forced him to examine why defeating the Turks was so important; as pope he could hardly answer the defence of culture or the pursuit of glory. Was his decision to go on crusade a sign that the spiritual side had won, and that he was looking to God for a miracle to support his crusade?

As his *Commentaries* and even his crusade bull reveal, he did not envisage his crusade as a solo, quixotic journey – at least not initially. Nor was he hopelessly naïve about the response he hoped to elicit. Pius's reasons for going on crusade were more clear-minded and rational, despite their drama. He spoke of the idea as early as 1461 in a secret letter to the doge of Venice, but it was not until March 1462 that he began to take steps in this direction.[44] He explained his thinking to a group of six trusted cardinals: by embarking on crusade he would force Philip of Burgundy to fulfil the vow made in 1453 to fight the Turks if another great Christian prince would accompany him. After years of failed attempts to produce that prince, Pius had decided that he would play the role: 'We will summon Burgundy to follow us who are both king and pontiff and we will claim the fulfillment of his vow and oath. No excuse will be open to him. A greater than king or emperor, the vicar of Christ will declare war.'[45] If he could only convince Philip to take the field, others would soon follow. The King of France would send at least 10,000 men; the Hungarians and the Venetians would also contribute forces given their interests in the region. Finally, soldiers from all over Europe would enlist.[46]

Where pressure did not succeed, he hoped a combination of goodwill and shame might do the trick. When he announced his plan to all of his cardinals in September 1463, he stated: 'We are determined to go at once into the war against the Turks and by deed as well as words to summon Christian princes to follow us. Perhaps when they see their master and father, the Pope of Rome, the vicar of Jesus Christ, going into the war old and ill they will be ashamed to stay at home.'[47] He repeated this idea, though rather more gently, in his bull *Ezechielis prophetae* when he asks what excuse will suffice when he 'old, weak, and sick proceeds on this expedition, and you who are young, healthy, and robust of body are hiding at home'.[48] Given these words, one might argue Pius was a master of persuasion, scheming to draw or coerce men into crusading. He begins to look less like a dreamer and more like a clever tactician gambling that honour and chivalry were not dead.

Pius was also realistic about how much the crusade could accomplish. He did not expect an enormous groundswell of recruits who would march off at his command to crush the Turks; he would have been satisfied with saving Hungary, the bulwark of Christendom, from any further losses.[49] Nor did Pius expect complete unity throughout the expedition. Other states began to grumble at Venice's lead in the proposed crusade, fearing that she would win all of Greece and set her sights on Italy. But Pius believed that if the crusade succeeded in wresting Greece away from the Turks, disenfranchised Balkan Christians would soon rise up to reclaim their lands, thereby keeping Venice from amassing too much power.[50] Without a doubt, Pius was good at public relations; his daring plan was starting to bear fruit. The Venetians arrived at Ancona, albeit late. Many individual crusaders from northern Europe also waited at Ancona until plague forced them to withdraw. Philip was dissuaded from going on crusade by Louis XI of France, but sent a force of 3,000 men. Even Francesco Sforza sent a small force.[51]

Still, there is something about Pius's decision to go on crusade that makes it seem more than a clever stratagem. Shrewd and dispassionate as he might have been regarding the benefits of such a deed for his cherished expedition, he appeared deeply troubled by how far he had to go in order to provoke a response from his Christian flock. He had not always been so discouraged. During the conclave in which he was elected pope in 1458, he demonstrated an awareness of the corruption within the higher ranks of the Church as well as a desire to staunch some of it through his own election. Another frontrunner, the Cardinal of Rouen, was fabulously wealthy and well connected, but not known for his probity of life. Aeneas, by way of contrast, was poor and sincere. He seemed optimistic about reforming the Church from within, albeit more by exhortation than by tough measures.[52] His words during the conclave as well as his disappointment in Nicholas V in 1453 for failing to save Constantinople suggest that he believed a strong-willed and upright pope could reverse setbacks in the Church and in crusade.

After a few years of occupying the see of Peter, this bravado was noticeably shaken; Pius could not help but recognize how sullied the image of the papacy and clergy had become. He explained this to his group of six trusted cardinals in March 1462. His envoys had been derided by princes; the imposition of tithes was met with threats of a council; the sale of indulgences was deemed greedy. 'People think our sole object is to amass gold. No one believes what we say. Like insolvent tradesmen we are without credit. Everything we do is interpreted in the worst way.'[53] Still, he was not willing to abandon finding 'some plan for the common salvation'. These circumstances did not lead him to abandon crusade, but to view it as even more important than it had once seemed. While crusade continued to stand as a means to protect Christendom from external enemies and simultaneously to unify it, it now offered a way to purify or reform it in one fell swoop. His personal participation in crusade, he hoped, would restore Christians' faith in their clergy while inspiring a sufficient military response to the Turkish advance.

What was Pius's emotional state in all of this? His disappointment in the morals of the clergy ran deep and affected him personally; he felt a strong obligation to help heal the Church through his own example. As he goes about this task, he generally seems calm and determined, if wearied by the constant opposition he faced, but he also reveals his vulnerability and uncertainty. As he tells his cardinals in 1462, 'We have spent many sleepless nights in meditation, tossing from side to side and deploring the unhappy calamities of our time ... during our silent days and nights, we have been coming more and more to this decision.'[54] He does not claim to have been directly inspired by God in his answer, but his searching suggests prayer and anguish as well as strategizing. A touching air of humility and humanity also appears in his crusade bull of October 1463 that was lacking in his oration at Mantua. He acknowledges that the Turks' power has grown and that the fight will not be easy but still exhorts the faithful to follow him.[55]

Pius's tone regarding crusade was even more humble in his private address to his cardinals (September 1463). In the same entry mentioned above where he talks of pressuring and shaming fellow Christians into joining him, he shows himself to be very human and a little hesitant: 'It is not good to say 'Go'; perhaps they will listen better to 'Come'. We are resolved to try.'[56] These words show him stepping outside of the powerful mantle of pope to occupy that of priest. They also show his uncertainty about the outcome but an equal resolve to keep trying and to put his trust in God. He no longer firmly believes that he can succeed where Nicholas and others failed, but he is willing to sacrifice everything in the attempt, even his life. While Pius had no intention of going into battle, he knew well that the journey itself was more than his delicate health could bear. He goes on to say, 'If this method does not rouse Christians to war, we know no other. This path we are resolved to tread. We know it will be a crushing burden for our old age and that we shall in a sense be going to certain death. We do not refuse. We trust all to God.'[57] His words about trusting all to God seem a prayer both for the preservation of his life during the rigorous journey and for the success of the crusade. Hence, towards the end of his pontificate, Pius's crusade had become a deeply personal act as well as a carefully considered show of faith to the flock he had determined to lead by example.

There is also something of the classical, epic model in Pius's decision to crusade – an idea that translates most strongly in the *Commentaries*. Pius has come to see himself as the lone hero or re-founder of Christian and secular Rome, restoring it to its former glory.[58] As he states in the *Commentaries*, 'We must die sometime and it matters not where so long as we die nobly.' These words show him seeking a warrior's death, ennobled by fearlessness and self-sacrifice. But that is not all he is after; he immediately adds, 'Blessed are they who die in obedience to the Lord. A noble death redeems an evil life.'[59] Here he envisages himself as the lone Christian penitent seeking salvation and reparation for all his sins from God. Whether or not his crusade launched a greater anti-Turk offensive or redeemed the Church, Pius seemed to be seeking martyrdom as a means to propitiate the God whom he had grown ever more desperate to please as his papacy dragged on with so few accomplishments.[60]

Pius's doubts about his ability to launch a sufficiently large crusade can be seen in other ways that point to a hedging of bets. The ceremony surrounding the reception of the head of St Andrew into Rome is one telling example. The spectacular arrival of this very important Greek relic, brought by the Despot Thomas Palaeologus as he fled the Morea, provided a dramatic demonstration of the endangerment of the Christian faith in the Turkish advance. Even the dead were not safe from the infidels. The timing of this event, however, is very important. Thomas had arrived with the relic several months before Pius sent for it, and the procession took place before the receptacle for the relic was ready. The only event with which the procession coincided was Pius's decision to go on crusade – both took place in the spring of 1462.[61] It seems that Pius hoped St Andrew would bring energy to his flagging crusade and inaugurate a new phase. Perhaps the Italians' devotion to the cult of saints might motivate them; by crusading they could incur the debt of the powerful apostle and receive his intercession. Another way that Pius hedged his bets was through the continuing threat of anathema. *Execrabilis* was one form of this type of coercion; the bull of 1463 featured others. Here, Pius utters forceful maledictions against those who hinder his crusade.[62] These actions stand in sharp, fascinating contrast to his gentle exhortations to would-be crusaders to come with him. They also show his lingering faith in the power of papal threats even as they reveal the opposition he expected to encounter.

Pius's decision to accompany his crusade, then, seems motivated by many desires, which all played more or less equal roles in his mind and heart. He saw the move in political terms as a means to inject new life into his stalled crusade. It was also a vehicle of reform for a jaded and abused society of Christians. Finally, it was a deeply personal and risky mission. By this act, he hoped to redeem himself and make satisfaction to God. Whether Pius intended to see his crusade through until the very end is a difficult question to answer. At least one contemporary believed he planned to find an excuse to take harbour in southern Italy where be would be detained indefinitely while the crusade carried on without him.[63] Still, Pius's decision to go as far as Ancona without Philip the Good is telling. If he knew in 1463 the journey was dangerous to his health, by 1464 there was little hope he would survive it.

In reviewing Pius's attitude towards crusade over the years a pattern emerges. He started with pronounced secular concerns about the defence of Western culture and civilization. After his election to the papacy, these specific concerns seemed to recede, while his commitment to crusade as a religious undertaking intensified. In answer to the question posed earlier about whether his shift to a religious emphasis in discussion of crusade was personally motivated or a mere stratagem, it seems to have been a little of both. In the beginning of his papacy, Pius's awkward shift was probably driven more by the needs of rhetoric and public relations, but his conviction in the divine righteousness of crusade and his attachment to traditional piety appear to have grown as his papacy progressed.[64] He may, indeed, have been hoping for a miracle, however undeserving of one he thought he was.

Perhaps the clearest message that emerges from Pius's twists and turns in his approach to crusade is his desperate search for a way to touch Christians' hearts and command their respect. He tried diplomacy, eloquence, coercion, his own good example, even martyrdom. Yet, despite his disappointments he never gave up hope completely; his death may be seen as a last great gesture to prove to the faithful that the clergy (and their requests) deserved to be honoured. Pius had no illusions about converting Mehmed and the Turks, much less the desire to try, but he truly believed in the power of Christianity. His efforts towards crusade can be read as attempts to translate that belief to the jaded fold. We will never know if Pius's gamble would have paid off and shamed or inspired an adequate number of recruits, but if he had possessed the strength, he might well have waited them out.

4
The German *Reichstage* and the Crusade

Johannes Helmrath

Crusades were not all alike. The concept, which in the central Middle Ages designated a series of armed pilgrimages to the Holy Land associated with expansionist goals, came as a result of the Turkish conquest of Constantinople in 1453 to assume a thoroughly defensive character. These traumatic losses called for concrete answers. But before a military response could be made, a process of mobilization was necessary, not least because of the wide-ranging nature of the problem, which affected the whole of Christendom.[1] In practice, however, the response to the Turks in the fifteenth century was above all rhetorical. At the German imperial assemblies in the wake of the fall of Constantinople a new and characteristic form of oration was fashioned, which in the literature acquired the name 'oration against the Turks' (*Türkenrede*) or 'oration for a war against the Turks' (*Türkenkriegsrede*). The aim was to persuade the German princes to commit themselves to a military expedition against the steadily expanding Ottomans by convincing them of its necessity, through the use of argument and emotion. The key figure in this development proved to be the humanist and imperial counsellor Aeneas Silvius Piccolomini, later Pope Pius II (1406–64). At the assemblies that took place at Regensburg, Frankfurt and Wiener Neustadt in 1454–5 he adapted anti-Turkish oration to the needs of the *Reichstage*; he was the first to shape classical rhetoric for such an arena, making it a medium for the politics of the day, and the exposition of a topical subject matter. As a more or less constant feature at imperial assemblies right up to the end of the sixteenth century, anti-Turkish oratory also reflected an essential component of Europe's lively but fearful engagement with an alien religion and culture, which were perceived as inherently hostile.

In the following essay the German *Reichstage* will be considered as a particular forum for a new type of rhetoric, one that was impregnated with humanism. We shall investigate how the anti-Turkish oration became established as a new form of oratory at assemblies, what its chief goals were and who were its protagonists. It is also important to ask how far this constantly recurring theme of a crusade against the Turks contributed towards a new culture of oratory at imperial assemblies, and towards the evolution of these assemblies and their procedures into formalized *Reichstage*.

Reichstag and rhetoric: methodological issues[2]

It is important first to outline some of the key concepts of rhetoric. The ancient world adopted a three-fold schema, dividing the *genera dicendi* into the *genus iudiciale* (oration in court; Greek *dikanikón*), the *genus demonstrativum* (oration of praise or festive oration; *epideiktikón*) and the *genus deliberativum* (*symbouleutikón*). The third category included the political 'oration of advice' delivered at a popular assembly or assembly of representatives, and it serves as the leading concept in this study.[3] The oration of advice sets out to weigh up the pros and cons for any political decision, but at the same time has the goal of persuading the audience to make a decision in a particular direction. From this point of view rhetoric means not so much a theory or system as their implementation in the *actio*, the speech and its effective delivery, or oratory. The full spectrum of contemporary forms and occasions for orations included funerals and other commemorative gatherings, weddings and festivals, welcoming ceremonies and assemblies of universities, estates and synods.[4] Again, so-called 'anti-Turkish oration' was just one genre of oration at assemblies, which could address other themes; the prototype, however, was the classical deliberative oration.

Without intending for a moment to ignore the most recent research into the concept of *Reichstage* (*dietae*) and their evolutionary model,[5] we shall here take the word *Reichstag* to be synonymous with the broad meaning of any imperial assembly. The concept of an oration at a *Reichstag*, again, is not intended to delineate a specific, formal genre, rather to encompass all orations that were delivered at *Reichstage* or in their milieu. In this light, it does not seem to me to be anachronistic to view the German imperial assemblies in a 'parliamentary' perspective, despite the concerns of many scholars who condemn any association of *Reichstag* and parliament as typologically or genetically misconceived. After all, orations took place everywhere and in all contexts: at meetings of estates (*Ständetagen*), *États*, *Cortes*, sessions of courts and regions (*Hof*- and *Landtagen*), town communes, councils and general chapters.[6]

What they all had in common was oratory, in the sense of counsel. It is no coincidence that the word *parlamentum* derives from *parlare*. In this light it is surely not contentious to single out the imperial assemblies as the pre-eminent location for political oratory within the Holy Roman Empire.

As far as I can see, forms of speech and communication have not been systematically explored to date in research into estates.[7] Thomas N. Bisson might open up the way with his concept of 'ritual persuasion' at assemblies of estates,[8] at the same time bringing about a linkage with the steadily increasing volume of research into political festivities, ceremonies and rituals in the Middle Ages.[9] 'Ritual persuasion' reconciles what at first glance seem to be opposites: on the one hand, repeated ritual, which has its *modus operandi*, on the other persuasion by argument, which can be more or less spontaneous in character. This involves the crucial question of the extent to which an oration, for example at a *Reichstag*, should be perceived as a ritual act, or rather was so perceived by contemporaries.

The quintessential examples of oratory in a ceremonial context are orations made at the festive openings of sessions of the Paris *Parlement*, the chief organ of justice, events associated with one of the most heavily symbolic representations of monarchy, the *Lit de justice*. On such occasions the president of the *Parlement*, and occasionally the king himself, would deliver a *harangue*.[10]

For a long time historians showed little interest in orations at the *Reichstage*.[11] In his studies on *Reichstag* literature during the baroque period, Friedrich Hermann Schubert noted that the oldest amongst the sparse descriptions of *Reichstage* came from the pens of Italian humanists: Aeneas Silvius Piccolomini in the case of Regensburg in 1454 and Riccardo Bartolini in that of Augsburg in 1518.[12] More than anything else, the first descriptions consist essentially of accounts of orations. It is well known that rhetoric held a place of honour for the humanists. In Italy the city-states converted the 'rhetoric of the Renaissance', in the sense of theory, into a 'renaissance of rhetoric', in the sense of political orations.[13] But as Schubert remarked, it was not just the typical humanistic world-view that the history of the *Reichstage* was more than anything else that of *Reichstag* oratory: humanists also recognized in oratory an element that was fundamental for the *Reichstag*'s operation as a political forum.

Even in the imperial assemblies of the fifteenth century, when procedure had not yet been stabilized, we can discern a group of 'set piece occasions' for orations, what Braungart described as 'basic acts'

(*Basisakten*).[14] On such occasions the clearest correlation and the most fruitful symbiosis were achieved between the classical rules of rhetoric on the one hand, and the issues being addressed on the other. During the normal business of the *Reichstage* this occurred in the first place at the (more or less ceremonial) oration given at the start or conclusion, and secondly, in orations by envoys, with the corresponding replies. In the latter the sphere of diplomacy came into play, exercising its own impact on the oratory.[15] A somewhat different occasion was the sermon given at the Mass for the Holy Spirit, with which a *Reichstag*, like its spiritual counterpart, a Church council, was inaugurated. Mertens made a useful distinction between an 'inner zone' of events at *Reichstage*, consisting of both the central core of negotiations and the formalities that accompanied them, and a flanking 'outer zone' made up of communications by courts and towns; at the latter too there were orations. Fixing a clear division between the two zones is not yet possible in the fifteenth century, given the open character of the imperial assemblies. For that reason the important cluster of issues relating to ceremonial, ritual and festivities, which increasingly preoccupies students of the Middle Ages and early modern period alike, has to include oratory; and it similarly has to be considered when *Reichstage* are studied as festive occasions.[16]

Not all speech constitutes oratory. Interventions, contributions to debates, even more so the reading out of proposals or letters, cannot really be considered to be oratory in any meaningful sense of the word. For the sake of methodological clarity, and notwithstanding the problems involved, an attempt should therefore be made to define an oration. It is the verbal delivery, to an audience, of a speech that encompasses a substantial script that has been composed in careful accordance with the rules of rhetoric. From the large corpus of orations that have thus far been collected, we have to focus on a small group of orations that meet two conditions. In the first place they achieved *actio*, they were actually presented: they do not exist simply on the page, but were delivered to an audience at an imperial assembly. And in the second place they survive in their entirety, which means that there was sufficient interest to preserve them. Only in such circumstances can genre and language really be analysed, subject to the vagaries of selections made during the process of transmission. From a written text alone it is often apparent neither that the oration actually took place and that the text was not written 'for the drawer', nor that the text contains the oration as given rather than the outcome of a later rewriting.

The most important compilation of sources is the *Deutsche Reichstagsakten*, the publication of which, inaugurated by Ranke, began in 1867.[17] For the period from 1409 to 1594 there exist about 80 orations that meet the criteria specified above, i.e. they were definitely delivered at an imperial assembly and then textually transmitted. But the phrase 'at an imperial assembly' is potentially misleading. In each case, as far as the sources permit, we have to ascertain the context in terms of the discussions that were occurring, the audience and its composition, and the location. In the assemblies of the fifteenth century there was as yet no such thing as a plenary session. And the precise location in which orations occurred can be sobering: as opportunity offered, this could be the hall of the local *Rathaus*, or even a parlour in the tavern where a prominent participant was lodging.

From 'oration as treatise' to 'oration as call to arms': the 'Turkish *Reichstage*' of 1454–5

An initial high point in *Reichstag* rhetoric, which there is space here only to mention, occurred in the years from 1438 to 1446, when the council of Basel acted as a forum for wide-ranging discussions about the authority of pope and council; the search for princely support caused the debates to spill over, as it were, into the imperial assemblies. Envoys from pope or council, men such as John of Segovia, Niccolò Tudeschi and Nicholas of Cusa, gave orations which typically were treatises constructed in accordance with juristic and scholastic norms.[18] The oration delivered by the Spanish theologian John of Segovia at Mainz on 28 March 1441 lasted seven and a half hours. To the best of my knowledge that was a record, the longest known oration given before a *Reichstag* audience in the late Middle Ages.[19] The treatise that the canonist Niccolò Tudeschi (Panormitanus) gave in the form of an oration in the following year contained almost 1,000 legal citations; it covers 100 printed pages in the *Reichstagsakten*.[20]

The Turks saw to it that after an eight-year pause a new wave of imperial assemblies took place. At the same time a new type of oration made its appearance there: the humanistic oration in the classical and above all Ciceronian mould. The fall of Constantinople made crusading a duty of the shocked Christian public. Like the Great Schism before it, the war against the Turks caused contemporaries, at least the 'opinion leaders' characterized by Mertens, to look for the leadership of a pan-Christian enterprise towards the emperor and the empire, authorities which were ancient, wide-ranging and universal, even if symbolic.[21] As in the conciliar period, the established forum was the embryonic *Reichstage*, which were evolving from special meetings of the royal court.

A sequence of three *Reichstage*, those held at Regensburg and Frankfurt in 1454 and Wiener Neustadt in 1455, have acquired the name in the literature of the 'Turkish *Reichstage*'. From this point onwards the history of the empire was to remain closely intertwined with the Turkish question for three centuries. The latter had a profound impact on the *Reichstage*, above all on oratory there. The oration against the Turks immediately became a standard element. As an oration delivered before princes it was disseminated over the whole of Europe;[22] by contrast, so far as we know the only meetings of estates at which it became embedded were the German *Reichstage*.

Clearly, the 'Turkish *Reichstage*' evolved from those held during the conciliar period: like their predecessors, they were platforms for oratory. Not this time, though, for 'orations as treatises'; at these *Reichstage* the modern, humanistic 'orations as calls to arms', with their enormous debt to Cicero, achieved their breakthrough. There had been precedents for this type of oration in the conciliar period, to the extent that humanists had appeared at councils as 'guest performers' – notably, Poggio Bracciolini at Constance and Gherardo Landriani, Ugolino Pisani and Aeneas Silvius Piccolomini at Basel.[23] But the *Reichstage* now functioned as the main forum for this modern oratory, whereas previously they had experienced only scholastic forms, which the humanists scourged as debased forms of rhetoric.

The secular topic of war found its natural home in the anti-Turkish oration, alongside the idea of forming minds through rhetoric. The target audience was essentially made up of the princes, in their capacity as military commanders, and the estates, as providers of manpower and tax revenue. In this respect the educational mission of the humanists, especially with respect to lords, became prominent, assimilating with the medieval Mirror for Princes tradition as well as with traditional crusade preaching. What was at stake was the Christian justification of warfare, and the best way to achieve this was to present the conflict archaically as a war against the heathen, a crusade, while at the same time depicting it within the rhetorical tradition of the ancient world, pragmatically stressing its feasibility. Anti-Turkish oratory at the *Reichstage* therefore had a number of goals: persuading the princes, demonstrating the emperor's willingness to take action, presenting information gained about the enemy, enabling the speaker to win renown as an orator and arousing cathartic reaction from the audience.

The rhetorical ambition of a man delivering an oration against the Turks drew on the persuasive rationale and the affective power of a goal for which, at the end of the day, there was no alternative. Who could afford to declare himself opposed to the protection of Christendom? Often the subject matter in the orations is manpower and taxes. In this respect anti-Turkish oratory fits into the tradition of princely orations before their estates, in which attempts are made to establish the *casus necessitatis* and validate the associated need for ad hoc funding. We are dealing with an early form of oration to parliament: for war and taxes were the earliest and most important issues that came within the competence of assemblies of estates.[24] Within the growing corpus of material relating to the Turks, anti-Turkish oratory represented a unique type of oration both in literary and in political terms. That contemporaries realized this is shown by the collection of orations that Nikolaus Reusner made at the end of the sixteenth century, which remains even today the most significant and complete such compilation of texts.[25]

It is worth underscoring Mertens's remark: 'it was, on the whole, through the medium of anti-Turkish orations in Latin that the professional culture of oration gained access to the imperial assemblies.'[26] In large measure this was the work of one person, the imperial counsellor Aeneas Silvius Piccolomini (1406–64). Recruited to the chancery in 1442 and crowned with the poet's laurels, appointed bishop in 1447, the humanist advanced at court to become an influential politician.[27] The three 'Turkish *Reichstage*' of 1454–5 were basically his achievement,[28] acting as diplomat and as orator. Aeneas Silvius had long been convinced of the need for war against the Turks, which later became the key theme of his pontificate. In addition, there was a strong convergence between his own identity, personal as well as humanistic and literary, and the oratory at the *Reichstage*.

His oration at Regensburg, *Quamvis omnibus*, given on 16 May 1454 during the third session, both acted as the prelude and established the parameters for what followed.[29] Then at Frankfurt and Wiener Neustadt there took place a unique encounter. Three of the stars in the humanistic firmament came together: as at Regensburg Giovanni da Castiglione (†1460), the bishop of Pavia, as papal legate,[30] Johannes Vitéz (†1472), bishop of Großwardein, as envoy of King Ladislas of Bohemia and Hungary,[31] and Piccolomini, bishop of Siena, as representative of the emperor. And there was a fourth orator, the Franciscan provincial Giovanni da Capistrano, who rushed from Breslau to Frankfurt in response to Piccolomini's urgings.[32] Capistrano represented charismatic preaching and may best be visualized as operating in the 'outer zone' of the *Reichstag*'s activities referred to above. It is reported that in Capistrano's audience even visitors to the *Reichstag* sat entranced on the wooden platform while the preacher, who it was said could have initiated a riot by raising his finger, railed on Frankfurt's market square against luxury and for the crusade.[33]

All four men were professional orators. Three of them, Piccolomini, Castiglione and Capistrano, came from Italy, the fourth, Vitéz, from Hungary. For all the heavy burdens carried by the legate Castiglione, his oration and that of Piccolomini bear unmistakable similarities. There was no repetition of the pro and con debates that had characterized the Basel Council. There was no alternative to a crusade, so the debate was not whether, but when and how. In this respect Piccolomini and Castiglione formed something akin to a pair of sparring fighters, in so far as the former lobbied for imperial sponsorship of a crusade and the latter for papal sponsorship, while sharing a common goal. Their orations ran like a chain through all three *Reichstage*, together making up a dense mass of humanistic oratory that was without precedent in the empire. Both spoke at Regensburg on 16 May; at Frankfurt Piccolomini spoke on 15 October, the legate on 16 October; at Wiener Neustadt Piccolomini spoke at the opening on 25 February (*In hoc florentissimo conventu*) and again on 23 March (*Si mihi*), Castiglione on 22 March. In the lead-up to the Regensburg meeting the legate had already spoken before the Emperor Frederick III at Vienna and before King Ladislas at Prague, then at Regensburg itself.[34] For a long time both his Frankfurt oration *Sollicitus* of 16 October 1454 and his Wiener Neustadt oration *Supervacuum puto* of 22 March 1455 were believed to be lost, but they did survive.[35]

The high degree of transmission is remarkable. Five orations of Aeneas Silvius Piccolomini, three of Castiglione (seven if we include those that he gave in the lead-up to Regensburg) and five of Vitéz[36] were preserved as texts. Never before had not just the orator himself, but also his audience, deemed so many orations to be worth recording. In the case of Wiener Neustadt alone, nine orations survive as texts out of a total of 18 that we know were delivered.[37]

The high point was Piccolomini's oration at Frankfurt, *Constantinopolitana clades*, an Incipit that was in itself programmatic. He gave it on 15 October 1454,[38] before an audience whose size is unknown, but which included the papal legate Castiglione, Markgraf Albrecht Achilles of Brandenburg, Archbishop Jakob of Trier, an assembly of high-ranking academics and envoys representing the empire, Hungary, Denmark and Burgundy, Capistrano and various town representatives. The oration lasted for two hours. Piccolomini had the brief of opening the *Reichstag* on the emperor's behalf with an oration containing a political emphasis. This he did. But he went further than duty prescribed, making the choice to use the occasion for a political discourse of great range. Frankfurt became Rome. The model for the structure was Cicero's oration before the Senate, *De imperio Cn. Pompei*, the classic deliberative oration from Latin antiquity. Piccolomini began with emotional references to the widely reported atrocities committed by the Turks in 1453, then moved the emphasis of his argument on to a moral plane. He drew a picture of Europe, the common *patria*, threatened, constricted and cornered (the *angulus*-syndrome).[39] Then he laid out in a classical manner the three arguments for a just war – what was *iustum*, what was *utile* and what was *facile* – established the distinctions between them, worked towards a passage of praise for the Germans (*Vos, Germani*) that was to have a profound impact on later German nationalism, and concluded with an allusion to the heavenly guide from Dante's *Paradiso*.

Piccolomini himself reported on his oration and its effect. There is a striking contrast between the restrained judgement passed in the letters that he wrote from Frankfurt immediately after the oration, and the hymn of praise that features in the later 'Commentaries' (*Commentarii*).[40] Had people generally understood him, given that, in his words, 'Cicero himself, or Demosthenes, would have found these hearts too hard to move'? The thought suggests itself that in the highly educated counsellors present, that 'rhetorically well-equipped leading group of the late-medieval princely state', [41] the humanistic orators at the *Reichstage* had the most receptive audience they could hope for. But what did the princes understand? What impact did the oration have on their political decisions? 'What are letters to us?' (*Quid nobis de litteris*), as Piccolomini himself described the princes asking at one point in the *Clades* oration.[42] And the oft-reiterated, unquestionable fact remains that despite the oratory of a Piccolomini, the war against the Turks failed to materialize. Yet to make any judgement of the success of the *Reichstage* rest on robust results and actions is to hold anachronistic expectations of these assemblies. They were not legislative or decision-making bodies: their principal function, at this point anyway, was to debate and advise. It is inappropriate also to measure the success of oratory, the 'effect of its assimilation in terms of the actions and behaviour of its audience',[43] solely through the political activity that it generates. The theory of rhetoric placed a high value on the immediate effects of a psychological nature, resulting in a change in behaviour, but there were other important functions: the building of consensus and the imparting of information, for example. The assembly at Frankfurt experienced no surge of enthusiasm, no cries of 'Deus vult!' as the council of

Clermont had in 1095. People kept their heads, and it was only two weeks after the oration, following tough negotiations between Piccolomini and the prince-electors, that a detailed military roll (*Heeresmatrikel, Anschlag*) consisting of an army of 55,000 men was drawn up for the war against the Turks, the third such roll since 1422.[44] Even Piccolomini had expected no more.

In addition, judging success solely in terms of action fails to take into account the indirect effect exercised by an oration through its written versions. Piccolomini reported that many who heard the *Clades* oration were visibly moved and made copies immediately after its delivery: 'orationem Enee ab omnibus laudatam multi transcripsere'.[45] At least two letters survive in which Piccolomini promised that he would send copies.[46] And he did: with exactly 50 known copies, above all of central European provenance, the oldest (the Dominican Library, Vienna, 235/293) dated 5 January 1455, the *Clades* was one of the most widely copied orations from the last phase of manuscript production.[47] Piccolomini's Frankfurt oration was, on the one hand, literally inscribed among the first semi-official acts of the *Reichstage*, and on the other, received as a literary work of art. In the latter respect it won wide dissemination, above all in humanistic circles, as a model and prototype for future orations against the Turks. It was highly valued and its effects were very considerable; even Sebastian Brant, in his *Narrenschiff*, made use of themes from it.[48]

A word on the origins of those who gave orations between 1409 and 1455: overall the majority were Italians, with Piccolomini holding centre stage. With the exception of Gregor Heimburg, the only German orators worthy of note were the Vienna theologian Thomas Ebendorfer, who gave four unequivocally scholastic orations at *Reichstage*,[49] and later Johannes Hinderbach, a pupil of Piccolomini. A humanistic impression is left by the orations (1444, 1454) of Bishop Guillaume Fillastre, the Burgundian envoy, who also spoke elsewhere, for example, before Pope Pius II.[50] The many German counsellors who are named usually made their appearance only as translators of the Latin orations; at Frankfurt and Wiener Neustadt in 1454–5 there were Ulrich Riederer, Ulrich Sonnenberger, Johannes Hinderbach and Hans Pirckheimer.[51] As yet there was no German Piccolomini amongst them.

The congress of Mantua, 1459, and its aftermath

Following Wiener Neustadt the short-lived blaze of glory of *Reichstag* oration came to an end, not least because its 'apostle', Piccolomini, finally returned to Italy in 1455. Following his election as pope, in 1459 he convened his princely congress at Mantua. The organization of the congress as a forum for oration was certainly inspired by two models: the pope's experience of the Basel Council on the one hand, and the German *Reichstage* on the other. Pius II had in mind a sort of Italian *Reichstag*, using the opening created by the Peace of Lodi to further his great goal of the war against the Turks, and while Mantua proved to be a bitter disappointment, it was a masterpiece of oratory,[52] with the pope as principal performer. He saw himself as a new Urban II, and this he certainly achieved in terms of oratory, though not in the impact that his oration enjoyed.

Thematically and structurally, the crusading oration that Pius II gave at Mantua in September 1459, *Cum bellum hodie*, was based upon the *Clades* oration and the orations that he had delivered at Wiener Neustadt. But in quality it surpassed them, establishing a new apogee,[53] and constituting a *summa* of Piccolomini's orations against the Turks. The Mantuan oration was transmitted in more than 120 manuscript copies and at least 16 printed versions. *Cum bellum hodie* could well be the most widely disseminated oration of all European humanism, above all because it was copied more than the *Clades* oration in Italy and France. One significant factor behind the multiple copying was that the most famous orations, like *Clades* and *Cum bellum hodie*, were included in different imprints of the pope's *Epistulae familiares*, which reached a particularly wide audience. They were included selectively in the great collections of councils and *Reichstage* (Labbe and Mansi; Müller's *Reichstagstheatrum*), in the *Annales ecclesiastici* of Baronius and his continuators, and of course in Reusner's collection of *orationes turcicae* (1595–8), besides individual works like the Burgundian Chronicle of Adrien de But.[54]

Piccolomini had delivered his previous orations as imperial envoy and bishop. Now he spoke as pope. This brought about, on the one hand, an increased emphasis on the pastoral and preaching element, which it is true had always been present to some degree, with the pope praying for God's help, and on the other, an appeal towards the Christian world in its entirety. Given our subject it is worthwhile briefly analysing the characteristic style of the oration *Cum bellum hodie*.[55] The pope began with a prayer, then much as in *Clades* he handled three topics: first, *justae causae*, second, *facultates belli gerendi*, and third, instead of *utile*, the *magna praemia* that the war would bring for the victor (209A). The justice of the war was approached from an historical perspective (*revolvite historias*; 211A). Pius described the extent of the Christian *Imperium Romanum* (*haec fuit olim*; 209D), its successive losses to Islam, the gains made by Islam up to its present phase, the expansion of the Turks, and the immediate threat that the latter posed (*aperta est Turcis Italia*; 211A). In this way the legitimacy of resistance was made crystal clear to the audience. The notorious cruelties perpetrated by the Turks were narrated in a manner calculated to elicit an emotional response.

To prove the *facilitas* of the war the orator evoked the alleged weakness and softness of the Turks, historic victories from the Old Testament and antiquity in which small armies had triumphed over larger ones, and recent successes against the Turks such as that at Belgrade in 1456. He included a short sketch *de Sarracenorum lege* (214E), which more than had been the case with his earlier orations linked *Cum bellum hodie* to traditional critiques of Islam. Here the pope anticipated the substance of his later *Epistula ad Mahometem*, establishing the key differences between Christianity and Islam in terms of *veritas fidei*. There followed an appeal to believe the witnesses to the faith: if the Greeks, Pius said, gave credence to their historians Herodotus and Thucydides, and the Romans to Livy, Sallust and Tacitus – 'why then do we not believe ours?' (*Cur nos non credimus nostris*), that is to say the martyrs, the Greek and Latin Church Fathers as well as *proximi aevo nostro*, Thomas Aquinas and Albertus Magnus (217A). Referring to the antetypes of the Old Testament prophets and the Sybils, the pope came to 'Christ's law' (*lex Christi*). Its message, the sufferings of Christ that brought mankind salvation, flowed out in the appeal: 'O reges, o duces, o viri potentes, surgite iam tandem et Christi dei vestri religionem ac honorem defendite' (218D). In expanding on his third point, the attainable *praemia* (i.e. *utilitas*), the pope referred only briefly to material booty, instead evoking at length the heavenly reward, the indulgence (*plenissima venia*; 219A), the True Life (*vera vita*) and the heavenly Jerusalem. All this was to be won through the *Turcense bellum* (219C). In his peroration Pius offered, despite his age, to give his own body to the crusade: 'Et nunc, si censetis, non recusabimus aegrotum corpus ... per castra, per acies, per medios hostes ... lectica vehi generosum putabimus' (220D). At the end of his pontificate he would make good this offer.

As products of high rhetoric, Pius II's two great bulls against the Turks should be ranked alongside his orations, which they resemble both in style and substance. The first was *Vocavit nos pius* of 13 November 1458, the invitation to the congress of Mantua; it was included in its entirety by the poet Lodrisio Crivelli in his unfinished prose work *De expeditione Pii Papae II contra Turcos*.[56] The second was the bull *Ezechielis*, which was dated 23 October 1463, and reached an even bigger audience than the oration *Cum bellum*.[57]

While the princely congress at Mantua has the appearance of a universal *Reichstag* meeting on Italian soil, the use of humanistic oratory in the assemblies north of the Alps subsided, a development that in some ways paralleled that of humanism in Germany generally. The initial thrust of the years dominated by Aeneas Silvius Piccolomini died down; not until the end of the century would there be a second great impetus, its major exponent being Conrad Celtis and its reach considerably greater. A broader, structural reason for the lull was the remarkable infrequency of *Reichstage*. Simply put, without *Reichstage* there could be no *Reichstag* orations. 1460 brought two separate meetings, at Nürnberg and Vienna, follow-ups to Mantua. Here the legate Cardinal Bessarion, visibly embittered and combatting growing obstruction to the pope's plans, gave four orations in which he called for the war against the Turks that had been gestating since 1454. After that a new series of meetings started in 1466, again because of the Turkish threat. But we look in vain for orations like those that had been given at Frankfurt and Wiener Neustadt. Even the momentous Regensburg *Christentag* of 1471,[58] where for the first time in 27 years an emperor again made his appearance and which is quite rightly seen as a landmark in a new phase in the development of the *Reichstage*, scarcely stands out for its oratory. There were indeed five orations, including three by the papal legate Francesco Todeschini, another member of the Piccolomini family. Two other orations, whose texts have come down to us, were not delivered: an oration of welcome by Antonio Lolli and the noted oration against the Turks by Giannantonio Campano. Campano had designed his oration as an overblown attempt to surpass the *Clades Constantinopolitana* of his patron Pius II, and it heavily relied on its predecessor.[59]

In the following decades, through to the *aetas Maximilianea*, the transmission of texts for orations at the *Reichstage*, including those against the Turks, is thin.[60] The yield is modest even in the case of the Worms *Reichstag* of 1495, which was so rich in ceremony and so innovative constitutionally.[61] Amongst the numerous verbal interventions that characterized the discussions, there were few striking orations. In the main they were made by envoys, and it appears that in no case did the text survive. The Venetian envoy Benedetto Trevisan made use of his audience with the emperor on 31 May to make 'a magnificent oration in the Latin tongue' before a large number of people attending the *Reichstag*, to which the king had his Italian advisor Ludovico Bruno make a reply.[62] Then, at a particularly ceremonial occasion, the elevation of Eberhard im Bart, count of Württemberg, to duke on 21 July 1495, Veit von Wolkenstein delivered on the king's behalf what the Württemberger

Werner Keller described as 'ain lang zierlich red', an oration of praise for King Maximilian and Count Eberhard.[63]

Recent research[64] has emphasized that at the Worms *Reichstag* structural changes, notably the growing use of written documents and the stabilization of procedure, were already making themselves felt. The same can be said of the progressive strengthening of the 'Three Court system' (*Dreikuriensystem*), and establishing in the form of registers the membership of the *Reichstag*, which hitherto had at best been volatile. It can be demonstrated that these factors were at work much earlier than 1495, especially at the Regensburg *Christentag* in 1471;[65] and according to Peter Moraw's well-known thesis they were instrumental in making the *Reichstag* a genuine institution enjoying a dualistic relationship with the emperor.[66] Since communication and formation were so interdependent in the case of the *Reichstage*, an important question arises in relation to these and future changes in the way the *Reichstage* were organized:[67] did the growth of a written culture damage oral proceedings, at the cost of oratory as much as anything else? The key point is that the question cannot be answered in the affirmative without close study. Written cultures are not autonomous processes and it is simplistic simply to equate them with modernization. It was quite possible also for oral cultures to experience a revival at the same time that written cultures expanded.

A second high-water mark of humanistic oratory: the *aetas Maximilianea*

Just such a revival occurred at the *Reichstage*, and it was the work of the monarch, Maximilian I. The Habsburg was the most skilled orator of all the German kings to date. In contrast to his taciturn father Frederick, Maximilian brought his requests before the *Reichstage* in person and gave an example of princely oratory which had rarely been seen before, indeed it had been viewed as incompatible with the princely and aristocratic ethos. Maximilian's battlefield oration to the nobility of the Upper Rhine at Colmar in 1498 impressed amongst others the Milanese humanist Erasmo Brasca,[68] and his oration at the Constance *Reichstag* in 1507 was so remarkable that Ranke thought it had been concocted by Guicciardini in the style of Livy.[69]

At the same time the Habsburg employed more professional men of letters at his court than any monarch before him. Poets, liberally created *poetae laureati* by Maximilian, historians and artists carried out their literary and rhetorical 'professional services' (*Dienstleistungen*), as Dieter

Mertens put it, against the background of what Jan Dirk Müller termed 'a differentiation in the functions of the lay intelligentsia'. As part of the propaganda process of the House of Austria, such men were engaged in the 'politicization of the myth' by giving orations at the *Reichstage*.[70] In at least eight out of 30 cases *Reichstage* served as stages for their coronations as poets.[71] One of the best known of these individuals was the above-mentioned Riccardo Bartolini from Perugia. In 1518 the theologian and artist made an oration at the emperor's request at the Augsburg *Reichstag*. The emperor's European wars and dynastic politics were legitimated as necessary preliminary measures for his great crusade against the Turks.[72] The fact that Bartolini's *Descriptio* of this *Reichstag* was immediately published may serve as a striking example of how book printing had come to serve the interests of publicizing such events throughout the empire in the *aetas Maximilianea*.[73] More generally, with a total of seven preserved orations against the Turks, this Augsburg meeting surpassed all previous ones. But while a campaign against the Turks was yearned for rhetorically, like the *Reichstage* of 1454–5 Augsburg yielded no practical results: the military effort was in inverse proportion to the rhetorical exertions. But Habsburg propaganda continued to place a premium on maintaining the emperor's leadership of the crusading cause, in terms of prestige and public opinion. The agenda for the orations was two-fold: first to deploy their rhetorical skills to win over the listening audience; and secondly, following their immediate printing, to operate more broadly in the context of public opinion.

The educational substratum of humanism in Germany had become more substantial since the days of Aeneas Silvius Piccolomini and his fellow orators of 1454–5. By the close of the fifteenth century humanism had established itself as an interdisciplinary culture common to all the learned estates. Maximilian's court-humanism can be interpreted as both a dynastic reflex and a motor contributing to a general trend. Yet it remains incontrovertible that the individuals who gave orations at the imperial assemblies in 1518, 1521–2 and again in 1530, were for the most part Italians: Riccardo Bartolini for the emperor, the lawyer Girolamo Balbi for Hungary;[74] then the most ambitious orators, the papal legates and nuncios Thomas Cajetan,[75] Francesco Chieregato,[76] Giovanni Tommaso Pico della Mirandola,[77] Lorenzo Campeggi and Vincenzo Pimpinella, the last *poeta laureatus* since 1512.[78] The German humanist Ulrich von Hutten composed a written oration in 1518, but like Campano in 1471 he was unable to bring it to *actio*, which made him very bitter.[79] In their argument and language, all these orations reveal the influence of the three 'classics', Piccolomini, Bessarion and Giannantonio Campano.

The 'Reformation *Reichstage*' of the 1520s and later decades remained stages for orations against the Turks, especially those at Worms in 1521, Nürnberg in 1522 and the momentous Augsburg *Reichstag* of 1530. From the latter, three orations have survived: that of the legate Campeggi,[80] the nuncio Pimpinella,[81] and the Croatian nobleman Bernardinus Frankapan.[82] Poles, Hungarians and Croatians, all driven from hearth and home by the Turks, for a long time enjoyed the right as guests at *Reichstage* to give lurid accounts of what they had experienced. Erasmus Vitellius (Ciolek), bishop of Plock, represented Poland in 1498 at Freiburg and in 1518 at Augsburg,[83] Andronicus Tranquillus Parthenius (Fran Trankvil Andreis) spoke in August 1518 at Augsburg,[84] Franciscus Josephit (Zsivkovich), bishop of Zengg, spoke in April 1522 at Nürnberg,[85] and a member of the Croatian Frangipani (Frankapan) spoke in November 1522 at Nürnberg, in 1530 at Augsburg and in 1541 at Regensburg.[86]

In the *aetas Maximilianea* the high point of *Reichstag* rhetoric coincided generally with that of German humanism. With all due caution we can say that by the time of the Augsburg meeting of 1530 at the latest, both the number and the significance of the orations were declining. The further one goes into the sixteenth century, admittedly following printed sources that become steadily more scarce, the less frequently one encounters them. Provisionally, one Heinrich Stephanus, speaking in 1594 at Regensburg, may be viewed as the last man in the century to deliver an anti-Turkish oration at a *Reichstag*; at least it won him a place in Reusner's *orationes turcicae*.[87] This may however be a coincidence, given the fact that *Reichstage* were occurring less and less frequently.[88] What is certain is the accelerating tendency to institutionalize and bureaucratize imperial assemblies.[89] The *Ausführliche Bericht, wie es uff reichstägen pflegt gehalten zu werden*, an official publication from around 1570, portrays an idealized world of minutely regulated and written procedures. Oral interventions, in the form of reading aloud discussion papers, continued to feature, but orations were at best given at set-piece occasions. *Reichstage* were opened, following a few words of greeting, by the routine reading out of the emperor's proposals. The arrival of foreign envoys, another set-piece occasion, was equally regimented; above all, orations were circulated in written form before they were delivered.[90] There was written traffic between the 'Three Courts' and with the emperor, in the form of *Relationen* and *Correlationen*, while intensive negotiations generated papers in duplicate, quadruplicate and sextuplicate.[91] Their deliberation in the Court councils, and the exchanges that occurred between Courts, had their own quasi-ritual characters, but the nature of the imperial assemblies as a whole altered from 'meeting of princes to committee of experts'.[92] The parliamentary standing orders (*Geschäftsordnung*) of the 'Eternal *Reichstag*' of Regensburg (1663 onwards) were not far in the future.

Conclusion

We may venture the following conclusions. The open organization of the older imperial assemblies had permitted orators of the stamp of Aeneas Silvius Piccolomini more freedom than the formalized 'court *Reichstage*' (*Kurienreichstage*), with their emphasis on hierarchy, function and written procedures. Oration at the *Reichstage* could never become as fully constitutive of the system as it became in English parliamentary oratory in the time of the Pitts. It would be anachronistic to expect anything else of the *Reichstage*, which remained aristocratic assemblies of magnates, with the towns acting in a subsidiary capacity. But it can be shown that during at least three phases in the history of the *Reichstage*, orations did play a more central role. The first was the *Reichstage* of the conciliar period, from 1438 to 1446, when the orations were essentially treatises expressing scholastic learning. The second was the professional, humanistic oration, which enjoyed its first efflorescence at the 'Turkish *Reichstage*' of 1454–5, and revived whenever the Turkish threat again became a major concern. And the third was during the *aetas Maximilianea*, when the second efflorescence of humanistic anti-Turkish orations took place in the context of shaping public opinion.

5
Burgundy and the Crusade
Jacques Paviot

By comparison with what happened elsewhere, above all in Italy, in connection with crusading in the fifteenth century, Burgundy appears as a repository of an older idea of crusade.[1] The crusading tradition in the house of the Valois dukes of Burgundy, seen by many as the heralds of the crusade in the fifteenth century, had been founded by Philip the Bold at the end of the fourteenth century. It was born out of the agreement between Philip,[2] Louis duke of Orleans, Philip's nephew and the brother of King Charles VI of France, and John of Gaunt duke of Lancaster, to lead such an expedition, following the truce of Leulinghem between France and England, in the Hundred Years War.[3] The trio subscribed to the Zeitgeist, since such individuals as Leo V, former king of Lesser Armenia,[4] Robert Le Mennot, known as 'L'Ermite',[5] and Philippe de Mézières,[6] were calling on Richard II of England and Charles VI of France to lead a new crusade to liberate Jerusalem.[7] From that perspective, it was possible to view the expedition planned by the dukes as a *passagium particulare*, and that of the kings as a *passagium generale*.

Philip the Bold held no such views. In 1394, he had sent embassies to Prussia and to Hungary, not yet having made up his mind if he wanted to fight against the pagan Lithuanians or the Muslim Turks.[8] It was Charles VI who decided to help the Hungarians. Then John of Gaunt ceased to show interest in such an expedition. Louis of Orleans was committed to acting as regent of the realm when his brother was mad and he could not go. Nor, realistically, could Philip the Bold, the most powerful man in France – something he must have known from the beginning, at least if we accept the judgement of his contemporary Jean Froissart, who wrote that Philip was a man of much imagination and foresight in his affairs.[9] The duke did not abandon his project, but he organized it in such a way that his eldest son, John, count of Nevers (future 'the Fearless') could earn his knighthood. Only then, at the last moment, in the spring of 1396, did Philip address himself to the Church in the person of the pope of Avignon, Benedict XIII, of whom he was a reluctant supporter, to get the necessary bulls for his son. From beginning to end, the 'crusade of Nicopolis' had been a chivalric entreprise for the duke of Burgundy, even if its participants were thinking of proceeding to Jerusalem once they had defeated the Turks.[10] The crusade as a chivalric war against the infidels had been a total failure, and those French knights who escaped death at Nicopolis in 1396, of whom Boucicaut was the most prominent, succumbed to the same tactics at Agincourt in 1415.[11]

After a captivity of several months among the Turks (September 1396 to August 1397), John of Burgundy (duke 1404–19) did not involve himself any further in the matter of the crusade. Later, his *legenda negra* even made him an agent of the Turks because of his role in the civil war in France.[12] His son Philip the Good was born in the *annus horribilis* of 1396, so he could have no memory of what happened, and returned to the patterns of the crusade as seen by his grandfather. His 'godfather' in crusading matters had been Henry V of England: acting together with Charles VI of France, Philip and Henry despatched Gilbert de Lannoy as a spy to the Levant in 1421.[13] Until the middle of the century, Philip acted in every sphere in defence of the Christian faith and of the Church. He nurtured projects against the Hussites in the late 1420s and early 1430s, in competition with Cardinal Henry Beaufort who was papal legate. He planned to achieve the conquest of the Morea with a Portuguese *infante* (Henry or Ferdinand) in 1436–7. He sent relief to Rhodes against the Mamluks in 1429, 1441, 1444, and to Constantinople against the Ottomans in 1444–5.[14] Throughout, his ultimate aim remained the liberation of the Holy Sepulchre, as proved by the pilgrimage/embassies of Guyot, Bastard of Burgundy, in 1426, of André de Toulongeon in 1432, by the reports of Gilbert de Lannoy (1421–3), and of Bertrandon de la Broquière on the Turks (1432–3).[15] The itineraries of these men indicate that the idea was to follow one of the routes of the First Crusade.[16]

Unlike his grandfather, Philip the Good had a theoretician of the crusade in his service.[17] Jean Germain, a native of Burgundy and the son of a serf, pursued his studies with the aid of Duchess Margaret of Bavaria, and became bishop of Nevers in 1430. Early in the same year, Philip the Good nominated him chancellor of the newly created Order of the Golden Fleece. In 1436, he was transferred to the see of Chalon-sur-Saône. He died in 1461.[18] We do not know why, when or how he became interested in the subject of the crusade or the state of the Holy Land and the condition of the eastern Christians, but as early as 1433 Philip the Good gave him for examination the copies of the Koran and the life of Muhammad that Bertrandon de la Broquière had brought back from Damascus, where he had had them translated by the chaplain of the Venetians.[19] Germain was a man who looked back to past times. He put forward his ideas publicly, in front of the court at Hesdin in 1437, at the chapter of the knights of the Golden Fleece at Mons in 1451, and in the same year, on several occasions, while acting as envoy for the duke of Burgundy to western sovereigns. At Hesdin in 1437 he delivered the homily on the Feast of Saint Andrew (30 November), Burgundy's patron saint. He reminded his ducal listeners, the duke and his duchess, Isabel of Portugal, of the apostle's conversion of the Morea (which was still in the hands of the Greeks at the time he spoke), of the conquest of Antioch during the time of Godfrey of Bouillon, and of the presence at the siege of Acre of the count of Flanders, Philip of Alsace.[20] As time passed, Jean Germain enlarged the aims of the duke: to reconquer all the lands which had been in the hands of the Christians in bygone days. He had the opportunity to expound these views during what was unquestionably his hour of glory, at the chapter of the Order of the Golden Fleece at Mons in 1451. There he delivered the collected fruits of his reflections: the *Mappemonde*, a list accompanied by a map of all the places which had been Christian, composed in 1449,[21] a treatise of apologetics, the *Trésor des Simples* or 'Debate of the Christian and the Saracen', written in 1450,[22] and other works not related to the crusade.[23] During the mass, he delivered in French a general homily, in the course of which he described the terrible desolation of the Church militant, the conquests of the Moors [sic] in Syria, the profanation of the Holy Places, the Muslim attacks on Cyprus and Rhodes, and the conquests of the Turks in Asia and Greece (i.e. the Balkans). He deplored the lack of interest shown by the Christians over the course of the preceding two centuries, and recalled the mighty feats of Godfrey of Bouillon, of the saintly kings of France, the wars of Wladislas[24] in Hungary and Wallachia, and the victories of John Hunyadi.[25] He exhorted the Christians to make peace between themselves, and called for an army that would obey its leader.[26] The homily was devoid of originality; furthermore Jean Germain set no precise aim for a crusade, and the duke took no notice. Philip the Good then sent embassies to the pope, the emperor, and the kings of France, England, Naples, Hungary and Poland, their *oratio* taking the form of a copy of Jean Germain's sermon.[27]

Meanwhile events came to the help of Philip the Good: Constantinople fell to the Turks in May 1453. The duke now had an aim for his crusade and the associated diplomacy, and a new historical figure to act as point of reference: Baldwin of Flanders-Hainault, who had become Latin emperor of Constantinople in 1204. Hence the duke might[28] claim rights to the Eastern imperial throne. For example, the town of Mons, anticipating Philip the Good's visit in 1454,[29] organized *tableaux vivants* about the feats of Baldwin, and the ducal secretary Louis Du Chesne mentioned him at the meeting of the estates of Holland-Zeeland at The Hague in 1456.[30]

This crusade had started as an initiative within the Order of the Golden Fleece, which comprised the sovereign, the chancellor and the knights. The Order had been founded for the honour and the increase of the true Catholic faith, and for the exaltation of the faith and holy Church;[31] but such goals lacked originality, given that the statutes of other orders of knighthood included similar prescriptions. We have looked at Germain's views; what of the knights, or more precisely the courtiers? As early as the chapter of Mons in 1451, the project was conceived of a great feast with the intention of uniting the nobility behind the duke in his new venture. Circumstances, notably the Ghent uprising, prevented the feast from occurring until the winter of 1454. What happened, in effect a dramatized version of knightly romances, is familiar to us from the works of Johann Huizinga[32] and Jean Rychner.[33] A team of three was appointed, the most famous of whom was Olivier de la Marche,[34] the other two being Jean de Lannoy, a newly elected knight of the Golden Fleece (the only one in the group),[35] and Jean Boudaut.[36] They were put in charge of organizing what became the *Banquet du Faisan* (Feast of the Pheasant), which was held in Lille, on 17 February 1454, bringing to a close a series of jousts in which the last ones referred to the Swan Knight, legendary ancestor of the House of Cleves (Duke Adolf of Cleves being Philip the Good's brother-in-law), and also, more to the point, of Godfrey of Bouillon.

The Feast of the Pheasant was a debauch of luxury, in a mixture of knightly values and popular amusements – some scenes could easily have been painted later by Hieronymus Bosch or Peter Bruegel – with the story of Jason played out at intervals on a stage. Notwithstanding the *entremets* of the Lamentation of Holy Church (acted by Olivier de la Marche dressed as a woman and roosting on a fake elephant), it was all very far from the Christian idea of the crusade; indeed no cleric or prelate played a part, not even Jean Germain, who by this point had fallen into disfavour. The *entremets* were followed by the ceremony of the vows upon a live pheasant, a re-enactment of the one in *Les Vœux du Paon* ('The Vows of the Peacock'), a novel by Jacques de Longuyon (written before 1312), itself a sequel to the *Roman d'Alexandre*. Many of the vows are serious, following the pattern set by that of Philip the Good, but several could have been delivered on the occasion of a knightly feast as a *pas d'armes*: for example, the lord of Pons vowed not to stay in a town for more than 15 days, and not to sleep in a bed on Saturdays, until he had fought hand-to-hand against a Saracen.[37] The lord of la Roche vowed not to wear armour on his right arm (Philip the Good did not accept this) and not to appear at table on Tuesdays, until he had fought in a battle where 1,000 fighters were killed. Hugues de Longueval vowed not to drink wine until he had spilled the blood of an infidel, and so on. We may note that the vows that were given afterwards in Hainault and Flanders were more sober and prudent.[38] Overall, the Feast of the Pheasant looks like a flight of fancy, an escape into an imaginary world, and non-noble contemporaries were shocked by the lavish expenses involved.[39]

There followed a decade of preparations, plans, projects and diplomatic missions. Pope Nicholas V had called for a crusade to begin on 1 March 1454. In the spring of that year, Philip the Good went in person to the imperial diet at Regensburg where he presented his offers, but neither the emperor nor the king of Hungary and Bohemia made an appearance. In spite of that, the duke of Burgundy send delegations to the series of diets that followed concerning the crusade.[40] On his return to his dominions, the duke made preparations to set out in spring 1455. There were delays, and the pope died. Calixtus III set a new date, 1 March 1456. In 1455, Philip sent an embassy to King Charles VII of France, but without success: the duke knew then he could not go on the crusade. Then the dauphin Louis, heir to the throne of France, took refuge at the court of Burgundy, and the duke had to wait until Charles VII's death. Meanwhile, aids continued to be levied, the Burgundian chancery and *chambre des comptes* drew up or received projects relating to the planned expedition, and Bertrandon de la Broquière finally submitted the report of his travels in 1432–3. Pius II, elected pope in 1458, organized a congress at Mantua in the following year to revive the project of a crusade against the Turks, and here Philip the Good's representatives presented the same proposals that had previously been made at Regensburg. When Charles VII at last died in 1461, Philip the Good thought that he was now free to embark on his crusade, but the new king, Louis XI, made it clear that he opposed the idea, without going so far as formally to forbid it. Pope Pius II continued to encourage Philip to fulfil his vow and, on 19 October 1463, brought him into an alliance with the republic of Venice and himself.[41] However the crusade aborted because Louis forbad Philip the Good to go at the end of the year, while Pope Pius II died before he could board his galley at Ancona on 15 August 1464.[42]

Coming back to the idea of crusade in the Burgundian dominions, we cannot discern in it the idea of penitence, nor can we say that there occurred any theological reflection on the penitential nature of the crusade. For the dukes of Burgundy, 'crusading' was all action. They thought about the crusade, and lived it, as a chivalric entreprise against the infidels (whoever these might be). That is not to say that they were only looking behind, and were unaware of what was going on, for example, within the Franciscan Order. Philip the Good and his wife Isabel of Portugal favoured the expansion of the Observance throughout their dominions. Following the example set by Duke John the Fearless and Duchess Margaret of Bavaria, Isabel of Portugal supported Saint Colette of Corbie (1381–1447) and her reform of the Order of the Clares.[43] Both Philip the Good and Isabel of Portugal met or exchanged letters with Giovanni da Capistrano, who spent time in Burgundy and Flanders in 1442–3.[44] The documentation relates only to the affairs of the Observance, shedding no light on crusading matters, although these may have been broached, given that Giovanni da Capistrano could have met Jean Germain in Besançon in 1442. However, the official chronicler Georges Châtelain praised the actions of the saint at the Turkish siege of Belgrade in 1456.[45] Philip the Good was also corresponding with Alberto da Sarteano, who became general vicar of the Order. Several letters of the former have been preserved. What Alberto da Sarteano, and also Giovanni da Capistrano, asked of the duke of Burgundy was the recovery of the Holy Sepulchre from the infidels. From Jerusalem, on 6 October 1436, Alberto da Sarteano wrote to Philip the Good to thank him for his donation of alms to the convent of Mount Sion, and expressed the wish to see him in the Holy Land not only carrying out a pilgrimage, but also fighting to increase the Christian religion, now that the peace of Arras had restored peace in the kingdom of France.[46] From Rhodes, on 26 December 1440, he wrote again to Philip, mainly on the subject of Church Union, but also to exhort the duke to imitate and emulate the virtues of his ancestors in the royal house of France, who had conducted wars under God's banner and the guardianship of the Church.[47] As late as 19 March 1454 Giovanni da Capistrano wrote to Philip the Good from Regensburg asking him to forgive the rebels of Ghent (who in reality had already been defeated) and to fight for the recovery of the Holy Land and the increase of the Christian faith.[48] One month before, the Feast of the Pheasant had taken place and Philip the Good had vowed to go and fight against the Turks for Constantinople. Thus even the men who were spearheading the movement for the new devotion were pushing Philip the Good into the old ways of the crusade.

Did the duke of Burgundy succeed in establishing and sharing his ideas relating to the crusade among his peers, his nobility and his subjects? As mentioned above, following the chapter of the Golden Fleece held at Mons in 1451, Philip the Good, without doubt following the advice of Jean Germain who was then basking in his moment of glory, despatched four embassies: the first to Pope Nicholas V and King Alfonso the Magnanimous of Naples, the second to King Charles VII of France, the third to King Henry VI of England, and the fourth to the king of the Romans Frederick III, King Ladislas the Posthumous of Bohemia and Hungary, and King Casimir of Poland. Charles VII was in the process of conquering Aquitaine, while Henry VI had lost Normandy and was losing Aquitaine, so the time was not well chosen. Alfonso of Naples, who was also titular king of Jerusalem, stole from Philip the idea of convening a big international conference. But the most damning indictment came from the Polish chronicler John Długosz, who wrote that the verbose embassy sent by the duke of Burgundy was vain and lacked sense; it was full of high-sounding rhetoric, but devoid of courage and remote from any effect or result.[49] The episode was a smarting diplomatic failure, and Jean Germain fell into disfavour and did not appear again at the court of Philip the Good. After this the duke of Burgundy treated only with the king of France and the Emperor, to both of whom he was a vassal, and with the pope.

This failure in the world at large was perhaps a further stimulus to seek refuge in the world of the imagination. It seems that Philip the Good hoped to appeal chiefly to the knightly feelings of the nobility from his dominions, and also in the kingdom of France. He had a lengthy report of the Feast of the Pheasant written down by Olivier de la Marche, with the aim of diffusing it, but it does not seem to have enjoyed any echo.[50] Moreover, he seems to have wanted to hold a new Feast of the Pheasant, though without the *entremets*, when he was in Paris in 1461, just after the coronation of Louis XI, whom he had accompanied to his capital city; but he did not succeed in getting the agreement of the new king of France.[51] The knightly spirit of distant and exotic adventures was kept up by an original literary production of historical novels, with no parallel in the French-speaking world: *Histoire d'Hélène, Charles Martel,*

Chroniques et Conquêtes de Charlemagne, Gillion de Trazegnies, Gilles de Chin, Jean d'Avesnes, Le Comte d'Artois, Louis de Gavre, Les Trois Fils de Roi.[52] Their effect was shortlived, only the last one being printed in the sixteenth century, and none secured the fame of Joannot Martorell and Martí Joan de Galba's *Tirant lo Blanc* (whose main character may be based on the Burgundian crusader Geoffroy de Thoisy),[53] *Curial and Guelfa* from Spain or Luigi Pulci's *Morgante* from Italy.

Jean Germain had noticed that, following his sermon at Mons, some of the knights of the Golden Fleece groaned and spoke saddened words. The enthusiasm for the crusade which we can detect in the way the Knight is presented in the Prologue to Chaucer's *Canterbury Tales* can be seen in the number of Burgundian knights who participated in the crusade of Barbary in 1390, in the *Reisen* of the Teutonic Knights, or in the crusade of Nicopolis.[54] During the fifteenth century, however, fewer individuals went to fight against the infidel. The best known is Geoffroy de Thoisy.[55] He took part in the pilgrimage of André de Toulongeon to the Holy Land in 1432, was chosen by Philip the Good to lead a small fleet to help relieve Rhodes in 1441, and supervised the building of galleys for the duke at Nice. He played a leading role in the defence of Rhodes against the Mamluks in 1444 and received there the order of chivalry. De Thoisy also joined the fleet sent by the pope, Venice and Burgundy to Constantinople, practised piracy in the Black Sea in 1445, and was made a prisoner for a few weeks in Mingrelia. He went on to supervise the building at Antwerp of new galleys which the duke intended to send to the Levant in 1446–9, made a vow at the Feast of the Pheasant, and supervised the building of three galeasses at Pisa in 1463. Jean de Rebreviettes also vowed to go on crusade at the Feast of the Pheasant; waiting for the departure of the duke, he went ahead to fight against the Moors in Spain and Morocco in 1457–8.[56] In March 1459 the duke made him a gift in order to help him to go back to Turkey.[57] Antoine de Payage went on board the fleet of Anthony, Bastard of Burgundy, which left Sluis in May 1464. He seems to have spent the following year with two other knights from the fleet, making war on the sea against the Saracens. In 1466, he left Marseilles, captured two ships (one Saracen, the other Catalan) near Tunis, but was obliged to sell them at Syracuse. He tried to enter the service of Venice, and, while waiting for an answer, went towards Egypt, came back to Rhodes, and encountered the pilgrims' galley from Venice; a fight took place and he seized it. He then wrote to the duke of Burgundy to ask for his protection.[58]

Philip the Good paid in part the expenses of the fleets that he sent to the Levant before the 1450s. One source of money was the tenth that

Pope Eugenius IV allowed him to raise in 1441 in the Low Countries, France and Germany, in the dioceses of Thérouanne, Arras, Amiens, Tournai, Cambrai, Noyon, Liège and Utrecht, under the supervision of the bishop of Tournai, Jean Chevrot, the head of the ducal council.[59] After the fall of Constantinople, Philip increasingly relied on the tenths. Nicholas V issued a bull on 30 September 1453 in which he offered the plenary indulgence to everybody who would go on crusade in person or through a substitute, for six months starting on 1 February 1454. At the same time a tenth would be raised throughout Europe. Clerics who agreed to participate in the expedition were exempt from the tithe, authorized to bear arms and to use them against the infidels. During the expedition, every crusader would have the right to choose his own confessor who could absolve him from his sins and any ecclesiastical sentences that he was carrying. Nicholas V issued two other bulls on 30 December 1455 in favour of the duke of Burgundy and his subjects. The first was a repetition of his former one, with some restrictions: the clerics could use their arms only for defence, and the laymen could receive absolution for the reserved cases only once. The second bull treated the tenth. Those clerics who handed over one hundredth of their annual income during the expedition received the plenary indulgence, or they could make a single payment of one hundredth of their movable assets. The poorer ones who could not pay could claim the plenary indulgence in exchange for visiting the churches of Malines and for placing an alm in the poor box set up for the Jubilee. In the Burgundian Low Countries, the tithe collector was again Jean Chevrot.[60]

In an attempt to bolster the zeal of the faithful for the crusade, the authorities, civic or ecclesiastical, adopted the practice of organizing processions, and we have information about some of those that occurred at Douai. For example, a procession took place on 9 October 1426, at the Church of Notre-Dame, for the defence of the Christian faith against the *Pragois* (Hussites); on 22 July 1439, at Notre-Dame, for the 'reduction' [*sic*] of the Greeks; on 23 May 1456, at Notre-Dame, by order of the pope, on account of 'the infidels' (the siege of Belgrade); on 14 September 1456, at Saint-Pierre, because of the Turks; in 1457 several processions because of the Turks, and a general procession, on 3 July, at Saint-Aubin, following the pope's order that a procession should be held each month, because of the Turks; on 17 April 1463, at the Franciscans' church, for the *voyage de Turquie*.[61] We may note that the chronology of these processions does not match the chronology of the projects pursued by the duke of Burgundy, with the exception of the last one.

As this last example shows, the crusade aroused popular emotion only in 1463–4, without doubt because the pope was scheduled to lead the expedition. We have some documentation about the great town of Ghent and the little town of Axel, in Flanders. At Ghent the crusade was preached on 18 March 1464, the Sunday preceding Palm Sunday, on the square of the Friday Market. There followed a general procession. Eighty men, whose names and armaments were written down in the Town Diary, took the cross and chose a captain, Hector Hughes, alias de Costere, to lead them to Venice, to board ships there.[62] In Axel, the crusaders put on their coat of arms wearing a cross of Saint Andrew (because of the duke of Burgundy), took their banners, bows and spears, and went to the church to hear the mass of the Holy Spirit. Everybody confessed his sins and the priest gave them the sign of the cross on their shoulder. Then the crusaders approached the altar, raising their spears in the air as a sign for the victory of Christ. A banner bearing the sign of the cross was blessed with the holy sacrament, indicating that the volunteers were ready to die for the cross. Once the mass had finished, there was a general procession during which the priest gave his benediction to the kneeling crusaders. Then the municipality offered wine, and tearful farewells took place.[63]

There is also the interesting case of Gérard Deschamps, a native of the diocese of Liège. After the fall of Constantinople, under the pontificate of Calixtus III (1455–8), he gathered 300 men on foot, and led them to Rome in the hope of going on to Greece. He went back to Savoy where he formed the project of the *Societas Jesus*, which received the approval of Pope Pius II in 1459. The aim was to recruit crusaders in four nations, Burgundy, Lorraine, Savoy and Liège, and to gather them at Bouillon (once again we go back to the First Crusade). Deschamps does not seem to have had much success, for the pope ordered an inquiry, but he persevered with his own military agenda. He fought in Bosnia in 1463; and three years later he was scheduled to lead men in Hungary.[64] These examples show that there existed a genuine desire or will amongst the populace at large, more so than in the nobility, to fight against the infidels. The latter seem to have had a very blurred definition, being Muslim, Moor, Saracen or Turk.

As for the definition of the crusade, Jean Germain, relegated in his disfavour to his new diocese of Chalon, had time to ponder it, but without changing his opinions. His *Trésor des Simples* had been translated into Latin and John of Segovia got hold of a copy of it, in his own exile at Aiton in Savoy. In 1455 Segovia entered into discussion with Germain, as he had in the previous year with Nicholas of Cusa, on the best way to deal with the 'infidels': should Christians use the 'spiritual sword' (*spirituale gladium*), as argued by Segovia and Cusa, or the 'temporal sword' (*temporale gladium*), as argued by Germain? A part of the debate between Segovia and Germain has been preserved, though we lack the most interesting letters from the bishop of Chalon. Meanwhile, Germain clung to his views.[65]

The dukes of Burgundy, then, nourished a traditional view of the crusade. The theologians with whom they came into contact comforted them with the idea of the liberation of Jerusalem. In contrast to some English or German princes, they never went on pilgrimage there, though Philip the Good sent several persons to do so in his name.[66] Such a view comforted them also in their chivalric dreams of Oriental adventures. This flight into the imaginative detached them from the piety of their subjects, and it locked their nobles into the staging of these dreams in a series of novels and knightly games, feasts and *pas d'armes*, for which they are remembered to this day.

6
An Obscure but Powerful Pattern: Crusading, Nationalism and the Swiss Confederation in the Late Middle Ages

Claudius Sieber-Lehmann

At first glance the 'great league of Upper Germany' ('magna liga superioris Alamaniae'), or *Eidgnoszschaft*,[1] as it took shape in the fourteenth and above all in the fifteenth centuries, seems to hold no link with the subject of crusading.[2] Nothing would appear to be more incongruous than bringing the stalwart confederates (*Eidgenossen*) into any arena of conflict against non-believers: there was no prince at hand who could undertake a commitment to a new *cruciata*, and no leagues of knights to celebrate the memory of past glorious deeds against the infidels,[3] while the Swiss lands themselves enjoyed the security of being relatively far removed from any non-Catholic powers. None the less, an intriguing series of links did exist, and they constitute the agenda of this essay.

Crusade and legitimation

In the year 1500 there appeared in print a chronicle of the Swabian War, compiled by Nikolaus Schradin, the town clerk at Lucerne. With immense pride Schradin handled in verse form the victory that the confederates had enjoyed over the Swabian League. Its third chapter carries the title: 'How the confederates came into being, and how they achieved such knightly deeds against the heathen that they were rewarded with their liberty, becoming free men and nobody's to command' ('Wie sich der eidgenosen stamen erhebt hatt / vnnd wie sy erholt habent mitt iren ritterlichen stritten gegen den heyden das man jnen den priß gab / do durch sy erholt habent das sy frey lüt vnnd niemantz eigen sin sollent / vnd darumb gefrigt sindt').[4] Schradin followed this with a description of how the confederates had migrated from Sweden southwards to the Alps, where they settled as

81

Figure 1 The Swiss defeat the heathens and occupy Switzerland, 387: Nikolaus Schradin, *Schwabenkrieg* (1500), fol. 5r.

devout Christians and cultivated the soil. In the year 387 they defeated the powerful heathen chief Eugenius and received the liberties mentioned above. A woodcut illustrates their glorious deeds, and in it their opponents are characterized as heathens, with turbans and scimitars (see Figure 1). It is on that account, Schradin comments as he brings his account of confederate origins to a close, that the confederates are able to manage their affairs in their ancestral lands without a nobility.

At first sight this reads like a simple origins myth, but the weighty role that the crusade against the heathen plays for Schradin merits closer attention. Clearly, he considered this long-past victory over unbelievers to be the best way to secure legitimation, to justify the independent way in which the confederates were running their own affairs. Nor was Schradin alone in this. Petermann Etterlin, who published the first printed history of the Swiss, borrowed from Schradin the idea that the conflict with the heathen was the greatest deed of the confederates' forefathers, tracing the Swiss cross back to their achievements on crusade.[5] In much the same way, past performance on a crusade may seem to have little to contribute to the justification of contemporary claims to power. It must have been apparent to nearly everybody in the West since the fall of Acre in 1291 that the *cruciatae* had failed as an undertaking. And when Schradin portrayed the ancestors of the confederates fighting against a prince called Eugenius, he was dealing with make-believe history, which carried a heavy risk, in this age of humanism and growing historical awareness, of being unmasked as nothing more than a fable.

In the case of the Swiss Confederation it is clearly important to remember that in addition to acting as an example of meritorious past services acknowledged with rewards that proved to be of long duration, the history of the crusades could also serve as a forerunner of the Confederation's own policies. The first armed expeditions to the Holy Land were carried out under the patronage of the pope rather than that of a single secular authority, not to mention that of an emperor from the house of Habsburg. The crusaders were recruited from all levels of society, and the leadership of the enterprise was entrusted to a group of princes. Levelled hierarchies, a broad-based participation by pious combatants on a military expedition, and the chance to attain a position equivalent to that of nobles through the display of courage: these were also characteristics of the way the Swiss waged war. So it is not surprising that St Maurice and his Theban Legion, and the 10,000 knights under Achatius, enjoyed great reverence in the Confederation, on the grounds that they represented 'a devout people in arms' in the period before the crusades themselves.[6]

Crusade and mobilization

As the example of the war with Burgundy in 1474–7 demonstrates, crusading ideas were also brought into play to mobilize the Confederation's population for a campaign against its Christian neighbours.[7] As early as August 1474 the Bernese called their fellow confederates to their aid, to combat raids by mercenaries who were in Burgundian pay. They appealed to the 'German nation' (*teutsche nation*), which they claimed was under threat. For a long time this was construed as indicating an identification on the part of the confederates with the 'German nation', an interpretation that found favour above all with National Socialist historians.[8] But the context in which *teutsche nation* was most frequently used in the second half of the fifteenth century has, at least at first sight, nothing to do with nationalism in the modern meaning of the word.[9] It was papal attempts to bring about a crusade of the 'German nation' against the Ottomans that suddenly caused references to the *teutsche nation* to multiply, and made the idea familiar within the Confederation. This development can be traced back to 1453, but the turning point was the Regensburg *Reichstag* of 1471, three years before the outbreak of the war with Burgundy. Its major concern was the organization of a campaign against the Ottoman Turks. The 'Latin nation' (*welsche nation*) was invited to proceed against the Turks at sea, while the 'German nation' was to conduct a land campaign.[10] And it is striking that the Confederation's authorities did not just borrow the idea of the *teutsche nation* from the calls to crusade, but also their image of the Ottoman foe. This they turned against their opponent, the duke of Burgundy, and his troops, especially his mercenaries from Lombardy. Charles the Bold was declared to be 'the Turk in the West', labelled as insane, hungry for conquest, unbelieving, perverse and hot-tempered: the classical mixture of stereotypes brought to bear in anti-Islamic propaganda, for example against Sultan Mehmed II, the conqueror of Constantinople.[11]

If war propaganda with its images of the enemy is to succeed, it has to correspond with a pre-existing body of ideas in the population, add to it and take it in the desired direction. What such ideas did the people who lived in the lands of the Confederation possess, with regard to the Turks and the crusade that was planned against them? To date there is no comprehensive account of the crusade propaganda of either the spiritual or secular powers in the Confederation. So as a first step there is no alternative to taking samples at random registering the presence within the community of the Confederation of printed literature about the Turks (*Turcica*) in the last decades of the fifteenth century. The period chosen covers the years between 1453 and the Reformation. With the arrival of the new faith the evaluation of the crusade against the Turks was transformed, as the example of Luther demonstrates.[12] This had an immediate impact on the *Turcica*. One Bernese supporter of the Reformation remarked that the town archive stored its papal bulls in 'the Roman junk-box [rubbish bin]'.[13] Clearly little care was taken with regard to the Catholic past in the towns of the Confederation, which for the most part adhered to the new faith; and this makes the work of today's historians more difficult, when they set about reconstructing the history of crusading publicity in the Confederation.

The most abundant records for measures against the Ottoman Turks are to be found, predictably enough, in the sphere of the Church. Without doubt the so-called 'Turkish indulgences' had a major impact, because following the fall of Constantinople Pope Calixtus III had suspended all the indulgences that had previously been issued.[14] Anybody who applied for an indulgence had to make a fresh application, and many of the faithful appear to have chosen to do so. In the second half of the fifteenth century there was an inexorable rise in the popularity of indulgences; and it applied to both sexes, as witnessed by the appearance of a printed indulgence formula for women.[15] The success of these indulgences is evidenced by those who battened on them, so that in 1458 one Rudolf Ment was advertising fake 'Turkish bulls' in Aarau.[16] Indulgences against the Turks conferred two benefits: they reduced the sufferings to be endured in the hereafter, while at the same time making it possible to carry out the Christian's duty to support the war against the heathen. But not all were content to take this convenient route, for there is evidence that both men and women from the Confederation set out on campaigns against the unbelievers.[17] The town authorities were very concerned to promote the granting of indulgences against the Turks, because only a third of the proceeds made their way to Rome, the remainder being set aside for the maintenance of the town's church buildings. This was commonly linked to the practice of persuading the pope to substitute local churches for the major Roman shrines, and extracting a fee from the population when they visited these churches as pilgrims to gain the associated indulgences. Between 1460 and 1466 the town of Basel managed its own 'Rome journeys' (*Romfahrten*) with great success,[18] and this persuaded the town of Bern to make its own application to the pope for a 'Rome journey' and to implement it in 1476.[19] The bull for this enjoyed a print-run of more than 1,000 copies at Basel, while at Bern it was interpreted to the audiences by qualified preachers, a 'media event' which must have exercised an impact in its own right.[20]

Crusade preachers, who toured the Confederation, were instrumental in publicizing the indulgence campaigns that the town authorities had organized. As proof of their success in carrying out their brief we can cite a decree from 1456, forbidding preachers against the Turks to initiate another campaign in the diocese of Constance, which included much of the Confederation; it was felt that they had collected too much money in the previous year.[21] In 1457 a Franciscan from Besançon and a parson from Courtion collected about 184 florins for the planned crusade in Freiburg im Üechtland, which lay in the diocese of Lausanne.[22] In the same year the papal nuncio Ludovico Cescases visited Bern and sanctioned the expenditure of the crusade money; other nuncios appeared at Solothurn and Freiburg im Üechtland.[23] At the broader level of the economy, textile manufacturing felt the effects of papal measures against the Turks. It is well known that the papal curia applied a pious gloss to the unexpected discovery of alum at Tolfa, to justify its establishment of a monopoly over the production of alum.[24] The hoped-for proceeds were to make it possible to finance the war against the Turks. There is evidence that Basel enjoyed imports of alum from Italy, a large proportion of which originated at Tolfa.[25]

The most persistent impression made by clerical propaganda for the crusade was the daily sound of the noon bell. In 1456 Pope Calixtus III had decreed that the bells should ring at noon not just on Fridays but every day, as a reminder to the population of the Ottoman threat, and to persuade them to pray to God for His protection.[26] In 1468 the Council at Bern additionally decreed that when the noon bell rang, each person should say five 'Our Fathers' and 'Hail Marys';[27] and in 1479 the same Council reiterated that the noon bell should sound.[28] Pope Calixtus III had also declared that the Feast of the Lord's Transfiguration on 6 August, which originated in the Eastern Church, should become an official feast-day.[29] The celebration of the Lord's Transfiguration is evidenced in the last decades of the century at Basel and in Switzerland.[30] Anyone who visited a church or owned sacred pictures was reminded of the threat from the Turks, for the wicked creatures who were shown torturing and tormenting Christ in the images of his Passion, were often characterized as unbelievers through their turbans and scimitars.[31] And it was quite possible that the beggar whom contemporaries encountered at the church door asking for alms said he was a refugee from Constantinople.[32]

Crusading propaganda emanating from the emperor and the imperial estates also grew in volume after the fall of Constantinople. As early as January 1455 the Habsburg Emperor Frederick III requested the confederates to set in motion military assistance for his planned campaign against the Ottomans.[33] In 1466 the imperial envoy Ulrich von Grafeneck visited the Confederation's members (*Orte*), to bring them up to date on the preparations for the crusade against the Turks.[34] In 1467 they were invited to take part in the *Reichstag* scheduled for that year at Nürnberg.[35] The *Orte* also invariably featured in the so-called 'Turkish notices' (*Türkenanschlägen*), the contingents that were expected for the crusade.[36] Letters from the emperor inviting the Confederation's *Orte* to take part in the crusade against the Turks increased from 1468 onwards. The successes of the Ottomans, who were invading and pillaging the Habsburg dynastic lands, had shocked Frederick III and caused him to summon another *Reichstag* after a long period without one; the outcome was the Regensburg *Christentag* of 1471 referred to above. The Swiss too attended this *Reichstag*, a remarkable occurrence given the fact that for many years they had stayed away from the *Reichstage* on account of their disputes with the Habsburgs. This event seemed so momentous to the Bernese chronicler Diebold Schilling that he noted it in his great chronicle of Burgundy and in his official chronicle of Bern, including a lengthy, aloof and ironic report by the chancellor of the bishop of Basel. This too dwelt at length on anti-Turkish propaganda, the speeches fitting the now-customary pattern: the Turks are inhumanly cruel, they slaughter or enslave the victims of their incursions, they will turn next to the Holy Roman Empire and appear in southern Germany, etc.[37]

Although the discussions with the emperor at Regensburg foundered and the delegation from Bern and Zürich made their way home with their task unaccomplished, the link between the empire and the towns of the Confederation was not broken. In the first place, on 16 August 1471 Basel invited the Bernese to the next meeting of town representatives (*Städtetag*) at Frankfurt, which was to concern itself exclusively with the Turkish question;[38] Constance similarly invited Zürich.[39] In September–October 1471 the imperial envoy Hugo von Montfort, together with Bishop Ortlieb of Chur, visited the meeting in Zürich, to communicate the decisions reached at Regensburg;[40] later the same imperial embassy appears to have fixed a *Städtetag* at Constance to discuss the threat from the Turks.[41] At the start of the meeting of the *Orte* (*Tagsatzung*) at Zürich Count Hugh described to the confederates the emergency created by the Turks. The envoys emphasized the duty of every Christian to take part in the preparations against the Turks, and then explained the decisions reached at Regensburg. As a quid pro quo they offered their help in the negotiations for 'a perpetual covenant' (*Ewige Richtung*). Unsurprisingly the confederates, at least the people of Lucerne, did not warm to the proposal of a comprehensive Turkish tax, as the conclusion attached to the decisions (*Abschieden*) showed: the councillors of Lucerne declined to contribute, 'because we are too poor for such things and too far away from such matters'. Characteristically, however, they hastened to add that they were loyal subjects of the empire and good Christians, an indication that the confederates could not simply shrug off their Christian duty towards the war with the Turks. On 20 November 1471 the confederates once more justified their conduct to Bishop Ortlieb of Chur.[42]

At the start of 1472 Frederick III wrote to the town of Schaffhausen, which at that point was in league with the confederates, about an expedition against the Turks,[43] which later attracted a remark in the *Abschieden*.[44] When imperial envoys told the towns at the Augsburg *Reichstag* of 1473 that the Hanse towns and the confederates alike were excluded from the projected campaign against the Turks, there was protest on the part of the invited town envoys. In consequence the emperor's orator promised that 'sein kayserlich majestatt wöllte durch bottschafft und schrifft unverczogenlich daran sein, das dieselben hennstett [Hansestädte], seestett und Aydgenössen so mergklichen anstössen der cristenhaitt widerstannd zetün helfen ... '[45] An imperial letter of credence for Bishop Ortlieb of Chur and Count Hugo von Werdenberg to the confederated towns and territories dates from 30 May 1473; presumably the business of this embassy to the confederates was also related to help against the Turks.[46] Two months later the confederates had once again to deal with requests on the part of the emperor, who summoned them under threat of punishment to visit the *Reichstag*.[47] News of the meeting of the emperor and the duke of Burgundy at Trier, on which the confederates were well informed, contained fresh reports of Turkish incursions.[48] On 11 December 1473 the emperor informed 'unsern und des reichs lieben getrewen burgermaister und rate der statt Zurich' that the *Reichstag* scheduled to meet at Augsburg to consider the Turkish question had been postponed, but he demanded of Zürich that, with the confederates, it unfailingly attend the *Reichstag*;[49] the confederates and Zürich were also invited to stay until the end of the *Reichstag*.[50]

The threat from the Turks was also deployed as an argument to label the confederates as disturbers of the peace; their aggressive policies would prevent the empire mobilizing its military resources and so impede the much-needed crusade. As Frederick III complained to St Gallen in 1456, Bern and Solothurn were hindering the campaign against the 'unbelieving Turks' with policies that favoured the enemy.[51] Later too the charge was directed against the confederates that they disturbed the peace, set themselves against measures for peace,[52] and so impeded peace-making within the empire, the most important precondition for a successful crusade against the Turks. In 1467 the bishop of Constance and 'ander erbar lüt' intervened between the duke of Austria and the confederates, who wanted to go to the aid of Schaffhausen, on the grounds that such internal disputes could only frustrate the war with the Turks.[53] Diebold Schilling incorporated this passage into his reworking of the Tschachtlan-Dittlingerschen Chronicle.[54] A mounting interest in the Turkish question was shown by Schilling's insertion into this work of other texts relating to *Turcica*: two lists of the sultan's titles and a letter from the sultan to the emperor, who is offered the sultan's daughter in marriage.[55] Schilling inserted this text from the Tschachtlan-Dittlingerschen Chronicle in both his official chronicle of Bern and his great chronicle of Burgundy, but not the material about the sultan's title and the sultan's letter.[56]

Both the protection of the Church and the struggle against unbelievers continued to feature among the central duties of the empire, and accordingly among those of the emperor's subjects.[57] From 1471 onwards, pursuing its dynastic interests but also conscious of its own pre-eminent status, the Habsburg imperial government increased its pressure on the estates, which were ceaselessly reminded of the essential support that the 'German nation' should provide for a crusade. Nobody could evade the emperor's arrangements. But the imperial estates and the towns delayed their payments or diverted the emperor's demands towards duties that were nearer or more pressing in character. The example of the war with Burgundy shows this well. Charles the Bold had first to be brought to heel, before an expedition could be mounted against the Turks. After the duke's death the crusade plans of the imperial government were revived and came to dominate the whole span of the late fifteenth and early sixteenth centuries.[58] To Maximilian I, Frederick III's son, a successful military campaign against the unbelievers represented one of his most important life goals; but it remained a dream.[59] In the decades that followed the war with Burgundy crusading ideas persisted, alongside a consciousness of the Turkish threat. For example, the confederates entered an alliance with King Matthias Corvinus of Hungary.[60] The examples quoted at the start of this essay, from Nikolaus Schradin and Petermann Etterlin, show that fictional achievements in long-forgotten crusades played a major role in the way the confederates legitimated themselves.[61] Typically, Cardinal Matthäus Schiner drew on classic motifs from crusading rhetoric to exhort mercenaries from the Confederation to fight for the pope in the Italian wars.[62]

A reflection of contemporary reactions towards *Turcica* is the appearance on the Swiss stage from the start of the sixteenth century onwards of Turks as figures of terror,[63] and there are continuing instances of *Turcica* in the sixteenth and seventeenth centuries in the Swiss interior (*Innerschweiz*).[64] Even a later chronicler such as the reformed Bernese

Valerius Anshelm constantly referred in his work to the threat of the Turks, which enabled him at the same time to direct criticism at the papacy's practice on indulgences.[65]

The example of the war with Burgundy shows of course that the image of the Turk as foe could be used for self-justificatory purposes. We have seen that between 1474 and 1477 the anti-Ottoman image was applied to Charles the Bold, the 'Turk in the West'. Negative stereotypes obviously lend themselves to such a process of transfer without great difficulty. It was characteristic that this should occur in the case of the Ottoman image. Shortly before the war with Burgundy the confederates were portrayed as the ideal opponents of the Ottomans, in the sense that the Devil could be driven out by using Beelzebub.[66] In 1477 the astronomer and doctor of Chur, Erhard Storck, published an astrological pamphlet with prophecies, which, as so often, failed to come about. Storck was subject to much disappointed criticism and in a second text of May 1479 he tried to justify his predictions. At the conclusion he formulated anew his vision of the future, whose last lines ran:

> The pope will soon die, the emperor will rule everywhere,
> And the vainglory of the clergy will come to an end.
> The Swiss people will overcome the Turks on this side of the
> Rhine.

> ['Papa cito moritur, Cesar regnabit ubique / Sub quo tunc vana cessabit gloria cleri. / Elveteus populus Theucros cis Renum prostrabit.'][67]

While it is true that this proposal flattered the military abilities of the confederates, it was but a short step from that towards equating the Swiss with the Turks. As early as the 1450s the faction that supported the Confederation at Rapperswil bei Zürich was insultingly labelled 'the Turks'.[68] During the Swabian war the equation Swiss = Turks became one of the favourite ways of abusing the confederates.[69] The anonymous 'Haintz von Bechwinden' began the pamphlet that he wrote shortly after the Swabian war programmatically with the following verses:

> 'The Swiss race is disobedient / towards the Roman empire, they despise its holiness/in the same way that the Turks do that of Christendom. / Just as the Turk has occupied much Christian land, / so have the Swiss acquired their status.'

> ['Der sweitzer stamm ist ungehorsam / dem römischen reich, durchechtet des hailikait / eben dem gleich, wie der Türck die

cristenhait. / Wie der türck ein hat genommen gar vil cristennland, / wie die sweitzer synd kommen in irren stand.']^[70]

By this point the description 'Turk' had been worked free completely from the crusading context; it had become a flexible and adjustable term of abuse. Visual examples also make this clear. In 1507, when the above-mentioned Petermann Etterlin portrayed the opponents of Bern during the Laupen war, these neighbouring Christians pointedly wore turbans (see Figure 2).[71] Finally, the universal availability of the Turkish stereotype was made apparent during the confessional conflict, when each confession hurled the abusive term 'Turks' at those on the other side.[72]

Crusade as 'concealed pattern'

The argument presented above shows that the Ottoman threat, and the constant renewal of plans to undertake a crusade, were familiar to the population of the Swiss Confederation. They constituted a background music, so to speak, one that sometimes sounded loudly and at other times quietly, but which was always audible. For a long time historical research failed to register the presence of crusading ideas in western Europe after the fall of Acre. Because nothing came of the *cruciatae*, they vanished from the field of vision of a historiography that mistakenly concerned itself only with events and outcomes. But recent research has been able to demonstrate that even after the failure of armed expeditions to the Holy Land, the concept of crusade exerted an influence far and wide.[73]

This approach accords with the methodology of the *nouvelle histoire*, which concerns itself with the *longue durée* of ideas and modes of conduct. It can be shown that patterns of thinking are not only very persistent, but also undergo processes of change and re-emerge in new contexts; they form collective points of reference that shape human activity.[74] In this sense we are dealing less with a phenomenon that lends itself to definition as understood in the classical history of ideas or ideologies, than with appearances that belong to a certain *mentalité*[75] or *Habitus*.[76] The formation of a mode of behaviour that is wrapped up with crusading ideology may be characterized as follows. In the age of the crusades to the Holy Land (1095–1291), the clergy shaped an anti-Islamic image of the foe (*Feindbild*) that was at once self-contained and far-reaching in scope. This stereotype became associated at the same time with a genuinely Christian pattern of legitimation, above all with the concept of the Chosen People of God. The best example of this is Guibert of Nogent's 'Dei Gesta per Francos'.[77] While the crusades ended in total

Figure 2   Bern defeats its opponents during the Laupen war, 1339: Petermann Etterlin, *Kronica von der loblichen Eydtgnoschaft, jr harkomen und sust seltzam strittenn und geschichten* (1507), p. 334.

failure, both the image of the foe and the self-legitimation that was associated with it remained within the thought processes of contemporaries. As the states of the early-modern period formed in the course of the late Middle Ages, the political authorities drew on definitions of both enemy and self that had been fashioned by the Church, in order to send their subjects to war against neighbours or confessional opponents. This sequence may be understood as part of a process of secularization, though in the light of the new 'crusades' that we are experiencing at the start of the twenty-first century, we must work with the assumption that the process of secularization could at any time be set into reverse.

Recent research by Norman Housley places these observations in a broader context. For Housley the recourse to crusading ideas was just one of the aspects that together made up a generic term that he describes as 'religious warfare', covering the period from 1400 to 1536.[78] Alongside 'crusade' as a concept Housley places 'sectarian apocalypticism, national messianism and defence of doctrinal truth', which made their mark on the conduct of war in Europe between 1400 and 1536 and generated a form of 'religious warfare' that characterized this period.[79] An impressive series of example serve as illustrations of Housley's thesis, a prominent place being given to Hussitism, which all too often gets overlooked in historical research. The examples given above, which illustrate the impact that crusading ideas exercised in the Swiss Confederation, Housley assigns to the 'pattern' of 'national messianism'.[80]

The four 'patterns of thought' that influence and change 'religious warfare' are without doubt highly suitable as heuristic categories to assess armed conflicts in the late Middle Ages in a comparative manner. The generic term 'religious warfare' will lead to discussion. Given a tendency to interpret religious behaviour in a purely functional way, it cannot be over-emphasized that in the late Middle Ages religion played an independent and powerful role in the waging of any war. But the adjective 'religious' leads to the question whether, on the whole, there was any 'non-religious warfare' in the Middle Ages. Even hardened mercenaries like the Armagnacs were accompanied by priests. Could they not perceive themselves to be executors of 'religious warfare', despite the fact that their deeds were anything but Christian? And generally speaking, was or is it ever possible to wage a war without ideas that are founded in belief? It is evident that both religion and the conduct of war changed during the late Middle Ages, whilst processes of religious legitimation served the purposes of widely differing groups. The afore-going reference to the concept of *Habitus* attempts to take this development into account: serviceable modes of speech and behaviour were at hand, which can be characterized very well with the help of Housley's four 'patterns of thought'. But how can we describe this process, containing as it does the paradox that 'patterns' that originated with the clergy finally came to be believed by the laity, and were independently used by them? Not only did 'faith and warfare' conjoin in an unholy alliance, but they nestled in the mentality of the population of Europe. The disastrous consequences can be seen and felt right up to the present day.

7

Giovanni da Capistrano and the Crusade of 1456

Norman Housley

Few events in the history of the crusades were as remarkable as the relief of Belgrade in the summer of 1456. It was extraordinary primarily because a Turkish army commanded by the sultan in person and equipped with formidable siege guns was repelled by an ad hoc force made up of John Hunyadi's soldiers, Belgrade's garrison and inhabitants, and above all the crusaders recruited and led by Giovanni da Capistrano. More broadly, both Capistrano's success in recruiting an army of crusaders, and that army's heterogeneous but predominantly non-noble nature, fly in the face of trends in crusading in the fifteenth century. Debate has raged about what happened in July 1456: was Belgrade saved by Hunyadi or Capistrano?[1] Whether or not he saved Belgrade, however, the achievement of this 70-year-old friar in mobilizing enthusiasm for a crusade against the Turks was in itself daunting. Does the explanation lie in the crisis which Hungary faced in 1456, or in Capistrano's own personality, experience and skill as a preacher? To place these issues in context I shall first establish the framework of Capistrano's preaching and his own itinerary. I shall then analyse, in so far as the sources permit, the themes of his preaching and the devotional atmosphere which it generated in the crusading host. Finally, I shall explore some of the later echoes of the 1456 campaign.

The origins of Capistrano's preaching lie in the shock waves created by the fall of Constantinople three years previously. Given the defeat suffered by Hunyadi in 1448 at the second battle of Kosovo, it was obvious that the immediate threat was to Hungary and in particular to its southern fortress town of Belgrade (Nandoralba), situated at the juncture of the Sava and Danube rivers. It is not clear from Capistrano's long and varied career why he threw himself with such energy into promoting Hungary's cause. His first known reference to the Turks in a letter came in February 1443, when he was 56 years old.[2] He took part in crusade preaching and negotiation in the mid-1440s, but it was a marginal involvement compared, for instance, with his work on behalf of the Franciscan Observance, his persecution of heretical groups and his harassment of the Jews. Indeed, when he expressed an interest in going to Hungary in 1451, it was to do some heresy hunting.[3] That said, his experience, reputation and authority made him a force to be reckoned with in the years following Constantinople's fall, though not even Capistrano could cut through the Gordian knot of self-interest and prevarication that characterized the imperial diets of 1454–5, dooming all hopes for a major military expedition. In the summer of 1454 Capistrano was in the central European lands, and he considered going to Hungary to preach the crusade in the kingdom's defence. But on 26 July Aeneas Silvius Piccolomini wrote urging him instead to attend the Michaelmas diet at Frankfurt and help rouse the Germans to action. Without outside support the Hungarians would do nothing.[4] Capistrano agreed, and Piccolomini gave further proof of his confidence in the friar's abilities when he asked him to persuade any of the German princes whom he encountered to come to the diet; even though the Emperor Frederick III was not planning to attend, much could still be hoped for.[5]

Capistrano's own commitment to the defence of Hungary, and his tendency to speak his mind openly, are clear in a sharp letter that he wrote to Pope Nicholas V on 28 October 1454. The third diet, to be held at Wiener Neustadt in February 1455, would be too late to organize help in the event of a Turkish invasion of Hungary in 1455. If the Hungarians made a truce and stood aside, the Turks could sweep through and then 'woe to you, Italy; woe to you, Rome'. The Italians could not afford their present nonchalance and Nicholas was being openly criticized for his inactivity. As for Capistrano himself, his way ahead was clear. Though eaten up by age ('consumptus senio') and without any money to offer, he would do what little he could for the faith. First he would visit Frederick III and beg him for an army of 12,000 horse and 30,000 foot. Then, responding to repeated entreaties from the Hungarian authorities, he would make his way to Hungary and do all he could to dissuade them from making a truce with the Turks. Capistrano concluded his letter to Nicholas with comments which came as close as discretion permitted to an open assault on the humanist pope's priorities. He was frustrated not to be able to work with a personalized version of the pope's crusade bull or indeed to have any clear idea of what Nicholas was trying to achieve. And his report of what 'all princes, all lords and the world at large' was saying was clearly shorthand for his own opinion: 'Why should we expend our efforts, our belongings, the bread from our children's mouths, on fighting the Turks when the pope is spending St Peter's treasure, which ought to be devoted to the defence of holy faith, on towers and fine walls, lime and stone?'[6] A few weeks previously Capistrano had written an encouraging letter to Philip of Burgundy, who had responded to the Frankfurt diet with a flurry of administrative preparations and whose enthusiasm for the crusade was clearly much more to Capistrano's taste.[7]

Given the tone of his October 1454 letter, Capistrano must have regarded the death of Nicholas V in March 1455, and the election of the energetic and fervent Calixtus III, as the clearing of a log-jam.[8] On 1 May 1455 he wrote to Calixtus congratulating him, urging him to pursue the crusade and reiterating his point that building projects must be stopped so that resources were available.[9] Soon afterwards the friar was in Hungary, and on 21 June he wrote again to the pope setting out in detail plans for a crusade which he had hatched together with Hunyadi at the diet of Raab. Close co-operation with Hunyadi was essential, for although his influence had been weakened by recent military defeats and political setbacks, he was captain general for the 15-year-old Ladislas V Posthumus and remained the most powerful magnate in Hungary.[10] In a remarkable flight of fancy, Capistrano described a paper army of 100,000 men. It would comprise 10,000 cavalry supplied by Hunyadi and 20,000 by the king, 10,000 by George Branković the despot of Serbia, 20,000 by Calixtus and 10,000 by Alfonso of Aragon/Naples and the cities of Italy; and 20,000 mixed horse and foot provided by Philip the Good of Burgundy. With such a force operating on land, and Alfonso of Aragon/Naples waging war at sea, Hunyadi was confident of clearing the Turks from Europe and of recovering Jerusalem: 'with such a big armed force he would hope also to recover Jerusalem'. This was an astonishing claim to make, and it is not surprising to find Hunyadi qualifying it with the remark that the army would have to be made up of 'not boys, but able men who are trained in the use of arms'. On the other hand, the army would not require pay: it would live off the captured spoils and lands of the Turks.[11]

This is an interesting letter on several counts. There is no reason to doubt that the reference to Jerusalem sprang from Capistrano's own hopes. He had visited the Holy Land in 1439–40, probably to observe the *custodia Terrae Sanctae* maintained by his order. But it also accorded with the aspirations of the new pope. Calixtus quoted Ps. 137:5 in the oath which he swore after his accession,[12] and viewed the recovery of the Holy Land as imminent in the aftermath of victory a year later.[13] The force of 10,000 cavalry which Hunyadi was to provide gives us a working figure for the captain general's personal *banderium*, important in the discussion of how many troops he may have had at Belgrade.[14] Most significantly, Capistrano's paper host gives us a good impression of the friar's conception of the sort of crusading army which was needed: a coalition of forces, each in itself substantial, fielded by the various Christian authorities which had an interest in the crusade. There was no reason why they should not include volunteers who had taken the cross but, as Hunyadi's remark confirmed, they should all be experienced fighting men, capable of facing soldiers whose abilities Hunyadi appreciated more than anybody else.[15] The captain general's concern that professionals be enlisted was reflected in an appeal sent by King Ladislas to the German lands in July 1456, in which he promised wages for soldiers who came to his assistance, a Hungarian florin per week for a horseman and 13 groschen for a footman.[16] That there should be some form of simultaneous naval operation had come to be emphasized in crusade planning since the 1440s.[17]

Capistrano spent the autumn and early winter of 1455–6 in Transylvania. He was prepared to put the defence of Hungary even before the interests of Observant reform, for the Conventuals were making use of Pope Calixtus's sympathy for their cause to try to secure the repeal of *Ut sacra*, Eugenius IV's bull of 1446 which granted them autonomous status within their order.[18] In Transylvania the focus of Capistrano's activities was still pastoral and missionary; in September 1455, for example, the people of Lipova (Lippa, co. Arad) invited him to preach there, assuring him that he would win over to the faith the 'many pagans, schismatics and unbelievers' who lived in the area.[19] He had been preaching the crusade intermittently since May 1454,[20] but his preaching campaign proper began in February 1456. At Buda on 14 February he received from the papal legate Juan de Carvajal a cross which the pope himself had blessed, 'with the greatest devotion and floods of tears', together with a commission to raise crusaders in anticipation of a Turkish invasion that year.[21] He left the capital in mid-April, and for the next three months most of his preaching took place in the towns and villages between the Drava and Tisza valleys in the south.[22] Given his age, his stamina was remarkable: it has been estimated that between his arrival in Hungary at the end of May 1455 and his journey to Belgrade early in July 1456, he covered nearly 600 km.[23] So too was the effect of his preaching. Writing to Calixtus III from Buda on 24 March, Capistrano commented that 'many prelates and barons have taken the sign of the life-giving cross, and a multitude of the lesser folk; and each day we are signing more people'.[24] On 4 May the archbishop of Kalocsa, Raphael Herczeg, wrote urging the friar to preach in his area, which was threatened by the Turks. For the past eight days a crowd had gathered at Bács expecting Capistrano's appearance, and there was a danger of food shortages.[25] A few days later he repeated his request, baiting his appeal with the promise that many people would take the cross: 'much fruit would come of it, numerous people would be aroused to take the holy cross and proceed with spirit against the enemies of the Christian faith.'[26] On 2 June Carvajal wrote to Capistrano suggesting that his services would be better employed lobbying with Frederick III at Vienna. The diet which convened at Pest in April had made insubstantial preparations to meet an Ottoman offensive and it is likely that the legate despaired of an effective Hungarian defence.[27] He himself claimed that Capistrano's preaching was dispensable since fear of the Turkish threat to hearth and home, combined with Hunyadi's authority, would be sufficient to arouse the south to arms. But he withdrew his suggestion on 15 June in response to Hunyadi's request.[28] From such letters we get a powerful impression of a successful preaching campaign by Capistrano and his fellow Observants. Those who took the cross gathered near Szeged, a town located on the Tisza mid-way between Buda and Belgrade, and designated as their assembly point by Hunyadi.[29]

News reached the Hungarian diet of Mehmed's march on 7 April, but it was only three months later, on 3 July, that the Turkish army arrived before Belgrade. Capistrano had entered the fortress the previous day. Initially his crusaders were encamped on the southern shore of the Danube, some distance west of the fortress; later they were based somewhat nearer, close to the left bank of the Sava.[30] It is not my purpose to enter into the debate mentioned earlier on Hunyadi's role in the successful defence of Belgrade. What matters for the purposes of this essay is the agreement amongst the sources that crusaders played a key part in all three encounters with the Turks which ended in their rout: Hunyadi's breaking of their naval blockade on 14 July; the repulse of their ferocious infantry assault on the fortress on 21–22 July; and the foray beyond the walls on 22 July, which precipitated a panicky Turkish retreat and the abandonment of much of their costly matériel. The point is that irrespective of how much help they received from Hunyadi's *banderium*, the fortress garrison commanded by the captain general's brother-in-law Mihály Szilágyi, and the inhabitants of Belgrade, the crusaders proved their worth as fighters.[31] Crucially, at the critical point in the desperate fighting which occurred on 21–22 July they stood alone.[32]

Capistrano's crusade came to an end when he fell ill and died in the autumn of 1456. This may seem odd, since our main text for the crusade, Giovanni da Tagliacozzo's *Relatio de victoria Belgradensi*, narrates that it came to a dramatic close somewhat earlier, on 23 July:

> Then the crusaders received licence to depart, and a blessing, from the most blessed father, acting as their captain. They all returned home in good heart, astounded and marvelling at the events which God had brought about through the ministry and offices of the most blessed father. And that was the end of the crusade.[33]

We shall return to the circumstances that caused Capistrano to dismiss his troops. But many were soon replaced. Carvajal started the journey south from Buda to Belgrade on the very day of victory with 4,500 crusaders.[34] And it is apparent from the third letter which he wrote to Calixtus III about his victory, on 17 August, that despite Hunyadi's death six days earlier the friar was far from regarding his crusade as finished.[35] On the contrary, he returned to his grand schemes of June 1455, asking for an army of 12,000 heavily armed horsemen from Italy, or at least 10,000, paid for six months' service by the pope. Fighting alongside his crusaders, and soldiers fielded by the Hungarians, this army would expel the Turks from Europe and recover the Holy Land. He revived the idea of their living off the enemies' spoils during their three years on campaign.[36] It was an approach with which the pope was fully in sympathy, urging Capistrano to exhort 'the prelates, barons, nobles and people of the whole kingdom of Hungary, to follow the cross of Jesus Christ'.[37] According to Nicholas of Fara, Capistrano and the legate Carvajal took the first step in this direction by reconstituting the crusader encampment near Belgrade, an initiative that foundered with the friar's death.[38]

From this it seems to follow that the *cruciata* referred to by Tagliacozzo as ending on 23 July was not the whole anti-Turkish enterprise, but something more specific: the body of men and women recruited in late April, May and June in Hungary's southern counties who had marched with Capistrano from Petervaradja, plus those who had gathered at Szeged and made their way down the Tisza to Belgrade, joining the crusader camp during the first three weeks of July.[39] Predominantly these were Hungarians, though even in this force there were some Germans and Austrians,[40] who had taken the cross from Capistrano and his fellow preachers in 1454–5. Pius II's biographer Lodrisio Crivelli wrote rhapsodically of 600 students at the University of Vienna who took the cross and fought like Leonidas's Spartans in the defence of Belgrade.[41]

The author of the revolutionary tract called *The Book of One Hundred Chapters* was one of these, taking the cross from Capistrano at the age of just 18.[42] Others from the German-speaking lands had only reached Vienna or Buda at the time of the battles and they came south later. On 14 June Carvajal wrote to Capistrano that many crusaders were gathering in Germany but lacked leadership.[43] According to a Breslau chronicler, the public reading out of King Ladislas's letter of 25 July had a considerable effect there: people wept with anguish and 800 took the cross either to go in person or to send deputies. Equipped by the town council with wagons and food supplies, this Breslau contingent joined the other German crusaders at Vienna.[44] A Nürnberg contingent, also 800 strong, and led by the Swiss captain Heinrich von Malters and Ott Herdegen, set out on the southwards march on 25 August.[45] A day later a returning crusader wrote of groups of crusaders kicking their heels in both Buda and Vienna, awaiting instructions.[46] On 29 July Carvajal wrote to Francesco Sforza that when the siege was broken 'those crusaders who were mounted and noble, and had been called to arms, had not yet arrived'.[47] Although it is possible that Carvajal was engaging in wishful thinking, when the king finally came south to Belgrade, in November 1456, he was accompanied by a strong retinue of German crusaders.[48] The historian Antonius Bonfinius later claimed that the king trusted these men more than he did the Hungarians left at Belgrade by Hunyadi; they became caught up in Hungarian domestic politics and for a time it looked as if there would be a second assault on Belgrade, this time by German crusaders fighting against Hunyadi supporters.[49]

Without losing sight of these later groups, it is natural to characterize the crusade of 1456 largely in terms of the individuals who made up the army which fought alongside Capistrano at Belgrade and whom he dispersed on 23 July; in Tagliacozzo's dramatic phrase, 'And that was the end of the crusade'. Most of these *crucesignati* were recruited in the spring of 1456 following Capistrano's own assumption of the cross in February. Estimating the size of this force is no easier than in the case of earlier crusades. Giovanni da Tagliacozzo and Nicholas of Fara referred to 60,000 crusaders,[50] but this is no more reliable than their estimates of 160,000 and 120,000 combatants in Mehmed II's army.[51] Jenő Szűcs's figure of 20,000–30,000 crusaders is more credible,[52] and Babinger argued that a countryside stricken by plague and harvest failure could have fed no more than 12,000.[53] But as Hofer and Held pointed out,[54] the army fluctuated a good deal in size. Because it was based outside the fortress, it was able to absorb fresh groups of recruits who arrived from the north throughout the first three weeks of July. When the crusaders initially placed in Belgrade to help defend it against the Turks were relieved, after the breaking of the blockade on 14 July, their wounded and sick were dispersed for care to towns further up the Danube.[55] And in the week that followed Capistrano took similar care to relieve the crusaders stationed within the fortress.[56] In such fluid circumstances, making any reasonable estimate of the size of the army must surely have been well-nigh impossible.

The main sources for the character of this army are the lives of Capistrano written in the early 1460s by his fellow Franciscans, Nicholas of Fara and Christopher of Varese, and four letters by Giovanni da Tagliacozzo, in particular one written at Udine in July 1460 and usually called the *Relatio de victoria Belgradensi*. All these sources were written with a view to securing Capistrano's canonization, and Tagliacozzo was writing in 1460 to put the record straight,[57] but these considerations do not render them unusable. It is helpful that the letters by Tagliacozzo span the period 1456–60, and that the first was written on 28 July 1456, before Capistrano's death on 23 October. It is hardly likely that just six days after the defeat of the Turks Tagliacozzo would be assembling a hagiographic portrait of his master, and by comparing Tagliacozzo's accounts Robert Lechat was able to test the biographer's veracity. Lechat concluded that in his *Relatio* Tagliacozzo engaged in a good deal of embroidery: 'The biographer permits himself to amplify a good deal, cites Scripture copiously, and indulges in explosions of lyricism.'[58] To take one example, the first letter marvelled that God protected Capistrano from the Turks' missiles in the thick of battle. In the second letter this was elaborated: the Turks realized that Capistrano was the crusaders' leader and made a special effort to kill him, which made his escape the more miraculous. In the *Relatio*, arrows were miraculously diverted from their course.[59] As Lechat remarked, this is precisely the kind of hagiographic addition which we would expect, and which we are equipped to set aside. 'A modicum of prudence is sufficient to weed out the suspect elements and retain a crop of information which we would be wrong to neglect.'[60] Much the same methodology can be applied to the *Vitae* of Nicholas of Fara and Christopher of Varese, who were not present at Belgrade but drew on the accounts of Tagliacozzo and Jerome of Udine, who were.[61]

No surviving source offers us the content of Capistrano's crusade preaching.[62] In 1451–5 he enjoyed spectacular success in preaching north of the Alps, in Bavaria, Franconia, Thuringia, Saxony, Silesia, Moravia and the Catholic parts of Bohemia.[63] Small urban centres, cities and university towns all fell under his spell, woven through spontaneity, improvisation, emotional appeals and an intuitive grasp of crowd psychology. As with previous great preachers, delivery mattered as much as message: Nicholas of Fara claimed that crowds listened to Capistrano preaching in Latin for three hours at a stretch but became inattentive when his interpreters began translating.[64] Even if exaggerated, this is a highly revealing comment, and it accords with much evidence that the crusaders regarded themselves as followers, almost disciples, of Capistrano. Christopher of Varese wrote that many Germans took the cross in 1456 on hearing the news that Capistrano was preaching the crusade in Hungary, because the memory of his preaching in their towns remained so fresh, and they wanted both to fight the Turks and to see the friar again.[65] This is confirmed by the comment of the Nürnberg *Creutzer*, that those who fought at Belgrade were 'common people' (*gemein volk*) who had assembled 'from cities, villages and market towns', and had 'no lord or noble' as their leader, only 'the holy father John Capistrano'.[66] In other words, the leadership vacuum created by the stupor of the Reich's authorities combined with Capistrano's powerful charisma and seemingly superhuman stamina to create a continuity of preaching and leadership in the field which was possibly unknown since the days of Peter the Hermit.[67]

The situation was replicated in the interior of Hungary in 1456. One of Tagliacozzo's 'explosions of lyricism' occurs when he describes the overwhelming loyalty which the crusaders felt towards Capistrano.

> They obeyed the holy father and no other as their captain, or rather as the lieutenant of Jesus Christ. And this was not surprising, for they had been aroused by his preaching and exhortation, they had taken the cross from him, and they had promised to follow him into captivity and death. He was the ruler, commander, judge, captain and emperor of all the crusaders.[68]

He embodied the crusade he had brought into being, and the crusaders would have gone through fire or water for him.[69] For Nicholas of Fara he was another Joshua, another Moses.[70] There can be no doubt that if one of the Turkish missiles referred to earlier had hit Capistrano, the crusade would have collapsed in much the same way that Pope Pius II's ended eight years later at Ancona. The difference is that whereas Pius worked through the bureaucratic machinery of the papal Curia, Capistrano had at his disposal nothing but a handful of followers. Small wonder that in his attempt to describe adequately his master's boundless energy in the midsummer heat of the Balkans, Tagliacozzo conjured up some bizarre images. One was that when Hunyadi gave him a horse to enable him to get around more quickly, the beast was rapidly worn to a frazzle.[71] Another was that the dust adhered so solidly to Capistrano's tongue that it had to be shaved off with a knife. Scorning the demands of the body and the dictates of old age, the friar would not stop to eat, drink, wash, shave, change his clothes or rest, and during the whole course of the siege he slept for just seven hours in total.[72]

An appreciation of the personal role played by Capistrano is no excuse for not trying to recreate the message he communicated, starting with the way he characterized the crusaders' enemy. It goes without saying that Capistrano would have preferred conversion to combat, but with the exception of the occasional prisoner and deserter, this was impracticable.[73] Tagliacozzo went out of his way to deny that his revered master encouraged hatred of the Turks,[74] but his own text shows that in the heat of the moment Capistrano dehumanized the enemy. He labelled them dogs and insisted, rather bizarrely, that Sultan Mehmed be referred to constantly as 'the biggest dog'.[75] The only biographer to give any idea of how Capistrano portrayed the threat which they collectively posed is Christopher of Varese, who wrote:

> he told them to reflect on how those dogs constantly blasphemed against the Lord's name, how they mocked Christ's faith, destroyed churches, profaned holy altars, how they delighted in deflowering virgins on altars dedicated to God, how they shed the blood of Christians in uncontrolled rage, how they led Christians away into captivity, and how they extolled, praised and exulted in their own faith, bestowed on them by that devilish man Muhammad, full of filth and shamefulness.[76]

Given that Varese did not witness the preaching, the similarity of such themes to the commonplaces of anti-Turkish rhetoric is suspicious, though that is not to dismiss them out of hand; one could argue that it was precisely such commonplaces that Capistrano, lacking direct experience of the Turks, would fall back on. It is possible that, like Tagliacozzo, Capistrano stressed the importance of Belgrade in the defence not just of Hungary, but of the whole of Christendom.[77] One recurrent idea has more credibility because it did spring from Capistrano's work. This was that the Turkish menace was so pressing that anybody who fought against them was welcome.

Anyone who wants to take our side against the Turks is to be counted as a friend. Whether they are Serbs, schismatics, Wallachians, Jews, heretics, even unbelievers, if they stand alongside us in this tempest, we shall embrace them in friendship. The battle now is against the Turks, and only against the Turks.

As Tagliacozzo emphasized, it was a remarkable moment: a man who for decades had relentlessly pursued and killed heretics, now looked benignly on as they stood shoulder to shoulder with devout Catholics.[78] It proved to be an astute approach, for Tagliacozzo himself praised the courage, ferocity and tenacity in combat of the Serb inhabitants of Belgrade.[79]

For the most part, however, it is the devotional aspect which is most to the fore in accounts of Capistrano's army, and there can be no doubt that both during his preaching campaign and in the sermons which he delivered to the army, the friar emphasized the redemptive process which they were engaged in. Thus before engaging the Turks on 22 July, he urged his followers: 'Behold, my children, now is the accepted time, behold, now is the day of salvation [2 Cor. 6: 2]. Behold, now the gate to paradise stands open, behold the [martyr's] crown, behold, now is the time for redemption of sins.'[80] Such a conflict imposed constraints on their own behaviour. They must fight for the faith and not for booty; indeed, for the time being all booty should be burnt. Provided their intention remained pure, all the goods of the Turks would eventually be theirs as well as eternal life.[81] This was fully in line with traditional crusading thought, but it also accorded with Capistrano's background of penitential preaching, in particular his condemnation of avarice, luxury and display. Perhaps Tagliacozzo's most colourful passage is the one in which he described the impeccably correct behaviour which reigned in the crusader camp.[82] Piety, harmony and brotherhood were the norms. Misdeeds were punished swiftly and with rough justice: a thief lost an ear, and a would-be profiteer narrowly escaped being thrown into the Danube alongside his overpriced loaves.[83] The contrast with, for example, the Nicopolis expedition of 1396 is striking, and in both cases a good deal has to be put down to exaggeration; but it remains true that in 1396 some of the motives which took the crusaders to the battlefield were conducive to pride, vanity and quarrelsome behaviour, whereas in 1456 the crusaders had responded to the preaching of a man who above all else demanded *reformatio vitae*.[84] It is likely that Capistrano's forceful presence and example, his apparent ubiquity and the overwhelming respect he enjoyed created a unique atmosphere.

As Hofer put it:

> What played itself out in the camp at Belgrade has to be understood
> in the light of the religious movement which Capistrano released
> everywhere he set foot. His camp at Belgrade was not so much a mil-
> itary encampment as a religious assembly, similar to those which
> sprang up around him throughout the previous six years in all the
> places to which his missionary journey led him.[85]

Naturally enough, the devotional tone of the crusade was that of the
Franciscan Observance. Capistrano's banner portrayed St Bernardino of
Siena, and the crusaders marched behind banners showing St Francis,
St Anthony of Padua, St Louis of Toulouse and St Bernardino.[86]
Capistrano emphasized again and again that those who died would win
not just salvation but martyrdom.[87] As Christopher of Varese put it,
'Fortunate are they who perish in this, Christ's battle, for straightaway
they shall be crowned by the angels with the holy martyrs who died for
the faith.'[88] According to Nicholas of Fara, this sort of language provoked some rash behaviour on the part of the crusaders, who after making their confession and receiving communion rushed into the Turkish
lines, meeting certain death.[89] Tagliacozzo recorded Capistrano's own
sadness when he realized that he was going to die peacefully in bed
rather than be martyred, 'which he had for so long longed for and
sought out'.[90] Most significantly, nearly all the sources emphasize the
multifarious use by Capistrano and his crusaders of the Name of Jesus:
it was a battle cry, an instrument of unity and a declaration of allegiance.[91] Its significance was well summarized in the advice given by
Capistrano to the crusaders who manned the galleys which broke the
Turkish blockade on 14 July: 'after publicly exhorting them to defend
the Christian faith and to achieve the full remission of all their sins and
martyrdom, he ordered them to invoke and acclaim none other than
the Name of Jesus, both on land and at sea.'[92] It was an exhortation he
would later reiterate to the whole army.[93] In Tagliacozzo's account, the
'holy and terrible Name of Jesus Christ'[94] achieved a central place alongside the cross. The two devotional symbols seem to command equal
devotion.[95] This is remarkable given that the theology and spirituality
of the cross were the hallmark of crusading. Quoting Galatians 6:14,
Capistrano insisted that everything from portable altars to priests' robes
be marked with red crosses.[96] The victory was won 'under the banner of
the most holy cross with the acclamation of the Name of Jesus Christ',
while Christ promised Capistrano success 'by virtue of my name and of

the most holy cross'.[97] Thirty years previously Capistrano had helped
Bernardino to defend the Name of Jesus against the charge of heresy.[98]
Its triumphant place in an expedition which enjoyed such an outcome
was a blazing affirmation of the legitimacy of the Observance, setting
the cap on one of Capistrano's lifetime goals.

The defeat of the Turks was of course regarded as a miracle, fully comparable with the greatest victories of the Old Testament Israelites.[99] As
Capistrano put it in his second letter to the pope, 'the entire community of the Christian religion should render thanks and praise to our
Lord Jesus Christ, who alone fought for his cause and ours, defeated and
destroyed the army of the Great Turk, to the latter's confusion and dis-
grace. Throughout all eternity this glorious victory of Jesus Christ
should be on the lips of every Christian.'[100] This central miracle was buttressed by other expressions of divine support. Nicholas of Fara wrote of
two comets which appeared in June 1456, presaging the Ottoman
invasion; Capistrano interpreted them as foretelling the defeat of
the Turks.[101] Tagliacozzo noted a series of miracles, some more impressive than others. Capistrano's decision to go to Hungary to preach was
the result of hearing voices calling 'to Hungary' ('In Hungariam').[102]
While praying in virtual despair at Petervaradja (Petrovaradin,
Peterwardein), on the way to Belgrade, he experienced a vision of an
arrow which hovered above the church altar, carrying an assurance of
victory written in letters of gold.[103] The vision was a turning point:
never again did Capistrano question the outcome of the campaign.
Following Capistrano's arrival at Belgrade on 2 July, when Hunyadi
called on him to journey downstream along the Danube to join him at
Keve, the friar was saved from capture and death by a freak storm.[104] It
was miraculous, in Tagliacozzo's eyes, that so few casualties were caused
by the enormous boulders which the Turks hurled into Belgrade.[105] That
the largest Turkish galley operating on the Danube should be sunk by a
stone fired from the Turks' own siege works was God's work.[106] Only
inspiration from St Mary Magdalene, on the vigil of her feast-day, could
have caused the crusaders who were manning the fortress's crumbling
outer circuit to throw incendiary material into the ditches at the critical
point of the Turkish assault, causing confusion in the enemy ranks and
turning the tide of battle.[107] Miraculously, the Turks perceived a boat carrying Capistrano and just five others across the Sava, on 22 July, to be
an entire army crossing the river.[108] During the battle that followed,
Turkish arrows were miraculously diverted from hitting Capistrano, and
Turks fell down dead when the Name of Jesus was shouted by their
opponents.[109]

The central characteristic of Capistrano's army was the absence of noble participation. In the letter he penned to the pope on the day of the victory, 'quickly and in haste, exhausted, on my return from the battle', Capistrano described his crusaders as 'poor and unskilled' ('pauperes et rudes').[110] Tagliacozzo made the point well: 'Now the crusaders began to assemble at the designated spot [Slankamen], the poor were aroused while the rich and the noble stayed at home.'[111] Later he helpfully expanded his characterization, writing of 'commoners, plebeians, the poor, priests, secular clerics, students, monks, brethren from various orders, mendicants, members of the third order of St Francis, and hermits'.[112] Not just Tagliacozzo but numerous other sources make this clear. Tagliacozzo and Nicholas of Fara, in a curious echo of a *topos* which went back to the First Crusade, had the retreating sultan bemoan the humiliation of his conquerors being both socially and militarily inferior to his own forces.[113] It was not a civilian army *per se* because for more than 50 years the *militia portalis* system had entailed drafting peasants for the defence of the realm.[114] The crusaders had an abundance of swords, cudgels, slings and staffs, together with military equipment. But they lacked artillery, cavalry, body armour and experience,[115] serious deficiencies which explain the despair which some felt at the chances of such a force repelling the Turks.[116]

This naturally causes us to ask whether Capistrano in his preaching specifically sought out the poor (*pauperes*) as chosen by God to defend Hungary. In 1514 a Hungarian crusade which was predominantly made up of peasants encountered active opposition from the nobles, and was transformed into a social revolt of great savagery.[117] Rumblings of discontent against the absence of Hungary's nobility certainly occurred in 1456. They are documented by Tagliacozzo, whose credibility on this issue there is no reason to doubt. He recorded that following the naval battle, the crusaders burned their booty 'lest it be carried off by the powerful, who had not been present' ('ne a potioribus, qui non interfuerunt, auferrentur').[118] Criticism subsequently focused on what the crusaders reckoned to be the lacklustre performance of Hunyadi, who remained on a ship in the Danube and Sava throughout the battles of 21–22 July.[119] In his earliest letter about the siege, which was hastily written and possibly unguarded, Tagliacozzo wrote that the crusaders had no time for him.[120] It is likely that the feeling was reciprocal. One German source went so far as to say that animosity between the crusaders and Hunyadi reached such heights that 'if the crusaders had caught him, they would not have let him live another second, while he would happily have seen them all cut to bits'.[121] The battle outside the walls of

Belgrade on 22 July was fought in open defiance of Hunyadi's command, and on the following day it looked as if fighting would break out between Hunyadi's men and the crusaders. The latter resented the vaivoda's veto of any pursuit of the fleeing enemy, and they vented their anger by having it publicly proclaimed (*praeconizari fecerunt*) that

> the victory which the Lord had bestowed on them the previous day, had owed nothing to the work or industry of any baron of the kingdom of Hungary. It had been due solely to the virtue of the most holy Name of Jesus Christ and of his most holy cross, and to the merits and hard work of the most blessed father, brother Giovanni da Capistrano.

Beside being an affront to Hunyadi's standing and honour, this brazen statement carried serious implications in terms of the disposition of the massive plunder which had been won. It was in these circumstances that Capistrano took the action described earlier, intervening forcefully and sending the crusaders home.[122] Only when they had all dispersed did Hunyadi set foot inside Belgrade.

There was clearly a big difference between what occurred in 1456 and in 1514. On the latter occasion some of the Franciscan Observants who preached the crusade threw in their lot with the rebels, supporting and justifying their revolt against their lords. In 1456, by contrast, Capistrano acted swiftly and decisively to staunch resentment against Hunyadi, and *a fortiori* against the rest of the Hungarian baronage, even at the cost of a delay in pursuing his own military agenda. This is the more striking because Capistrano was not afraid to speak his mind, and in the past he had characterized the rapacity of lords as one of his greatest foes; it complemented their reluctance to take up arms in defence of the common cause.[123] Nor had he spared the king and nobility of Hungary, for on 3 July, the day of the Turks' arrival at Belgrade, he wrote that if Ladislas V and his nobles did not want a visit from the Turks, they had better save the city.[124] When bloodshed between Christians seemed imminent, Capistrano rapidly drew a line. None the less, the question can be asked whether Capistrano had not himself, during the preaching and even more during the crowded first three weeks of July, deliberately countered the defeatism generated by the all too apparent deficiencies of his crusaders by playing up the theme that God had chosen them for this venture because of their poverty and humility. Tagliacozzo wrote that Capistrano frequently used such exhortations as 'My children, most devout Hungarians! O poor ones! To Turkey!'[125] Nicholas of Fara quoted him as preaching 'Fear not, my weak flock, and do not tremble. For God will give us the longed-for victory over our enemies, just as the path of the stars has foretold.'[126] And Tagliacozzo reported a conversation between Hunyadi and Capistrano, on the eve of the Turkish assault, in which Hunyadi's advice that the fortress be abandoned was countered with the words: 'Don't worry, my lord! God is great and he will overcome the might of the Turks with the few and the unarmed. He will defend our fortress and cast his enemies into confusion.'[127] There are strong grounds for believing that such a conversation occurred.[128] Capistrano had much the same answer for those who questioned whether the crusaders could take on the Turks outside the walls on 22 July.[129]

If the poor were chosen for this venture, it was virtually inevitable that some observers of the crusade would ask awkward questions about social obligations.[130] On 3 August 1456 Johann Goldener, dean of St Stephen's in Vienna, commented excitedly in a letter to Mattheus Schlick that the social order was turned upside down, with clerics and manual workers (*mechanici*) fighting, while knights (*milites*) prayed and laboured.[131] Tagliacozzo's views seem to have been broadly similar. He was genuinely puzzled by the failure of the Hungarian nobility to appear when their country was in such danger.[132] And he saw a moral in the fact that Hunyadi's most powerful war galley, 'that ship, so large and well-equipped, in which all human hope had been placed, rather than in the vessels of the poor', sank when its powder was accidentally ignited.[133] But Tagliacozzo was aware of the danger of misinterpreting a crusade preached by the mendicants as *ipso facto* a crusade of the poor. He reflected with commendable discretion on the various possible reasons why the bands (*turmae*) which arrived between 14 and 21 July carried banners representing the Franciscan saints:

> so that from this it would become apparent that the crusaders had been brought together by a man who was a distinguished member of the Franciscan Order; or to make it clear that this was a crusade just of the poor and not of the rich; or maybe they did this to conform with the banner of their father, or so that combatants would obtain the assistance of those saints under whose banners they fought.[134]

One historian has commented that in eastern Europe crusading belonged above all to the peasantry.[135] It is certainly the case that so far as one can see the Hungarian nobility's neglect of its legal obligations, and the rapacious assaults on royal fiscality carried out by the most powerful lords, were accompanied, in 1456 as in 1514, by a dramatic failure to respond to the crusading message. Tagliacozzo stated that all groups in Hungarian society welcomed the friar on his arrival in 1455,[136] but it would seem that despite Capistrano's claim in his letter of 24 March 1456,[137] relatively few members of the elite took the cross or honoured that commitment if they did. The reason for their apparent indifference may lie in a revealing passage in Tagliacozzo's *Relatio*. He believed that many nobles had taken the cross, and laid the blame for their non-appearance at the door of the magnates: in Hungary it was the custom ('mos est') for the lesser nobility to proceed to war only in the company of their lords.[138] There is support for this in Martyn Rady's recent study of the Hungarian nobility, in which he emphasized the remarkably limited means of some two-thirds of the nobles; unless they took service in a baronial *banderium* such men could not fight in a crusade in a manner befitting their status even if they were personally fired up by Capistrano's preaching to take the cross.[139] As for the members of the higher aristocracy, with the sole exceptions of Hunyadi and Jan Korogh, the region's chief landowner and office-holder, their interpretation of Hungary's *antemurale* image was couched not in terms of personal commitment but of the raising of external support; it should be added that they took their cue from the king, Ladislas V Posthumus, who spent the critical weeks of 1456 in safety at Vienna. It is tempting to deduce that the crusaders of 1456 were more patriotic than their lords, but it must be admitted that the sources do not refer to the existence of such feeling or even to Capistrano making reference to it.[140] Overwhelmingly, the message to which the crusaders responded was the two-fold one of defending the faith and earning their own salvation. The surge of disdain which some experienced towards the lords was expressed not in terms of national conceptions of identity and obligation but of social ones.

It is natural to treat the paeans of praise with which Tagliacozzo showered his hero with scepticism, and to conclude that he must have exaggerated Capistrano's role not just in saving Belgrade but also in raising his army of crusaders: 'O most blessed father Giovanni da Capistrano! Surely it was by your ministry, your hard work, your deeds, your command, and your prayers, that all this came about?'[141] Yet in large measure, the success of Capistrano's preaching in 1456 does have to be attributed to the man's own qualities. The same common sense that makes us sceptical of Tagliacozzo leads us to assume that at least some of the recruits who flocked to Belgrade, especially those from the south, were responding to the threat posed to their own farms, homes and families. But we must remember Hunyadi's rejection of Carvajal's argument that this should be enough in itself to rouse the southern counties to action. Hunyadi clearly did not believe that it was: Capistrano's preaching was essential.[142] Nor does the Turkish threat explain the considerable agitation in Germany and Austria, especially at places which had experienced the friar's preaching earlier. The excitement of events in 1456 could not therefore readily be replicated elsewhere, unless the preaching was entrusted to a group of men who shared some of Capistrano's extraordinary skills.

The relief of Belgrade was celebrated throughout western and central Europe. Thomas Gascoigne preached a sermon in its honour at Oxford, and Nicholas of Cusa preached twice at Neustift.[143] For contemporaries, who were still coming to terms with the fall of Constantinople in 1453, the victory was significant above all because it showed that God was still prepared to intervene on behalf of his people *in extremis*. On the Feast of Peter and Paul (29 June) 1456 Calixtus III had issued a general appeal for prayers, fasting and penance. Christians should 'return to the Lord, that he may return to us'. There should be intercessory processions on the first Sunday of each month. The *Missa contra paganos* should be sung, and at every Mass priests should pray to God to 'protect thy Christian people, and crush by thy power the pagans who trust in their fortunes'.[144] Such a *Gebetskreuzzug*, as Hofer termed it, was a highly traditional response to adversity; recently it had been used in reaction to the defeats suffered by the Catholic armies during the Hussite crusades.[145] On this occasion, however, it seemed to have worked, worked moreover in so dramatic a manner as to make the miraculous nature of the victory incontrovertible. In its honour Calixtus III in 1457 ordered the general observance of the Feast of the Transfiguration (6 August), the day on which news of the victory had reached him at Rome. Moreover, God continued to show his support, for in August 1457 the papal fleet enjoyed a victory at Mytilene, capturing more than 25 Turkish vessels.[146]

By this point the high hopes nourished by the pope, Capistrano, Carvajal and Hunyadi in the immediate aftermath of the victory had evaporated. Death intervened to bring the *tempus acceptabile* to an end. Hunyadi died on 11 August 1456, Capistrano on 23 October 1456, the pope on 6 August 1458. The triumph at Belgrade passed from being the first stage in an agenda of strategic recovery, to being an abiding inspiration, proof of the possibility of renewed success if only the faith and energy which had been displayed in July 1456 could be kindled anew amongst Christendom's leaders. Enthusiasts like Benedetto Accolti, Francesco Filelfo and Flavio Biondo were well used to citing the First

Crusade as proof of divine intervention on the side of Christians.[147] Belgrade was useful because it was a contemporary example which could be deployed to counter arguments that the First Crusade had happened a long time ago. For example, in 1513, in a letter to the king of Hungary, Pope Leo X cited the relief of Belgrade alongside the Hospitaller defence of Rhodes in 1480, recent successes in Bosnia and the deeds of Old Testament warriors, to show that God assisted his people.[148]

More pragmatically, the relief of Belgrade showed that the Turks were not such tough opponents as they seemed to be. This mattered because commentators stood in awe of Turkish military prowess and it was necessary for crusade enthusiasts not to play up the Ottoman threat so much that it induced despair rather than generating action.[149] The problem was confronted in a forthright manner by Pope Pius II in 1459 in *Cum bellum hodie*, his address to the delegates at the Congress of Mantua.

> Godfrey [of Bouillon] and the others who fought with him in Asia often destroyed huge numbers of enemies with a handful of men, slaughtering the Turks like cattle. But maybe you think the Turks of today are better than they once were, now that they have conquered Greece? Well, their calibre was shown in the battle of Belgrade, just three years ago ... Those Christian soldiers who defended the town consisted of a few crusaders, not noble or rich, unused to war, poorly armed, unskilled, disordered, rustic. None the less, they defeated the Turks, meeting their adversaries not so much with iron as with faith. The puffed-up Emperor of the Turks, previously believed to be invincible and dubbed 'the terror of the nations', was by such people defeated in the field, repulsed from the siege, driven from his camp, and compelled to undertake a shameful retreat.[150]

Nor were the Turks the only enemies of the faith against whom the relief of Belgrade could serve as an inspiration and example. What is very likely to be the most detailed, artistically impressive and contemporaneous representation of the repulse of Mehmed's army is a fresco measuring 46 square metres in the choir of the Observant church at Olomouc (Olmütz) in Moravia. Dating from 1468, the fresco clearly shows a dramatically oversized Capistrano standing in a citadel packed with heavily armed soldiers, clutching the Bible in his right hand, and raising with his left hand a picture of the Man of Sorrows. Further along the walls a captain (probably Hunyadi) carries a standard with the sign of the cross, while outside the fortress walls, on the right of the fresco, other Christian soldiers are engaging the Turks amidst siege-works studded with the barrels of cannon. The fresco was painted shortly after the church was consecrated by the papal legate Lorenzo Rovarella when King Matthias Corvinus was staying in Olomouc during his war against George of Poděbrad. As Stanko Andrić pointed out, this depiction of a great crusading success in a staunchly royalist and Catholic town at a time when the crusade was again being deployed against the Bohemian Utraquists, was scarcely likely to be a coincidence. 'The besieged and ardently defended town was a metaphor of the country occupied by the Hussites. Capistran, tirelessly preaching the word of God, showed the way to victory.'[151]

The other context in which the relief of Belgrade played a major role was the attempts to secure Capistrano's canonization. It was only in 1690 that Capistrano was finally declared a saint, following a series of campaigns of which the first began immediately after his death. At this point a number of factors worked against Capistrano's supporters. They included some which would have operated irrespective of what happened in 1456, including the isolated and precarious location of his body and nascent cult at Ilok, in the far south of Hungary, and the recent canonization of Bernardino of Siena, for whom Capistrano himself had been a strenuous lobbyist.[152] Belgrade, however, did not help Capistrano's cause. On the one hand, discrepant accounts of what had occurred began with the letters written by Capistrano and Hunyadi immediately after the Turkish retreat. We have seen that Tagliacozzo wrote his longest account of events, at Udine in July 1460, partly in response to denigration of Capistrano; indignantly he referred to 'the various letters and songs' in which the friar's role had been ignored.[153] A few years later Nicholas of Fara adopted a similarly defensive tone: 'This most happy and most glorious victory over the Turks was won by the blessed Giovanni, and by nobody else, let them say what they will.'[154] The difference in the accounts was picked up immediately by contemporaries, including Aeneas Silvius Piccolomini, and in practice it ruled out using the relief of the city to promote Capistrano's cause. As Stanko Andrić eloquently put it, this 'troublesome and polyphonic tradition' meant that 'there was no vigorous and solitary (vigorous because solitary) text, one of those prerequisites so characteristic for earlier centuries, to ensure the supremacy of the adverb *divinitus*'.[155]

In one sense, indeed, Belgrade hindered Capistrano's case. Juan de Carvajal took against the friar and of the three negative qualities which he attributed to him, rashness, vanity and irascibility, the first two were allegedly demonstrated by events at Belgrade. Thus Capistrano had shown rashness (*temeritas*) in taking part in the sortie outside Belgrade on 22 July and vanity (*vanitas*) in claiming the lion's share of the credit for the victory. The theme of vanity, which particularly appealed to humanists, was seized on by Aenea Silvius Piccolomini in two works written in 1458, *In Europam* and *Historia Bohemica*, in which similarly phrased comments occur to the effect that hunger for fame was Capistrano's Achilles's heel.[156] It seems likely that when he became pope, Piccolomini was already disposed not to accede to the lobbying of Capistrano's supporters; and the situation was not helped when Capistrano's close friend James of the Marches was tried for heresy in 1462.[157]

On the later occasions when canonization was promoted, the relief of Belgrade played a much less contentious role. When the official canonization process opened in 1519, its members, all Hungarian prelates, were certainly aware of the parallels between the situation in 1453–6 and that currently facing their country. Capistrano's cult was immensely popular in Hungary, and his canonization could be expected to boost morale. The fall of Belgrade to the Turks in August 1521 made the process yet more timely. In the letter he wrote in support of the process in 1523, the bishop of Csanád described Capistrano as 'an intrepid warrior of God, he was unwilling to be confined to cloisters, but for Christ's faith he fearlessly exposed himself to the cruel battlefield and to mortal danger'.[158] But events overtook the process. Ilok fell to the Turks on 8 August 1526, just a few weeks before Mohács. Capistrano's body disappeared and was never rediscovered.[159] Amidst such calamities the canonization process collapsed. When the canonization finally succeeded, the relief of Belgrade received its due share of attention.[160]

Making a definitive judgement on the crusade of 1456 is difficult, not so much because of the debate over 'ownership' of the victory as because events both fitted established patterns of crusading activity and yet did not. Viewed from certain angles, Capistrano's army looks like the 'popular' crusades of 1212, 1251, 1309 and 1320.[161] Yet Capistrano's commission to preach the crusade, his close links with Calixtus III, Aeneas Silvius Piccolomini, Carvajal and Hunyadi, his unimpeachable orthodoxy and reverence for papal authority, and his firm control over the crusaders, make such a resemblance superficial. So while a recurrent characteristic of 'popular' crusades had been their anti-Semitic behaviour, Capistrano in 1456 held out the hand of friendship to Jews and other non-Catholics who would join his crusaders against the Turks.[162] So far as we know, there was nothing in any way heterodox or subversive, in doctrinal terms, about the crusaders in 1456.[163] The challenge which circumstances led some of them to pose to the social order was at best incipient, and Tagliacozzo went to great pains to stress their instinct for sound organization and orderly behaviour.[164] Allowing for the vast social changes which had taken place, they resemble rather more the 'People's Crusade', the armies which made up the initial wave of the First Crusade, which like them lacked noble participation. The foray beyond the walls of Belgrade on 22 July 1456 could well have brought about disaster, in the same way that the followers of Peter the Hermit and Walter Sansavoir were massacred during an ill-judged advance from Civetot (Kibotos) in Asia Minor in October 1096.[165] Hunyadi's veto on provoking the Turks was sound, and to a large extent the difference in outcome in 1456 and 1097 was down to luck. Everybody involved in the crusade wanted noble participation; without it they muddled through, and had death not intervened, the next stage in the crusade would probably have enjoyed a rather more conventional military profile.

This, of course, begs the question of what was a 'normal' military profile for a crusade in the fifteenth century. That we have relatively little comparative evidence to work with is in itself a testimony to what Capistrano and his fellow Observants achieved in their crusade preaching during the early months of 1456. Success on this scale had not occurred for many generations, and it would not recur until, in analogous circumstances, the Franciscan Observants again raised an army of Hungarian peasant *crucesignati* in the spring of 1514. That the preachers of 1514 could repeat the success of 1456 (albeit with tragic results) is a warning not to ascribe the army of 1456 solely to Capistrano: be it a patriotic response to the Turkish threat to home and hearth, an unusual willingness to engage in combat which derived from the *militia portalis* system, or a particular chemistry between Observant preaching and the sensibilities of the Hungarian population, the fact is that in Hungary the call to take the cross still achieved results which could only be dreamed of elsewhere. The irony was that the responsiveness comprised the *laboratores* and *oratores*, not the *bellatores*, the men to whom popes since Urban II had primarily looked to answer the crusading call. As Johann Goldener put it, 'Behold, what a transformation! Alas, so much confusion ... '.[166]

8
Hungary and Crusading in the Fifteenth Century

János M. Bak

The Hungarian 'long fifteenth century' – in this case, from the defeat of the crusaders at Nicopolis in 1396 to the crusade-turned-rebellion of 1514 – was characterized more by the political use of crusading ideas than by actual military actions against 'enemies of Christendom', supported by papal indulgences. Late medieval crusade in this part of the world meant almost exclusively the fight against the advancing 'infidels', the Ottoman Empire. The rhetoric of crusading in this age began with the reforms introduced in the wake of the failure at Nicopolis, became significant during the interregna between 1439 and 1458, and constituted the central element in the diplomacy of King Matthias I Corvinus (1458–90). Actual crusading campaigns were rather few: one leading to the defeat at Varna (1444), the other relieving Belgrade in 1456. Both have been extensively studied and described, as have the events of 1514, in which the 'peasant' *crucigeri* (in Magyar: *kurucok*) turned against the 'enemies inside', that is, the lords and prelates, who, in their eyes, were not just failing to defend them against the infidel, but were actually worse than the latter.[1]

Once he managed to return home after the disaster of Nicopolis, King Sigismund called a diet to Temesvár (today: Timişoara, Romania), which met and approved a number of reforms some time in October 1397.[2] This decree contained a renewal of the Golden Bull of Andrew II, first issued in 1222, and a few other specific rights and privileges of the nobility. However, Article 7 of the old text was expanded by a fairly long arrangement for military obligations. The reference was usually to the present war (*guerra presens*), but the obligations remained in force essentially until the end of the medieval kingdom. They specified the obligation of landowners (noblemen) on the occasion of a general levy, and imposed heavy fines for those who proved reluctant to fight.

The radical innovation was, however, the duty of all landowners to equip and send to war a number of 'archers in a soldierly fashion' (*pharetrarii more exercituancium*), according to their holdings. One such soldier was to be supplied for every 20 peasant plots, the so-called *portae*; hence, the name of this auxiliary force, *militia portalis*. Considering that in Sigismund's time the kingdom may have had some 400,000 tax units (plots), such an infantry (or light cavalry?) would have been quite a valuable force. It is unclear whether the idea was to arm peasants (1 in 20?), or to expect landowners to hire warriors according to their means, in the manner of some sort of 'scutage'. In subsequent decades the ratio of peasants to militiamen was altered more than once, but we have, unfortunately, no unequivocal evidence of the *portalis* troops' participation in any campaign. What is important, nevertheless, is the attempt at a widespread arming of commoners (or, alternatively, the hiring of professional soldiers), reflecting the perception that the kingdom's defence called for a constant supply for troops. Other types of evidence suggest that a good percentage of the peasantry, especially those engaged in animal husbandry, were quite well-trained fighters.[3] Whether this was due to the *portalis* system or other reasons cannot now be specified.

Article 63 of the 1397 Temesvár diet also addressed military necessities and adumbrated a reform, albeit a temporary one, of finances. The assembly decreed that 'all clergy give and render half of their income for the defence of the realm' and that this half (essentially half of the tithe) was to be retained by the landowners, handed over to special collectors of this 'war tax', and not be employed for anything else.[4] This was the first step towards an 'extraordinary' taxation for anti-Ottoman defence, and it was followed by many more, becoming almost regular by the second half of the fifteenth century. Had it been collected, such a levy would have been a significant contribution to defence expenses, but there is no evidence that the clergy and the papacy ever agreed to repeat it until the very last years of the medieval kingdom. It has also been pointed out that the allocation of income to specific purposes should be seen as a first step towards establishing a regular budget, which was unknown in medieval states. The Hungarian estates attempted more explicit reforms of state finances, mainly for defence, in the early sixteenth century, and this example pointed in a direction that was elaborated later.[5]

Soon after this diet, Sigismund and his barons, above all his Florentine counsellor and general, Pipo Scolari and later the Ragusan brothers Tallóci (Tallovac), began to build up an elaborate system of defences on the kingdom's southern border.[6] The backbone of this system was a line of border fortifications beginning (in the south-east) along the lower Danube and ending, once it was finally completed in mid-century, at the Adriatic. After the fall of Serbia and then Bosnia, the system came to include fortresses beyond the immediate border of the kingdom; and a second line of forts was also established, situated some 80–100 km further north, deep inside the kingdom. Aside from the most significant castles, the defensive perimeter as a whole was garrisoned by the *banderia* ('private armies') of the lords of the region, such as the bans of Croatia-Slavonia, the *ispán* (*comes*) of Temes and the voivode of Transylvania. These individuals were assigned sizeable incomes from several other counties, or royal revenues such as the salt monopoly. In addition, increasing numbers of South Slav lords and their retainers and peasants (or warrior-peasants, called *vojniki*), found refuge in the kingdom and they supplied defensive mobile forces of considerable value, especially because they were highly familiar with the Ottoman tactics of raids and marauding auxiliaries. All in all, this system, usually under unitary command, withstood Ottoman advance for some 60–70 years; its last outpost, Jajce, fell only years after the defeat of the royal army at Mohács in 1526. Of course, this success was not unconnected to fluctuations in the priorities of Turkish expansion, and the internal conditions of the Ottoman Empire.[7]

I list these steps, which can be regarded as lessons learned from the defeat at Nicopolis, because I wish to argue that in the fifteenth century the central theme of Hungarian politics was what I should like to call 'defensive crusading'. The key term in this cluster of ideas was the claim that Hungary functioned as the bastion, the shield, the wall against the infidel: *antemurale Christianitatis*. This may sound paradoxical, since we usually understand crusading ideas as justifications for offensive military campaigns against the enemies of faith (or at least of the accepted version thereof). But if one also considers, for example, St Augustine's arguments concerning the 'just war', one that is waged in defence of the Christian world, or even the early crusading sermons that had emphasized the danger posed by the infidels to the Christian commonwealth, it may perhaps be accepted.

It is not quite clear when and in what context this notion first emerged. It is already adumbrated in a letter of King Béla IV from 1242 to the pope after the Mongol devastation of Hungary, and connected, as it was usually to be later as well, with complaints that the country was left alone to defend 'the West'.[8] In the fifteenth century both the popes of Rome and the Hungarian chancellery used a wide range of expressions defining Hungary as the bastion of Christendom. One of the earliest may have been a letter of Pope John XXIII to Sigismund of Luxemburg in 1410, in which the pontiff characterized Hungary as *scutum atque murus inexpugnabilis nostreque et christianae fidei fortitudinis brachium* ('the shield and insurmountable wall and the arm of our strength and that of the Christian faith').[9] King Wladislas, who fell at Varna, introduced the twin expression, also to have a long history into modern times, of both Hungary and Poland constituting 'the wall and shield' (*murus et clipeus*) of the faithful.[10]

The functions of these metaphors were manifold. In 1440 the Hungarian estates argued that they had to elect an adult king instead of Ladislas, the already crowned posthumous baby of Albert of Habsburg; otherwise the kingdom, surrounded as it was by enemies, especially the heathen, would lack a suitable leader (*idoneum rectorem*). That is why they invited Władisław Jagiełło to be king.[11] Five years later Aeneas Silvius Piccolomini tried to convince the archbishop of Esztergom to accept the young Ladislas as their king, because 'our Christian faith cannot be protected unless its wall, which is Hungary (*murus eius qui est Ungaria*), is firm'.[12] The later Pope Pius II seems himself to have coined the formula *murus et antemurale sive clipeus* ('wall, bastion or shield'), which later became widespread, in a letter that he wrote to Pope Calixtus III in 1458.[13] In 1447 Pope Nicholas V warned Emperor Frederick III to make peace with Hungary, 'that has always offered itself as a shield ... and fought for the defence of the Christians.'[14] The papacy used these *topoi* most frequently in connection with attempts at securing peace for the Hungarians, so that they could wage the war against the infidel: in this sense it fits well into the many similar concerns connecting crusading with peace among the Christian powers. The Hungarian chancellery usually inserted these expressions into letters asking for financial assistance, mainly from Rome. For the most part their efforts met with some success, even if the sums that were finally sent were mere fractions of the needs.

In concert with the defensive rhetoric, the Hungarian leadership was not promoting offensive crusading projects in the Balkans, despite the fact that the Ottomans increasingly threatened the kingdom's southern border. The dominant strategy, in so far as one existed at all, was to assist the 'buffer states' of the northern Balkans, and to attempt to secure their loyalty to Hungary, in other words, to encourage them to resist Ottoman subjection. This worked well enough when the Hungarian forces seemed to be strong enough, but less well when the Porte appeared to gain the upper hand. One element of religious warfare, though not explicitly a 'crusading' programme, was, however, detrimental to this attempt: Hungarian advances, above all in Bosnia, were often connected to efforts to force the 'heretics' to return to obedience to Rome. This made the local population and its leadership suspicious of their northern neighbour, to the extent of preferring Muslim tolerance to Latin 'persecution'.[15] It seems that in regard to the Serbian and Wallachian Orthodox 'schismatics' who fled to the kingdom from the Ottoman occupation, the policy pursued was, or became in the course of time, a wiser one. Royal legislation protected them from overzealous Hungarian bishops.[16]

On the other hand, Hungarian nobles were in no way 'pacifists'. It has been pointed out that offensive warfare, mainly into the northern Balkans, was highly popular among them, not only because of the general medieval ethos of heroic combat, but also because these campaigns were the best ways to earn royal favours and the land grants that went with them. The highly positive image enjoyed by Louis of Anjou, characteristically the only Hungarian king who was traditionally called 'the Great', was mainly due to his leading Hungarian troops into Italy, Wallachia and Bosnia. In contrast, Sigismund's 'bad press', which has lasted into our own time, was partly due to his defensive stance, well considered though it was.[17] There is a more material explanation. After the decline of the royal domain in the thirteenth and fourteenth centuries, the estates available for royal grant shrank to almost none. To earn donations from the Crown, it was necessary to wait for the extinction of noble lineages, and these escheated possessions were granted almost exclusively on the basis of military merits.[18] On the other hand, the spiritual rewards that were offered for crusading do not seem to have mobilized the nobility; or at least, there is no evidence that they did. Mention should be made here of the crusades against the Hussites. In the first two, in 1420–1, Hungarian troops took an active part, but as far as one can see, they fought, as usual, within the context of baronial contingents under their king's command. In the first anti-Hussite crusade Sigismund was accompanied by the private troops (*banderia*) of those great lords who belonged to his trusted entourage, together with a few lesser nobles who tried their luck in the campaign. In 1421 the general levy was called up and command entrusted to the able Scolari, but they accomplished little, and there does not seem to have been much enthusiasm. No Hungarians are known to have participated in the subsequent three crusades, all defeated by the Taborites.[19]

The most conspicuous instance of Hungarian ambivalence towards a crusade was that of the campaign that ended in the disaster of Varna.

The general history of this campaign is well known: on 10 November 1444 an international force, led by the young Polish king, Wladislas, the experienced general John (János) Hunyadi, and the papal legate Cardinal Cesarini, was defeated by the army of Sultan Murad II at the shores of the Black Sea. Of the commanders only Hunyadi survived. The background is, perhaps, less well known. It is, however, interesting in so far as it sheds some light on the person and motives of the most famous commander of Hungarian (and allied) armies in the mid-fifteenth century, John Hunyadi.[20] More than two decades ago, Pál Engel called for a closer scrutiny of the image of Hunyadi that had been handed down by scholarship and national tradition ever since his death, that of the 'hero who had only virtues, no vices'.[21] Hunyadi, son of a lesser nobleman of Romanian (Wallachian) origin, began his career under Sigismund and spent some time learning the craft of war in Italy. Aside from some successful campaigns against the Turks, he established his reputation as a victorious general in decisive encounters with the Habsburg party after the dual royal coronation of 1440–1. Once Władisław I had established his rule in Hungary, Hunyadi became voivode of Transylvania, then also ban (commander) of Severin. In 1442 he scored a victory against Shehabeddin Pasha, the beylerbei of Rumelia, the head of the Ottoman forces in Europe. Next year, at the encourage-ment of Pope Eugenius IV, the Hungarian army went onto the offensive, for the first time since Nicopolis. During this, so-called Long Campaign, Hunyadi led the Hungarians, together with some of their Balkan allies, almost as far as Sofia, and returned undefeated. The offensive had achieved nothing of military or political significance: no territory was recovered or occupied. But it boosted the reputation of the general and made the idea of driving the Ottomans out of Europe once again con-ceivable. Whether it was a realistic objective remained to be seen.

Politicking and planning began as soon as the army returned to Belgrade in January 1444. It seems that the sultan was ready to make concessions, as he was involved in a domestic conflict. Despot Đurađ (George) Branković of Serbia, whose daughter was married to the sultan and who had lived in Hungary since his expulsion from his country in 1439, was eager to do anything to bring about his return to his native land. Most likely, he was offered this and the release of his two blinded sons from Ottoman captivity, should he manage to dissuade the Hungarians and their allies from war. Burgundy, Venice and Genoa, were seen as likely participants in a crusade. The hawks in Hungary were very influential; let us remember that the diet had elected Wladislas through the use of the argument that he would be the leader of the struggle against the Ottomans. But on 25 April 1444 the king agreed that Branković should send an envoy to the Porte. Preparations for war, on the other hand, continued apace, and were very actively promoted by the papal legate Cesarini. A preliminary peace was signed in Edirne on 12 June, promising Branković Serbia and the Hungarians a tribute of 100,000 ducats. The details of the ensuing double-deal are quite complicated. The king swore an oath to keep to the truce with the Turks, but this was secretly annulled, as one given to infidels, by the cardinal. Peace negotiations continued, but letters from Wladislas were dispatched to the allies and to his Polish subjects arguing the 'necessity to go to war'. The Ottoman envoys were moved to Várad (Oradea) from Szeged, probably to conceal from them the evidence of military preparations. What was significant was the oath sworn on the peace treaty by Hunyadi on 15 August 'in the name of the king, himself, and the whole Hungarian people'.[22]

Clearly, the Ottomans knew full well that Hunyadi's reputation, influence and military fame were the best guarantee of peace, even better than that of the young king. The question arises, why this famous commander took the risk of the damnation of his soul for a false oath, however sophisticated the cardinal's canonical arguments may have been. 'No matter how much he trusted the wily prelate,' writes Engel, 'Hunyadi had to have a very serious reason for his action. It can only be surmised that his reason was a previous agreement with Branković.'[23] A property dispute which began in 1448 between the despot and the, by that time regent of Hungary, sheds light on what might have happened four years previously. According to this lawsuit, Hunyadi held sizeable properties, including an important castle and several towns, which rightfully belonged to Branković. The contested estates amounted to about half of the very extensive properties bestowed on the despot after his flight from Serbia. The conflict was finally resolved in 1451 with an agreement that allowed the regent to hold a good part of the estates 'for a certain appropriate reason'.[24] The details of all this are unclear, but the usually well-informed Polish historian Jan Długosz maintained that there was an *occulta pactio* between Hunyadi and Branković to the effect that the former would support the peace that allowed the latter to return home.[25]

What is of interest here is that the acclaimed hero of Christendom could apparently be convinced to give up crusading plans in return for a number of villages and towns that would be added to his, already quite impressive, landed property. In turn, this possible exchange makes the modern student of events raise the question of the famous warrior's motives and aims. However, it would be anachronistic and also futile to ask whether Hunyadi was driven by his desire for property, fame and power or by Christian crusading ideals. The two did not exclude each other, especially if one takes into account that most of Hunyadi's campaigns were fought by his 'private' army, his retainers as landowner and voivode, and as ban, and that the prerequisite for fielding it was the possession of royal office and material wealth. These could be augmented both by such merits as victories and successful defence, and by transactions that were usual for his time, even if they sometimes became questionable in the eyes of a post-Renaissance morality. Engel was surely right in pointing to the dangers of a one-sided romanticization of Hunyadi's image: he was a man of his age, condottiere, politician, warrior and crusader, all at the same time. And his memory as a hero in shining armour was transmitted not only by national historians, but also by popular memory, not unlike that of the similarly contradictory figures of King Marko or Skanderbeg.

Of course, the only successful crusading event of the age was connected to Hunyadi's name: the relief of Belgrade by the peasant crusaders led by Giovanni da Capistrano.[26] Reacting in all likelihood to the news of the fall of Constantinople, Capistrano asked for a crusading bull and began to recruit people all the way from Bohemia. This crusade was not a strictly 'Hungarian' matter: it was part of the Franciscan's wide-ranging activities in central Europe, from inciting to pogroms, burning the corpses of dead heretics and other inquisitorial acts, typical for popular preachers.[27] It was, however, a highly successful recruiting project, and, finally, even a military success, however 'unorthodox' in terms of siege tactics: the crusaders, eager to fight and trained in the rudiments of warfare by Hunyadi, attacked the besiegers who, apparently surprised by the massive force, retreated.[28]

There was an intensive debate, mainly à propos the events of 1456, among Hungarian historians in the 1960s about the 'patriotism of the masses' in the Middle Ages. Surely, those contributors were right who denied anything comparable to modern 'national' feelings amongst the thousands equipped with sticks and scythes who finally made the sultan give up the siege. However, many of them had already experienced the horrors of Ottoman raids, the burning of their villages and the dragging of their fellows or kinsmen into slavery. They were ready to fight for their *patria,* which in those times meant the village or town of one's birth.[29] Additionally, or perhaps even in the first place, the dramatic preaching of Capistrano mobilized their feelings, inculcated by many a Sunday sermon, of the Christian's 'duty' to fight against the infidel. Finally, as the events that followed the siege proved, there was some kind of eschatological fervour about the 'poor and downtrodden' bringing about the final victories. At any rate, the aftermath of 1456, when the 'peasant crusaders' became restless because they felt that the lords had claimed credit for the victory that they had achieved, and were sent home by the commanders, foreshadowed the last crusade on Hungarian soil, the one that less than 60 years later turned into overt insurrection.

The son of Hunyadi, King Matthias (1458–90), assisted by able chancellors, was a past master of crusading rhetoric. This is not the place to rehearse the centuries' old debate about the 'final aims' of the king's policies. In fact Matthias, whom the Hungarians expected to follow in his father's footsteps, led only a few, limited and (therefore) mostly successful, campaigns against the Ottomans, spending most of his reign in wars and diplomacy that were aimed at acquiring territories in the north and west.[30] Many historians argued that these expansionist efforts were prerequisites for a major anti-Ottoman project, and that the king aimed to establish the wide power base necessary for its success. These theories of the older schools of historians were to serve above all as 'excuses' for the king against the charge of power hunger and self-aggrandisement.[31]

As late as 1931 Elemér Mályusz wrote: 'The new empire [of Matthias] was to include all those territories whose riches and population would guarantee the success of a Turkish war.'[32] A generation later, the best expert on Matthias's army, Gyula Rázsó, was somewhat more sceptical in his judgement of the king's long-term policy:

> The beginning of his Bohemian campaign in 1468 marked a decisive turn. His aim now, and in all likelihood to the end of his life, was to establish a European, or at least central European, power under Hungarian leadership. Had he succeeded, the Ottoman threat would indeed have been blunted with the resources of such a Hungarian empire … . It was a great concept, but essentially misguided – though Matthias may not have recognized its defects.[33]

No doubt, the lesson of his father's life was that Hungary alone stood little chance of stopping the Ottoman advance, to say nothing of expelling the Turks from Europe. But it is also true that Matthias's main concern was to establish his own position as a *homo novus* vis-à-vis the 'historical' dynasties of Habsburg and Jagiełło.[34] It cannot be decided whether Matthias would have fulfilled his many promises, to the popes and others, to march against the sultan, once a wider territorial base had been established and an efficient standing army had been built up, because he died in the midst of his victories.[35]

The king's correspondence, mainly his letters to the popes, did not spell out this 'grand design' in so many words. Rather it reiterated his unwavering commitment to the Turkish war, if only his enemies within and outside his realm would not hinder him in marching south. At the very beginning of his reign, Matthias even called on Emperor Frederick III, the obvious, though not yet open, opponent to his succession to the throne, to fight together with him *pro communi causa fidei Christiane*, and his uncle, Michael Szilágyi, the regent for the young king, requested the papal legate to call a crusade against the Ottomans.[36]

Interestingly, the diplomatic correspondence, mainly with Rome, contained many more personal formulations referring to the king's role than statements of the general *antemurale* topos. Pope Paul II called Matthias 'the unique column of Christian hope and strength', or 'the most powerful champion of Christ'.[37] The king, in turn, pointed out that, as a son of the hero, he was destined by 'birth and education' to be *perpetuus Turci hostis*. That said, however, he added in one letter that 'if the pope does not want him to make peace with the Turk, then he should take care that he [Matthias] is able to sustain the fight'.[38] The 'remnants' of crusading ideas show up above all in Matthias' insistence that his wars, wherever they were fought, were waged in the interest of the *respublica Christiana*, thus positing an imaginary unity of Christendom, which may have been a reality only in the true Age of Crusades.

One anti-Ottoman crusade Matthias did take seriously: that of the Sienese pope, Pius II. Like many late medieval crusading projects, this one was combined with attempts to establish peace between warring kings and princes, so that they could join forces against the infidel. Initially, it seemed to succeed at the meeting in Mantua (1459), but the pope's death in 1464 had the effect of cancelling everything. Matthias was prepared to send troops in support of this venture, and he conducted a campaign into Bosnia during the autumn of 1464, but normally he preferred to remain at 'peace' with the sultan as long as the Ottomans did not attack. This 'peace', of course, was qualified on both sides by the fact that border skirmishing and minor incursions never ceased. None the less, Matthias received from Pius's successor, Paul II, all that was left in the papal treasury at Pius's death, 40,000 gold florins, augmented by another 17,000 florins.[39] The popes regularly sent subsidies 'for the Turkish wars' to Buda, for example, between 1469 and 1471 all told 43,000 florins.[40] Such sums, however, have to be compared with the 150,000–200,000 florins that constituted the minimal amount required annually for the upkeep of the southern defence perimeter.[41]

The crusade that Matthias fought with quite some success was the one against King George of Bohemia, denounced as a heretic. To be sure, Hungarian troops were already moving into Moravia when on 19 April 1468 Pope Paul II called for a crusade against the recalcitrant and 'perjurious' George. Matthias had offered his services to the Holy See against his former father-in-law for some years,[42] and was only too happy now to have formal sanction for his campaign in support of the Catholic estates that offered him the crown of Bohemia. As far as the record allows us to judge, little 'crusading fervour' was involved in the ten-year war, fought for the most part by the king's new mercenary army, in the course of which Matthias acquired a good part of the lands of the Crown of St Wenceslas.[43]

After Matthias's death, under the Jagiełło kings, the country's defences deteriorated. This was partly due to financial problems and partly to the lack of able commanders. In these decades even the traditional rhetoric of Christian militancy decreased. It is, for example, remarkable that the crusade called for in the Jubilee of 1500 had no resonance in Hungary, at least as far as one can see. The rhetoric in the noble diets, summoned almost every year, and sometimes twice a year, came to emphasize a new ideology: that of Scythian valour and national greatness. The decree passed at the 1505 diet about the succession to the throne described the Hungarians as *Scythica gens,* one that had conquered and defended its country by blood and iron, and whose native kings had spread the Scythian virtues far and wide in the world. True, the *antemurale clypeusque* formula was also mentioned, but the key argument was not, as in 1440, that of needing an able war leader against the Turks, but the inadmissibility of electing a 'foreign' king.[44]

As is well known, the crusade of 1514 originated in the political ambitions of Archbishop Bakócz. Having failed to convince the other cardinals to elect him pope, he did not want to return home empty-handed. Once again the call to crusade, this time even more actively supported by Observant Franciscans, was followed by masses of commoners, peasants and town dwellers.[45] It is understandable that after the most murderous and widespread rural uprising in Hungarian history, usually called the peasant war of Dózsa, during that summer, the Hungarian prelates and nobles did not want to hear any more about a crusade. In the last decade of the independent kingdom, the nobility did all it could to rid itself of defence duties, while the treasury was less and less able to maintain the *antemurale Christianitatis.*

At the bitter end, crusade or not, the noble levy, most of the magnates and all the prelates gathered with their retainers and hired soldiers under the king's flag to oppose the Ottoman imperial army. How can one explain the strange and tragic paradox that after years of haggling about military duty and trying to place the entire burden on the Crown, when it came to the moment of truth, the country's elite heroically fought and fell within less than two hours on 29 August 1526 at the field of Mohács? Seven out of the ten bishops and archbishops, more than 20 *barones*, the cream of the aristocracy, and uncounted lesser noblemen in their train lost their lives, and the king died while trying to flee. The Ottoman danger was well known to all of the country's inhabitants. Nobles had to fear the loss of property, status, political role; burghers their houses and towns, peasants their villages, their cattle and their lives. There were plenty of Balkan refugees everywhere to tell the tale even to those who had not themselves experienced Ottoman raids. But, as several historians have put it, the 'natural reflex of self-preservation' of the thousands of nobles who annually, or more frequently, gathered at tumultuous diets, did not preclude their refusal to take effective action, which bore a cost to themselves, for the defence of the realm. No one has yet offered an answer to this conundrum.[46] But it may be worthwhile considering the opinion of the papal nuncio, Baron Burgio, who resided in Hungary during the kingdom's last fateful years. In 1525 he described the elements of the nobility that alone had the right to decide about action or inaction in the following words:

> The first part is soldiering, fighting on the borders in the pay of the magnates; they are the best and the most courageous ... Another part consists of those nobles who live on their country estates, pursue husbandry and trade, never go to town, and do not attend the diet but merely cast their vote on the delegates sent by the county to the national assemblies. The third part is made up of those eight or ten wealthy and well-bespoken noblemen who take part in public affairs and are sincerely concerned with the affairs of the country.[47]

Maybe what happened was that *la bona parte et la più audace* did come to the aid of its country under the banner of its lords, and died for it. But that was not enough, except for establishing a *lieu de mémoire* for the centuries to come.[48]

9

Poland and the Crusade in the Reign of King Jan Olbracht, 1492–1501

Natalia Nowakowska

Introduction

On the blank pages at the back of a 1484 printed missal for the diocese of Kraków, an anonymous fifteenth-century Polish cleric has inscribed an additional text, a votive mass against pagans. Written in red and black ink, the liturgy pleads for divine protection in the face of imminent cataclysm:

> Strike from on high, without delay, at these profane dogs the Turks and make them flee across the land and sea, for yours is the power, King of Heaven. Without you we are nothing, without you, we cannot resist ...[1]

At first glance, the geography of fifteenth-century central Europe does not seem to bear out the urgent concerns of the anonymous scribe, as the kingdom of Poland lay far from the frontiers of the Ottoman Empire. To the north-east, Poland was sheltered by the vast Grand Duchy of Lithuania, to which she was linked by the ruling Jagiellonian dynasty and a series of treaties of close alliance; to the south-east lay the Orthodox princedom of Moldavia; and, beyond, the Ottoman satellite of Vallachia. These buffer zones were not, however, all that they seemed and the threat to the Polish state suddenly became acute in the last decades of the century. In 1478, the Tartar Khan of the Crimea, Mengli-Girej, married his daughter to the son of Sultan Bajezid II, creating a potent alliance and providing the Ottomans with an aggressive agent on the Jagiellonians' eastern flank: political frontiers made little difference to Tartar raiding parties, which could move at great speed over considerable distances, cutting across Lithuania to menace Poland directly.[2]

Moldavia, meanwhile, was an unstable and fickle neighbour: its ruler, Stefan the Great (1457–1504), liberally swore homage to the three states which claimed sovereignty over his lands, to the sultan in 1481, to King Kazimierz IV of Poland in 1485, and to King Matthias Corvinus of Hungary in 1490.[3] The fear of a direct Ottoman assault from the south, through the Moldavian–Vallachian corridor, became compelling after 1484, when Bajezid II seized the deltas of the Dniester and Dnieper rivers from Moldavia, and with them the key trading ports of Kilija and Białogród.[4] Not only were these cities crucial to Poland's trade routes, but they also gave the sultan a critical strategic foothold. As Bajezid himself boasted: 'This victory will facilitate our future conquests, it opens up the road to Poland, to the Czechs and the Hungarians, our progress will now be much easier …'[5]

It was to Jan Olbracht Jagiellon, first as prince then as monarch from 1492, that the task of formulating Poland's response fell, deciding how – and whether – to apply the crusade model to the local situation. Not only is this dilemma interesting in itself, as a case-study of contemporary Catholic responses in a kingdom rarely considered in English-language crusade scholarship, but Jan Olbracht's policies were themselves so puzzling as to invite closer investigation. During his reign, Poland exhibited a marked unwillingness to deploy the crusade, instead developing a unilateral understanding of national defence, characterized by a lack of religious language, and a reluctance to court papal involvement. Here, the three phases of Jan Olbracht's anti-infidel policy will be analysed, in order to see what they reveal of Polish attitudes towards the crusade, both within and beyond the royal court. These are the anti-Ottoman campaign of 1497, the search for international aid in the face of Ottoman–Tartar raids from 1498, and Poland's involvement in Pope Alexander VI's crusading league of 1501–3 and subsequent appropriation of papal crusading funds. It will then be asked why Poland's ruling dynasty, political elites, leading humanists and even Franciscan commentators came to exhibit such peculiar understandings of what has been called 'one of the most important components, and defining characteristics, of late medieval western culture'.[6]

The new king

Jan Olbracht, born in December 1459, was the third son of Kazimierz IV, Grand Duke of Lithuania and King of Poland (1446–92), and his wife Elizabeth Habsburg, and the fourth Jagiellonian monarch to sit on the Polish throne; the originally pagan Lithuanian dynasty had held

Poland's elective crown since 1386. Sixteenth-century writers saw Jan Olbracht as an erudite, independent-minded military leader, bent on chivalric glory. The chronicler Maciej of Miechów (known as Miechowita), a physician and professor at Kraków University, wrote in his 1519 *Chronica Polonorum*:

> He was blessed with wisdom and shrewdness, and gifted in languages, for he spoke Latin, Polish and German beautifully. He read histories and loved academic disputations. Mature in his bearing, when aroused he would indulge in voluptuous and libidinous behaviour, being a military man.[7]

Writing a decade later, the Kraków canon Bernard Wapowski stressed the king's hunger for fame:

> He was full of majesty, and by day and night he thought of nothing else but how to link his name with fabulous deeds for all eternity. ... His great soul was tortured night and day as he waited for an opportunity ...[8]

These readings are not simply retrospective, written in the light of the king's later wars, because even before his coronation Jan Olbracht was esteemed for his campaigns against Islamic forces; some commentators claimed that it was precisely this reputation that endeared the prince to the kingdom's electors in 1492.[9] After the fall of Kilija and Białogród in 1484, it was Jan Olbracht who had led his father's armies to the Moldavian border in order to secure Poland's southern frontier.[10] In 1487, moreover, armed with a crusading bull granted by Pope Innocent VIII to King Kazimierz, Jan Olbracht headed a royal army assembled for the purpose of reconquering the lost ports: in the event, this force, mustering at Lwów, instead clashed with a horde of advancing Tartars, whom the prince soundly defeated at Kopystrzyn in August, executing their leaders on the battlefield.[11] Kopystrzyn was a rare example of Polish military success against Tartar forces.

King Kazimierz IV died in Lithuania in June 1492, and in August Jan Olbracht was elected king of Poland at Piotrków castle.[12] In spite of the precarious strategic situation inherited by the new king, the prospects for a robust response to the Ottoman advance were promising. Not only was Jan Olbracht himself experienced in anti-infidel campaigns, but the Jagiellonians had recently achieved dynastic supremacy in central Europe. To the east, Jan Olbracht's younger brother Aleksander had inherited the Grand Duchy of Lithuania in 1492, Prince Zygmunt was Duke of Glogau in Silesia, while Prince Fryderyk had embarked on an ecclesiastical career, becoming bishop of Kraków in 1488. Most importantly, the oldest sibling, Władysław Jagiellon, king of Bohemia from 1472, had in 1490 succeeded Matthias Corvinus as king of Hungary. This conglomeration of Jagiellonian states, stretching from Zagreb to Smolensk, presented a formidable Catholic front against the Ottomans. There was apparently every reason to hope for a grand Jagiellonian crusade in the 1490s.

The 1497 war

The precise genesis of Poland's 1497 campaign – 'hoc improspere expeditionis' – is unclear.[13] In the early years of his reign, Jan Olbracht was unable to contemplate major military initiatives owing to the entanglements of his royal brothers: from 1492 to 1494, Lithuania fought a difficult war with Muscovy, while Władysław struggled to retain the Hungarian Crown in the face of Habsburg ambitions and magnate dissent.[14] It gradually became clear that these persistent difficulties would prevent Hungary from becoming an active ally – Jan Olbracht may finally have become convinced of this at the dynastic summit held in the Slovakian town of Levoća in the spring of 1494.[15] There, Jan Olbracht and Władysław held secret negotiations over several weeks, with Princes Zygmunt and Fryderyk in attendance.[16] The earliest Polish commentator on the summit, Miechowita, declared that although a joint Polish–Hungarian war against the Turks had been discussed, there was an impasse and 'all the proposed articles were rejected'.[17]

Faced with the continuing Ottoman occupation of the Black Sea ports and regular Tartar raids carried out at the sultan's instigation on the south-eastern province of Podolia, Jan Olbracht began to undertake preparations for an aggressive Polish response on a major scale. The king called on his vassal states of Mazovia and Teutonic Prussia to send forces, and met Aleksander Jagiellon in November 1496 to devise a strategy for reconquering Kilija and Białogród.[18] In January 1497, the Polish diplomat Michał Strzeżowski was sent to Constantinople, to demand the return of the ports. The sultan refused, and a truce between the states, dating from 1489, was allowed to lapse.[19] Crucially, there is no evidence that Jan Olbracht made any overtures whatsoever to Rome on the eve of the campaign; this deliberate exclusion of the papacy is strongly in keeping with the monarch's later policies.

Within Poland, civil taxes were raised for the anti-Ottoman war in May 1496. The wording of these proclamations is telling, because they tend to describe the forthcoming campaign as a war waged to defend the kingdom rather than the Catholic faith. Many royal tax dispensations, for example, simply refer to the campaign as an 'expeditioni bellica' designed to prevent Ottoman occupation of Poland.[20] Only two taxation proclamations make any reference to the religious dimension of the Ottoman threat, explaining that the war was necessary 'for the freedom of our faith and the salvation of our republic', and for 'defence ... against the powerful enemies of the faith of Christ'.[21]

The Crown also raised money from the Polish clergy through the good offices of Prince Fryderyk, who in 1493 had been elected primate of Poland and elevated to the cardinalate.[22] Using the 'subsidium charitativum', the 'voluntary' levy which bishops could raise from their clergy for special needs, Cardinal Fryderyk demanded contributions towards the future war in August 1494 and June 1497 – these comprised taxes of up to 25 per cent on ecclesiastical incomes.[23] Significantly, even diocesan accounts of these taxations describe the forthcoming war purely as a campaign for national defence. The Gniezno cathedral chapter, for example, noted that it had agreed to pay towards the king's actions 'against the Turks and Tartars for the defence of the realm and his subjects', with no explicit reference to the religious character of the struggle.[24]

By the summer of 1497, Jan Olbracht had assembled the second largest Polish army of the fifteenth century, an estimated force of some 80,000 men and heavy artillery.[25] Stefan of Moldavia watched these preparations with disquiet, concerned that Jan Olbracht's imminent campaign to recapture the Moldavian ports would involve an armed assertion of Polish sovereignty over his princedom. In spring, Stefan had warned the sultan of Polish machinations and received 800 janissaries with whom to defend himself.[26]

On 7 August 1497, the Polish army reached the banks of the Dniester, which marked the limits of the kingdom. Crossing onto Moldavian soil, Jan Olbracht was met by Stefan's chancellor, Isaac, who informed the king that Stefan had refused the Polish royal army permission to enter his territories because he was the sultan's loyal vassal. Jan Olbracht, incensed, ordered that Isaac be dispatched in chains to the dungeons of Lwów castle. The army was now faced with a serious dilemma: such a large force could not proceed several hundred miles through enemy territory without secure supply routes, and the fateful decision was made to march on the Moldavian capital of Suceava, to force Stefan to cooperate.

Although Stefan had escaped from the city, Jan Olbracht laid siege to its citadel on 24 September. The king's problems rapidly escalated, as disease ravaged the army and Jan Olbracht himself became bed-ridden. Only a few days into the siege, a Hungarian envoy arrived from King Władisław, claiming that the Polish campaign was no more than a thinly veiled attempt to conquer Moldavia and a flagrant challenge to Hungary's sovereignty over the principality. Jan Olbracht was warned to leave immediately or face hostile action from Hungarian royal forces. Embroiled in a diplomatic and military mess, Jan Olbracht reluctantly negotiated a truce with Stefan and lifted the siege of Suceava on 19 October 1497.[27]

The Polish army then began a humiliating retreat north. A week after leaving Suceava, it entered a narrow tract of forest in the Bukowina region, by the village of Codrul Cosminului. There, a motley force of Turks, Tartars, rogue Hungarian magnates, Vallachians and Moldavians ambushed the king's army – all the forces to whom Stefan had earlier appealed for aid. The attack in the Bukowina forest is traditionally seen as a massacre, although the true scale of casualties is extremely difficult to ascertain. Miechowita lists senior nobles who had perished and describes how knights were carried off into Turkish slavery, tied in pairs by their long hair.[28] This account was quickly censored after its publication in 1519, indicating how sensitive the government still was about the episode 20 years later. The earliest contemporary comment on the ambush is found in a letter written by Cardinal Fryderyk in November 1497. Fryderyk, having recently received Jan Olbracht's version of events, wrote as follows to Bishop Lucas Watzenrode, a leading member of the royal council: 'our army, at the hands of the Turks and Vallachians, suffered losses of equipment and men. Some of the nobility were captured there, and this and the other set-backs occurred largely because of His Majesty's poor state of health.'[29] Cardinal Fryderyk's account is sparse and ranks the loss of military hardware as more serious than the casualties sustained. It is possible, however, that Fryderyk himself had received a sanitized version of events from Jan Olbracht, or even that the cardinal toned down the gravity of the situation to save face for the Crown and stave off panic within the royal council.

A Polish army officially bound for Turkish territory had ended up besieging a Christian capital and suffered defeat at the hands of a mixed force of Catholic Hungarians, Orthodox Moldavians and Vallachians, and Muslim Turks and Tartars. After a century of dispute, Polish and Romanian historians are now generally agreed that Jan Olbracht was probably genuine in his stated desire to reach the Black Sea coast: he had after all drawn up detailed plans for the recapture of the ports and deliberately antagonized Bajezid II.[30] However, it is likely that the conquest or pacification of Moldavia had been a secondary objective.

The Polish campaign of 1497 provides an extremely rare example of a Catholic ruler attacking the Ottomans without a crusade bull. Just as revealing as Jan Olbracht's implicit rejection of the crusade is the total lack of comment which this feature of the campaign provoked among his Polish contemporaries. There is evidence of dissent from the war in the royal council – significantly, leading advisors seem to have objected to the military dangers of the planned campaign, but not to the lack of a crusading bull. Miechowita's chronicle, for example, describes the royal chancellor, Krzesław of Kurowązek, travelling to the army camp in Lwów and begging the king not to provoke Stefan, a man of legendary military prowess; in Wapowski's rendition, Krzesław does not act on his own initiative, but is instead sent by Cardinal Fryderyk.[31]

While wider evidence for elite attitudes towards the 1497 war is fragmentary, it is none the less telling that neither of the two key contemporary chroniclers of these events – Miechowita and the Observant Franciscan Jan of Komorowo – expressed any surprise or unease at the decision not to consult Rome.[32] The failure of these writers to ascribe any higher purpose to the 1497 campaign is even more striking given their clear belief that divine providence was at work during the war. Both Miechowita and Jan of Komorowo pointed to the open sexual debauchery of Jan Olbracht's army, and saw the attack at Codrul Cosminului as divine punishment for these sins.[33] Miechowita also recorded that when the army celebrated mass at Lwów before embarking south, the priest dropped the host: a terrible omen.[34] The deportment of the army, then, was seen as inviting religious commentary, while the nature of the campaign itself was not – a clear indication of how far the crusade was from the minds of these writers.

When we consider how little even the Venetians – seasoned observers of the region – knew about the 1497 war, it seems likely that papal Rome knew even less. In September 1497, the Venetian diarist and senator Marino Sanudo recorded the rather fantastical report that Jan Olbracht had set out with 'one hundred thousand horse and an infinite number of foot', successfully captured Kilija and Białogród, and was marching on the Crimean port of Kaffa.[35] Poland had no desire to broadcast news of its defeat and a narrowly avoided dynastic war, and Alexander VI probably had little inkling of the non-crusade waged against the sultan by the Polish king.

Interlude: Poland in crisis, 1498–9

Jan Olbracht's act of aggression was heavily punished by Bajezid II, and the years 1498 and 1499 saw the first direct Ottoman raids on Polish soil. These attacks were not serious attempts to annex territory, but rather retributive expeditions sent to loot and intimidate. In April and May 1498, a Turkish force led by Bali-Bej appeared before the walls of Lwów and raided the city's environs.[36] The vast quantities of booty and slaves acquired led to the campaign being nicknamed 'the war of abundance' by the Turkish troops.[37] There was mass panic when news of the raids reached Kraków: the populace tried to flee and Jan Olbracht hastily threw up new defences, including the city's celebrated barbican.[38] The Turkish raids were witnessed by the Franciscan friar Jan of Komorowo, who has left us a vivid account of peasants warding off Turks with axes and of his own cross-country escape. In hiding on a forested hill, he watched former neighbours led off into slavery:

> Ahead of us, the Turks plundered some towns and a wood, in which many noblemen, including the treasurer of the province of Podolia, were hiding along with their households, offspring and families. They were betrayed by their peasants, and the Turks captured them. They stretched their bound arms out ahead of them, like a flock of sheep, falling over and crying out. We found boys and old men slain on the road, and saw many wounded men and women.[39]

In July, the Crimean Tartars in turn launched a major raid on southeastern Poland.[40] In November, the Turks returned and again raided the regions of Lwów and Halicz. This time, however, unusually fierce frosts and snows decimated the Turkish army on its return journey – Jan of Komorowo heard reports that of the original force of 40,000 Turks, only 8,000 survived.[41]

Jan Olbracht's actions in response to this crisis give us considerable insight into the king's understanding of national defence. Faced with the possibility of a repeated Ottoman assault on Poland, the king turned for aid first to the Holy Roman Empire and only later, under some duress, to Pope Alexander VI. In the wake of the Moldavian debacle, Poland and Hungary had signed a peace treaty in which they agreed to combine their diplomatic efforts in the search for international assistance.[42] The Polish diplomat Mikołaj Rozemberg, acting as the representative of both kingdoms, made official pleas for aid before the

Emperor Maximilian at the diets of Freiburg in July 1498, Worms in January 1499 and Uberlingen in July 1499.[43] Rozemberg's brief was to stress that the Jagiellonian kingdoms, by forming a barrier, were fighting to protect Germany herself.[44] The Jagiellonians were asking the Empire for a very specific kind of aid:

> On the manner of help – soldiers from Your Majesty's [Empire] are not needed, but rather a financial subsidy, because the distances involved are such that both men and horses will be exhausted long before they reach our kingdoms; and because the Turks will learn of the advent of such a force. ... And so that the Electors and His Majesty [the Emperor] do not think we are trying to make money out of this, let those Electors select one or two representatives who can be in charge of distributing this money to us.[45]

This plea for cash rather than manpower is in itself an implicit rejection of the classic, medieval crusading model, predicated as it was on large international forces marching against the infidel. Here we have a preliminary glimpse of the ways in which Poland's strategic position in the 1490s was not easily compatible with traditional crusade practice. Raiding parties, particularly those composed of Tartars, were unpredictable and exceptionally difficult to force into pitched battle: the crusading tract composed in circa 1490 by the Polish courtier and Italian humanist Callimachus (Filippo Buonacorsi) dwelt at length on the difficulties of fighting such an elusive enemy.[46] In 1498, Jan Olbracht's first response had been to position a royal muster army along the southeastern frontier. Nobles, however, refused to serve in remote border regions indefinitely.[47] In 1499, the Crown instead established military camps along the border under the command of Piotr Myszkowski. Civic and clerical taxes had succeeded in paying salaries for only three months, before soldiers began to desert *en masse*.[48] From 1499, therefore, Poland's overwhelming need was for foreign financial aid.

The Emperor Maximilian offered Rozemberg no more than evasive replies, repeatedly postponing discussion of the Jagiellonian requests to another diet. In the summer of 1499, a thoroughly disenchanted Rozemberg asked Jan Olbracht if he could be recalled.[49] It was only at this point – over a year after the first Ottoman raids on Poland – that King Władisław of Hungary suggested to Jan Olbracht that the pope might be approached. In a letter to his brother, Władisław proposed that an orator be sent to Alexander VI, asking him to assign the money raised during the jubilee holy year of 1500 towards an anti-Turkish war, as well as the income from the annate taxes raised in the two kingdoms.[50] Jan Olbracht, replying in May 1499, was lukewarm. The Polish king wrote at length of his deep cynicism about Maximilian, and turned to the matter of Rome only in his last paragraph. In this key passage, Jan Olbracht set out his views on Rome's role in the Ottoman issue:

> Your Majesty [Władisław] should consider what we should ask the pope to do in order to support our actions against the Turks. Now, Your Majesty can see that the income from the Jubilee and from annate remissions will not bring us much money. ... For, truly, this my kingdom of Poland stands to gain very little from annates, unless His Holiness is willing to assign to us the annates and jubilee income from the whole of Germany for this public necessity. Our orators can also try to persuade the pope to make some financial contribution for this action out of his own riches, for the love of holy religion.[51]

It is striking that, in this passage, Jan Olbracht pointedly fails to invoke the crusade at all, referring instead in general terms to 'public necessity'. In his survey of the fund-raising mechanisms in the pope's gift, the king notably fails to mention the tenth, the traditional cornerstone of crusade finance. This suggests that the absence of any references to the crusade, the 'expeditio generalis', was no mere accident of terminology, but instead a quite deliberate omission. The crusade indulgence and the spiritual dimensions of holy war are similarly absent. Devotion as a motive – 'love of holy religion' – is mentioned only in the last line, and ascribed solely to the pope, with what may even be ironic intent. This correspondence, in its lack of attachment to the crusade, sets out a little more explicitly the assumptions that had underpinned the 1497 campaign; it also suggests that Jan Olbracht had been dissatisfied with the benefits of the crusade bull which had legitimized his 1487 campaign, as prince.

King Jan Olbracht's personal disinclination to involve Pope Alexander VI is thrown into relief by the actions of some of his subjects. On 22 October 1498, three Poles appeared before a public consistory in Rome, Canon Andrzej Jan of Lwów, Canon Tomasz of Poznań and an anonymous soldier from Podolia. They presented to the pope and cardinals a letter written from one canon of Lwów to another, which described the Turkish and Tartar raids on south-eastern Poland, 'of which the king was aware'.[52] This humble delegation appears to be a diocesan initiative, a desperate attempt to seek aid after the devastation of the lands around Lwów; it is unclear if the Crown was even aware of their mission. The episode shows that, royal policy notwithstanding, certain members of Polish society did still look to the pope as their natural protector against infidels.

Poland and Alexander VI's crusading league

The Jagiellonian decision to turn to Rome in 1499 happened to coincide with the sudden outburst of hostilities between the sultan and the Venetian Republic, triggered by Ottoman attacks on Venice's Greek ports that August.[53] Frenetically, diplomats in Venice, Buda and Rome began to hammer out the terms of a putative papal–Venetian–Jagiellonian crusading league. Jan Olbracht sent two representatives to Alexander VI's Roman crusade conference of spring 1500, the Kraków canons Mikołaj Czepiel and Mikołaj Wróblowski.[54] Poland was represented at the Buda talks by a single delegate, the royal advisor Piotr Kmita.[55]

On 1 June 1500, Alexander VI published the universal crusade bull *Quamvis ad amplianda*, thereby launching the first papal crusade against the Ottomans since Pius II's ill-fated attempt of 1464.[56] In full anticipation of Polish military participation in the league, the pope also drew up two additional bulls for Hungary and Poland. The first raised a tenth on the clergy of both kingdoms; the second granted a plenary indulgence to all those who fought, sent proxies, equipped the army or donated funds.[57] Significantly, because the crusade coincided with the jubilee year of 1500, the second bull promised supporters of the campaign the full, potent jubilee indulgence, conferring the same spiritual benefits as a pilgrimage to Rome. The bulls stipulated that the three custodians of the Polish crusade funds, with keys to the storage chests, would be the king, Cardinal Fryderyk and the papal collector, Gaspardus Golfus, bishop of Cagli. Jan Olbracht, having hitherto avoided the crusade, now found himself at the heart of a major papal crusading league.

Golfus arrived in Kraków in August 1500, where he published the crusade bulls with some pomp, processing with them around the city.[58] At court, the nuncio drew up detailed instructions for local collectors and confessors, which were copied into the royal registers.[59] Golfus was assisted in his collection and preaching campaign by the local Observant Franciscans, and reactions in the city bear testament to the appeal which the crusade still held for the capital's population. The preaching of August 1500 immediately prompted a small-scale popular crusade: an armed crowd set out from Kraków in search of infidels, killing 20 Jews in the ghetto town of Kazimierz, and unsuccessfully trying to break into the house where the terrified Turkish ambassadors were lodged.[60] Miechowita's chronicle furnishes further evidence of the residual power of crusade preaching in Poland: the professor claimed that many citizens well remembered Giovanni da Capistrano's preaching in the city decades earlier, and himself quoted Capistrano's prophecies in his work.[61]

The urban disturbance aside, an optimistic and possibly credulous Golfus reported to his superiors in September and December 1500, and again in March 1501, that Jan Olbracht was full of enthusiasm for the crusade.[62] Poland's subsequent ignominious exit from, and subversion of, the papal league occurred in three stages. The first sign that the government might have a liberal approach to papal instructions came during Golfus's collection campaign of 1500, when Cardinal Fryderyk, in rather opaque circumstances, unilaterally converted the papal tenth into an episcopal 'subsidium charitativum', a move which placed the monies squarely under his control and which he claimed was approved by the king.[63] Golfus left Poland in December 1500, denouncing Cardinal Fryderyk in both Buda and Rome.[64]

In another blow, in January 1501, King Jan Olbracht comprehensively removed himself from the crusading league when he sent an envoy to Constantinople to conclude a new truce with the sultan.[65] Venice, Hungary and the papacy finally ratified the league in May 1501, expressing the hope that Poland would join the campaign as and when her strategic situation allowed.[66] The official – and highly compelling – reason for Poland's exit was the unfolding and ominous situation on her frontiers. In June and September 1500, Tartars had launched devastating raids on eastern Poland: a shocked Golfus reported that 200,000 people had been carried off to the slave markets of the Crimea.[67] In addition, in May 1500, Ivan III of Muscovy had attacked Lithuania. Aleksander Jagiellon's war effort fared badly, and Poland had to be on standby to rescue the grand duchy.[68]

In these circumstances, Poland's decision to abstain from the crusade appears perfectly unremarkable. None the less, royal documents show that King Jan Olbracht was in any case highly reticent about the league, suggesting that the geopolitical situation provided a welcome excuse. The king and council had deep reservations about the project, chiefly concerning their putative Italian allies. In May 1500, for example, the king voiced his cynicism about the Venetians in a letter to Lucas Watzenrode, bishop of Ermland:

> They will not commit themselves to any treaty which might oblige them to undertake any onerous task, and they are clearly searching for ways to transfer the war from their lands to ours, if they can.[69]

An anonymous memorandum written for the king by a high-ranking advisor is even more telling, as it expresses concern about Alexander VI's involvement.[70] The author warned that a papal league was a dangerous phenomenon, because signatories who breached any clause could face excommunication. The pope, it was argued, wished only to find allies to help him entrench his son, Cesare Borgia, in northern Italy, while the Venetians simply wanted to avoid fighting by any means possible. The Polish royal council, it seems, was unwilling to entrust its security to Venice, Hungary or the pope.

Another unorthodox aspect of Poland's involvement in the league was the Crown's appropriation of the monies collected to fund the crusade effort. After the kingdom's (technically temporary) withdrawal from the alliance, the crusade/jubilee funds passed into a legal and political limbo. As we have seen, Jan Olbracht's principal objective in his attempt to raise international aid had been to secure external funding for frontier defence. Royal registers reveal that, by June 1501, King Jan Olbracht had already borrowed 3,000 florins from the Polish jubilee funds.[71] This pattern continued during the interregnum following the king's sudden death in June, while holding court at Thorn. Days after his death, Cardinal Fryderyk, as primate the automatic regent or 'interrex', wrote to the royal council lamenting the kingdom's strategic vulnerability. He urged the lords to 'consult with each other what is to be done to secure the defence and tranquillity of these lands ... we will of course need money'.[72] During his regency, the cardinal went on to spend large sums employing mercenaries to deploy on the kingdom's frontiers.[73] Some of this expenditure – 4,000 florins – was met by loans from the magnates Spytek of Melsztyn and Mikołaj of Kurowązek.[74] The remainder of the Polish lay crusade contributions were, however, at this point also seized by the cardinal.

In the winter of 1501, news reached the papal crusade legate in Buda, Cardinal Pietro Isvagli, that Cardinal Fryderyk had illegally opened the crusade chests and spent their contents.[75] With great indignation, Isvagli wrote to Fryderyk warning him of the dire consequences of such actions and exhorting him to put the money back.[76] Fryderyk, in polite and measured missives, assured the legate that nothing illegal had occurred – he had simply, in the absence of both Golfus and the late king, acted in his capacity as the last remaining key-holder and spent the money 'on the ends to which it was granted'.[77] Fryderyk's seizure of the crusade funds for the Crown was arguably the closing act of Jan Olbracht's foreign policy.

Polish anti-infidel strategy in the reign of Jan Olbracht was characterized by indifference towards, and subsequently exploitation of, the

Poland and the Crusade in the Reign of King Jan Olbracht, 1492–1501   141

crusade. The decision to wage an independent national defensive war against the Ottomans in 1497, the clear perception of the emperor rather than the pope as the principal source of international aid, the distaste for Alexander VI's league and the willingness to appropriate funds collected by the Holy See are all evidence of a deep ambivalence towards the institution of holy warfare. Why, then, did the Polish royal government display such attitudes? Were they confined only to the royal court? Polish historians have tended to view Jan Olbracht's policies as part of an intricate European diplomatic game, in which the crusade was largely a rhetorical device manipulated to serve the interests of cynical Renaissance states.[78] There are, however, distinct peculiarities in Polish anti-infidel policy, and their causes can be sought in the kingdom's particular political culture: the convictions of individual members of the Jagiellonian dynasty, elite anti-papal sentiment, and the lack of a strong crusading tradition.

The dynasty: Jan Olbracht and Fryderyk

In the first instance, Poland's reluctance to crusade between 1492 and 1501 can be attributed to short-term factors, such as the personalities, convictions and powers of the two leading members of the dynasty, King Jan Olbracht and Cardinal Fryderyk. In the case of Jan Olbracht, there is a significant correlation between the king's independent approach to national defence and the views of his confidant and former tutor, the Italian humanist Callimachus.[79] In around 1490, possibly on the occasion of Innocent VIII's crusading conference, Callimachus had composed the most important Polish crusading tract of the fifteenth century, *De Bello Turcis Inferendo*.[80] The tract, noting the papacy's failure to act against the Turks, describes the flaws in the existing crusade model, declaring it impossible and futile to induce monarchs to march their armies across continental Europe in order to meet the Ottomans in battle. Callimachus argues that a far more logical solution would be for one powerful kingdom to take on the empire – which he describes as under-populated and unarmed – alone, concluding that Poland was ideal for the task. This work, although addressed to a pope, is a manifesto for a one-nation crusade and as such prefigures Jan Olbracht's later policies: in 1497 the monarch arguably took the lessons of *De Bello Turcis Inferendo* one step further, dispensing with the mechanism of the crusade altogether. Contemporaries were in no doubt as to Callimachus's influence over the king and, significantly, specifically blamed the Italian for the 1497 debacle. Miechowita complained that Jan Olbracht heeded

Callimachus above all his other councillors, and that it was the human-ist who had turned the king's mind to this war: 'it was above all the fault of the Florentine'.[81] In Callimachus, we have a likely source for some of the monarch's defensive policies.

Cardinal Fryderyk Jagiellon also undermined the crusade in Poland, in two distinct ways. It was Fryderyk's ability and willingness to tax the clergy so punitively, at rates of up to 25 per cent, which enabled Jan Olbracht to ignore the papacy, by providing significantly higher yields than the traditional crusade tenth. Fryderyk's coercive powers as royal primate made Poland financially independent in the first years of the reign, arguably underpinning the independent national war policy. Monarchs elsewhere, such as Henry VII of England, rarely received more than a tenth through the 'subsidium charitativum' raised by pliant bish-ops.[82] After 1497, Fryderyk also became one of the loudest anti-crusade voices in government, repeatedly urging his brother to make peace with the sultan before further calamities befell the kingdom, so that 'we may have some respite from these evils'.[83] In 1503, Fryderyk wrote to Pope Alexander VI, setting out the reasons why Poland should preserve her Ottoman truce.[84] The papal chancellery, in its instruction of 1500 for Cardinal-legate Isvagli, had demanded Fryderyk's active support for the crusade; it seems, instead, that the Polish prince saw anti-Ottoman cru-sading, and the concomitant antagonization of the sultan, as highly reckless.[85]

Elites and political culture

Indifference towards the crusade was not, however, confined to mem-bers of the ruling Jagiellonian dynasty in the 1490s. As we have seen, there is no evidence of widespread elite dissent from Jan Olbracht's decision to wage an independent war rather than a crusade in 1497, and no trace of a political backlash at the monarch's defensive policies immediately after his death, suggesting a degree of silent assent. The political elite's apparent complicity in these policies can be explained in two ways.

Above all, Poland differed from most European kingdoms in having a weak crusading tradition. The political disintegration of Poland into small warring polities in the thirteenth and early fourteenth centuries had prevented any meaningful Polish participation in the crusades of the 'classical period', the campaigns in Asia Minor, Palestine and North Africa. There are only isolated examples of Polish knights taking the cross in this period, such as Henry of Sandomierz and Jaks of Miechów, both of whom had fought the Saracens in the 1150s.[86] It was only with the reunification of the kingdom that King Kazimierz the Great (1333–70), of the Piast dynasty, adopted the crusade as a state-building tool, creating the beginnings of a royal crusading tradition. With papal support, he conquered the Orthodox princedom of Halicz and incorporated it into the Crown, receiving crusade bulls in 1351, 1352, 1363 and 1369 to defend his gains from the Tartar Golden Horde and their pagan Lithuanian allies.[87]

With the accession of the Jagiellonians in 1386, however, the nascent Polish crusading traditions created by Kazimierz were quietly quashed. Although King Władisław Jagiełło (1386–1434) constructed a colourful chivalric court at Kraków, presenting himself as the ideal Christian knight, Dariusz Piwowarczyk has claimed that crusading elements were deliberately played down because of a Polish foreign policy which diligently avoided any involvement in anti-Hussite crusades.[88] When Władisław III, king of Hungary and Poland, led an international crusader army at the battle of Varna in 1444, he acted solely in his capacity as ruler of Hungary, and Poland remained officially neutral.[89] King Kazimierz IV too consistently refused to crusade against Hussites, or to involve himself in anti-Ottoman papal plans. The 1487 crusade, led by Jan Olbracht, was a notable exception and arguably an anti-Hungarian rather than an anti-infidel ploy – an attempt further to undermine Matthias Corvinus, the Jagiellonians' great rival and the papacy's long-standing crusade champion in Central Europe, at a time when Hungary had intervened against Innocent VIII in the Neapolitan Barons' War.[90] For the Polish knightly classes, therefore, emotive collective memories of the Holy Land and later crusades were simply not a long-standing component of national tradition or identity, as they were in England, France, Burgundy or Iberia. In this context, it is understandable that Poland's magnates were content to fight the Ottomans without a crusading bull, an institution of which they had negligible experience.

A defining feature of the crusade was the active involvement of the papacy: it was essentially a holy war waged under the direction of spiritual authorities. It is therefore significant that there are strong signs of anti-papal sentiment within the Polish elite in this period, a second source of crusade weakness in Polish political culture. Polish anti-papalism was fuelled by decades of bitter diplomatic disputes which had, crucially, hinged on crusading issues. Rome had refused to accept Władisław Jagiełło's conversion of 1386, and continued to sanction Teutonic Order crusades against Catholic Lithuania and the Polish king until as late as 1422.[91] During Poland's Thirteen-Year War with the Order

(1454–66), the pontiffs had backed the German knights and placed those areas of Prussia controlled by Poland under interdict. In the 1470s, Kazimierz IV had been excommunicated for pursuing his rivalry with Matthias Corvinus, and thereby undermining a putative anti-Ottoman crusade. Rome was also bitterly disappointed when Kazimierz IV allowed his son Władisław to be elected king of Hussite Bohemia in 1472.[92]

A tract presented to the Polish parliament in the 1470s by the leading magnate Jan Ostroróg, entitled *De Monumenta Reipublica*, offers a sharp insight into the anti-papal feelings which these events engendered. Ostroróg stressed that the Polish king need not defer to the pope in Rome and argued that all papal taxes were illegitimate, a fraud perpetrated by cunning and avaricious Italians.[93] As we have seen, Jan Olbracht's councillors in 1501 were the heirs to this tradition, rejecting the pontiff as a credible protector or ally and refusing to ascribe to him any altruistic motives whatsoever. Tellingly, when Alexander VI's compromising letters to Bajezid II were intercepted and published in Italy in 1494, copies were filed with key diplomatic papers in the Polish royal chancellery.[94] While Jan Olbracht's reign saw no open disputes with Rome on the scale of those experienced by his predecessors, a powerful legacy of distrust remained within royal government.

The Polish crusade and Rome

The ambivalent, pragmatic and ultimately muddled approach to the crusade visible in King Jan Olbracht's policies was, as we have seen, in large measure the product of local political and cultural factors. However, the actions of papal Rome are also a crucial part of the picture in explaining the waning of the crusade in Poland; not only had the popes directly engendered Polish elite cynicism towards the Holy See through decades of diplomatic disputes, but Rome's inflexible and Italocentric understanding of the holy war was particularly damaging to the cause of the crusade in Poland.

Popes of this period remained strongly attached to the military crusading model developed in the Middle Ages, which was predicated upon the collective action of large, international fleets and armies. Innocent VIII's crusading conference of 1490 and Alexander VI's league of 1501 both drew up battle plans for huge multinational forces of this kind, in which Poland was cast in a minor supporting role, as a subsection of an imperial army marching from Vienna, and an adjunct to Hungarian forces respectively.[95] As we have seen, both Callimachus and the

Jagiellonian diplomat Rozemberg had stressed that such templates were not useful in the central European context.

Secondly, papal policy glossed over the unpalatable fact that Polish and papal strategic interests might be incompatible in the face of the Ottoman threat. Rome made no secret of the fact that it placed more emphasis on the dangers of the Adriatic theatre of war, which threatened its own security, than on that of south-central Europe. Cardinal-legate Isvagli, explaining Alexander VI's rationale for the crusade league to the Buda court in 1500, stressed that the Turks 'are now trying to penetrate the interior of Italy, which would lead to the fall of the peninsula and of all Christendom – may God prevent it!'[96] The well-honed language of papal crusade bulls continued to stress the necessity of defending the Catholic faith, the 'sanctum opus defensionis fidei'. This curial rhetoric masked the fact that, by 1500, the 'sanctum opus' could carry conflicting meanings: there were multiple frontiers and theatres of war, several potential military models and more than one Islamic enemy. The responses formulated by the High Renaissance papacy were, therefore, a very particular interpretation of the strategic problems facing Latin Christendom. In the late fifteenth century, Rome showed little sensitivity to the particular strategic problems of central Europe, and limited willingness to adapt the crusade to suit that region's local situation.

The crusade model advocated by the papacy in these years served Poland's national interests poorly, as Poles were quick to perceive – the kingdom required permanent border garrisons rather than international relief armies, and was far more alarmed by Tartar–Ottoman raids than by the strategic threat to central Italy. As early as the 1470s, Jan Ostroróg had forcefully argued that papal crusade mechanisms were detrimental to Polish interests. In *De Monumenta Reipublica*, he wrote that 'while the pope has every right to extort money from other nations on the pretext of defending the faith, Poland is free from such contributions', due to the amounts spent locally on anti-infidel defence.[97] Almost identical sentiments were expressed by Cardinal Fryderyk Jagiellon in 1502. Writing to the Kraków cathedral chapter, Fryderyk explained that he had converted the papal crusade tenth into a local episcopal subsidy because there was a danger that Rome would make a claim on the funds, whereas 'our church is far more afflicted [than others] and we cannot carry the burden both for foreigners, and for ourselves and our own kingdom, at the same time'.[98] Much of the anti-infidel policy of Jan Olbracht's reign reveals a similar unwillingness to subvert Polish national interests to those of Rome, or to allow the pope (rather than those living on the front-line) to define the defensive interests of Christendom.

In the face of this implicit rejection of papal crusade leadership, what we see in the years 1492 to 1501 is instead a tentative local reinvention of the crusade in the absence of Roman direction, where Poles from various sections of society came to equate the crusade wholly with national defence. The notion that all crusading action should serve Polish needs first and foremost is explicit in the actions of Jan Olbracht and implicit in the writings of Callimachus, but it can also be detected well beyond the royal court. In 1500, for example, local nobility attending a regional parliament (*sejmik*) in western Poland openly called upon the king to spend the jubilee/crusade funds on hiring mercenaries for national defence, without the slightest concern that this might be illegal or a misdirection of the papal cash.[99] Particularly telling is a comment made by the Observant Franciscan, Jan of Komorowo, who had personally witnessed Golfus's collection campaign. Writing of the events of summer 1500, Komorowo concluded that 'much money was raised for the defence of Podolia'.[100] In other words, even those close to Golfus assumed, and presumed, that the money raised in the pope's name was intended for the defence of Polish frontiers, rather than for an international league.

Polish attitudes during the reign of Jan Olbracht therefore offer an intriguing insight into how the crusade might function, or malfunction, in circumstances where papal leadership had been tacitly rejected. As such, this interlude in Polish policy might be seen as a step towards the radical conception of the crusade developed by another central European monarch, the Hussite king George Podiebrady of Bohemia. In 1462, Podiebrady proposed an international crusade council run by a league of princes, which would organize anti-Ottoman action independently of the papacy.[101] Arguably, Jan Olbracht's 1497 war came closer than any other anti-Ottoman campaign of the period to implementing Podiebrady's vision. At the end of the fifteenth century, Poland briefly moved in the direction of the non-papal crusade not as a result of any theological radicalism, but because of a widespread belief that Rome could not, and would not, offer genuinely useful assistance in the urgent matter of national defence.

The near-absence of a crusading ethic in Polish fifteenth-century chivalry, the rule of a studiously non-crusading dynasty and a century of highly damaging quarrels with Rome meant that, in Poland, the crusade was hard-pressed to survive as a viable defensive model, particularly when contemporary papal initiatives overlooked, or minimized,

Poland's own strategic needs. It is this convergence of factors which gave birth to the Polish government's abject lack of faith in the crusade by 1492. The Polish case illustrates that although the papal monarchy could be the making of the crusade – providing leadership, vision and finance – it could also be its undoing.

The crusade's dependence upon good relationships between national monarchs and popes is well illustrated by the subsequent history of the Polish crusade. The unusual attitudes which characterized Jan Olbracht's anti-infidel policies were relatively short-lived, visible only in this very first phase of Poland's two centuries-long struggle against the Ottomans. In the early sixteenth century, King Zygmunt I Jagiellon (1506–48) began a keen diplomatic rapprochement with Popes Julius II and Leo X. In his reign, Poland was an active participant in the Fifth Lateran Council, the papal nuncio Zaccharias Ferrarius travelled to the kingdom to investigate the possible beatification of the Jagiellonian prince Kazimierz (d.1484), and Polish diplomats in Rome discussed elaborate crusading schemes with papal courtiers.[102] The new warmth in papal–Polish relations led to a considerable shift in elite attitudes, which is best encapsulated by the words of Primate Jan Łaski, King Zygmunt's chancellor and a veteran of crusade negotiations in Rome.[103] Censoring Miechowita's *Chronica Polonorum* in 1521, Łaski not only deleted the compromising sections detailing the humiliation of Jan Olbracht's army in Bukowina in 1497, but also inserted the following comment into the text:

> the realm decided never again to permit its kings to organize general expeditions, nor to let the kingdom's nobility take up arms against the infidel Turks and Tartars, unless the Holy See was first consulted, and unless other Christian kings and kingdoms also participated.[104]

This condemnation of the royal policies of the 1490s illustrates how, by 1521, the actions of Jan Olbracht and his government appeared to their successors to be foolhardy, curious and a little difficult to comprehend.

10
The Hospitallers at Rhodes and the Ottoman Turks, 1480–1522

Nicolas Vatin

Technically speaking, the Knights of St John of Jerusalem were not crusaders. But while retaining the name of Hospitallers, the Order became militarized and it was expected that its members would wage constant war against the 'infidels'.[1]

In the early fourteenth century, at the moment when the Templars were removed from the scene, the Hospitallers achieved an impressive reorientation. By developing a crusade project and bringing about the conquest of Rhodes, Grand Master Fulk of Villaret justified the survival of his Order. None the less, the unpopularity of the Knights lasted for the whole of the fourteenth century, as they lived off revenues collected in the West, where there was no clear perception of what they were achieving in the East.[2] It was therefore important for the Order to maintain its crusading activity, circumscribed though this was by its limited military resources. Without going into detail, one should mention the Knights' naval victories over the Turks during their first years at Rhodes, and their participation in the papal league of 1332, the capture in 1344 of Smyrna, whose defence was imposed on the Order in 1373, the sack of Alexandria in 1365 and the Nicopolis crusade in 1396. Also significant were interventions in Greece (1377–8, 1387–1403), the construction at Halikarnassos (Bodrum) of the castle of St Peter that started in 1408, the shelter given to the papal fleet in 1457 and the role played by the Order in the defence of Venetian Euboea in 1470.

However, the Order was now in charge of a small state and it was crucial to safeguard its prosperity. The Rhodian period was therefore marked as much by agreements with Muslim neighbours, whether the Mamluks of Egypt, the Anatolian Turkish emirates, then the Ottoman Empire, as by military activity against Islam. Maritime areas subject to the Order's protection were delineated and commerce developed. With the exception of the Mamluk attacks of 1440 and 1444, the first half of the fifteenth century was peaceful enough. But the fall of Constantinople in 1453 changed the situation. Mehmed II demanded tribute payments that the Order refused, exposing itself to Ottoman attacks. Hostilities continued, aggravated without doubt by the *corso* sponsored by Rhodes. Finally, Mesih Pasha laid siege to Rhodes in May 1480. Protected by its great walls and defended by the garrison and civilian population, the city held out, and the pasha had to raise the siege after the failure of the final assault launched on 28 July.[3]

The subject of this essay is the ambiguous stance of the Order of St John towards the ideal and practice of crusade in the years 1480–1522. While there was continuity with the Order's policies in the preceding years, there were features too that were particular to this period. To make the argument as clear as possible, it is important first to examine the Knights' relations with their Ottoman and Mamluk neighbours.[4]

Following Mehmed II's death, his successor Bayezid II concluded a treaty with the Knights in 1482 that was highly favourable to them. His brother and rival Djem had fled to Rhodes, and the sultan granted the Order a second agreement by which he undertook to hand over an annual payment of 40,000 ducats in exchange for the Order's undertaking to keep Djem in custody.[5] A long period of friendly relations ensued. In fact, the treaty between the two powers was renewed on a regular basis at the death of each sultan and grand master right up to the arrival on the throne of Suleiman the Magnificent in 1520. On the whole, relations were equally good with the Mamluks, with whom a treaty was concluded in 1484. The Order maintained prudent neutrality throughout the Ottoman – Mamluk war of 1485–90. Djem was transported to Europe, where he resided in France and then at Rome. It was there that the king of France, Charles VIII, took him into his household, but the Ottoman prince died at Naples on 24 February 1495. These events put the Knights' relations with the Porte under some strain, but not excessively so. Four years later, when the Veneto-Ottoman war of 1499–1503 broke out, the Order again opted for a public stance of neutrality. This it had to give up in 1501, when the pope placed the grand master in command of the Christian fleet. However, peace was re-established with the Porte in 1504 without any alteration to the status quo. Shaken anew by an internal political crisis that was worsened by the threat posed by the Safavids in the East, the Ottoman Empire was eager for peace. On the other hand, relations between the two parties were characterized by growing distrust, even by an underlying hostility manifested in the activity of corsairs. The situation of the Hospitallers became much more problematic after Selim I's conquest of the Mamluk territories in 1516–17. It was plain to see that at some point another attack on Rhodes would be attempted and in 1522 it occurred. After a long and difficult siege, Suleiman the Magnificent won the prize that had eluded his great-grandfather, Mehmed II. The Knights were forced to leave Rhodes and the Dodecannese.[6]

It is in this geopolitical context that I shall attempt to outline what were, in reality, the crusading policy and activity of the Order at Rhodes between 1481 and 1522, and what its limits were. Having done that, I shall try to interpret other features of the Hospitallers' activities in this period, which enabled them to convince the West of the usefulness of their mission in the East and to justify their costly presence at Rhodes.

*   *   *

The retreat of the Ottomans after they had been forced to lift their siege of Rhodes in July 1480 was a great victory. Vigilance remained essential, for the Knights were convinced that the sultan would soon attempt a fresh assault. But, while setting out on campaign for an unknown destination, wrongly suspected to be Rhodes once more,[7] Mehmed II died a few miles outside Istanbul on 3 May 1481. His death unleashed a civil war between the supporters of his two sons, Bayezid and Djem. The quality of verifiable information in the memoirs of Guillaume Caoursin, the Order's vice-chancellor,[8] shows that the Knights followed these events closely. The welcome news of the sultan's unexpected death enabled them to seize the initiative.

In the weeks that followed, the Genoese, reassured about the fate of Chios, nourished the idea of recovering territories that the deceased sultan had conquered (Caffa, Pera, Mytilene).[9] The Hospitallers too immediately planned to profit from events. Starting on 23 May, Council discussed an operation aimed at the conquest of Mytilene. Preparations were made in great secrecy, but according to Bosio the expedition came to nothing because of the earthquakes that devastated Rhodes that year.[10] The reasons put forward for the conquest of Lesbos are revealing of the frame of mind of the Knights: the island was rich, fertile and prosperous, but it also occupied a strategic position at the entrance to the Sea of Marmara.[11] The Knights were envisaging its use for crusading purposes.

It was impossible to construe Mehmed II's death as anything other than a sign from God. In the extravagant address which he delivered before the 'Rhodian senate' to celebrate the occasion, Caoursin made his views crystal clear:

> It is our belief that the earth was unable to stomach a corpse so crim-
> inal, fetid and savage. Opening in a gigantic fissure, its viscera gap-
> ing, it despatched the body to its core and hurled it to the perpetual
> chaos of the damned. Its stench affects even Hell, aggravating the suf-
> ferings inflicted on the damned. For it was around the time of his
> demise that there took place, in Asia, on Rhodes and the neighbour-
> ing islands, repeated tremors in the earth. Two were particularly vio-
> lent, so powerful and terrifying that they brought down several forts,
> citadels and palaces. The sea itself, rising more than ten feet, crashed
> onto the beach, only to recede to its former level, finally, in its own
> time, regaining its calm.[12]

Naturally enough, Caoursin knew that these earthquakes, the worst of which were yet to happen, were natural phenomena that could be sci-
entifically explained. But as a good Aristotelian, he knew too that it was possible to interpret them in various ways, at different levels. So there is no reason not to take his approach seriously. The signs were building up around the death of the 'most bitter enemy of the orthodox faith, the persecutor of Christians, the constant foe of the life-giving cross and of the Order that bears the cross'. The time had arrived for a crusade, which he called for in a vibrant peroration, once he had outlined his proposal:

> The divided empire can be occupied without difficulty ... . For if an
> army based on land were to make its appearance from Hungary, and
> if a fleet bearing and displaying the sign of the life-giving cross were
> to sail in the Aegean Sea, the Dardanelles and the Sea of Marmara,
> these sick dragons would be immediately destroyed by the forces
> of the faith.[13]

This sweeping project for a combined land and sea operation was constantly to recur in the Order's debates and it possessed little origi-
nality. Once Djem had placed himself in the hands of the Knights, Grand Master Pierre d'Aubusson did not fail to write to the pope and the Christian sovereigns to underline that it was in their interests to seize the opportunity to combine forces in an attack on the sultan. By backing an offensive led by the pretender on European soil, while profiting from the problems caused in Anatolia by the Karamanids, it would prove possible to recover Greece and the Aegean islands without difficulty.[14]

The same strategy resurfaced 20 years later, when the course taken by the Veneto-Ottoman conflict of 1499–1503 induced the pope to construct an anti-Turkish league and to propose to Grand Master Pierre d'Aubusson that he should assume command of the Christian fleet as a papal legate.[15] Following a debate in Council on 23 April 1501 d'Aubusson accepted, and next day he wrote to the pope in these terms: he did not doubt that by bringing together the forces of the Christian princes and the Holy See, it would be possible to defeat the Turks, provided that the fleet's operations were backed by a substantial land-based expedition mounted by the king of Hungary. It was important too that constancy should be displayed and that the resources that were necessary should be made available.[16] Pierre d'Aubusson reiterated this analysis at the time of the Council held on 17 July 1501:

> It is imperative that His Holiness, His Royal Majesty [the king of France] and the other Christian sovereigns encourage and persuade the most serene king of Hungary to wage war manfully against the Turks and to persist in it with constancy. For the Hungarian people is bellicose by nature, and thanks to their proximity to the Turks and their expertise in fighting them, they can do a good deal to hold the Turk's attention, causing him to divert large numbers of troops to resist them. There is even a hope that the tyrant himself [the sultan] will take the field against them. That would give the fleet an opening and a splendid chance to achieve great things to the honour of the Christian name.[17]

Some months later, following the failure of the siege of Mytilene,[18] the aged Pierre d'Aubusson still wanted to believe that all was not lost. Reviewing the operations of the past months, and forgetting that it was not long since he had himself considered the capture of Lesbos to be the first stage in a programme of reconquest, on 1 December 1501 he wrote to Pope Alexander VI:

> We[19] have readily arrived at the same conclusion, that it is neither expedient nor profitable to the Christian religion to attack the islands held by the Turks, given that it would inflict little or no damage on them, and that their proximity would allow them to recover the lost lands without much effort. On the contrary, all our efforts should be concentrated on a strong assault on one of the two forts in the Dardanelles, which could be captured quickly. Afterwards we could

enter the Sea of Marmara and attack and sack Gallipoli, which is densely populated, and we could burn the greater part of the Turkish fleet, which is normally anchored there. We can then proceed without diversion or opposition towards Constantinople, destroy whatever is left of the fleet and capture the city, especially if it is subject to pressure from a strong army sent by the most serene king of Hungary ... [20]

These were truly big schemes, and I do not intend to examine whether they were practicable. It is true that on 30 December 1501 a representative of the king of Hungary arrived at Rhodes to announce that Hungarian troops would soon be attacking the Ottoman frontier.[21] But little happened, and in the following year the naval conflict moved westwards, with the capture by the Venetians of Sainte-Maure. Pierre d'Aubusson seems none the less to have remained at heart a crusader. In August 1502 he was still rejecting the sultan's peace overtures and hoping to profit from the Porte's difficulties provoked by the Safavid sovereign Shah Ismail. If the pope kept his promises, then for his part d'Aubusson was ready to dedicate to the struggle his own body and goods, and those of his Order and Knights.[22]

But Pierre d'Aubusson died on 3 July 1503, while Venice and Hungary were both concluding peace treaties with the Porte. The lieutenant who assumed the management of the Order's affairs, Gui de Blanchefort, seems to have considered that these noble plans for a crusade were no longer viable, and once more peace was sought.[23] The Order's relations with the Porte were far from being unclouded in the two decades that followed. Quite apart from *corso*/piracy, which was either directed from Rhodes or protected by it, and to which we shall return briefly below, the Knights remained suspicious and anxious. It is possible that they considered securing possession of Prince Korkud, in the hope of recovering the advantages that they had formerly extracted from holding Djem. And it is certain that they believed the presence on Rhodes of one of Djem's sons was useful as leverage on the Porte, even though he had converted to Christianity.[24] After 1514 they maintained diplomatic contacts with the Safavid enemies of the Ottomans, partly on behalf of Pope Leo X, who was pursuing new crusade projects.[25] They did not hesitate to try to stop the Ottoman–Mamluk rapprochement, expressed in Bayezid II's provision of technical help for the fitting out of an Egyptian fleet in the Red Sea.[26] If we can believe Grand Master Aimery d'Amboise, the Order's attack on the Mamluk flotilla that was taking on board timber in the gulf of Alexandretta in August 1510 was conceived as an act in defence of the whole of Christendom:

> In these last years, the sultan of Syria and Egypt has poured all his energy, attention and resources into the construction and equipping of a naval fleet; every year he has transported timber from the gulf of Alexandretta to Alexandria to enlarge this fleet. His goals are to harm the Christians who live in this, our Mediterranean Sea, and to build ships in the Red Sea so as to expel the Portuguese forces. In this situation, knowing from experience that such cargoes of timber constitute a threat to the whole of Christianity, are used for evil ends, and permit the enemy fleet to grow year after year, we have decided to do all that lies within our power to forestall this future blaze, by putting out the fire near its start.[27]

These fine words, however, should not cause us to forget that the Knights had behaved with prudence. They had taken care not to attack the Ottomans, who were much more dangerous at this time than the Mamluks; with the latter, indeed, the Knights were shortly to reach agreement to the extent of supplying them with some help against Selim I.[28] All this formed part of the subtleties of the Order's policy towards the Ottomans between 1503 and 1522, a policy which overall aimed for peace.

Returning to the crusading rhetoric of the grand masters, several remarks need to be made. In the first place, it does not envisage the immediate reconquest of the Holy Places, but that of the Byzantine Empire, meaning the eradication of the Ottoman dynasty at a moment when it had become a menace to the whole of Christianity.[29] Above all, all the crusading projects that were proposed were predicated on the mobilization without fail of all of the Christian states. And this appeared very difficult to achieve. The siege of Mytilene in 1501 had shown that in the right circumstances western powers were prepared to go beyond simple rhetoric, and if these operations proved inconclusive in the event, one of the causes was that the pope himself failed to keep his promises. On other occasions rhetoric suited all concerned, including the Knights. Thus in 1482 the kings of Naples and Hungary had both replied in the negative, using various pretexts, to the proposals made to them following the arrival of Djem.[30] Caoursin was in a strong position when he justified the Order's decision to make peace with the sultan in 1482 on the grounds of the divisions amongst the

Christian kingdoms:

> Failing to open eyes that are clouded by the mists of passions, the
> Christians reject the opportunity offered to them, and each is preoc-
> cupied with his own affairs. For sure, the blood of Christ is colder in
> the spirits of Christians than the Sarmatic Sea; those who should be
> boiling are frozen by a more than glacial cold.[31]

Naturally enough, Pierre d'Aubusson harboured no illusions. In his
instructions of 5 August 1482, already cited, he said that he doubted the
effect of his calls to crusade when people's hearts were not in it: he said
it was like talking to deaf people, quoting the proverb 'Nobody is deafer
than one who doesn't want to hear'.[32] He himself had not waited for the
arrival of the belated responses of the kings of Naples and Hungary
before opening negotiations with the Ottoman sultan.[33] Besides, a truce
had already been concluded on 26 November 1481.[34]

We should add that the agreement finally reached with the Porte on
the fate of Djem specified that he was to be carefully guarded, and that
on the whole the Knights kept their word. When Charles VIII seized the
hostage during his journey to Rome in the course of his Neapolitan campaign of 1495, claiming his intention to be that of leading a great expedition against the Ottomans, the grand master replied to the requests of
the young king of France in a very evasive way.[35] Similarly, to the extent
that the Order wanted to help the Venetians once they were fighting the
sultan in the years following 1499, it had to be as discreetly as possible
and never on an official basis.[36] In fact, it seems clear that as long as it
remained possible, the Order chose to stay neutral in this conflict.

But it was difficult to refuse the honour and obligation of replying to
the pope's demands in 1501.[37] From that point onwards, the grand master and his Council did the best they could, without ever forgetting their
interests: the Hospitaller fleet was forbidden to pass Cape Malio, and the
threat posed by the Turkish corsairs was enough to delay its departure for
Mytilene. Yet it remains the case that we have the impression of real conviction underpinning the crusading rhetoric used at this moment.
Perhaps this was because, once the die was cast, there was nothing to win
from conciliating the enemy and it was more worthwhile to acquire decisive gains; perhaps also because Pierre d'Aubusson, who was 79 years old
in 1501, experienced in his last years a renewed burst of religious zeal. It
is certainly the case that his death counted for a good deal in effecting
the Order's return to its policy of good relations with the Porte.

The Order's officers at Rhodes put on a fine show when the occasion for it arose, but with the exception of certain periods of excitement, it would appear that they judged the crusading ideal to be as impracticable as it was noble. No more than in previous periods did they possess the resources to fight alone.[38] In addition, they had other duties, as Caoursin put it to the ambassadors sent in 1482 to negotiate at Istanbul:

> Peace is known to be a gift of such a celebrated and excellent nature that it is easy to persuade the spirit to embrace it. But while everyone welcomes it with open arms, the yearning is strongest amongst the multitude who earn their living in the cultivation of the fields. For generous soldiers, accustomed to arms, pursue glory in military action … . But circumstances often demand that we take pity on the troubles of the peasants whose sweat enables food to reach the princes and soldiers.[39]

For the grand master was also the sovereign lord of a small state whose prosperity it was his duty to guarantee.[40]

Thus, reviewing the activities of the Knights of Rhodes between the victory of 1480 and the defeat of 1522, one is left wondering what importance the ideal of crusade possessed in the image that they held of themselves and in the image that others held of them.

*   *   *

But the Hospitaller Dodecannese did not constitute just another little Latin state in the Levant. From the start it had resisted the Ottoman advance: Constantinople, the Morea, Trebizond, more than one island in the Aegean had fallen; Venice had lost Euboea. By contrast, Rhodes had withstood a dreadful siege at the very same time that Otranto fell into Ottoman hands, if only momentarily. The prestige that the Knights and their Grand Master Pierre d'Aubusson culled from this was considerable. The Order did not fail to exploit it for its propaganda in the West: the account of the siege, composed in pompous Latin by Guillaume Caoursin, was published four times in 1480, once in 1481 and twice in 1482. It was immediately translated into Italian, German and English.[41] This military victory served to confirm the exceptional standing of a small state which, alone among the Catholic lands surviving in the East, had always refused to pay tribute. The report of the Council held on 27 August 1482 at which it was decided to send envoys to Bayezid II reiterated this theme with insistence: there was to be no tribute, annual gift or embassy, matters on which the Order's representatives were in no way to grant their consent.[42] Caoursin, of course, lost no chance to underscore this point. If the Hospitallers had dealings with the tyrant, they did so with heads held high:

> It is quite proper [Caoursin has one of the envoys say] that we disdain a treaty that would be unjust. For our prince and our companions-in-arms are determined to live only in the dignity of the Catholic religion that they profess, whether they are at war or at peace. If something is honourable, we can do it; if something is shameful, we cannot. Each person must be asked to contribute to the full.[43]

In fact, the Knights had been able to dictate terms to Bayezid II, whose brother Djem they held. Was it glorious to be the gaolers of the prince in exchange for an annual payment of 40,000 ducats? 'Certain envious individuals have not failed to twist the whole matter with their corrosive teeth,' Caoursin acknowledged.[44] On the contrary, he asserted, it was the more glorious to snatch tribute from someone who customarily demands it of others:

> Oh, the inscrutable providence of God! What unutterable justice! What ineffable goodness! This very rich, powerful and proud scion of the cruellest of tyrants has handed over an agreed sum of gold to the crusader-prince ('principi crucesignato') of the Rhodians, in whose company his brother clings onto life, a man whom their criminal father loved so much! ... By this glorious treaty, agreed between equals, he has showered distinction on the Rhodians. [45]

Maybe the high moral value that the Order's envoy placed on these diplomatic successes was not always appreciated as he would have wished. That said, the success itself certainly was admired and the grand master, Pierre d'Aubusson, acquired considerable stature. Henceforth he was considered in Europe as a specialist, to be consulted on matters to do with the crusade or relations with the Ottoman Turks. In 1484 and 1486 he intervened, more or less at the request of the pope or the king of Naples, to persuade the sultan not to make his fleet leave for the Mediterranean, or to obtain his indulgence regarding the people of Chios. On each occasion, he did not fail to make the best of his services.[46] As we have seen, when Charles VIII wanted to undertake a crusade in 1495, he turned with insistence towards the Grand Master, to whom he wrote: 'More than anybody else you understand Turkish affairs and what can be done.'[47] And it was again to his services that Louis XII in turn appealed when he embarked on a maladroit intervention between Venice and the Porte.[48]

A specialization of the Hospitallers at Rhodes was the systematic organization of one semi-military activity that would later be considerably developed, when the Order was installed at Malta. This was the *corso*.[49] In effect, Rhodes became the principal port in the region for corsairs. The Order's ships, but above all private vessels, once they had received a corsair's licence from the Hospitaller authorities, could attack 'the unbelieving enemy' by land or by sea. Their targets included Christian ships carrying Muslim merchandise or products of strategic significance that were to be sold to Muslims. This is not the place to describe the procedures of the *corso* in detail. It is enough to say that the Order's members exercised a preponderant role, and that their own activity, coupled with the fact that pirates and corsairs knew that they could dispose of their prizes on the market at Rhodes, favoured the development of piracy in the eastern Mediterranean. It is always difficult to assess the economic consequences of piracy, and it is easy to exaggerate them. But there is no doubt that the captivity of Muslims taken by Rhodian corsairs or by corsairs protected by Rhodes made the Order extremely unpopular in the East.[50]

The *corso* was under the Order's control, and the granting or refusal of licences was subject to circumstances. A practice which was certainly ancient,[51] but is especially well attested in this period, was that of attaching conditions protecting vessels, including Muslim ones, that were navigating in a maritime zone which *grosso modo* went from Castellorizo to Patmos. The result was to safeguard the security of the maritime frontiers of the Hospitaller Dodecanese, a situation that favoured commercial traffic with Anatolia. The Order's archives show that Council took these instructions seriously and reacted severely against contraventions. In addition, the Order's fleet, which was small but of high calibre, contributed to the maintenance of order in this zone through its presence and patrols.[52] Beyond its boundaries the corsairs could operate legitimately. In practice, there is evidence that the Order tried, with some success, to restrain them during the two decades that followed the peace agreements of 1481–2. The war of 1499–1503 caused a considerable intensification of *corso* activity, both Rhodian and Ottoman, it should be stressed, nor did the restoration of peace bring with it the return in full of the situation that had previously existed. Without doubt it was difficult to rein in an activity that had experienced substantial growth and contributed to the prosperity of the market at

Rhodes. But peaceful merchants paid the price for it in their relations with their Ottoman or Mamluk partners.[53] So it is probably necessary to look for a second explanation for this activity, which continued to enjoy some support in the first two decades of the sixteenth century. One is struck by the geographical coherence of Rhodian *corso* activity in this period: by attacking the routes that connected Istanbul with Alexandria, Euboea and Attica, the corsairs seem to have been carrying out specific policies. It is certain that they were harassing the provisioning of the Ottoman capital at this time; and at certain points the Porte experienced difficulty in guaranteeing the basic security of its waters.

So on a small scale, the Order was devoting itself to an unceasing war against the enemies of the faith. It was a type of holy war that caused more delicate temperaments to experience some distaste. The knight Sabba de Castiglione, for example, wrote in 1507 to his patroness Isabella d'Este: 'But the most remarkable thing is that I, who once professed the holy law, have now become a sea-pirate!'[54] Others reacted with enthusiasm. The Czech pilgrim Lobklovic, who passed by Rhodes in 1494, greatly appreciated the activity of Pierre d'Aubusson:

> Here the Master of Rhodes has his galleys, naves and fustas. When he doesn't have a truce with the Turks or King Zoldan [the Mamluk sultan], he orders his courtiers – one, two or three hundred, according to the need – to board those galleys and ships and to sail to the Turkish mountains located some 12 or 14 miles from Rhodes. And if they meet on the way a Turkish ship and catch it, they remove all the Turks from it: if they encounter nothing at sea, they disembark on the coast and raid the nearby Turkish villages; having gathered prisoners and animals and whatever else is worthwhile, they load all that on their ships and return home.[55]

As for Francesco Suriano, whose text was published in 1524 but had been written in 1485 with some later additions, he wrote:

> The city renders the Levant safe from the depredations of the infidels, by sending all along Egypt, Syria and Turkey their armed galleys, light galleys, brigantines, giarme and nave: navigation in the East is therefore safe.[56]

It is striking that these two authors made no distinction between the official fleet of the Order and the corsairs. For them, the *corso* against the 'infidels' was a highly praiseworthy activity that redounded entirely to the credit of the Knights. For Suriano, they were without doubt champions of the faith, as is shown by the following passage, the imprecision of which leads one to think that it refers both to their victory in 1480 and to their ongoing control over the seas:

> And they are there [at Rhodes] to this day, combating and storming manfully the Turks and the Saracens, the arch-enemies of the Christian faith. And so bravely do they stand up to them that they dare not approach nearer than 300 miles. And if these were not present the Christians could no longer visit the Levant. Nay, the Turks would long since have possessed themselves of Crete, Cyprus, Scio, with all the other islands of the Archipelago, if not guarded by these knights.[57]

To Michel Fontenay, it seemed clear that in the seventeenth century the *corso* practised by the Knights, now installed on Malta, had no other *raison d'être* than to justify the existence of the Order and its revenues in Europe.[58] Up to a point, the same conclusion can be drawn about the end of the fifteenth and the beginning of the sixteenth century, to the extent that the *corso* was the only regular activity that displayed the irreducible hostility of the Hospitallers towards the Muslims. The passages quoted show that it served this purpose. On the other hand, this judgement calls for some qualification. By contrast with periods which followed, the Order reached agreements with the Muslim states and, in certain circumstances, it protected their subjects. As much as a propaganda theme, the *corso* was an instrument of policy that it tried, with varying degrees of success, to control.

In fact, what was of paramount importance for Suriano was the security of the seas, which he attributed to the Knights. In this they rediscovered, in a sense, their original vocation, which was not military but hospitable. Thanks to their presence on Rhodes they could protect the numerous pilgrims who passed the island and were accommodated there.[59] These pilgrims constituted the majority of the travellers who have left us accounts of their visit. Naturally enough, the Order's propaganda had never failed to insist on the importance and usefulness of this Hospitaller mission, and when circumstances called for it, to give it pride of place over the military mission.[60]

Other Christians had a specific debt to the Knights: captives of the Ottomans who had made use of the presence of the Hospitallers to escape. This was a highly delicate issue. In 1393 the Order had refused to come to terms with Bayezid I because it declined to agree to a clause specifying that fugitive slaves would be handed back to the Ottomans.[61] Following this, an acceptable compromise was devised. The agreement concluded in 1482 contained a specific clause, already classic in treaties reached by the Ottomans: a runaway slave would be returned if he was a Muslim but redeemed for 1,000 aspres if he was Christian. The sultan, of course, agreed to reciprocate.[62] The existence in Anatolian territory of a Hospitaller bridgehead was clearly crucial in facilitating these escapes. Previously Smyrna had played this role.[63] Smyrna was lost in 1402, but the fortress built at Halikarnassos (Bodrum), which replaced Smyrna and like it was dedicated to St Peter, also exercised such a function. Its garrison kept a pack of large dogs,[64] which had an ability often wondered at by travellers: if they encountered Muslims they attacked them, but if they found Christians who were coming to seek refuge, they welcomed them and brought them safely back.[65] For this wonder-working too the Knights received the credit. In any case, they did not hesitate to emphasize the value of the service that they were performing to the whole of Christendom by saving these unfortunates from a servitude all the more dreadful because, having lost their liberty, they also ran the risk of losing their souls should they suffer the ill-fortune of converting to Islam.[66] With justice could the grand master describe the Castle of St Peter as the *refugio de li christiani oppressi de la servitute turchesce*.[67]

Surely such service was enough to justify the existence of the Order of St John and the efforts made in the West to ensure that it could maintain itself on Rhodes?[68]

*   *   *

For Anthony Luttrell, the installation of the Knights at Rhodes at the start of the fourteenth century should cause us to think that they had accepted that the reconquest of Jerusalem was no longer an objective, and that they had realized that the crusade was going to become a defensive war against the Ottomans. The Order could not abandon the crusade, which was its *raison d'être*, but it could 'in its own ways divert, or even pervert, it'.[69] As we have seen, subsequent events seem to support this conclusion.

It seems certain that after the failure of the Ottoman siege of 1480, nobody in Europe seriously considered challenging the Hospitaller presence at Rhodes. The glory that the Order had derived from the victory was buttressed by the personal prestige of Pierre d'Aubusson, whose magistracy lasted for more than half of the period covered by this essay, from 1476 to 1503. The Venetians could denounce him as a 'friend of the Turk',[70] and not without apparent reason: but it remains the case that he had fashioned Rhodes into a bastion of Christendom in the East, the only one capable of standing fast against the Turk and of dictating terms to him. After 1480, maintaining the Hospitaller presence constituted an end in itself, not only for material reasons that do not concern us here, but also for moral reasons.

More through diplomacy perhaps than through arms, the Knights kept themselves busy, and they let no opportunity slip to make propaganda use of it in the West. Does this lay them open to the charge of duplicity? Without doubt Pierre d'Aubusson realized that the crusade projects he developed were impracticable, unless it proved possible to unite Christendom. But it would be unjust to question his personal desire to bring them about. The attitude that both he and the Knights assumed in 1502–3 tells in favour of his sincerity. But it was surely necessary to take into account the objective situation. And if the Order's military activity was in the nature of things limited, surely their hospitable activities in the Levant should also be brought into the equation?

11

Reconquista and Crusade in Fifteenth-Century Spain

John Edwards

When Western European 'crusaders', mostly from France or Germany, set off towards Jerusalem in 1096, the Spanish Christian war against Islam had been in progress, often intermittently, for nearly four centuries. From the eighth century until the present day, controversy has raged over whether there was indeed, from the start, a coherent movement of *Reconquista* – reconquest – since it involved regaining for Christendom territory that had been captured and occupied by Muslim rulers.[1] What cannot be denied, though, is that over a period of nearly 800 years, between the occupation by Muslim forces in the years 710–20 of nearly the whole of the Iberian peninsula, and the fall of the emirate of Granada at the beginning of 1492, intermittent warfare took place between Christian and Muslim forces. It is equally undeniable that this warfare, in its latter stages, explicitly took on the character of a holy war waged by Christians against Muslims – a 'crusade'. This lengthy episode had begun in 711, when mixed Arab and Berber forces crossed the Straits of Gibraltar, and rapidly gained control of the great bulk of the territory of the Christian Visigothic monarchy. Muslim supremacy in the peninsula lasted until 1031, when the caliphate of Córdoba began to disintegrate into a set of small kingdoms, known from the Arabic as *taifas* (pieces). Yet Córdoba, as the Spanish capital, was situated well to the south of its Visigothic predecessor, Toledo, and Muslims, who until the tenth century remained a fairly small minority of the peninsula's population, had little effective control over large stretches of the north. Thus it was possible, in that period, for a set of separate mini-states – Asturias, León, Castile, Navarre and Catalonia – to become viable units, and begin the southward expansion which would eventually create the political geography of late medieval Spain.

Initially, the northern ranges of the Cantabrians and Pyrenees provided protection for these weak groupings, and indeed, for about three centuries, the Christian 'kingdoms' and counties remained on the defensive against the overwhelming military, political and cultural superiority of the Muslims. Nevertheless, the caliphs' armies, while marching north each summer across an extensive 'no-man's land' to ravage Christian territory, never succeeded in subduing it. Eventually, in the second half of the ninth century, on the central and western sectors, Christians began to settle permanently in the valley of the Duero, though in the eastern sector, Muslim settlement would continue until the eleventh century to confine the Christian Catalans to the foothills of the Pyrenees, in the Carolingian 'Frankish March'. The break-up of the Cordoban Caliphate shifted the balance of power in favour of the Christian side, but this too was divided, and would remain so until the end of the Middle Ages. In the meantime, the Visigothic Castilians and Leonese moved southwards, across the Meseta, or central plateau, in 1085 achieving the symbolically important capture and extensive resettlement of the former capital, Toledo, which enabled the settlement of the Tagus valley to begin as 'New Castile', and opened the way to the Muslim heartland in Andalusia. The immediate, and reactive, invasion from North Africa of the fundamentalist Almoravids, followed by that of their successors, the Almohads, prevented any further significant Christian advance until the middle of the twelfth century. Early in the thirteenth century, though, the breakthrough into the Guadalquivir valley was finally achieved when, in 1212, a combination of Castilian, Aragonese and extra-peninsular forces defeated a Muslim army at Las Navas de Tolosa. Once more, further progress was not immediate, but, by 1250, the great cities of Córdoba (1236) and Seville (1248) had fallen into the hands of Ferdinand III of Castile, and all of Muslim Andalusia was in Christian hands, except for the southern and eastern sectors, which now became the Nasrid emirate of Granada. In parallel, James I of Aragon achieved the conquest (1238) of what became the kingdom of Valencia, which he added to his existing Aragonese and Catalan territories. These victories initiated a long period of Christian consolidation and settlement, before, in 1344, Alfonso XI of Castile captured the strategic site of Algeciras, dying during the siege of Gibraltar six years later, probably from bubonic plague. In outline, then, by the mid-fourteenth century, about two-thirds of Spain, together with a still higher proportion of its population, was under Christian rule, in the Crown of Castile, the Crown of Aragon, which included both Aragon and the Catalan territories, and the kingdom of Navarre.[2]

Given the nature of the conflict, it was inevitable that, rightly or wrongly, warfare between Christian and Muslim forces in Spain, and in Portugal up to the mid-thirteenth century, would come to be connected with the specific notion of 'crusade', as it began to evolve in the latter part of the eleventh century. Probably from its very beginning in the eighth century, but certainly after about 880, when documentary sources begin to become more readily available, the religious aspect of the Christian war against Islam, in which the bulk of the combatants on both sides descended from the earlier Christian population, was constantly emphasized. The early Asturian kings were praised by contemporary chroniclers for expanding Christendom, and this view was fully developed in Spain by the mid-eleventh century, before Urban II had preached the First Crusade. Sancho I Ramírez of Aragon and Navarre (1063–94) is recorded as explicitly combining the notions of territorial and religious conquest:

Let it be known to all the faithful that for the amplification of the Church of Christ, formerly driven from the Hispanic regions, I, Sancho ... took care to settle inhabitants in that place [Montemayor], for the recovery and extension of the Church of Christ, for the destruction of the pagans, the enemies of Christ, and the building up and benefit of the Christians, so that the kingdom invaded and captured by the Ishmaelites [Muslims], might be liberated to the honour and service of Christ, and that once all the people of that unbelieving rite were expelled, and the filthiness of their wicked error was eliminated therefrom, the venerable Church of Jesus Christ our Lord may be fostered there for ever.[3]

There would be no significant change from this approach to that of the conqueror of western Andalusia, Ferdinand III of Castile, when in newly captured Seville in 1252, in the midst of a fully developed European crusading movement, he issued his deathbed instructions to his son, about to become Alfonso X:

My lord, I leave you the whole realm from the sea hither that the Moors won from Rodrigo king of Spain. All of it is in your dominion, part of it conquered, the other part tributary. If you know how to preserve in this state what I leave you, you will be as good a king as I, and if you win more for yourself, you will be better than I, but if you diminish it you will not be as good as I.[4]

There seems here to be an explicit echo of God's commission to Joshua to enter and possess the land of Canaan (Deuteronomy 34 and Joshua 1: 1–9), and indeed a contemporary chronicler, Lucas of Tuy, referred to Ferdinand as the 'new Joshua'. Explicit papal involvement with Christian campaigns against Muslims in Spain first appeared when Alexander II (1060–73) and Gregory VII (1073–85) urged French knights to enter the Christian war against Muslims in Spain. Also, probably in 1063, Alexander issued a bull to southern Italian knights who proposed to fight in Spain. In it, he claimed the authority of the Holy See to relieve them of penance and remit all their sins, in accordance with what would soon become the standard grant of spiritual privileges to crusaders. In a letter addressed to Spanish bishops and to the province of Narbonne, which had episcopal jurisdiction over part of Catalonia, Alexander, while asking for Jews to be protected, explicitly authorized war against Muslims, on the grounds that 'one may justly fight against those [the "Saracens"] who persecute Christians and drive them from their towns and from their own homes'.[5] In O'Callaghan's view, 'There seems no significant difference ... between [Alexander's] concession to "the knights destined to set out for Spain" and later bulls of crusade to the Holy Land'.[6] During the Spanish campaigns of 1064, in which there were numerous foreign participants, the Aragonese town of Barbastro fell to those who may reasonably be described as 'crusaders before the letter'. Having massacred the Muslim inhabitants the Christians fell into luxurious ways, and the town was soon recaptured by Muslim forces, only becoming permanently Christian in 1100. Yet this inauspicious start to 'reconquest as crusade' had the effect of illustrating, to those French knights present, both the economic and the spiritual benefits of the war against Islam in Spain. Gregory VII took up his predecessor's agenda with vigour, in this as in other ways, characteristically using the 'Donation of Constantine' to justify the growing number of campaigns in Spain as a means of restoring the country to its rightful place as a possession of the Holy See. By the time Urban II preached the Holy Land crusade at Clermont, in 1095, the uneasy pattern of 'crusading' relations between Spanish rulers and popes had largely been set, until well into the sixteenth century.[7]

The period between the accession of Peter of Castile in 1350 and the beginning of the Granada war in 1481 has generally been seen as a 'decadent' period in the history of 'holy' or 'religious' war against Muslims in Spain. In the words of José Goñi Gaztambide, the historian of the papal bull of the crusade, which was so prominent a feature of Spanish history during these years, 'The religious idea of holy war seems to have gone to sleep'.[8] Instead, between 1350 and 1369, the Christian warriors of Spain, and their allies from England and France, largely ignored the emirate of Granada, except as a possible ally, instead devoting themselves to internecine conflict, within and between the Christian kingdoms.[9] Even after Henry of Trastámara had overthrown Peter of Castile and founded a new dynasty under that name, the conflict went on, as Castile fought, especially against Portugal, for peninsular hegemony, and Edward III's son, John of Gaunt, continued to pursue the Crown of both kingdoms. In the process, the concept of 'crusade', which since the thirteenth century had been employed from time to time in warfare between Christians, came to be attached to wars between the peninsular kingdoms, and matters were further complicated when the Great Schism of the Western Church began in 1378. In 1385, for instance, before the battle of Aljubarrota (Batalha), the archbishop of Braga and primate of Portugal blessed the Portuguese troops and gave them the cross, thus making them 'crusaders' (*cruzados*). The pretext was that the Castilians were 'schismatics', because they supported the Avignon pope, while the new ruling house of Avis gave Portuguese allegiance to the 'Roman' Urban VI. Meanwhile, two bishops and some friars fortified Castilian troops with indulgences from Clement VII, who duly wrote a letter of consolation to John I of Castile, after his defeat on 14 August 1385.

Traditional crusading had not been forgotten, however. The Avignon pope also supported Castilian warfare against the Muslims, on 22 June 1386 granting the military order of Santiago (St James) a plenary indulgence for three years to defend some of its southern Spanish castles against the 'Moors'. Then, in the summer of 1397, North African ('Barbary') pirates attacked the Valencian port of Torralba, burning it down and carrying off the inhabitants to slavery. In the eyes of the ecclesiastical authorities, though, the worst offence was the theft of consecrated Eucharistic hosts from the parish church. On 1 March 1398, the Spaniard Benedict XIII, by now 'anti-pope', issued a bull ordering a crusade for the recapture of the hosts, in which he granted the traditional indulgences to participating soldiers and chaplains and to benefactors, as well as appointing keyholders (*claveros*) to guard the expedition's funds. This was to be an Aragonese effort, and by 14 August 1398, 70 ships and 7,500 men had been assembled to attack the North African town of Tedeliç, capturing, sacking and burning it. Over 1,000 Muslims are said to have been killed, and 300 prisoners taken, but it is not recorded whether the lost hosts were found. Inspired by this success, the councillors (*jurats*) of Valencia organized another expedition to maraud in North Africa, this time with 90 ships, some Valencian and the rest Majorcan, and with the participation of the bastard prince Lionel of Navarre. On this occasion, though, nothing was achieved. Subsequently, it was not until 1408 that Martin I of Aragon suggested to Benedict that another crusade should be organized against the 'Saracens' of North Africa.[10] The pope was ready to oblige but, by this time, the main Iberian focus had shifted once again to Granada.

By 1409, all of Europe was aware that Ferdinand 'of Antequera', as he would later be generally known, uncle of and regent for the child-king of Castile, John II, intended to attack Muslim Granada. The duke of Austerlitz and the count of Luxembourg offered their crusading services to Ferdinand and to his fellow regent, the king's mother, Catherine of Lancaster, while, from France, the count of Claremont and the duke of Bourbon volunteered to serve for six months, with 1,000 men-at-arms and 2,000 archers. In the first six months of 1407, the Castilian parliament (*Cortes*) had granted the Crown a subsidy (*servicio*) for war in Granada, amounting to the considerable sum of 45 million *maravedíes*, and, during the rest of that year, the war consisted mainly of raids into enemy territory, and attacks on castles. Hostilities drifted on in this manner until 1410, when Ferdinand decided to seek greater glory by planning a large-scale campaign aimed at besieging and capturing the strategic town and fortress of Antequera, which dominated communications in the central part of the emirate. The town fell on 25 September 1410, after a five months' siege in which siege engines and artillery had been used on a scale that would not be seen again in Spain until Ferdinand and Isabella's campaigns of the 1480s. On this occasion, though, the 'crusade' ended in the negotiation of a truce with Emir Yusuf III, which would last until 1428.[11]

Once John II of Castile came of age, in 1420, he appears to have seen the emulation of his uncle in warring on Granada as a means of demonstrating his manhood. Crusading bulls issued by Martin V were already in place, and the newly reunited papacy had set a tariff for financial contributions in return for the relevant indulgences. This approach, evidently aimed at increasing the proceeds, was to be followed in all subsequent crusading bulls for Spain. Martin fixed the minimum contribution at the excessively high level of eight ducats, but succeeding popes 'widened access' by reducing the price progressively – Eugenius IV to five florins and Nicholas to three, where it was to remain throughout Ferdinand and Isabella's Granada war. Martin V reacted enthusiastically when told that John intended to renew the crusade against the Nasrid emirate. In a bull dated 8 October 1421, he immediately appointed as his commissioners the archbishops of Toledo and Santiago, as well as the bishop of Burgos, with instructions not only to organize the sale of the bull but also to place the cross on as many men as possible. Martin added a set of indulgences which, he obligingly declared, would remain in force even if king and emir arranged a truce lasting up to six months. He also granted to John, *and to his successors*, the third share of the ecclesiastical tithes (*tercias reales*) which was traditionally given to Spanish rulers who involved themselves in 'reconquest' and crusade. This would become a valuable source of revenue.

Internal conflict in Castile delayed military action until 1431, when the crusade was finally preached, and Eugenius IV appointed Cardinal Alfonso Carrillo as his legate to assist the war effort and also to work for the conversion of Granada's Muslims. In a bull dated 13 June 1431, Eugenius granted the full Holy Land indulgences to the crusaders and instructed Carrillo to seek from the Castilian clergy a further subsidy of a tenth (*décima*) of their revenues, this also being a precedent for later expeditions. After further wrangling between the Spanish Christian rulers, the campaign began, culminating in a Christian victory, in the battle of La Higueruela, in the Sierra de Elvira near Granada itself. On this occasion the papal crusading banner was carried by Alonso de Estúñiga, a member of the household of Álvaro de Luna, constable of Castile and intimate counsellor of the king. Processions and *Te Deums* were ordered throughout the kingdom, but John failed to exploit his success, and, despite his best efforts, the financially strapped Eugenius failed to induce a further crusading effort. Finally, on 30 October 1437, the pope appointed Cardinal Jordan as legate for all the Spanish kingdoms, with the power to issue a full set of relevant bulls of indulgence, but again results were limited. Not for the last time in this conflict, the next significant victory, the capture of the border town of Huelma on 20 April 1438, was the result not of royal, let alone papal, initiative, but of a local venture by Iñigo López, marquis of Santillana, in his capacity as chief captain (*capitán mayor*) of the frontier of Jaén.[12]

This lack of activity did not prevent the distinguished bishop, diplomat and scholar Alonso de Cartagena, from employing the continuing *Reconquista* as a justification for Castile's precedence over England at the Council of Basel (1434), on the grounds that it was a holy war with full indulgences, and supported by the entire first estate of clergy.[13] Yet Castile, in particular, was still not living up to these pretensions, and John II's subjects were to remain liable until the end of his reign 20 years later to sporadic Muslim attacks from Granada and North Africa. It was not until 1448 that the Castilian king began to agitate once more for a campaign in Granada. On 30 May Nicholas V agreed to issue a new crusading bull, aimed mainly at potential soldiers, but allowing others to obtain indulgences for a minimum fee of three gold florins. Monetary values were in flux, though, in this disturbed period of Castilian history, and on 9 June 1449 the pope instructed his Spanish representatives to adjust the tariff accordingly. Nicholas was concerned that abuses were occurring in the sale of the bulls and that there were excessive contacts, including the handover of castles and lands, between Christians and Muslims on the frontier of the emirate. As John II's reign approached its end, in a climate of increasing internal instability and external Muslim aggression, the pope issued indulgences to the city of Seville and the duke of Medina Sidonia, to 'crusade' defensively against Muslim Granadans. The reign of his son Henry IV (1454–74), would scarcely improve on this situation.[14]

Henry IV of Castile has come down to posterity, largely thanks to propagandists working for his successors, Isabella and Ferdinand, with a reputation for impotence, both personal and political. Like the murdered King Peter before him, he was accused by his enemies of an excessive affection for Islam and Muslim customs. Yet, at the beginning of his reign, his advisor and royal treasurer Diego Arias Dávila, who was, like Bishop Alonso de Cartagena, of Jewish origin (*converso*), urged him to undertake a new crusade into the emirate of Granada in order to unite the dissident nobility, who had so troubled his father, with the Crown. Thus on his coronation day, 20 April 1455, Pope Calixtus III, a member of the Valencian Borja (Borgia) family, granted him a new crusading bull on the customary terms. Yet all the froth and publicity resulted only in a large raid (*tala*) of the traditional kind, in the Vega, the plain around the city of Granada. There was no field battle, and the king appears, if the hostile royal chronicler, Alonso de Palencia, is to be believed, to have wanted as little damage as possible to be done to Muslim property.[15] At this time, leading Castilians seem to have persuaded the king that such limited 'crusading' activity would not dry up the sources of papal funding, but would serve to restore the royal finances and hence the prospect of further grants of lands and vassals to hungry aristocrats, both actual and aspiring. Yet it was in 1456 that Calixtus made an innovation, in the terms of crusading bulls, which would have huge theological as well as material consequences. This was the grant of the crusading indulgence, in return for cash, to those already dead, as well as to the living who participated in or else supported a crusade.

The possibility of granting indulgences to the dead had been hotly debated since at least the thirteenth century, notably by Albert the

Great, Alexander of Hales, Thomas Aquinas and Bonaventure, who responded to the natural desire, once the doctrine of purgatory had been developed, to do something to assist their deceased relatives and friends in their torment.[16] The fundamental doubt was whether, even if the idea of papal indulgences was accepted in principle, a pope had the power to issue such dispensations to those who had passed on from the earth. Already, before 1200, pardoners were beginning to tout such wares, but they were firmly rebuked by the Fourth Lateran Council in 1215, and by the Council of Vienne in 1312. Nevertheless, the issue would not go away. Yet when Calixtus issued his bull for Spain, on 14 April 1456, he seems to have been going against prevailing official and general opinion. Thus Goñi Gaztambide cites the view expressed in a manuscript, apparently intended as a manual for confessors, which was found in the library of the Castilian count of Haro (1455):

And there are some counsellors so simple-minded that they believe whatever lies some pardoners (*demandadores*) tell them, saying that they gain so many pardons when they die. And this the pope does not say, nor does he ever grant pardon to the dead, if they did not gain them while they were alive, because as soon as the soul leaves the flesh, the Church cannot absolve or release them, because that is in the power of another and higher Lord.[17]

The practice did have some learned supporters, notable among them the Spanish theologian Alfonso de Madrigal ('Tostado'), who died in 1455. In his commentary on Matthew's gospel (Quaestio XC), he accepted indulgences for the dead as a natural extension of those given to crusaders. Nevertheless, when Calixtus III's bull was published in Spain, it met stiff opposition on the traditional grounds that the pope on earth had no power over the dead. In terms of the *Reconquista*, everyone knew that the pope had produced an innovation, and Tostado's view was not generally accepted. According to the *converso* military man, courtier and writer, Mosén Diego de Valera, one of those who did preach the 1456 bull in Castile was the Observant Franciscan, Fray Alonso de Espina, of whom more will be said in due course. In Valera's words, '[Espina] warned the monarch [Henry IV, who was his penitent] that such an indulgence had never been granted, to be applied to the departed', but nevertheless he urged that the money had to be collected and spent on the war, on pain of major excommunication.[18] In the event, the considerable sum of 100 million *maravedíes* was assembled, but, once again, no significant military action took place against the

Granadans, who continued their raids on Christian territory. This was despite the fact that Calixtus had done everything he could to support Henry IV as a crusader. On 10 January 1456, in anticipation of favours that would later be received by Ferdinand and Isabella, the pope appointed the king as administrator and governor, for no less than 15 years, of the spiritualities and lucrative temporalities of the military orders of Santiago and Calatrava, so that he might better confront the 'Saracens'. Henry ostentatiously took the habit of a knight of Santiago, as well as the cross of 'holy war', while his treasurer, Diego Arias, collected the revenues which Calixtus had granted, and little or no fighting took place on the ground. The same procedures were followed in 1457, this time with the sending of a blessed sword by the pope, but it is interesting to note that John II of Aragon refused to allow the publication of the relevant bull (dated 23 February 1457) in his domains.

Henry IV's evident reluctance to do any more than amass crusading revenues irked both Calixtus and his successor, Pius II, who were both ever more preoccupied by the advances of the Ottoman Turks (see below). Nevertheless, Pius allowed Henry to retain crusading benefits and rights for use in Spain, though he instructed his new nuncio, Antonio de Veneriis, to try to curb abuses in the sale of pardons, many of which were the responsibility of members of the Mercedarian and Trinitarian orders, whose main function was to ransom Christians from captivity in Muslim lands. After further years of royal inaction, though, Pius felt constrained, in a bull dated 9 March 1462, to instruct the Carthusian prior of Las Cuevas (Seville), to absolve the king for his misuse of crusading funds. This may have been just a slap on the wrist, but the serious message contained in the gesture was clear enough, both inside and outside Castile. There is no doubt, though, that Pius regarded crusading against the Turks as the main priority of Christendom, and he caused ill-will in Spain by allowing collectors of the crusading funds to take their salaries out of the resulting revenue. This measure was attacked by the royal confessor Espina, on the grounds that preachers should work for God alone and not for financial gain. Thus the latter years of Henry's reign saw growing abuses by pardoners, as well as the diversion of crusading funds into the royal coffers, without any notable military result. Given the chaotic political situation in Castile at the time, with a weak king and largely uncontrolled noble factions warring for patronage and power, the low priority given to the Granada war was hardly surprising.[19] Things would be very different when Henry's half-sister Isabella, who in 1469 had married Ferdinand, the heir to the Aragonese throne, seized the Castilian Crown at Segovia, on 13 December 1474.

This change was not immediately apparent, as Isabella had first to defend her throne against internal and external attack, as Alfonso V of Portugal supported the claim of his young wife, and Henry IV's supposed daughter, Juana. Yet even before peace with the neighbouring kingdom was concluded, on 12 September 1478, Ferdinand and Isabella approached Pope Sixtus IV with a request for a new grant of the crusade bull and a tenth of Castilian clerical revenues. The Franciscan pope urged the monarchs to complete the Reconquest, but quickly realized that he was dealing with a new kind of ruler in Castile, who would demand much but also deliver much. No doubt influenced by the unfortunate experience of the previous two reigns, Sixtus confined himself in his first crusading bull, dated 13 November 1479, to the grant of a plenary indulgence only to those who directly participated in a crusade against Granada. This did not satisfy the petitioners, and the Spanish ambassadors in Rome, by now jointly representing Castile and Aragon for the first time, repeated the demand for the clerical tenth in addition. At this point there was a renewal of the dispute between Spain and Rome over whether crusading funds should be spent in war against the Granadans and North Africans or against the Turks. The Curia insisted that a third of all the money raised in Spain should go to the Ottoman crusade, but events on the Granadan frontier now supervened. At the end of 1481, Muslim forces captured the frontier town of Zahara, and a regional magnate, Rodrigo Ponce de León, marquis of Cádiz, successfully retaliated by taking Muslim Alhama at the end of the following February. Ferdinand and Isabella now felt able to renew the largely defunct war, and negotiations quickly became practical rather than theoretical. At the new rear base in Córdoba, on 3 June 1482, the two rulers and the papal representative, Domenico Centurione, agreed a joint attack on the Islamic states, in which the pope would take charge of operations against the Turks, and Ferdinand and Isabella of the Granada front. The resulting bull, issued on 10 August 1482, which still provided for a third of the revenue raised to go to the war against the Ottomans, also further lowered the financial threshold for those absentees who wished to purchase a crusade bull, the minimum fee henceforth being just two silver *reales*. The king and queen set the ball rolling by offering 100 *reales* each for their bulls. For the participants, including army chaplains, the benefits on offer were generous, and even existing legacies, given for the ransoming of captives held in Muslim territory, were to be diverted to the current war effort. Somehow, though, the papal collector did not manage to lay his hands on the funds earmarked for the projected Turkish crusade.[20]

As Ferdinand and Isabella struggled through the earlier years of the Granada war, papal finances continued to weaken and, in 1484, Innocent VIII inherited a full-blown crisis. He thus tried to insist on his rights, which included funds from Spain to mount campaigns against the Ottomans and a request for troops to serve in Italy. Faced with a firm refusal, though, he renewed Sixtus IV's bull, on 29 January 1485, ready for the new campaigning season, still retaining a third of moneys raised for campaigns against the Turks. This elicited from Isabella and Ferdinand an unusually direct statement of what they at least claimed to be their aims in the Granada war, and their understanding of what constituted crusading:

> We have not been moved to this war, nor are we moved, by the desire to increase our kingdoms and lordships, or greed to acquire greater rents than we have, or a wish to gather treasures. If we wanted to expand our lordship and increase our rents with much less danger and effort and expense than we are putting into this [war], we could do so. But the desire we have for the service of God, and zeal for his holy Catholic faith, makes us put aside all these interests and forget the labours and continual dangers which for this cause are growing once again for us. We are able not only to hold on to our treasures but even to gain many others from the Moors themselves, who would very willingly give them to us in return for peace, yet we refuse those which they offer us, and spend our own, only hoping that the holy Catholic faith may be increased, and Christendom be rid of such a continual danger as is here at the gates, if these infidels of the kingdom of Granada are not rooted up and thrown out of Spain (*arrancados y echados de España*).[21]

The king and queen professed themselves to be astonished that the pope felt able to demand money from Spain simply to pay the expenses of those who raised funds for the crusade. Their subjects, too, would be appalled to know of this and would probably respond by not purchasing the bull and thus damaging Innocent's finances. The monarchs pointedly suggested that, if the pope was short of money, he ought to approach other European kingdoms, since, of the Catholic powers, only Hungary faced a domestic problem with militant Islam which was comparable with Spain's. If, on the other hand, Innocent retaliated by cancelling the bull altogether, not only would the Granada war come to a halt, but Sicily would not be properly defended against the Turks and North Africans either. Ferdinand's instructions to his ambassadors in

Rome, in March 1485, survive, and are a typical example of his robust approach to diplomacy. The king instructed Fernando de Rojas and the apostolic protonotary Antonio Geraldino to seek an audience with the pope, in the presence of pro-Spanish cardinals, or even in the presence of the whole Sacred College, to state that their royal master and mistress would on no account accept the diversion of a third of the crusading revenue raised in Spain, under the terms of the bull, to the war against the Ottomans. Events on the ground in the 1485 campaign, notably the Christian capture of Ronda, were to change the situation, however. Rojas and Geraldino were naturally instructed to pass the news on to the Curia as soon as possible. On the strength of this significant strategic victory, Isabella and Ferdinand demanded yet more money from Innocent, who duly succumbed, granting a new bull (26 August 1485), in which all the revenue was allocated to the Granada war, with the Castilian clergy being required to supply a tenth of their revenues as an additional subsidy. The 'Cardinal of Spain', Pedro González de Mendoza, was entrusted with the collection of the subsidy, which was calculated at 100,000 Aragonese florins. Ten per cent of this was to go to the pope, even if the proceeds of the bulls were to remain with the royal treasurers. This pattern of grant was to be repeated for the remainder of the war against the Nasrid emirate, with further bulls being issued in 1486, 1487, 1488, 1489 and 1491. Throughout this final period, Ferdinand and the pope continued to argue over the allocation of funds between Spain and the Turkish crusade.[22] As for the yield from the crusade bull, the clerical tenth (*décima*) and other less important ecclesiastical revenues, only incomplete figures survive. Allowing, though, for the diversion of funds to Rome, to the salaries of collectors and for normal leakage in collection, and excluding the sums collected by the Church on other bases, Ladero estimates that the bulls and the tenth amounted, between 1482 and 1492, to the enormous sum of approximately 800 million *maravedíes*, three-quarters of which are accounted for in surviving documents. On this basis, Ladero has no hesitation in affirming that 'With the money from the crusade [bull] and the tenth, the Crown financed the greater part of the war'.[23] The fall of the city of Granada, on 2 January 1492, was not, however, to be the end of the specifically Spanish war against Islam.

Even so, although successive rulers of Castile, between 1400 and 1492, had generally resisted the diversion of crusading funds from Spain to the war against the Ottomans, this is certainly not to say that there was no direct Spanish response to the threat they posed. In this area of concern, the Crown of Aragon was more active, in relation to Castile, than in the

Granada wars. Thus with a bull dated 6 December 1403, Benedict XIII attempted to raise money for a crusade to help the struggling Byzantines against the Turks, though most of the money raised seems to have arrived in the pockets of fraudulent pardoners (*questores*). Much later (indeed too late), on 1 January 1443, Eugenius IV ordered the raising of a tenth from the clergy of Navarre and Castile, for warfare against the Ottomans in the Balkans. Both politics and geography made it likely that the strongest response would come from Ferdinand the Catholic's uncle, Alfonso V of Aragon, even before he also acquired the Crown of Naples, in 1455. There has been considerable debate among historians over the extent to which the size of the Ottoman threat was realized by contemporaries, before the fall of Constantinople in 1453, but Alfonso's record before that date was ambiguous. Although Aragonese (i.e. Catalan) ships were fighting in the eastern Mediterranean at least from 1444, no Spaniards seem to have taken part in the final defence of the Byzantine capital. It seems that, although Alfonso apparently had a clear understanding of Ottoman aims, and even grandiose plans to counteract them, he was frequently diverted by the complexities of Italian politics, and this situation did not significantly change after he became king of Naples. Although he continued to show a Spanish self-confidence in dealing with Islamic powers, he inevitably acquired the traditional Neapolitan and Sicilian preoccupation with regaining the Holy Land for Christendom.

Alfonso's mind seems, though, to have been refocused on the Turks by the Valencian Calixtus III's arrival on the papal throne, in April 1455. Reluctantly, the Neapolitan king, sick with fever, told the general council of the Church, on 26 August 1455, that he would take the cross in the 'Turkish enterprise'. He promised that, by the end of that year, he would have assembled 15 galleys in Naples, for use against the Turks in the Balkans, but in July 1456 the fleet was still not in existence. In the event, Alfonso's ships never set sail, and the pope branded him a traitor to the cause.[24] There was a similar lack of enthusiasm in Aragon and Catalonia. Calixtus congratulated his legate in Serbia, Cardinal Bernardino López de Carvajal, on his major part in the defeat of the Turks at Belgrade, in October 1456, and buoyed by this unusual and signal victory, in April 1457 he asked the Aragonese and Catalan clergy for a tenth. There was strong resistance, though, led by the cathedral chapters of Girona and Tarragona and, as a result, the papal demand was reduced. Indeed, a succession of nuncios and collectors sent by Calixtus, Pius II and Sixtus IV, including Joan de Margarit, Antonio de Veneriis and Rodrigo Borja (the future Alexander VI), continued to experience severe difficulties in collecting money in Spain for the Balkan and eastern Mediterranean crusade, up to the eve of the renewal of hostilities in Granada. Borja was even unable to collect what was owed in his own diocese of Valencia, which somewhat disingenuously pleaded poverty, and three years later, Sixtus IV was still trying to obtain the Valencian tenth.

Calixtus III had momentarily been buoyed by Henry IV of Castile's protestations of crusading zeal, but although small amounts were collected in that kingdom for the crusade against the Turks, there was no military action by the Castilians. What is more, in a bull dated 18 January 1460, Pius II conceded that such revenues might be diverted to the equally mythical Granada war. Eventually, Rodrigo Borja arrived as legate in Castile in November 1472; amidst political and social chaos he plodded on in pursuit of his clerical tenth, there as well as in the Crown of Aragon. The kingdom's clergy finally agreed to hand over 100,000 florins, but only in return for the endowment by the pope of two new canonries in each Castilian cathedral, for teachers of theology and canon law respectively. Borja soon found that this was not an auspicious time to preach the Turkish crusade in Castile, and disputes over Sixtus IV's demands rumbled on into Isabella's reign. In July 1478, at the Church council held in Seville, the new rulers tried to exclude from Castile papal nuncios and collectors sent to raise money for war against the Ottomans, evidently having Granada in their sights. The Turkish capture of Otranto, in southern Italy, in 1480, forced a response, but even then their fleet of 24 ships and 11 pinnaces arrived too late to take part in the successful Christian naval action.[25]

Foreign participation was the hallmark of a crusade, and the wars in Spain were no exception. At earlier stages of the Reconquest, foreign knights, especially from France, had been prominent, for example in major events such as the capture of Toledo in 1085 and the battle of Las Navas de Tolosa in 1212. This would continue to be the case in the fifteenth century, but the visiting crusaders were not always popular. In 1406, for example, the Franciscan friar Diego de Valencia wrote, in a poem on the death of Henry III of Castile:

> I believe [Castile] will be very disconsolate
> If the foreigners come to serve her.
> For it's being loudly bellowed that they want to come
> On their own initiative if there is granted
> By the Holy Father a proper crusade,
> So that there would be absolved of all their sins

> Those who die with the [Christian] renegades,
> The unfaithful vassals of the king of Granada.[26]

Such strictures did not, however, prevent foreigners from seeking service with the Christian armies in Granada until its conquest in 1492, in return for the traditional indulgences. Nevertheless, as Goñi Gaztambide pointed out, it is hard to measure the contribution of foreigners to Ferdinand and Isabella's war. The most notable contingent from abroad consisted of Swiss infantry, either hand-gunners (*espingarderos*) or pike-men (*piqueros*). Strictly speaking they were mercenaries, but the royal chronicler Hernando del Pulgar nonetheless regarded the '*soyços*' as worthy crusaders, because they did not adopt the normal practice of forcibly living off the land. Together with some Germans, they took part in various campaigns throughout the war, on occasions being personally commended by the Spanish sovereigns. 'Chivalric' visitors from north of the Pyrenees were almost impossible to find in the Christian armies, but the tale of the Englishman Edward Woodville, brother of Edward IV's wife Elizabeth, partly fills the gap between the romances of chivalry and Ferdinand and Isabella's artillery and infantry war in Granada. Having been Edward IV's admiral, Edward Woodville fell out of favour under Richard III, but was restored by Henry VII after the battle of Bosworth (1485). Avowedly in expiation for the bloodletting of the English 'Wars of the Roses', Woodville then led a small multinational force to Lisbon and thence to Córdoba, where Isabella received him and his men with lavish gifts and despatched them to the war-front. In May 1486, they took part in the siege of Loja, where Edward, having apparently usurped his older brother Anthony's title of 'Lord Scales', insisted on dismounting 'in the English style' and charging the Muslim defenders. At the cost of numerous casualties, the English force succeeded in storming the town, though their commander had some teeth removed by a flying boulder and thereafter withdrew his force.[27] Fundamentally, the Spanish crusades were an indigenous affair.

The fifteenth century saw a wide-ranging debate in Spain, and particularly in Castile, about the nature of knighthood (*caballería*) and nobility (*nobleza* or *hidalguía*), which rarely explicitly, but often implicitly, involved the 'crusade'.[28] Chivalric exercises, for example in the form of jousts and tournaments, were very much a part of the Trastamaran courts in both Castile and Aragon, and particularly in that of John II of Castile. Eloy Benito Ruano notes, in Spain in the early fifteenth century, 'a progressive loss of authenticity in the "heroic" values, which runs in parallel with an exacerbation and intensification of all its accompanying manifestations'. Thus chivalry became 'a great farce, a gigantic fiction, with an agreed language and keys of interpretation, with everyone who took part or watched the performance being in the secret'.[29] John II's court lived in such a world, in which knightly festivities would be ordered at the least provocation, and in any case every spring. As in other European courts of the period, an entire industry of heraldry, weaponry and care of horses surrounded these activities, the attempted merger between real life and chivalric romance being best represented, in this period, by the 'Book of the Honourable Passage' (*Libro del Passo Honroso*), containing the real-life exploits of Suero de Quiñones, which was published by Pedro Rodríguez de Lena in 1434.[30] Such ordeals, in literature or in practice, often bore no relation to the level of military activity on the ground. While the Granadan situation stagnated, and John II's regime experienced faction and civil violence, heralds and knights errant, notably from Burgundy in 1440 and 1448, linked Castile directly with the fantasy world of European chivalry.[31]

Despite the determined efforts of the royal chronicler, Alfonso de Palencia, to portray his master, Henry IV, as an inadequate and unchivalrous ruler who conspicuously failed to live up to the image of a Christian warrior-king, the culture of chivalry survived into the reign of his half-sister Isabella, and was paralleled in the other Iberian kingdoms.[32] Having, in the late 1470s, largely brought an end to the internecine strife among noble factions, especially in Castile, which had crippled the crusading effort in the previous two reigns, Ferdinand and Isabella attempted, with considerable success, to convert the chivalric culture, with its stress on war for the Christian faith, into an intrinsic part of monarchy. In the words of Palencia's successor as royal chronicler, Hernando del Pulgar:

> I do not say that the constitutions of chivalry (*caballería*) must not be observed because of the general inconveniences which may arise once again from their not being observed. But I say that they must be added to, diminished, interpreted and in some way moderated by the Prince, having respect for the time, the place, the person, and the other circumstances and novelties which occur, and which are so numerous and of such a nature that they cannot be incorporated within the terms of the law'.[33]

Thus the reigns of the 'Catholic Monarchs' saw a series of jousts, tournaments and other chivalric games, such as the 'game of canes' (*juego de cañas*), in which knights fought on horseback using sticks instead of lances. The difference was that everything now revolved around the monarchs themselves. In accordance with the new fashion for humanistic 'individualism', mass tournaments tended, during the Granada war, to be replaced by individual combat, in which an increasingly tamed nobility literally battled for the royal favour.[34]

On the basis of what is known about the literary resources of the queen in particular, it has with justification been said that chivalric literature, including Arthurian legends and historical romances concerning Greece, Rome and Troy, was consciously used by both monarchs 'to galvanize the forces of the anxious Castilian aristocracy towards the military projects, and those of religious reform, which were pushed forward by the Catholic Monarchs'.[35] Alongside the European chivalric literature there was a ballad tradition, which was, largely for stylistic reasons, not admitted to court until Ferdinand and Isabella's time. Part of this genre was the so-called 'frontier ballad' (*romance fronterizo*), referring to the interaction between Castilians and Granadans. Paradoxically, these ballads, even in their late fifteenth- and sixteenth-century forms, largely concerned episodes from the reign of John II. Consequently, they say little about kings, and much about local nobles and their forces, both Christian and Muslim, having more a literary than a historical character. They are striking for their sympathetic portrayal of defeated Islamic enemies. Nevertheless, by concentrating on conflict rather than peace between the two sides, they formed a proper adjunct to Ferdinand and Isabella's crusade, in parallel with the verse history of Juan Barba, which praised Isabella in particular as the 'consolation' of Castile, not least for her initiative in the reconquest of Granada.[36]

It only remains to consider two aspects of fifteenth-century crusading in Spain which reflect trends elsewhere, the first being the influence of reformed Franciscans and the second the effect of the new 'humanism'. By the middle of the fifteenth century, the 'Observant' movement in the Franciscan first order of friars had begun to acquire influence in Spain, and this was only strengthened after 1474, by the active support of Isabella and Ferdinand.[37] The Observants in Spain, like their Italian equivalents, focused much attention on the conversion of the Jews, but put much of their effort into seeking an Inquisition to ensure the orthodoxy of the *conversos*. Thus Fray Alonso de Espina, for example, was an implacable opponent of Henry IV's treasurer, Diego Arias.[38] The Order's great days of mission in the New World were still to come, after 1520, but one of its members made a massive contribution to Spanish crusading. This was Francisco (born Gonzalo) Jiménez de Cisneros, cardinal, archbishop of Toledo, Inquisitor General and regent of Castile. Apart from his activity in post-war Granada, in which, contrary to the surrender agreement, he enforced severe policies against the Muslim population, including forced baptism and the destruction of Arabic books, he also worked to pursue the war against Islam into North Africa. There, his most spectacular achievement was the capture by an army under his personal command, and the occupation for six years of the port and corsairs' nest of Oran. In addition to the practical conflict with Islam, Cisneros always had in mind a combination of the goals of Spanish and general crusading, in which the Granadan and North African wars would culminate in the recapture of Jerusalem itself, and possibly his own acquisition of the office of pope.[39] This characteristically Franciscan combination of crusading zeal and desire for Church reform would last well into the sixteenth century and be transferred to Spain's worldwide empire. The reception of the Renaissance in fifteenth-century Spain is still under debate, but there is no doubt that humanists at Ferdinand and Isabella's court actively supported the Granada war, and applauded subsequent Spanish conquests, both in Islamic lands and in the 'New World'. Characteristic of the genre is a letter written to Cardinal Giovanni Arcimboldi, archbishop of Milan, on 11 March 1492, by the Milanese humanist known in Spain as Pedro Mártir de Anglería (d'Anghiera), on the conquest of Granada:

> This is the end of the calamities of Spain, this is the end of the happy fates of that barbaric people which, they say, some eight hundred years ago, at the command of Count Julian, came from Mauretania, where they always retained the name of 'Moors' and cruelly and arrogantly oppressed conquered Spain. Oh, pain! How great up to now was their cruelty, their savagery and inhumanity with Christian prisoners. At last, my Kings, accepted by God, are demolishing to the ground that cruel tyranny, broken by whole years of disasters.[40]

Thus was the triumphalism which arose in the Spain at the end of the fifteenth century, and would carry on through the country's 'Golden Age' (*Siglo de Oro*). The continuing undercurrent of resistance, among Christians as well as the survivors of the Jewish and Muslim minorities, is another story, that of what is sometimes known as 'the Other Spain' (*la otra España*).[41]

Notes

1 Introduction

1 L. Mohler, 'Bessarions Instruktion für die Kreuzzugspredigt in Venedig (1463)', *Römische Quartalschrift* 35 (1927), 337–49, trans. N. Housley, *Documents on the Later Crusades, 1274–1580* (Basingstoke, 1996), pp. 147–54, no. 48.

2 Quoted in N. Housley, *The Later Crusades, 1274–1580. From Lyons to Alcazar* (Oxford, 1992), p. 107. See also J. Helmrath, 'Pius II. und die Türken', in *Europa und die Türken in der Renaissance*, ed. B. Guthmüller and W. Kühlmann (Tübingen, 2000), pp. 79–137, at 122–3.

3 For events and historiography see my *Later Crusades*.

4 S. Runciman, *A History of the Crusades*, 3 vols (Cambridge, 1951–54), 3: 427–68.

5 N. Iorga, *Notes et extraits pour servir à l'histoire des croisades au XVe siècle, quatrième série (1453–1476)* (Bucharest, 1915), p. iii. See also M. M. Alexandrescu-Dersca, *Nicolae Iorga – A Romanian Historian of the Ottoman Empire* (Bucharest, 1972), pp. 11–34.

6 N. M. Nagy-Talavera, *Nicolae Iorga. A Biography* (Iaşi, 1998), pp. 132–3. He points out (p. 80) that in 1897–8 Iorga taught a seminar at the University of Bucharest on 'the sources of the crusades during the fifteenth century'.

7 See Nagy-Talavera, *Nicolae Iorga*; W. O. Oldson, *The Historical and Nationalistic Thought of Nicolae Iorga* (Boulder, Co., 1973). Neither work constitutes a satisfactory study of this extraordinary man, but there is a useful collection edited by D. M. Pippidi, *Nicolas Iorga, l'homme et l'oeuvre* (Bucharest, 1972), esp. the essays by M. M. Alexandrescu-Dersca Bulgaru, M. Berza, Virgil Cândea and Andrei Pippidi.

8 Alexandrescu-Dersca, *Nicolas Iorga – A Romanian Historian of the Ottoman Empire*, passim.

9 Iorga, *Notes et extraits … quatrième série*, pp. v–vi. The meaning of the passage is confused: note the use of inverted commas, distancing its author from this view of the Ottomans; and cf. M. M. Alexandrescu-Dersca-Bulgaru, 'N. Iorga et l'histoire de l'empire ottoman', in *Nicolas Iorga*, pp. 175–86, at p. 180; V. Cândea, 'Nicolas Iorga, historien de l'Europe du Sud-est', ibid., pp. 187–249, at pp. 188–9.

10 V. P. Borg, *The Rough Guide to Malta and Gozo* (London, 2001), p. 98.

11 'To the Vatican and Venice I have made almost annual archival pilgrimages for more than twenty years': *The Papacy and the Levant*, vol. 2, p. vii.

12 For example, 'Lutheranism and the Turkish Peril', *Balkan Studies* 3 (1962), 133–68, and 'Pope Leo X and the Turkish Peril', *Proceedings of the American Philosophical Society* 113 (1969), 367–424.

13 *The Papacy and the Levant*, vol. 1, p. vii.

14 See my *Later Crusades*, pp. 470–2.

15 P. Russell, *Prince Henry 'the Navigator'. A Life* (New Haven, 2000).

16 R. Black, *Benedetto Accolti and the Florentine Renaissance* (Cambridge, 1985), ch. 9 *passim*; J. Hankins, 'Renaissance Crusaders: Humanist Crusade Literature in the Age of Mehmed II', *Dumbarton Oaks Papers* 49 (1995), 111–207, important both for its published texts and for the commentary. For Bisaha, Helmrath and Meserve, see their essays in this volume.

17 D. Goffman, *The Ottoman Empire and Early Modern Europe* (Cambridge, 2002); C. Imber, *The Ottoman Empire, 1300–1650. The Structure of Power* (Basingstoke, 2002); C. Kafadar, *Between Two Worlds. The Construction of the Ottoman State* (Berkeley, 1995).

18 On the debate about 'Turkishness', see my *Religious Warfare in Europe, 1400–1536* (Oxford, 2002), ch. 5 *passim*.

19 See my *Later Crusades*, ch. 10.

20 See my article, 'Indulgences for Crusading, 1417–1517', in *Promissory Notes on the Treasury of Merits: Indulgences in the Late Middle Ages*, ed. R. N. Swanson, forthcoming.

21 *Le Banquet du faisan. 1454: l'Occident face au défi de l'empire ottoman*, ed. M.-T. Caron and D. Clauzel (Arras, 1997).

22 On liturgy, see now the fundamental study by Amnon Linder, *Raising Arms: Liturgy in the Struggle to Liberate Jerusalem in the Late Middle Ages* (Turnhout, 2003).

2 Italian Humanists and the Problem of the Crusade

1 R. Schwoebel, *The Shadow of the Crescent: the Renaissance Image of the Turk, 1453–1517* (Nieuwkoop, 1967); J. Hankins, 'Renaissance Crusaders: Humanist Crusade Literature in the Age of Mehmed II', *Dumbarton Oaks Papers* 49 (1995), 111–207; N. Housley, *Religious Warfare in Europe, 1400–1536* (Oxford, 2002), esp. 131–59.

2 Aeneas Silvius Piccolomini, *Opera omnia* (Basel, 1551), p. 657: 'Intuere deinde mores hominum, ac nostrorum principum facta considera, quantus avaritiae sinus patet, quanta inertia, quanta voracitas? … Et tu cum hisce moribus deleri posse Turcorum exercitus putas?'

3 Ibid., p. 656: 'Quare, inquam, bone sperem? Christianitas nullum habet caput, cui parere omnes velint. Neque summo sacerdoti, neque imperatori quae sua sunt dantur. Nulla reverentia, nulla obedientia est. Tanquam ficta nomina, picta capita sint, ita papam imperatoremque respicimus. Suum quaeque civitas regem habet. Tot sunt principes quot domus. Quomodo tot capitibus, quot regunt Christianum orbem, arma sumere suadebis?'

4 Coluccio Salutati, letter to Jobst, margrave of Moravia, in *Epistolario*, ed. F. Novati, 4 vols (Rome, 1891–1911), 3: 197–217, at 208–9.

5 Ibid., p. 209: 'Nos autem Christiani traditi luxui et inertie, luxurie et gule intendimus.'

6 Ibid., p. 211: 'Expectabimusne donec ista contentio, proh dolor!, accendatur in bellum, vel usque quo Teucrorum audacia … in Christianos irruat et moveatur? Serum erit reconciliationem querere … '

7 See, especially, Justin, *Epitome of Pompeius Trogus*, 2.2.14–15.

8 For his life and works, see R. Arbesmann, 'Andrea Biglia, Augustinian Friar and Humanist (†1435)', *Analecta Augustiniana* 28 (1965), 154–85.

9   But see D. Webb, 'The Decline and Fall of Eastern Christianity: A Fifteenth-Century View', *Bulletin of the Institute of Historical Research* 49 (1976), 198–216; G. Fioravanti, '*Commentarii Historici de defectu fidei et Orientis* di Andrea Biglia', *Rinascimento*, 2nd ser., 19 (1979), 241–6; M. Meserve, 'From Samarkand to Scythia: Reinventions of Asia in Renaissance Geography and Political Thought', in *Pius II 'El Piu Expeditivo Pontefice'. Selected Studies on Aeneas Silvius Piccolomini*, ed. A. Vanderjagt (Leiden, 2003), 13–39, esp. 31–2.

10 On late medieval pundits in the last decades before print, see D. Hobbins, 'The Schoolman as Public Intellectual: Jean Gerson and the Late Medieval Tract', *American Historical Review* 108 (2003), 1308–37.

11 On these, see D. Webb, 'Andrea Biglia at Bologna, 1424–7: A Humanist Friar and the Troubles of the Church', *Bulletin of the Institute of Historical Research* 49 (1976), 41–59.

12 Vatican City, Biblioteca Apostolica Vaticana, MS Vat. lat. 5298, fol. 108r–v: 'Sic cecidimus mutata Romani imperii sede, quasi simul ac Romana cepit esse ecclesia, fides desierit esse catholica ... Sic se res habet, postea quam Constantinopolim fasces abiere, claves deserte sunt ... Coepit inde pessum ire Romanum imperium ac prorsus res Romana dissolvi ubi nec liberalitatis memoria nec ordinum tituli fuere.'

13 Biglia makes clear that in his opinion the Arabs *were* barbarians, unruly subjects of the proper, civilized rulers of the ancient East, namely Assyria and Persia.

14 N. Daniel, *Islam and the West: The Making of an Image* (Edinburgh, 1960), chapter 4; idem, 'Crusade Propaganda', in *A History of the Crusades*, ed. K. M. Setton, 6 vols (Madison, 1969–89), 6: 39–97, esp. 39–53. J. V. Tolan, *Saracens: Islam in the Medieval European Imagination* (New York, 2002).

15 Vat. lat. 5298, fol. 83^v: 'Hinc data late licentia imperii simul ac fidei hostibus, quicumque vellent, iugum ac religionem detrectare; quo factum est postea, ut utriusque vires plus in hoc orbe valerent, coniunctatis fide ac potentia principum.'

16 Ibid., fol. 87^v: 'Tam absurdos illa Machometi superstitio effecerat, ut penitus viderentur humanitatem repudiavisse. Omnis illa veterum ... memoria exciderat, ut ne vestigium quidem cognite aliquando virtutis superesset.'

17 Webb, 'Decline and Fall', pp. 213–15, argues convincingly that Biglia's hopes for Sigismund had soured by the time of his actual coronation, a fact which explains the pessimistic note on which the work concludes and may also account for the multiple dedications of the work.

18 Ibid., pp. 203–5.

19 R. Fubini, 'Biondo, Flavio', *Dizionario biografico degli Italiani*, 10 (Rome, 1968), pp. 536–59, esp. 573–4; D. Hay, 'Flavio Biondo and the Middle Ages', *Proceedings of the British Academy* 45 (1960), 97–128; E. Cochrane, *Historians and Historiography in the Italian Renaissance* (Chicago, 1981), pp. 34–40.

20 A draft may have been complete by 1442, but the work was not published for another two years: Hay, 'Flavio Biondo', pp. 103–5. It is unclear whether Biondo knew Biglia's *Commentaries*, though there are strong similarities between the two works.

21 See the opening lines of the book (*Decades*, p. 150): 'Scribentem hactenus decimo volumine non magis Romanorum imperii inclinationem, quam ipsius urbis Romae atque Italiae desolationem, ad quam superius eas

ostendimus perductas, saepe moestitia, saepe pavor invasere. Nunc tanquam ipse in periculi parte versor, horreo consyderare atque recensere, quam gelido trementique corde, Romani et suarum partium Itali regis Aistulfi saevitiam formidabant.'

22 Biondo, *Decades*, p. 151: 'Sed dum tantis fluctuat angiturque vel detrimentis vel periculis Roma et Italia, Constantinus imperator nullam subveniendi curam suscepit, quanquam varia tunc, et sibi ipsi contraria usus est fortuna. Et quidem hinc eam habuit imperator secundam, quod Turci tunc primum Asiam invadentes, Halanos primo, post Colchos, et Armenios, inde Asiae Minoris populos et ad extremum Persas, Saracenos agrorum direptionibus, et mortalium magnis repertorum aut congredi ausorum caedibus infestarunt.'

23 Hay, 'Flavio Biondo', p. 120, citing Biondo, *Decades*, pp. 163–4 and 166; E. Fryde, *Humanism and Renaissance Historiography* (London, 1983), pp. 8–9.

24 Biondo, *Decades*, pp. 207–9.

25 Ibid., p. 207: 'Paucos ante annos, gens e Perside Agarena (quam vos corrupte Saracenam dicitis) sanctam civitatem Hierosolymam, sanctae terrae loca invadens cepit ... Omnes Romano quondam imperio, et post Romano pontifici, parentes a Turcis Saracenisque nostris (imo Christi domini et immortalis Dei) hostibus possideri, neminem esse vestrum qui ignoret certum habemus ... '

26 Ibid., p. 208: 'Fuit hactenus in extremis ad septentriones Europae partibus Constantinopolitanum imperium obex, et tanquam murus, qui maiores omnia prostraturas Turcorum Saracenorumque alluviones continuit prohibuitque, ne Hungaros, Polonos, Bohemos et ipsos Alemannos primo, deinde caeteros obruerent Christianos. Pulsus vero ante paucos annos Asia imperator, de retinendis Constantinopoli propinquis Europae regionibus laborat.'

27 Ibid., p. 208: 'Melius, filii, et maiori cum gloria nostri progenitores inchoatam, ut altiuscule repetamus, Romae, et in Italia et viribus Europae auctam dignitatem ad totius orbis monarchiam extulerunt, per cuius omnes provincias et regiones nomen floruit Christianum – quod nomen nostris temporibus ad parvum orbis angulum coangustari, et quotidie de excidio periclitari videmus.'

28 Quoted in notes 2 and 3, above.

29 See the introduction to Pius II, *Commentaries*, ed. M. Meserve and M. Simonetta (Cambridge, Mass., 2003), p. xiv.

30 Pius II, *Commentaries*, 2.2.5. For Aeneas's crusading ideology see J. Helmrath, 'Pius II und die Türken', in *Europa und die Türken in der Renaissance*, eds B. Guthmüller and W. Kühlmann (Tübingen, 2000), pp. 79–138, with an exhaustive survey of the previous literature.

31 See, e.g., R. Rubinstein, 'Pius II and St. Andrew's Head', in *Essays in the History of Architecture presented to Rudolph Wittkower*, ed. D. Fraser *et al.* (London, 1967), pp. 22–33.

32 B. Nogara, *Scritti inediti e rari di Flavio Biondo* (Rome, 1927), pp. cxlix–clvi.

33 Flavio Biondo, *Roma triumphans* (Basel, 1531), p. 1: 'Exciti enim a te ingentes Italiae, Galliarum, Hispaniarum, Germaniae, populi in magnam praeclaramque expeditionem quam paras in Turcos ... Nonnulla in ipso opere edocebuntur, aliquando alias simile in rerum difficultate gesta, ut ipsa priscorum virtutis imitatio ... sit ad rem capessendam stimulos additura.' See

also his meditation on the subject at p. 217, discussed by A. Mazzocco, 'Rome and the Humanists: The Case of Flavio Biondo', in *Rome in the Renaissance: The City and the Myth*, ed. P. A. Ramsey (Binghamton, NY, 1982), pp. 185–95, at 191–2.

34   Bessarion, Letter to Doge Francesco Foscari, 13 July 1453, in L. Mohler, *Kardinal Bessarion als Theologe, Humanist und Staatsman*, 3 vols (Paderborn, 1923–42), 3: 475–7, at 475: 'Urbs, quae modo tali imperatore, tot illustrissimis viris, tot clarissimis antiquissimisque familiis, tanta rerum copia florebat, totius Graeciae caput, splendor et decus orientis, gymnasium optimarum artium, bonorum omnium receptaculum, ab immanissimis barbaris, a saevissimis Christianae fidei hostibus, a truculentissimis feris capta, spoliata, direpta, exhausta est.'

35   Francesco Filelfo, Oration at the Congress of Mantua, 18 September 1459, in *Orationes* [Milan, 1483–4], sigs H1ᵛ–H5ᵛ, at H2ᵛ: 'Eo enim omnis indignitas ducenda est indignior, quo ab indignioribus infertur hominibus; si homines quidem potius quam efferatae prorsus et truculentissimae quaedam belluae Turci sunt appellandi, cum nihil in se humanitatis habeant praeter hominis figuram, et eam sane ob flagitiossimam turpitudinis foeditatem depravatam ac nequam.'

36   A. Pertusi, 'I primi studi in occidente sull'origine e potenza dei Turchi', *Studi Veneziani* 12 (1970), 465–515; Hankins, 'Renaissance Crusaders', pp. 135–44; M. Meserve, 'The Origin of the Turks: A Problem in Renaissance Historiography', PhD diss. (Warburg Institute, 2001).

37   Flavio Biondo, *Decades*, p. 151: 'Fueruntque et ipsi Turci Scythae ex iis quos Alexandrum Macedonem intra Hyperboreos montes, ferreis clausisse repagulis, quum alii tradunt scriptores, tum beatus Hieronymus affirmat.' Biondo also quoted Jerome's letter to account for the emergence of the Huns: *Decades*, p. 6.

38   Francesco Filelfo, Letter to Wladyslaw III of Poland and Hungary, 5 November 1444, *Epistolae* (Venice, 1502), fols 37ʳ–38ʳ.

39   Aeneas Silvius, *Oratio de Constantinopolitana clade*, in *Opera omnia* (Basel, 1551), pp. 678–89, at 681: 'Scytharum genus est ex media Barbaria profectum, quod ultra Euxinum Pyrrichiosque montes (ut Ethico Philosopho placet) ad septentrionalem Oceanum sedes habuit; gens immunda et ignominiosa, fornicaria in cunctis stuprorum generibus.'

40   Niccolò Sagundino, 'De origine et rebus gestis Turcarum', in L. Chalcocondyles, *De origine ... Turcorum libri decem* (Basel, 1556), pp. 186–90.

41   Filelfo, *Orationes*, sigs. H2ᵛ–3ʳ: 'Quis unus omnium Turcos ignoret fugitivos esse Scytharum servos eosque pastores, qui ex ergastulis illius vasti et inhospitabilis montis Caucasi ... in Persida ac Mediam latrocinatum descendissent nullumque certum incolerent domicilium praeter obsoleta lustra et horrentes sylvarum latebras?'

42   Nicola Loschi, *Constantinus supplex*, in A. Pertusi, *Testi inediti e poco noti sulla caduta di Costantinopoli. Edizione postuma*, ed. A. Carile (Bologna, 1983), pp. 274 ('... Si Scythico iuveni tantarum pondera rerum/excussisse datum est?') and 276 ('Caspia gens').

43   Aeneas Silvius, *Oratio de Constantinopolitana clade*, p. 681: 'Et quamvis sub miti coelo et mundiori terra per tot saecula parumper excultam se praebuerit, sapit tamen adhuc multum pristinae deformitatis, neque omnem barbariem detersit. Carnes adhuc equorum, vesontium, vulturumque comedit, libidini servit, crudelitati succumbit, literas odit, humanitatis studia persequitur.'

44 M. Meserve, 'Medieval Sources for Renaissance Theories on the Origins of the Ottoman Turks', in *Europa und die Türken in der Renaissance*, eds B. Guthmüller and W. Kühlmann (Tübingen, 2000), pp. 409–36; also 'From Samarkand to Scythia'.

45 Aeneas Silvius Piccolomini, 'Oratio habita in conventu Mantuano', in *Opera omnia* (Basel, 1551), pp. 905–14, at 906–7. See also his discussion of the decline of Christianity in the East in *Asia, ibid.*, pp. 281–386, at 385–6.

46 F. Cardini, 'La crociata, mito politico', *Il Pensiero Politico* 8 (1975), 3–32, esp. 31–2; Hankins, 'Renaissance Crusaders', pp. 123–4, 142, 145–6; K. Fleet, 'Italian Perceptions of the Turks in the Fourteenth and Fifteenth Centuries', *Journal of Mediterranean Studies* 5 (1995), 159–72, esp. 167–9; Helmrath, 'Pius II', p. 106. N. Bisaha, 'New Barbarian or Worthy Adversary? Renaissance Humanist Constructs of the Ottoman Turks', in *Western Views of Islam in Medieval and Early Modern Europe: Perception of Other*, eds D. R. Blanks and M. Frassetto (New York, 1999), pp. 185–205, esp. 187–94.

47 The Latin translation of Herodotus, the foremost ancient authority on the Scythian peoples, which Lorenzo Valla completed shortly after the fall of Constantinople (in 1455: see G. Mancini, *Vita di Lorenzo Valla* [Florence, 1891], pp. 321–3; S. I. Camporeale, *Lorenzo Valla: umanesimo e teologia* [Florence, 1972], pp. 202–3 and 447–8) is often taken as a fundamental document for this revival (Schwoebel, *Shadow*, p. 148; Göllner, 'Legenden', pp. 50–1); however, I have found no evidence that any fifteenth-century humanist used or even more indirectly invoked the text of Herodotus, in Greek or Latin, in their discussions of the Scythian origins of the Turks.

48 Filelfo, letter to Theodore Gaza, 1470, in *Epistolae* (Venice, 1502).

49 For synopses of these texts, see H. Vast, *Le Cardinal Bessarion* (Paris, 1878), pp. 386–92; Schwoebel, *Shadow of the Crescent*, pp. 157–60; R. Manselli, 'Il cardinale Bessarione contro il pericolo turco e l'Italia', *Miscellanea francescana* 73 (1973), 314–26, and my 'Patronage and Propaganda at the First Paris Press: Guillaume Fichet and the First Edition of Bessarion's *Orations against the Turks*', *Papers of the Bibliographical Society of America* 97 (2003), 521–88, esp. 521–8. The text is printed, together with various letters and prefaces, in J.-P. Migne, *Patrologia Graeca* (hereafter PG), 161, cols 647–76. For the date of composition and various manuscript redactions, see J. Monfasani, 'Bessarion Latinus', *Rinascimento*, 2nd ser., 21 (1981), 165–209, at 179–81 and 196–204.

50 'Quis illum a tanto victoriae cursu retardabit? ... Quis erit impedimento? ... Italine, quibus hostis imminet, quibus caedem, ferrum, servitutem, exsilia denuntiat et ostentat? At nolunt, negligent, non possunt adduci ut credant sese adeo propinquos esse periculo.' PG 161: 650–1.

51 'Quid ad nos? Venetis curae sit. Recte cum iis actum. Utile enim esset, si gravioribus incommodes conflictarentur: quietius caeteri et securius viveremus. Tantum otio nostro accedit, quantum illis imperii demitur; si quis qui malis istis ingemiscat, is Venetus, Venetorum partibus favet, non audiendus, contemnendus. O turpem hominum ignorantiam ... ' PG 161:649.

52 See, for example, the account of his oration at the 1462 ceremony of St Andrew's head in Rubinstein, 'Pius II and St. Andrew's Head'. The instructions he provided for Venetian crusade preachers in 1463 also demonstrate his broad command of the traditional arguments for crusade. For barbarity, see his letter to Doge Foscari, in Mohler, *Kardinal Bessarion*, 3: 475–7.

53 'Turci ... sanguinem Christianum anhelantis': PG 161: 650.

54   Ibid., 651–9, esp. 652–3.

55   Nicephorus Gregoras in PG 148: 370–1; Pachymeres, ibid., 426–7; and Ducas in PG 157: 755–64.

56   Aeneas Silvius, *Opera omnia*, p. 908. See also Niccolò Sagundino's oration to Alfonso of Aragon, 25 January 1454, in A. Pertusi, *La caduta di Costantinopoli. Le testimonianze dei contemporanei*, 2 vols (Verona, 1976), 2: 128–41.

57   '[Turcus qui] solet Alexandro suam aequare virtutem. Nam Alexandrum macedonum regem ad res gerendas, ad aemulationem gloriae sibi imitandum proposuit.' PG 161: 656.

58   'Toto animo ac tota mente in nos dies noctesque feriatur.' Ibid., 653.

59   'Nullam ad id tutiorem esse viam intelligit, quam cum aliena jactura vires suas augere.' PG 161: 654.

60   'Nonne ita natura comparatum esse intelligit, ut nihil eodem situ permaneat, sed cuncta jugi, vario, novo motu agantur? Quod si amplum habet imperium, idque rerum omnium lege moveri oportet, nonne imminuetur, nisi augeatur? Ne putaveris Turcum augendi imperii studiosum et cupidum; at certe sit conservandi. Conservare vero non poterit, nisi augeat. Siquidem regressurum est quod non progrediatur, lapsurum quod non surgat, ruiturum quod non majus efficiatur. Qua confirmatus opinione exercitum suum auget in dies, quem habet amplissimum. Aliena invadit, ne sua amittat.' PG 161: 655.

61   Ibid., 655.

62   Ibid., 653–6.

63   'Habet enim non paucos Asianos populos infensos et in suam perniciem imminentes; quos in se impetum facturos aperte intelligit, si aut arma deposuerit, aut exercitus famam in contemptum ludibriumque adduci permiserit. Quem ut laudibus ornatissimum reddat, ut Asianis hostibus formidolosum efficiat, quo tandem transmittere cogitat? Ubi sui consilii alendi segetem uberiorem videt? Ubi magis admiranda conari potest? Non excident gladii; non fluent arma de manibus. Nam socios in officio ac fide continere studet, et eos ipsos quicum quotidie vivit. Maxime est suis omnibus invisus; oderunt socii, non amant familiares; parvo momento ad ipsius excidium ac necem omnes impellerentur. Id quoniam exploratum habet et compertum, bella peregrina suscipere, gerere, conficere statuit, ne domesticam civilemque dissensionem experiatur.' Ibid., 657–8.

64   Ibid., 659–69.

65   'Nihil aliud miseram exstinxit Graeciam, nisi discordia; nihil aliud eam orbis partem delevit, nisi bella civilia.' Ibid., 662.

66   Ibid., 662.

67   On movements for conciliation with the Turks (both political and spiritual) see R. Schwoebel, 'Coexistence, Conversion, and the Crusade against the Turk', *Studies in the Renaissance* 12 (1965), 164–87, esp. 166–70, 174–81; Daniel, *Islam and the West*, pp. 114–22.

3   Pope Pius II and the Crusade

1   R. Schwoebel, *The Shadow of the Crescent: The Renaissance Image of the Turk (1453–1517)* (New York, 1969), p. 65.

2   Kenneth Setton calls Pius's determination to go overseas on crusade, 'come hell or highwater ... one of the nobler pictures of the Quattrocento'. See *The*

Papacy and the Levant (1205–1571). Volume II. The Fifteenth Century (Philadelphia, 1978), p. 261.

3   For an overview of Pius's thought and works on this topic, see J. Helmrath, 'Pius II. und die Türken,' in *Europa und die Türken in der Renaissance*, ed. B. Guthmüller and W. Kühlmann (Tübingen, 2000), pp. 79–137. I also address Pius's views of the Turks in *Creating East and West: Renaissance Humanists and the Ottoman Turks* (Philadelphia, 2004).

4   Setton, *Papacy and the Levant*, p. 201, n. 12.

5   R. Wolkan, ed., *Der Briefwechsel des Eneas Silvius Piccolomini*, in *Fontes rerum austriacarum*, vol. 68 (Vienna, 1918), p. 200.

6   Ibid., p. 209.

7   On humanist views of the Turks, see Bisaha, *Creating East and West*; see also J. Hankins, 'Renaissance Crusaders: Humanist Crusade Literature in the Age of Mehmed II', *Dumbarton Oaks Papers* 49 (1995), 111–207.

8   Or as Gioacchino Paparelli states, 'it added new leaven to his ecclesiastical career'. See *Enea Silvio Piccolomini: l'umanesimo sul soglio di Pietro* (Ravenna, 1978), p. 114.

9   Zweder Von Martels and R.J. Mitchell state that the oration at Frankfurt was printed. See Martels, ' "More Matter and Less Art." Aeneas Silvius Piccolomini and the Delicate Balance between Eloquent Words and Deeds', in *Pius II 'El più expeditivo pontifice': Selected Studies on Aeneas Silvius Piccolomini (1405–1464)*, ed. Z. Von Martels and A. Vanderjagt (Leiden, 2003), p. 220; R. J. Mitchell, *The Laurels and the Tiara: Pope Pius II 1458–1464* (Garden City, NY, 1962), p. 102. Margaret Meserve and Marcello Simonetta say that the oration at Regensburg was printed. See Pius II, *Commentaries*, ed. Meserve and Simonetta (Cambridge, Mass., 2003), 1: 396, n. 105.

10   *Opera quae extant omnia* (reprint, Frankfurt, 1967), p. 681. On the Turk/Trojan issue and other perceptions of Turkish origins, see M. J. Heath, 'Renaissance Scholars and the Origins of the Turks', *Bibliothèque d'humanisme et renaissance* 41 (1979), 453–71; M. Meserve, 'Medieval Sources for Renaissance Theories on the Origins of the Ottoman Turks', in *Europa und die Türken in der Renaissance*, ed. Guthmüller and Kühlmann, pp. 409–36.

11   *Opera omnia*, p. 681; Von Martels, ' "More Matter and Less Art" ' p. 220.

12   Mitchell, *Laurels and the Tiara*, pp. 103–5.

13   N. Housley, *The Later Crusades, 1274–1580: from Lyons to Alcazar* (Oxford, 1992), pp. 102–4.

14   On this question and the protean nature of Aeneas's identity and self perception, see T. M. Izbicki, ' "Reject Aeneas!" Pius II on the Errors of his Youth', in *Pius II 'El più expeditivo pontifice'*, ed. Von Martels and Vanderjagt, pp. 187–203.

15   On Mantua, see Setton, *Papacy and the Levant*, pp. 201–14; Paparelli, *Enea Silvio Piccolomini*, pp. 157–71; Mitchell, *Laurels and the Tiara*, pp. 119–46.

16   See *Commentaries of Pius II*, trans. F. A. Gragg, ed. L. C. Gabel (Northampton, Mass., 1951), 2: 117.

17   Ibid., 2: 191.

18   Ibid., 2: 192–3. For an analysis of Florence's concerns at Mantua and following, see R. Black, *Benedetto Accolti and the Florentine Renaissance* (Cambridge, 1985), pp. 249–59.

19   Sforza would later bitterly disappoint Pius by backing out of his promise to lead the crusade and blocking crusade preaching efforts in his territory. See

M. Simonetta, 'Pius II and Francesco Sforza. The History of Two Allies', in
Pius II 'El più expeditivo pontifice, ed. Von Martels and Vanderjagt, pp. 147–70.

20 See *Opera omnia*, pp. 905–14.

21 Pius cites examples of just war in Troy and Carthage and Rome's assistance
of allies. He also discusses ancient victories of Western powers over the effem-
inate East. It should also be noted that the very structure of the oration is
classical; see M. J. Heath, *Crusading Commonplaces: La Noue, Lucinge and
Rhetoric against the Turks* (Geneva, 1986).

22 *Opera omnia*, p. 909. On the battle of Belgrade, see Setton, *Papacy and the Levant*,
2: 173–81; Housley, *Later Crusades*, pp. 103–4, and his essay in this collection.

23 The purpose of Clermont was reform, not crusade. Urban called a large gathering of laymen as well as clergy at the end of the council and gave his
famous rousing speech. The context of Urban's speech, then, came as a stir-
ring surprise to many in the crowd.

24 *Opera omnia*, p. 905. Elsewhere he uses the term 'civilia bella'; ibid., p. 907.

25 Von Martels, ' "More Matter and Less Art" ', p. 222.

26 *Commentaries*, trans. Gragg, 2: 251. Pius made similar claims about other orations' effect on the audience.

27 *Opera omnia*, p. 914. Pius also claimed to have told Philip of Burgundy's
envoys, *before* he delivered this oration, not to expect another crusade on the
level of Godfrey's or Conrad's. See *Commentaries*, trans. Gragg, 2: 215.

28 Setton, *Papacy and the Levant*, p. 214.

29 For a discussion of Pius's sincerity, see R. Schwoebel, 'Pius II and the
Renaissance Papacy', in *Renaissance Men and Ideas*, ed. R. Schwoebel (New
York, 1971). For more critical views of Pius, see F. Cardini, 'La repubblica di
Firenze e la crociata di Pio II', *Rivista storica della chiesa in Italia* 33 (1979),
471–2; F. Babinger, *Mehmed the Conqueror and his Time*, trans. Ralph Manheim
(1953; revd edn, Princeton, 1978), pp. 198–9.

30 While some have viewed Pius as using crusade as a means to achieve papal
power, Meserve and Simonetta opine that he could just as easily have been
using the doctrine of papal supremacy to achieve European unity and a crusade against the Turks. As promising as conciliarism and imperial leadership
had once seemed, they had long since failed, while his goal of crusade never
abated. See *Commentaries*, ed. Meserve and Simonetta, 1: xiv.

31 See *Commentaries*, book 12 for Pius's description of his recent preoccupations
and belief that the way was now clear for crusade.

32 For more on the *Commentaries*, see M. Pozzi, 'Struttura epica dei
Commentarii'; J. Lacroix, 'I *Commentarii* di Pio II fra storia e diaristica', both
in *Pio II e la cultura del suo tempo*, ed. L. R. Secchi Tarugi (Milan, 1991).

33 *Commentaries*, trans. Gragg, 2: 115.

34 Ibid., 5: 822.

35 See ed. Meserve and Simonetta, *Commentaries*, 1: xvii; see also Lacroix, 'I
Commentarii di Pio II.'

36 B. K. Vollmann, 'Aeneas Silvius Piccolomini as a Historiographer: *Asia*', in *El
più expeditivo pontefice*, ed. Von Martels and Vanderjagt, pp. 42–3.

37 Ibid., p. 54.

38 *Opera omnia*, p. 307. Pius believed Aethicus to be an ancient authority, but
he was actually a seventh-century writer. See Heath, 'Renaissance Scholars',
pp. 456–7.

39 M. Meserve, 'From Samarkand to Scythia: Reinventions of Asia in Renaissance Geography and Political Thought', in *Pius II 'El più expeditivo pontefice'*, ed. Von Martels and Vanderjagt, p. 24.
40 *Opera omnia*, p. 385.
41 Vollmann, 'Aeneas as a Historiographer', p. 53.
42 See my article, 'Pope Pius II's Letter to Sultan Mehmed II: a Reexamination', *Crusades* 1 (2002), 183–200. For a recent edition and translation of the letter, see Pius II, *Epistola ad Mahomatem II (Epistle to Mehmed II)*, ed. and trans. A. R. Baca (New York, 1990).
43 Von Martels, ' "More Matter and Less Art" ', pp. 205–17; L. C. Gabel, in *Commentaries*, trans. Gragg, 5: xxviii.
44 Setton, *Papacy and the Levant*, p. 235.
45 *Commentaries*, trans. Gragg, 4: 517.
46 Ibid., 4: 517.
47 Ibid., 5: 824.
48 *Opera omnia*, p. 918.
49 See Schwoebel, *Shadow*, pp. 60–1; *Commentaries*, trans. Gragg, 2: 214.
50 *Commentaries*, trans. Gragg, 5: 816.
51 See Housley, *Later Crusades*, pp. 108–9; Mitchell, *Laurels and the Tiara*, p. 233.
52 See book 1 of the *Commentaries* for Pius's lively account of his remonstrations with cardinals regarding the election of a morally fit candidate. On Pius's aborted attempts to reform the Church, see Ludwig Pastor, *The History of the Popes from the Close of the Middle Ages*, vol. 3 (London, 2nd edn 1900), 269–78.
53 *Commentaries*, trans. Gragg, 4: 516.
54 Ibid., 4: 516.
55 *Opera omnia*, pp. 915, 917.
56 *Commentaries*, trans. Gragg, 5: 824.
57 Ibid., 5: 824.
58 See Pozzi's intriguing and cogent reading of Pius's *Commentaries* as epic, in 'Struttura epica dei *Commentarii*'.
59 *Commentaries*, trans. Gragg, 5: 824.
60 Gabel, in *Commentaries*, trans. Gragg, 5: xxxi.
61 Ibid., 4: 525, 542; Gabel calls the whole event 'too calculated'. Ibid., 5: xxix.
62 *Opera omnia*, p. 922; see also *Commentaries*, trans. Gragg, 4: 517–18.
63 Von Martels, ' "More Matter and Less Art" ', pp. 226–7; Simonetta, 'Pius II and Francesco Sforza,' pp. 169–70.
64 Setton believes Pius's crusade was driven more by religion than by politics or humanism. See *Papacy and the Levant*, p. 270.

4 The German *Reichstage* and the Crusade

1 See C. Göllner, *Turcica*, vols 1–2, *Die europäischen Türkendrucke des 16. Jahrhunderts*, vol. 3, *Die Türkenfrage in der öffentlichen Meinung Europas im 16. Jahrhundert* (Bucharest, 1961–78); K. Setton, *The Papacy and the Levant (1204–1571)*, 2 (Philadelphia, 1978); N. Housley, *The Later Crusades, 1274–1580. From Lyons to Alcazar* (Oxford, 1992). For recent German publications, see F. R. Erkens, ed., *Europa und die osmanische Expansion im*

ausgehenden Mittelalter (Berlin, 1997); B. Guthmüller and W. Kühlmann, eds, *Europa und die Türken in der Renaissance* (Tübingen, 2000). See also below, note 21. I would like to thank Harald Müller (Berlin) for his assistance in preparing this text.

2   Generally see J. Helmrath, 'Parlamentsrede. Mittelalter', in *Historisches Wörterbuch der Rhetorik*, ed. K. Ueding, vol. 6 (Tübingen, 2003), cols 589–97. See also J. Helmrath, 'Rhetorik und "Akademisierung" auf den deutschen Reichstagen im 15. und 16. Jahrhundert', in *Soziale Kommunikation im Spannungsfeld von Recht und Ritual*, ed. H. Duchhardt and G. Melville (Cologne, 1997), pp. 423–46; id., 'Reden auf Reichsversammlungen im 15. und 16. Jahrhunderts', in *Licet preter solitum. Ludwig Falkenstein zum 65. Geburtstag*, ed. L. Kéry, D. Lohrmann and H. Müller (Aachen, 1998), pp. 266–86; id., 'Pius II. und die Türken', in *Europa und die Türken in der Renaissance*, pp. 79–137. Reference should also be made to my Cologne *Habilitationsschrift* (1994): *Die Reichstagsreden des Enea Silvio Piccolomini 1454/55. Studien zu Reichstag und Rhetorik* (forthcoming). An edition of the *Reichstage* orations of Aeneas Silvius Piccolomini in 1454–5 will appear in *Deutsche Reichstagsakten* 19.2 (ed. J. Helmrath) and 19.3 (ed. G. Annas).

3   H. Lausberg, *Handbuch der literarischen Rhetorik. Eine Grundlegung der Literaturwissenschaft* (Stuttgart, 3rd edn 1990), paras 224–38; H.-J. Schild, 'Beratungsrede', in *Historisches Wörterbuch der Rhetorik* 1 (Tübingen, 1992), cols 1441–54 (literature); S. Matuschek, 'Epideiktische Beredsamkeit', ibid., 2 (1994), cols 1258–67; 'Gerichtsrede', ibid., 4 (1996), cols 770–815; H. F. Plett, *Systematische Rhetorik* (Munich, 2000).

4   For a survey of the occasions, kinds and functions of oratory, see D. Mertens, 'Rede als institutionalisierte Kommunikation im Zeitalter des Humanismus', in *Soziale Kommunikation*, pp. 401–21. To date no systematic analysis exists of the collections of humanistic orations, which contain numerous orations against the Turks, though a start was made by P. O. Kristeller *Iter Italicum*, vols 1–6 (Leiden, 1964–92). Fundamental on the *genus demonstrativum* are J. O'Malley, *Praise and Blame in Renaissance Rome. Rhetoric, Doctrine, and Reform in the Sacred Orators of the papal Court, c. 1450–1521* (Durham, NC, 1979), pp. 232–5; J. M. McManamon, *Funeral Oratory and the Cultural Ideals of Italian Humanism* (Chapel Hill, NC, 1989), pp. 106–7, 342; G. J. Schenk, *Zeremoniell und Politik. Herrschereinzüge im spätmittelalterlichen Reich* (Cologne, 2003), pp. 403–48. See also Lausberg, *Handbuch*, paras 239–54.

5   P. Moraw, 'Versuch über die Entstehung des Reichstags', in *Politische Ordnungen und soziale Kräfte im Alten Reich*, ed. H. Weber (Wiesbaden, 1980), pp. 1–36, repr. in Moraw, *Über König und Reich. Aufsätze zur deutschen Verfassungsgeschichte des späten Mittelalters*, ed. R. C. Schwinges (Sigmaringen, 1995), pp. 207–42. See also H. Angermeier, 'Reichstagsakten', in *Handwörterbuch zur deutschen Rechtsgeschichte* 4 (Berlin, 1990), cols 794–7; J. Helmrath, 'Reichstagsakten', in *Lexikon des Mittelalters* 7 (Munich, 1996), cols 643–5; H. Müller, 'Die Reichstagsakten (Ältere Reihe) und ihre Bedeutung für die europäische Geschichte', in *Fortschritte in der Geschichtswissenschaft durch Reichstagsaktenforschung*, ed. H. Angermeier and E. Meuthen (Göttingen, 1988), pp. 17–46. Most recently on this issue see P. Moraw, ed., *Deutscher Königshof, Hoftag und Reichstag im späteren Mittelalter* (Stuttgart, 2002).

6   Helmrath, 'Parlamentsrede', with literature. Most recently, see P. Mack, *Elizabethan Rhetoric. Theory and Practice* (Cambridge, 2002), pp. 215–51 on 'parliamentary oratory'.

7   For research into estates, reference can here be made only to A. Marongiu, *Medieval Parliaments, a Comparative Study* (London, 1968); J. B. Henneman, 'Representative Assemblies and the Historian', *Legislative Studies Quarterly* 7 (1982), pp. 161–76; P. Moraw, 'Zu Stand und Perspektiven der ständischen Vertretungen im spätmittelalterlichen Reich', in *Die Anfänge der ständischen Vertretungen in Preußen und seinen Nachbarländern*, ed. H. Boockmann (Munich, 1992), pp. 1–33, repr. in Moraw, *Über König und Reich*, pp. 243–76; W. Eberhard, 'Herrscher und Stände', in *Pipers Handbuch der politischen Ideen*, 1 (Munich, 1993), pp. 467–542; J. Rogister, 'Some New Directions in the Historiography of State Assemblies and Parliaments in Early and Late Modern Europe', *Parliaments, Estates & Representation* 16 (1996), 1–16.

8   T. N. Bisson, 'Celebration and Persuasion: Reflections on the Cultural Evolution of a Medieval Consultation', *Legislative Studies Quarterly* 7 (1982), 181–209.

9   For the early and central Middle Ages see G. Althoff, 'Colloquium familiare – colloquium secretum - colloquium publicum. Beratung im politischen Leben des früheren Mittelalters', *Frühmittelalterliche Studien* 24 (1990), 145–67, repr. in id., *Spielregeln der Politik im Mittelalter. Kommunikation in Frieden und Fehde* (Darmstadt, 1997), pp. 157–84; T. Haye, *Oratio. Mittelalterliche Redekunst in lateinischer Sprache* (Leiden, 1999), with editions. Amidst the swelling volume of literature for the later period see J. J. Berns and T. Rahn, eds, *Zeremoniell als höfische Ästhetik in Spätmittelalter und Früher Neuzeit* (Tübingen, 1995), esp. G. Braungart, 'Die höfische Rede im zeremoniellen Ablauf: Fremdkörper oder Kern?', pp. 198–208; W. Paravicini, ed., *Zeremoniell und Raum* (Sigmaringen, 1997); B. Stollberg-Rilinger, 'Zeremoniell, Ritual, Symbol. Neue Forschungen zur symbolischen Kommunikation in Spätmittelalter und Früher Neuzeit', *Zeitschrift für Historische Forschung* 27 (2000), 384–413.

10 S. Hanley, *The 'Lit de Justice' of the Kings of France. Constitutional Ideology in Legend, Ritual, and Discourse* (London, 1983), pp. 53–5; E. A. R. Brown and R. C. Famiglietti, *The Lit de Justice: Semantics, Ceremonial, and the Parlement of Paris 1300–1600* (Sigmaringen, 1994), pp. 50–1, 64–7, 97. Cf. for the unusual oratory by rulers at the Aragonese *Cortes* M. D. Johnston, 'Parliamentary Oratory in Medieval Aragon', *Rhetorica* 10.2 (1992), 99–117; S. E. Cawsey, *Kingship and Propaganda. Royal Eloquence and the Crown of Aragon, c. 1200–1450* (Oxford, 2002).

11 F. H. Schubert, *Die deutschen Reichstage in der Staatslehre der frühen Neuzeit* (Göttingen, 1966); D. Mertens, 'Europäischer Friede und Türkenkrieg im Spätmittelalter', in *Zwischenstaatliche Friedenswahrung in Mittelalter und Früher Neuzeit*, ed. H. Duchhardt (Cologne, 1991), pp. 45–90, esp. pp. 46–55, 72–6; id., ' "Europa, id est patria, domus propria, sedes nostra ... " Zu Funktionen und Überlieferung lateinischer Türkenreden im 15. Jahrhundert', in *Europa und die osmanische Expansion im ausgehenden Mittelalter*, pp. 39–58.

12 Aeneas Silvius Piccolomini, 'De dieta Ratisponensi', in the form of a letter to Cardinal Carvajal: R. Wolkan, ed., *Der Briefwechsel des Eneas Silvius Piccolomini*, 3.1, Fontes rerum Austriacarum 68 (Vienna, 1918), no. 291, pp. 492–563, as well as numerous sections of RTA 19.1. Riccardo Bartolini,

'De conventu Augustensi descriptio', in E. Böcking, ed., *Ulrichi Hutteni Opera*, 5 (Leipzig, 1861, repr. Aalen, 1963), pp. 264–80. See also Schubert, *Reichstage*, pp. 105–15, 177–9, 619 (under Enea Silvio), pp.193–6, 199–203, 606 (under Bartolini); and below, note 72.

13   H. F. Plett, 'Rhetorik der Renaissance, Renaissance der Rhetorik?', introduction in Plett, ed., *Renaissance-Rhetorik/Renaissance Rhetoric* (Berlin, 1993), pp. 1–20; T. M. Conley, *Rhetoric in the European Tradition* (Chicago, 1990), pp. 109–50, 'Rhetoric and Renaissance Humanism'; B. Vickers, 'Rhetoric and Poetics', in *The Cambridge History of Renaissance Philosophy* (Cambridge, 1988), pp. 715–45; P. Mack, 'Humanist Rhetoric and Dialectic', in *The Cambridge Companion to Renaissance Humanism*, ed. J. Kraye (Cambridge, 1996), pp. 82–99; Q. Skinner, *Reason and Rhetoric in the Philosophy of Hobbes* (Cambridge, 1996), pp. 19–211, on Renaissance rhetoric in England; *Historisches Wörterbuch der Rhetorik*, ed. G. Ueding, vol. 1–(6) (Tübingen, 1992–(2003)); *Encyclopedia of Rhetoric*, vol. 1, ed. T. O. Sloane (Oxford, 2001).

14   G. Braungart, *Hofberedsamkeit. Studien zur Praxis höfisch-politischer Rede im deutschen Territorialabsolutismus* (Tübingen, 1988), p. 151, in the context of courtly requirements.

15   There is no comprehensive study of this topic. See J. G. Russell, 'Language: A Barrier or a Gateway?', in his *Diplomats at Work. Three Renaissance Studies* (Phoenix Mill, 1992), pp. 1–50, with many examples. For the ceremonial literature of the Baroque, see Stollberg-Rilinger, 'Zeremoniell'. G. Mattingly, *Renaissance Diplomacy* (London, 1955) remains indispensable.

16   See A. Dunning, *Die Staatsmotette 1480–1555* (Utrecht, 1970), who takes all the European courts into account. R. Aulinger, *Das Bild des Reichstags im 16. Jahrhundert* (Göttingen, 1980), neglected the role played by orations in ceremonial.

17   *Deutsche Reichstagsakten*, ed. Historische Kommission bei der Bayerischen Akademie der Wissenschaften (Ältere Reihe) vols 1–19.1, 22.1–2 and Index to vol. 22 (Göttingen, 1876–2001) (hereafter RTA). See also Angermeier, 'Reichstagsakten'; Helmrath, 'Reichstagsakten'; Müller, 'Reichstagsakten'.

18   Helmrath, 'Reden auf Reichsversammlungen', pp. 271f.; id., 'Kommunikation auf den spätmittelalterlichen Konzilien', in *Die Bedeutung der Kommunikation für Wirtschaft und Gesellschaft*, ed. H. Pohl (Stuttgart, 1989), pp. 116–72, esp. pp. 143–6, with literature. On the academic tradition of oratory, see J. Miethke, 'Die mittelalterlichen Universitäten und das gesprochene Wort', *Historische Zeitschrift* 251 (1990), 1–44.

19   RTA 15, pp. 640–1, no. 345, Segovia's oration at pp. 648–739, no. 349. Cf. Helmrath, 'Kommunikation', pp. 148–9.

20   RTA 16, pp. 439–538, no. 212. Even if part of the oration as we now have it derives from a later reworking, a recorded delivery time of seven hours (see preceding note) testifies to a good deal of elaboration in the course of the *actio*. Cf. Helmrath, 'Kommunikation', pp. 151–3.

21   See E. Meuthen, 'Der Fall von Konstantinopel und der lateinische Westen', *Historische Zeitschrift* 237 (1983), 1–35, lightly reworked in *Mitteilungen und Forschungsbeiträge der Cusanus-Gesellschaft* 16 (1984), 35–60; H. Müller, *Kreuzzugspläne und Kreuzzugspolitik des Herzogs Philipp des Guten von Burgund* (Göttingen, 1993); Mertens, 'Europäischer Friede', esp. pp. 46–55, 72–6; id., 'Europa'. A fundamental study is J. Hankins, 'Renaissance Crusaders: Humanist

Crusade Literature in the Age of Mehmed II', *Dumbarton Oaks Papers* 49 (1995), 111–207, repr. in id., *Humanism and Platonism in the Italian Renaissance* (Rome, 2003), pp. 293–424, with editions of 12 texts, though omitting the German literature. See also N. Bisaha, ' "New Barbarian" or Worthy Adversary? Humanist Constructs of the Ottoman Turks in Fifteenth-Century Italy', in *Western Views of Islam in Medieval and Early Modern Europe: Perceptions of Other*, ed. D. R. Blanks and M. Frasseto (Basingstoke, 1999), pp. 185–205; S. Hohmann, 'Türkenkrieg und Friedensbund im Spiegel der politischen Lyrik', *Zeitschrift für Literaturwissenschaft und Linguistik* 28 (1998), 128–58; M. Meserve, 'Medieval Sources for Renaissance Theories on the Origins of the Ottoman Turks', in *Europa und die Türken*, pp. 409–37; J. V. Tolan, ed., *Medieval Christian Perceptions of Islam. A Book of Essays* (New York, 1996), with rich bibliography; C. T. Maier, *Crusade Propaganda and Ideology: Model Sermons for the Preaching of the Cross* (Cambridge, 2000).

22 A good example is Flavio Biondo, 'De expeditione in Turchos ad Alphonsum Aragonensem serenissimum regem' (1452), published in B. Nogara, *Scritti inediti e rari di Flavio Biondo* (Rome, 1927), pp. 31–51. For numerous other examples, see Hankins, 'Renaissance Crusaders'.

23 Helmrath, 'Kommunikation', pp. 141–2; id., ' "Non modo Cyceronianus, sed etiam Iheronymianus". Gherardo Landriani, Bischof von Lodi und Como, Humanist und Konzilsvater', in *Vita Religiosa im Mittelalter. Festschrift für Kaspar Elm zum 70. Geburtstag*, ed. F. J. Felten and N. Jaspert (Berlin, 1999), pp. 933–60; id., 'Diffusion des Humanismus und Antikerezeption auf den Konzilien von Konstanz, Basel und Ferrara/Florenz', in *Die Präsenz der Antike in Mittelalter und früher Neuzeit*, ed. K. Grubmüller (forthcoming 2004).

24 On the 'Turkish taxes' (*Türkensteuer*) see S. Wefers, 'Türkensteuer', in *Lexikon des Mittelalters* 8 (Munich, 1997), cols 1108–9; F. Schanze, 'Türkenkriegsanschläge', in *Verfasserlexikon. Die deutsche Literatur des Mittelalters* 9 (Berlin and New York, 1995), cols 1164–7.

25 N. L. Reusner, ed., *Selectissimarum Orationum et Consultationum de bello Turcico vol. primum et secundum, ad reges et principes christianos* (Leipzig, 1595); id., *Selectissimarum Orationum ... vol. tertium, ad reges et principes christianos* (Leipzig, 1595); id., *Selectissimarum Orationum ... vol. tertii pars altera ad Sigismundum III regem Poloniae et Sueciae* (Leipzig, 1595); id., *Selectissimarum Orationum ... de bello Turcico variorum et diversorum auctorum vol. quartum bipartitum ... Altera consilia sive discursus Quomodo bellum Turcicum sit administrandum complectitur* (Leipzig, n.d.). These are supplemented by the collections of letters, N. L. Reusner and Nicolaus Leorinus, eds, *Epistolarum Turcicarum variorum et diversorum Authorum libri V, in quibus epistolae de rebus Turcicis summorum pontificum, imperatorum, Regum, Principum, aliorumque mundi procerum, iam inde a primordio regni Saraceni et Turcici usque ad haec nostra tempora leguntur* (Frankfurt, 1598); Reusner and Leorinus, eds, *Epistolarum Turcicarum ... rebus Turcicis a Baiazete I. usque ad haec nostra fere tempora exaratae: ex ipsis originalibus scriptis et actis fideliter in hunc ordinem translata ...* (Frankfurt, 1599).

26 Mertens, 'Europa', p. 49.

27 J. Helmrath, ' "Aeneae vestigia imitari". Enea Silvio Piccolomini als "Apostel des Humanismus". Formen und Wege seiner Diffusion', in *Diffusion des Humanismus. Studien zur nationalen Geschichtsschreibung europäischer*

Humanisten, ed. J. Helmrath, U. Muhlack and G. Walther (Göttingen, 2002), pp. 99–142. For the personnel and structure of the imperial court and chancery, see P.-J. Heinig, *Kaiser Friedrich III. (1440–1493). Hof, Regierung und Politik*, vols 1–3 (Cologne, 1997), esp. pp. 296–9, 527–33, 737–40, 1739 for Piccolomini. For Piccolomini see also the essays in this volume by Bisaha and Meserve.

28 On the *Türkenreichstage* see G. Voigt, *Enea Silvio de' Piccolomini als Papst Pius der Zweite und sein Zeitalter*, 2 (Berlin, 1862, repr. 1967), pp. 100–48; Müller, 'Reichstagsakten', pp. 32–9; id., *Kreuzzugspläne*, pp. 64–80 (literature); Helmrath, *Reichstagsreden*, pp. 163–310; id., 'Reden auf Reichsversammlungen', pp. 272–7.

29 RTA 19.1, no. 34.1, pp. 265–70; extracts in A. Pertusi, ed., *Testi inediti e poco noti sulla caduta di Costantinopoli*, edizione postuma a cura di A. Carile (Bologna, 1983) pp. 181–7, no. 20. I do not share Pertusi's opinion that this was 'forse la piu interessante' (sc. of all Piccolomini's orations against the Turks). Its significance for what followed was first recognized by Mertens, 'Europa', pp. 49–51.

30 Castiglione's life has received scant attention. See F. Petrucci, 'Castiglioni, Giovanni', in *Dizionario biografico degli Italiani* 22 (Rome, 1979), cols 156–8; B. Katterbach, *Referendarii utriusque signaturae a Martino V ad Clementem XIII* ... (Vatican City, 1931), p. 23, no. 5, p. 28, no. 12; A. A. Strand, 'Francesco Todeschini-Piccolomini. Politik und Mäzenatentum im Quattrocento', *Römische Historische Mitteilungen* 8/9 (1964–6), 101–425, esp. pp. 136–7, 193 note 157; M. Ansani, 'La provvista dei benefici (1450–1466). Strumenti e limiti dell'intervento ducale', in *Gli Sforza, la Chiesa lombarda, la corte di Roma*, ed. G. Chittolini (Naples, 1989), pp. 1–114, esp. pp. 11–14, 369; H. Wolff, 'Päpstliche Legaten auf Reichstagen des 15. Jahrhunderts', in *Reichstage und Kirche. Kolloquium der Historischen Kommission bei der Bayerischen Akademie der Wissenschaften 1990*, ed. E. Meuthen (Göttingen, 1991), pp. 25–40, esp. pp. 28, 35.

31 For Vitéz see [J. P. Kraljic], 'János Vitéz (1408?–1472)', *American Cusanus Society Newsletter* 8.1 (1991), 22–6 (literature); RTA 19.1, pp. 556–8; I. Boronkai, *Die literarische Tätigkeit von Johannes Vitéz* (Munich, 1979), pp. 136–48; *Iohannes Vitéz de Zredna opera quae supersunt*, ed. I. Boronkai (Budapest, 1980), pp. 11–16; *Matthias Corvinus und die Renaissance in Ungarn 1458 bis 1541. Ausstellungskatalog* (Vienna, 1982), pp. 138–54, nos 11–30; K. Csapodi-Gárdonyi, *Die Bibliothek des Johannes Vitéz* (Budapest, 1984).

32 For Capistrano at Frankfurt and Wiener Neustadt, see J. Hofer, *Johannes Kapistran. Ein Leben im Kampf um die Reform der Kirche*, revd edn ed. O. Bonmann, 2 (Rome, 1965), pp. 307–11, 324–33; K. Elm, 'Johannes Capistrans Predigtreise diesseits der Alpen (1451–1456)', in *Lebenslehren und Weltentwürfe im Übergang vom Mittelalter zur Neuzeit*, ed. H. Boockmann, B. Moeller and K. Stackmann (Göttingen, 1989), pp. 500–19, esp. p. 513; Mertens, 'Europa', p. 55; RTA 19.2 (forthcoming), provisionally no. 66. It seems that Capistrano's Frankfurt sermons have not survived.

33 *Quellen zur Frankfurter Geschichte* 1, ed. H. Grotefend (Frankfurt, 1884), pp. 59, 101, 159, 191–2. Most recently P. Monnet, *Les Rohrbach de Francfort. Pouvoirs, affaires et parenté à l'aube de la renaissance allemande* (Paris, 1997), pp. 101–2, 322–4, 370, 400.

34 The orations have been published for the first time in RTA 19.1, pp. 49–55, no. 92, pp. 77–80, no. 13a.2, pp. 82–6, no. 13a.5, pp. 270–5, no. 34.2.

35 Castiglione's Frankfurt oration survives in two manuscripts at Salamanca and Lambach. a) Salamanca Bibl. universitaria, Cod. 19, fols 154r–157v. The manuscript is contemporary and derives from the estate of the Basel conciliar theologian and cardinal of Felix V, John of Segovia; in part the *tituli* are in Segovia's own hand. On the handwriting, see Nicolai de Cusa, *De pace fidei cum epistula ad Ioannem de Segobia*, ed. R. Klibansky (Leipzig, 2nd edn 1970), pp. XXIIf., 91–102: a letter from Nicholas of Cusa to Segovia dated 18 December 1454; F. Marcos Rodríguez, 'Los manuscritos pretridentinos hispanos de ciencias sagradas en la Biblioteca Universitaria de Salamanca', in *Repertorio de las ciencias eclesiásticas en España*, 2 (Salamanca, 1971), pp. 289–90; B. Hernandez-Montes, *Biblioteca de Juan de Segovia. Edición y comentário de su escritura de donación* (Madrid, 1984), pp. 93–4, with commentary at pp. 195–201. b) Lambach Stiftsbibliothek, Cod. 221, fols 183r–188v (ch. 193 fol. 4°, 15th. c) This oration will be published in RTA 19.2, provisionally no. 67.2. His oration at Wiener Neustadt, *Supervacuum puto* of 22 March 1455, will be published in RTA 19.3. It was transmitted in six manuscripts: Basel Universitätsbibliothek, 581 no. 5, fols 41v–54v; Breslau Bibliothek des Ossolineums/Zaklad Narod. im. Ossolinskych, 601 fols 343r– 358v; Cambridge University Library, H h I 7, fols 3r–30r; Munich Staatsbibliothek, Clm 4016, fols 70r–75r; Solothurn Zentralbibliothek, Cod. S I 177, fols 182r–198r; Stuttgart Landesbibliothek, Q 171 Theol. et Philos., fols 98r–120v. To date Piccolomini's two great orations at Wiener Neustadt can most easily be found in *Pii II P. M. olim Aenae Sylvii Piccolominei Senensis orationes politicae et ecclesiasticae*, 1, ed. I. D. Mansi (Lucca, 1755), pp. 288–314 (*In hoc florentissimo* and its revision), pp. 316–28 (*Si mihi*).

36 For Vitéz's orations, composed in a highly elevated humanistic style, and replies, see Boronkai, *Vitéz opera*, pp. 252–82, nos 7–11.

37 Forthcoming in RTA 19.3. For the moment see Helmrath, *Reichstagsreden*, pp. 275–81, 289–304, 426–64, 491–501.

38 There are more than 15 printings, the best being *Pii ... orationes* 1, ed. Mansi, cols 263–73. For analysis of the manuscript and printing traditions, interpretation and a commented edition, see Helmrath, *Reichstagsreden*, pp. 180–289, 350–411, with full details forthcoming in RTA 19.2, provisionally no. 67.1. On the oration see above all J. Blusch, 'Enea Silvio Piccolomini und Giannantonio Campano. Die unterschiedlichen Darstellungsprinzipien in ihren Türkenreden', *Humanistica Lovaniensia* 28/29 (1979–80), 78–138; Helmrath, *Reichstagsreden*, pp. 177–273; id., 'Pius II. und die Türken', pp. 93–4, 104–17; Hankins, 'Renaissance Crusaders', pp. 111–46 passim.

39 This feature has attracted much attention in the recent literature: see above all Mertens, 'Europäischer Friede', pp. 48–54; id., 'Europa', pp. 54–5. More broadly, see W. Schulze, 'Europa in der Frühen Neuzeit – Begriffsgeschichtliche Befunde', in *Europäische Geschichte als historiographisches Problem*, ed. H. Duchhardt and A. Kunz (Wiesbaden, 1997), pp. 35–65, with treatment of Piccolomini's Frankfurt oration at pp. 44–5.

40 Piccolomini to Cardinal Carvajal, 16 October: 'Heri cepimus rem defensionis fidei agitare. ego nomine caesaris orationem habui quasi ad horas duas. an placuerit, nescio. multi, ut puto per adulationem, eam petunt. fui tamen

auditus screante nemine. sunt qui dicant illam profuisse. quod si verum erit, deo agam gratias et semper ago, qui me dignatur in rebus uti magnis. puto tamen, etiamsi Cicero aut Demostenes hanc causam agerent, dura haec pectora movere non possent'. See J. Cugnoni, ed., *Aeneae Silvii Piccolominei Senensis … Opera inedita descripsit ex Codicibus Chisianis vulgavit notisque illustravit* (Rome, 1882–3, repr. Farnborough, 1968), pp. 319–686, also printed separately with different pagination 1–367, here p. 419 (103). Contrast the *Commentarii*: 'Oravit ille duabus ferme horis, ita intentis animis auditus, ut nemo unquam screaverit, nemo ab orantis vultu oculos averterit, nemo non brevem eius orationem existimaverit, nemo finem non invitus acceperit … Orationem Enee ab omnibus laudatam multi transcripsere et secundum eam Ratisponense decretum de bello gerendo innovatum est, et Hungaris auxilium promissum equitum decem milium, peditum triginta duorum militum'. See A. van Heck, ed., *Pii II Commentarii rerum memorabilium que temporibus suis contiguerunt*, 1 (Vatican City, 1984), c. 27, pp. 83–4.

41 This was the characterization of J.-D. Müller, *Gedechtnus. Literatur und Hofgesellschaft um Maximilian I.* (Munich, 1982), p. 296 note 11.

42 *Pii II Orationes* 1, ed. Mansi, p. 268.

43 Thus H. U. Gumbrecht in a stimulating model for assessing the varied receptions that could be accorded to texts, *Funktionen parlamentarischer Rhetorik in der französischen Revolution. Vorstudien zur Entwicklung einer historischen Textpragmatik* (Munich, 1978), esp. pp. 5–24, with quote at p. 15.

44 Forthcoming in RTA 19.2, provisionally no. 71. For the reception of medieval crusade traditions by humanists, see Hankins, 'Renaissance Crusaders'; D. Mertens, ' "Claromontani passagii exemplum." Papst Urban II. und der erste Kreuzzug in der Türkenkriegspropaganda des Renaissance-Humanismus', in *Europa und die Türken*, pp. 65–78.

45 *Commentarii*, 1, ed. van Heck, c. 27, p. 84.

46 On the day following the *actio*, 16 October 1454, in a letter to Cardinal Juan de Carvajal ('faciam orationis mee quamvis inepte copiam'), and on 31 October, shortly before his departure from Frankfurt, to his friend Goro Lolli ('orationis mee, cum fuero in Novacivitate, copiam tibi faciam'): see J. Cugnoni, ed., *Aeneae Silvii Piccolominei Senensis … Opera inedita*, pp. 419 (103), 427 (111); forthcoming in RTA 19.2, provisionally nos 64.1 [2] and 64.2 [6]. A third such letter possibly went to Nicholas of Cusa, which would explain the transmission of the *Clades* oration in the Salamanca MS: see note 35 above.

47 The transmission received a major impetus from its inclusion in a printed edition of his *epistulae* in 1478 (Stuttgart, Michael Greuff) which reached at least ten imprints: see K. Häbler, 'Die Drucke der Briefsammlungen des Aeneas Silvius', *Gutenberg-Jahrbuch* 14 (1939), 138–52; Helmrath, *Reichstagsreden*, esp. pp. 177–99; forthcoming in RTA 19.2, provisionally no. 68.1.

48 For the manuscript transmission of Piccolomini's *Opera*, including the orations, see Helmrath, *Reichstagsreden*; P. J. Weinig, *Aeneam suscipite, Pium recipite: Aeneas Silvius Piccolomini. Studien zur Rezeption eines humanistischen Schriftstellers im Deutschland des 15. Jahrhunderts* (Wiesbaden, 1998); T. J. Mauro, *Praeceptor Austriae. Aeneas Sylvius Piccolomini (Pius II) and the Transalpine Diffusion of Italian Humanism before Erasmus*, 2 vols, University of

Chicago dissertation (Chicago, 2003). On Brant see also W. Ludwig, 'Eine unbekannte Variante der *Varia Carmina* Sebastian Brants und die Prophezeiungen des Pseudo-Methodius. Ein Beitrag zur Türkenkriegspropaganda um 1500', *Daphnis* 26 (1997), 263–99.

49 RTA 10, pp. 526–32, no. 326; RTA 15, pp. 630–4, no. 340; RTA 16, pp. 130–6, no. 80, pp. 544–7, no. 214. See additionally the replies given at audiences at the royal court at Vienna: RTA 13, pp. 107–9, no. 44; A. Lhotsky, 'Zur Königswahl des Jahres 1440. Ein Nachtrag zu den Reichstagsakten', *Deutsches Archiv für Erforschung des Mittelalters* 15 (1959), 163–76.

50 We have the text for orations that he gave at Nürnberg in 1444 and Regensburg in 1454: RTA 17, pp. 342–51, no. 166; RTA 19.1, pp. 291–3, no. 37.1b and no. 37.3 (French and German text, though only paraphrased). For Fillastre's oratory, see the monumental biography by M. Prietzel, *Guillaume Fillastre der Jüngere (1404/07–1473). Kirchenfürst und herzoglich-burgundischer Rat* (Stuttgart, 2001), pp. 407–16, esp. 512–19 for a list of all 40 documented orations, the orations at the *Reichstage* being nos 1 (1444), 9, 11–13 (1454/55); also M. Prietzel, ed., *Guillaume Fillastre d. J. Ausgewählte Werke* (Ostfildern, 2003), pp. 9–42, with studies on the transmission (pp. 71–84) and an edition with commentary of five later orations of 1459–65 (pp. 111–253).

51 For an exemplary study, see C. Reinle, *Ulrich Riederer (ca. 1406–1462). Gelehrter Rat im Dienste Kaiser Friedrichs III.* (Mannheim, 1993). On Hans Pirckheimer, see now the unpublished Mannheim *Habilitationsschrift* of F. Fuchs, *Hans Pirckheimer am Hofe Friedrichs III. (1458–59)* (Mannheim, 1993). On Hinderbach's orations against the Turks and their themes, see now D. Rando, 'Fra Vienna e Roma. Johannes Hinderbach testimone della guerra turca', in *RR. Roma e Rinascimento. Bibliografia e note 1997* (Rome, 1998), pp. 293–317; id., *Dai margini la memoria. Johannes Hinderbach (1418–1486)* (Bologna, 2003), pp. 430–57, esp. 431–4.

52 The oratory at Mantua has attracted little attention, but on the congress generally see J. G. Russell 'The Humanists Converge: The Congress of Mantua (1459)', in his *Diplomats at Work*, pp. 51–93, and the collection of essays by A. Calzona et al., eds, *Il sogno di Pio II e il viaggio da Roma a Mantova* (Florence, 2003), including, on the crusade oration, S. Dall' Oco, ' "Mantuam ivimus … non audiverunt christiani vocem pastoris": Fede, politica e retorica nelle "orazioni" e nelle "reazioni" mantovane', pp. 503–16.

53 Cugnoni, ed., *Aeneae Silvii Piccolominei Senensis … Opera inedita*, pp. 905–14, no. 397; Reusner, *Orationes de bello Turcico*, 1, pp. 20–40; Mansi, *Orationes*, 2, pp. 9–29, no. 2; I. D. Mansi, ed., *Sacrorum conciliorum amplissima collectio* 32 (repr. Paris, 1901), cols 207E–221A. *Cum bellum* calls for close analysis. On the basis of its structure John O'Malley established its adherence to the *genus deliberativum*, noting that it was 'an indisputable example of a classical *genus* self-consciously used by a pope': *Praise and Blame*, p. 81.

54 For Reusner see above, note 25. See K. de Lettenhove, ed., *Chronique d'Adrien de But [1488], complété par les additions du meme auteur* (Brussels, 1870), pp. 367–94 (oration *Responsuri* to the French embassy at Mantua, December 1459), pp. 398–414 (*Cum bellum hodie*), pp. 414–19 (bull *Vocavit nos pius*). Cf. Häbler, 'Die Drucke', passim.

55 Figures in parentheses refer to the edition in Mansi, ed., *Sacrorum conciliorum collectio* 32, cols 207E–221A.

56 Ed. G. C. Zimolo, in *Rerum Italicarum Scriptores*, 23 pt 5 (Bologna, 1950), pp. 91–6. On Crivelli see F. Petrucci, 'Crivelli, Lodrisio', in *Dizionario Biografico degli Italiani* 31 (1985), cols 146–52. On his poetry, see R. Bianchi, *Intorno a Pio II: Un mercante e tre poeti* (Messina, 1988), pp. 161–93; P. Garbini, ed., 'Poeti e astrologi tra Callisto III e Pio II: un nuovo carmine di Lodrisio Crivelli', in *Studi umanistici* 2 (1991), 151–70.

57 For a critical edition, with the text of a French translation by the Burgundian bishop and chancellor Guillaume Fillastre, see Prietzel, ed., *Werke Fillastre*, pp. 158–208; on the transmission of the translation, ibid., pp. 81–2. For some older versions, see Cugnoni, ed., *Aeneae Silvii Piccolominei Senensis … Opera inedita*, pp. 914–23, no. 419; Reusner, *Orationes de bello Turcico*, 1, pp. 40–59; A. Theiner, ed., *Baronius-Theiner, Caesaris S. R. E. Card. Baronii Od. Raynaldi et Jac. Laderchii Annales Ecclesiastici denuo excudi et ad nostra usque tempora perducti, vol. 29: 1454–1480* (Bar-le-Duc, 1876), pp. 356–61; A. Vigna, ed., 'Codice diplomatico delle Colonie Tauro-Liguri, 2.1: 1435–1475', in *Atti della Società Ligure di storia patria* 7 (1869), pp. 189–204. See also Setton, *The Papacy and the Levant*, 2, p. 261.

58 See now RTA 22.2, ed. H. Wolff (Göttingen, 2000), *Register* by G. Annas and H. Wolff (Göttingen, 2001). On Bessarion and the MS tradition of his orations against the Turks see J. Monfasani, 'Bessarion latinus', *Rinascimento* 2nd ser. 21–22 (1981–82), 165–209, esp. pp. 183–96, 201–7. See also Hankins, 'Renaissance Crusaders', pp. 116–17, 120–1.

59 See the important study by Blusch, 'Enea Silvio und Campano'. Why Campano did not speak, or was not allowed to speak, remains unclear. The oration was hailed, when it eventually appeared in print (Rome 1487? and 1495) as a written work of art, and was adopted as a model by German humanists, striking indications of how influential such orations could become.

60 See the survey by Helmrath, 'Reden auf Reichsversammlungen', pp. 278–81.

61 On the Worms *Reichstag* of 1495, see, in addition to H. Wiesflecker, *Maximilian I.*, vol. 2 (Munich, 1975), pp. 217–49, the Exhibition Catalogue *1495 – Kaiser, Reich, Reformen. Der Reichstag zu Worms* (Koblenz, 1995), with literature. Also C. Goebel, *Der Reichstag von Worms 1495. Zwischen Wandel und Beharrung. Eine verfassungs- und institutionengeschichtliche Ortsbestimmung*, Phil. Diss. (Gießen, 1992, available only as fiche), esp. pp. 335–66: 'Der Wormser Tag als kommunikatives Ereignis'. Goebel wrote this under Peter Moraw's supervision on the basis of the material in RTA m. R. 5.

62 RTA m. R. 5, p. 1741, no. 1812 (a comprehensive Venetian report).

63 Ibid., p. 921, no. 1172. See also *1495: Württemberg wird Herzogtum. Begleitbuch zur Ausstellung des Hauptstaatsarchivs Stuttgart* (Stuttgart, 1995), with edition, esp. p. 86; D. Mertens, 'Eberhard im Bart und der Humanismus', in *Eberhard und Mechthild. Untersuchungen zu Politik und Kultur im ausgehenden Mittelalter*, ed. H.-M. Maurere (Stuttgart, 1994), pp. 35–81.

64 Particularly Goebel, *Der Reichstag von Worms 1495*.

65 See now RTA 22.2.

66 See Moraw, 'Versuch über die Entstehung des Reichstags'.

67 H. Neuhaus, 'Wandlungen der Reichstags-Organisation in der ersten Hälfte des 16. Jahrhunderts', in *Neue Studien zur frühneuzeitlichen Reichsgeschichte*, ed. J. Kunisch (Berlin, 1987), pp. 113–40; H. Neuhaus, *Das Reich in der frühen*

Neuzeit (Munich, 1997), pp. 3–43, 64–77; W. Schulze, 'Der deutsche Reichstag des 16. Jahrhunderts zwischen traditioneller Konsensbildung und Paritätisierung der Reichspolitik', in *Im Spannungsfeld von Recht und Ritual*, pp. 447–61. On procedure at the *Reichstage* in the sixteenth century, see the concise account by P. Moraw, 'Hoftag und Reichstag von den Anfängen der deutschen Geschichte bis 1806', in *Parlamentsrecht und Parlamentspraxis der Bundesrepublik Deutschland. Ein Handbuch*, ed. H.-P. Schneider and W. Zeh (Berlin, 1989), para. 1, pp. 32–3.

68 A similar oration was given at Ensisheim. See D. Mertens, 'Maximilian I. und das Elsaß', in *Die Humanisten in ihrer politischen und sozialen Umwelt*, ed. O. Herding and R. Stupperich (Weinheim, 1976), pp. 177–201, esp. pp. 183–4; Mertens, 'Rede als Kommunikation', p. 418 (with literature).

69 An opposing position was taken by H. Wiesflecker, *Kaiser Maximilian I.*, vol. 3 (Munich, 1977), pp. 359–63, 564–5 note 47 (supported by the transmission of the oration in Georg Spalatin, *Historischer Nachlaß und Briefe* 1, ed. C. G. Neudecker and L. Preller (Jena, 1851), pp. 204ff.: 'Gewiss ist die Rede bei Guicciardini entstellt, aber sie wurde doch gehalten'. On Maximilian's oratory, see P. Diederich, *Kaiser Maximilian I. als politischer Publizist*, Phil. Diss. Jena, 1933 (Heidelberg, 1933), who considered the Constance oration to be a form of memorial (pp. 16, 49–50 and elsewhere), and see ibid., pp. 103ff., for a list of orations, mandates and pamphlets; H. Fichtenau, 'Maximilian I. und die Sprache', in *Beiträge zur neueren Geschichte Österreichs*, ed. H. Fichtenau and E. Zöllner (Cologne, 1974), pp. 32–46, esp. pp. 35–8; H. Wiesflecker, 'Die diplomatischen Missionen des venezianischen Gesandten Zaccaria Contarini an den Hof Maximilians I.', *Römische Historische Mitteilungen* 31 (1989), 155–79, esp. pp. 177–8.

70 Schubert, *Reichstage*, pp. 174–212; Mertens, 'Europäischer Friede', pp. 84–7 (quote); also Müller, *Gedechtnus*, pp. 48–79 (quote on p. 48), 251–80. I have not seen F. Römer and E. Klecker, 'Poetische Habsburg-Panegyrik in lateinischer Sprache. Bestände der Österreichischen Nationalbibliothek', *Biblos* 43 (1994), 183–98.

71 This began in 1442 with the coronation of Piccolomini during the Frankfurt *Reichstag*. On the subject generally, see A. Schmid, 'Poeta et orator a Caesare Laureatus. Die Dichterkrönungen Maximilians I.', *Historisches Jahrbuch* 109 (1989), 56–108, and the groundbreaking article by D. Mertens, 'Zur Sozialgeschichte und Funktion des poeta laureatus im Zeitalter Maximilians I.', in *Gelehrte im Reich. Zur Sozial-und Wirkungsgeschichte akademischer Eliten im Reich des 14. bis 16. Jahrhunderts*, ed. R. C. Schwinges (Berlin, 1996), pp. 327–48.

72 Augsburg, August 1518: 'Cum sacratissimum conspectum tuum', ed. Reusner, *Orationes de bello turcico*, 1, pp. 86–107. Details in A. Lhotsky, *Quellenkunde zur mittelalterlichen Geschichte Österreichs* (Graz, 1963), pp. 461–2; Schubert, *Reichstage*, pp. 193–9 (important for its description of the Augsburg *Reichstag*). On Bartolini, see F. H. Schubert, 'Riccardo Bartolini', *Zeitschrift für Bayerische Landesgeschichte* 19 (1956), pp. 95–127; Müller, *Gedechtnus*, p. 413; S. Füssel, *Riccardus Bartolinus Perusinus. Humanistische Panegyrik am Hofe Kaiser Maximilians I.* (Baden-Baden, 1987), esp. pp. 44–9 (with an important bibliography of Bartolini's writings at pp. 316–37); D. Mertens, ' "Bebelius ... patriam Sueviam ... restituit." Der poeta laureatus

zwischen Reich und Territorium', *Zeitschrift für Württembergische Landesgeschichte* 42 (1983), 145–73, at pp. 159–65; Schmid, 'Dichterkrönungen Maximilians', pp. 103–4, no. 24; Mertens, 'Zur Sozialgeschichte und Funktion des poeta laureatus', pp. 333–5, 341.

73   Müller, *Gedechtnus*, passim. For the *Descriptio* see notes 12 and 72.

74   Worms, 3 April 1521: 'Quod omnium votis', ed. Augsburg (Silvan Otmar) 1521; ed. Reusner, *Orationes de bello Turcico*, 1, pp. 94–107; *Hieronymi Balbi veneti, Gurcensis olim episcopi, Opera poetica, oratoria ac politico-moralia*, ed. J. Retzer (Vienna, 1791), pp. 547–61. Referred to in M. Okál, 'Hieronymus Balbus', *Zprávy. Jednoty klasických filologu* 13, 1–3 (1971), 91–117, esp. pp. 103–4; Schubert, *Reichstage*, p. 208 note 43; H. Lutz, *Conrad Peutinger. Beiträge zu einer politischen Biographie* (Augsburg, 1958), pp. 175–6; Rill, *Dizionario Biografico degli Italiani* 5 (1963), p. 372.

75   Augsburg, 5 August 1518: 'Boni adsumus nuntii', ed. E. Böcking, *Ulrichi Hutteni Equitis Germani Opera/Ulrichs von Hutten Schriften*, vol. 5, *Reden und Lehrschriften* (Leipzig, 1861, ND Aalen, 1963), pp. 162–7, no. 3. Mentioned in Bartolini, 'De conventu', pp. 267–8.

76   Nürnberg, 19 November 1522: 'Rede an die deutschen Fürsten', ed. *Oratio habita Nurimbergae in senatu principum Germaniae* [1522] (Nürnberg 1522, Augsburg 1522).

77   Speyer, 13 April 1529: 'Cum intellexisset d.n. conventum mature opus est', ed. RTA j.R. vol. 7.2, pp. 1244–6, appendix 128; vol. 7.1, pp. 726–8 (contemporary echo with paraphrases). Mentioned in J. Kühn, *Geschichte des Speyrer Reichstags* (Leipzig, 1929), pp. 162–3; H. Jedin, *Geschichte des Konzils von Trient* 1 (Freiburg, 1949), p. 201.

78   Schmid, 'Poeta et orator', pp. 59–60, 82. Amongst the active orators the dominance of the Italians is striking; on the other hand, of the 29 *poetae laureati* crowned by Maximilian, just six were Italians: ibid., p. 62.

79   For the printed version, see *Ulrichi Hutteni Opera* 3, ed. Böcking, pp. 167–81. See also Schubert, *Reichstage*, pp. 176, 205–8.

80   Augsburg, 20 June 1530: ed. Reusner, *Orationes de bello Turcico*, 1, pp. 141–54. Mentioned by Schubert, *Reichstage*, p. 208 note 42.

81   Augsburg, 20 June 1530: 'Quod felix, faustum, fortunatumque sit', ed. (respectively in Latin and German versions) Augsburg (Alexander Weissenhorn) 1530 and Nürnberg (Georg Wachter) 1530; ed. Reusner, *Orationes de bello Turcico*, 1, pp. 124–41. See generally, G. Müller, 'Vincenzo Pimpinella am Hofe Ferdinands I. (1529–1532)', in *Quellen und Forschungen aus italienischen Archiven und Bibliotheken* 40 (1960), 65–88.

82   Augsburg, 24 August 1530: Wolfgangus de Frangipani (Bernardin Ozalsjski Frankapan): 'Serenissime ac Sacratissime Caesar ... Placuit illorum opinioni per me licet insufficientem oratorem ipsorum et recommendo tanquam domino gratiosissimo, ed. Oratio ad serenissimum Carolum V. ... Caesarem inclytum: Ac ad illustrissimos et potentissimos Principes Romani Imperii, facta ex parte regnicolarum Croaciae', Augsburg (Alexander Weyssenhorn) 1530 (Facsimile: *Govori Protiv Turaka*, ed. V. Gligo [Split, 1983], pp. 614–19). Mentioned by Schubert, *Reichstage*, p. 207; I. N. Goleniscev-Kutuzov, *Rinascimento italiano e letterature slave dei secoli XV e XVI*, a cura di Sante Graciotti e Jitka Kresálková, vols 1–2 (Milan, 1973), esp. vol. 2, p. 17;

M. B. Petrovic, 'The Croatian Humanists and the Ottoman Peril', *Balkan Studies* 20 (1979), 257–73, at p. 268.

83 Freiburg, 1498: 'Postquam coniunctio sanguinis' (appeal for help against the Turks), ed. M. Freher, *Rerum Germanicarum Scriptores aliquot insignes, hactenus incogniti*, 1 (Frankfurt, 1602), pp. 235–7. See also S. W. Rowan, 'A Reichstag at Freiburg, 1497–1498', in *The Old Reich. Essays on German Political Institutions 1495–1806*, ed. J. A. Vann and S. W. Rowan (Brussels, 1974), pp. 31–57, here p. 53. Augsburg, 20–22 August 1518: 'Venimus a rege nostro', ed. Reusner, *Orationes de bello Turcico*, 1, pp. 65–85. Mentioned by Bartolini, 'De conventu', p. 271, paras 30–9; Schubert, *Reichstage*, pp. 198, 203 note 29; *Maximilian I. Ausstellungskatalog* (Innsbruck, 1969), p. 60, no. 236; Wiesflecker, *Kaiser Maximilian I.*, 4, pp. 389, 395, 618 note 24, 619 note 12.

84 'Consideranti mihi', ed. Augsburg (Johannes Miller) 1521; ed. Böcking, *Ulrichi Hutteni Opera*, 5, pp. 217–27. Mentioned by Göllner, *Turcica*, 1, nos 103–4; Bartolini, 'De conventu', pp. 277–8, paras 73–9; Petrovic, 'The Croatian Humanists', p. 267.

85 1 April 1522, MS Vienna, HHStA, Mainzer Erzkanzler Archiv Reichstagsakten fasc. 4a fols 37a–40a; RTA j.R. 3, pp. 76–7, no. 12 (summary of contents). See also H. Neuhaus, *Reichstag und Supplikationsausschuß* (Berlin, 1977), pp. 128–9.

86 Nürnberg, 19 November 1522: Bernardinus de Frangepanibus (Bernardin Ozalsjskli Frankapan): anti-Turkish oration, appeal for help for Croatia, ed. Nürnberg 1522. Augsburg, 24 August 1530: see above, note 82. Regensburg 1541: Franciscus Frangipani, archbishop of Kolossä: 'Quamvis natura mea semper abhorruit a turbidis consiliis non deficiet laus vestra de ore hominum usque in sempiternum', ed. Augsburg (Heinrich Steiner) 1541; (facsimile, *Govori Protiv Turaka*, ed. Gligo, pp. 623–35). All referred to by Petrovic, 'The Croatian Humanists', p. 268. See also the article 'Gesandte IX: Ungarn', *Lexikon des Mittelalters*, 4 (Munich, 1989), col. 1381.

87 Schubert, *Reichstag*, p. 467, comments on the seventeenth century, ' ... Reden, die allmählich aufhörten'.

88 Ed. Reusner, *Orationes de bello Turcico* 1, pp. 230–65. See Schubert, *Reichstage*, p. 208 note 43.

89 See E. Laubach, 'Habsburgische Reichstagspolitik 1528/29', *Mitteilungen aus dem Österreichischen Staatsarchiv* 40 (1987), 61–91, esp. on the problem of the imperial proposals. On the increasing effectiveness and rationality of diplomatic correspondence, see H. Stratenwerth, 'Aktenkundliche Aspekte der politischen Kommunikation im Regierungssystem Karls V.', in *Karl V. Politik und politisches System*, ed. H. Rabe (Constance, 1996), pp. 41–70.

90 K. Rauch, ed., *Traktat über den Reichstag im 16. Jahrhundert. Eine offiziöse Darstellung aus der kurmainzischen Kanzlei* (Weimar, 1905), pp. 54, 90. For this text see Schubert, *Reichstage*, pp. 224–61; Aulinger, *Bild des Reichstags*, pp. 44–9.

91 For an example, see F. Edelmayer, 'Kursachsen, Hessen und der Nürnberger Reichstag von 1543', in *Reichstage und Kirche*, pp. 190–219, esp. pp. 217–18.

92 H. Duchhardt, *Deutsche Verfassungsgeschichte 1495–1806* (Stuttgart, 1991), p. 94.

5   Burgundy and the Crusade

1   H. Müller, *Kreuzzugspläne und Kreuzzugspolitik des Herzogs Philipp des Guten von Burgund*, Schriftenreihe der historischen Kommission bei der bayerischen Akademie der Wissenschaften 51 (Göttingen, 1993) and J. Paviot, *Les Ducs de Bourgogne, la croisade et l'Orient (fin XIVe siècle-XVe siècle)*, Cultures et civilisations médiévales (Paris, 2003).

2   We may note that Philip the Bold had until then shown a very limited interest in the crusade. For example, he sent only a few men on the 'Barbary crusade' of 1390, which was led by his cousin Louis, duke of Bourbon.

3   For the context, see J. J. N. Palmer, *England, France and Christendom, 1377–99* (London, 1972); C. J. Phillpotts, 'John of Gaunt and English Policy towards France, 1389–1395', *Journal of Medieval History* 16 (1990), 363–86; A. Goodman, *John of Gaunt. The Exercise of Princely Power in Fourteenth-Century Europe* (Harlow, 1992); N. Saul, *Richard II* (New Haven and London, 1997); F. Autrand, 'La paix impossible: les négociations franco-anglaises à la fin du XIVe siècle', in 'Nicopolis, 1396–1996. Actes du Colloque international … Dijon, 18 October 1996', ed. J. Paviot and M. Chauney-Bouillot in *Annales de Bourgogne* 68 (1996), 11–22; Paviot, *Les Ducs de Bourgogne*.

4   H. Kühl, *Leon V. von Kleinarmenien. Ein Leben zwischen Orient und Okzident im Zeichen der Kreuzzugsbewegung Ende des 14. Jahrhunderts*, Europäische Hochschulschriften, Reihe III, Geschichte und ihre Hilfswissenschaften 893 (Frankfurt am Main, 2000).

5   L. Puiseux, 'Robert l'Ermite. Étude sur un personnage normand du XIVe siècle', *Mémoires de la société des antiquaires de Normandie* 24 (1859), 123–52.

6   N. Jorga, *Philippe de Mézières, 1327–1405, et la croisade au XIVe siècle*, Bibliothèque de l'École des Hautes Études 110 (Paris, 1896, repr. Geneva-Paris, 1976).

7   See, e. g., *Philippe de Mézières, Letter to King Richard II. A Plea made in 1395 for Peace between England and France*, intr. and trans. G. W. Coopland (Liverpool, 1975).

8   Cf. my *Les Ducs de Bourgogne, la croisade et l'Orient*.

9   Jean Froissart, *Œuvres*, ed. Kervyn de Lettenhove (Brussels, 1867–77, repr. Osnabrück, 1967), vol. 15, p. 109.

10   A. S. Atiya, *The Crusade of Nicopolis* (London, 1934); Paviot, *Les Ducs de Bourgogne, la croisade et l'Orient*, pp. 17–57.

11   Boucicaut drew up the French plan of attack at Agincourt; he did not notice that Henry V had followed the same tactics as Bayezid. I owe this remark to the late Nicoara Beldiceanu.

12   See my *Les Ducs de Bourgogne, la croisade et l'Orient*, pp. 54–6.

13   See my *Les Ducs de Bourgogne, la croisade et l'Orient*, pp. 63–6.

14   See Müller, *Kreuzzugspläne und Kreuzzugspolitik*, pp. 22–3, 32–48; J. Paviot, *La politique navale des ducs de Bourgogne, 1384–1482*, Économies et sociétés (Lille, 1995), pp. 105–23; Paviot, *Les Ducs de Bourgogne, la croisade et l'Orient*, pp. 72–109.

15   But not written down until 1457.

16   For the details, see my *Les Ducs de Bourgogne, la croisade et l'Orient*, pp. 59–115. The reports of the two spies have been published: 'A Survey of Egypt and Syria, undertaken in the year 1422, by Sir Gilbert de Lannoy … ', ed. J. Webb

in *Archaeologia* 21 (1827), 281–444 (report to Henry VI); *Œuvres de Ghillebert de Lannoy, voyageur, diplomate et moraliste*, ed. Ch. Potvin and J.-C. Houzeau (Louvain, 1878) (report to Philip the Good); *Le Voyage d'Outremer de Bertrandon de la Broquière ...* , ed. Ch. Schefer, Recueil de voyages et de documents pour servir à l'histoire de la géographie ... 12 (Paris, 1892).

17 Even though he wrote an 'Epistre lamentable et consolatoire sur la deconfiture' (to be published in the near future by Professor Philippe Contamine and myself), addressed to Duke Philip the Bold, the great theoretician of the crusade in France at the end of the fourteenth century, Philippe de Mézières, was a familiar not of the duke of Burgundy, but of King Charles VI and his brother Duke Louis of Orleans.

18 For his life and works and a bibliography, cf. *Dictionnaire des lettres françaises. Le Moyen Âge*, dir. G. Grente, new ed. G. Hasenohr and M. Zink, Encyclopédies d'aujourd'hui (Paris, 1992), pp. 781–2. I have not seen the thesis of Thomas Leist (University of Cologne).

19 *Le Voyage d'Outremer*, pp. 58, 261.

20 Philip died at Acre in 1191, during the Third Crusade. The homily is published in J. Mangeart, *Catalogue descriptif et raisonné des manuscrits de la bibliothèque de Valenciennes* (Paris-Valenciennes, 1860), app. 33, pp. 687–90.

21 See the edition of the prologue of this work in my article 'Les cartes et leur utilisation à la fin du Moyen Âge. L'exemple des principautés bourguignonne et angevine', in *Itineraria*, forthcoming 2004.

22 There is no edition; see Y. Lacaze, 'Un représentant de la polémique antimusulmane au XVe siècle. Jean Germain, évêque de Nevers et de Chalon-sur-Saône (1400?–1461). Sa vie, son œuvre', in *Ecole nationale des chartes. Positions des thèses soutenues par les élèves de la promotion de 1958 ...* , pp. 67–75; F. Berriot, 'Images de l'Islam dans le Débat manuscrit de Jean Germain (1450)', in *RHR. Réforme Humanisme Renaissance*, 14 (December 1981), 32–41.

23 Cf. S. Dünnebeil, ed., *Die Protokollbücher des Ordens vom Goldenen Vlies, vol. I: Herzog Philipp der Gute, 1430–1467* (Stuttgart, 2002), p. 105 (Instrumenta, 9); for the 'Mappemonde', cf. J. Paviot, 'Les cartes et leur utilisation à la fin du Moyen Âge. L'exemple des principautés bourguignonne et angevine', *Itineraria*, forthcoming 2004 (with the edition of the prologue).

24 Wladislas, king of Poland from 1434, and of Hungary from 1440, who was killed at Varna in 1444.

25 He had been fighting the Turks since 1440. However, he had been defeated at Varna in 1444 and at Kosovo in 1448. He died in 1456 after repelling the Turks at Belgrade.

26 Translated by himself into Latin in his 'Liber de virtutibus ... Philippi Burgundiae et Brabantiae ducis', in Kervyn de Lettenhove, ed., *Chroniques relatives à l'histoire de la Belgique sous la domination des ducs de Bourgogne (Textes latins)* Commission royale d'histoire (Brussels, 1876), chs 50–57, pp. 79–96.

27 To the king of France: Ch. Schefer, ed., 'Le Discours du voyage d'oultremer au très victorieux roi Charles VII, prononcé, en 1452 [*sic*], par Jean Germain, évêque de Chalon', *Revue de l'Orient latin* 3 (1895), 303–42; to the emperor: cf. N. Jorga, ed., *Notes et extraits pour servir à l'histoire des croisades au XVe siècle*, 3e série (Paris, 1902), pp. 343–4.

28 But without documentary evidence this remains a hypothesis.

29 L. Devillers, 'Les Séjours des ducs de Bourgogne en Hainaut: 1427–1482', *Compte rendu des séances de la Commission royale d'histoire, ou Recueil de ses bulletins*, 4ᵉ série 6 (1879), pp. 352 and 419.

30 Georges Chastellain, *Œuvres*, ed. Kervyn de Lettenhove, 3 (Brussels, 1864, repr. Geneva, 1971), pp. 69–78.

31 See Dünnebeil, ed., *Die Protokollbücher*, pp. 196–7.

32 *The Waning of the Middle Ages*, 1st Dutch edn, 1919.

33 *La littérature et les mœurs chevaleresques à la cour de Bourgogne* (Neuchâtel, 1950). See also M. Stanesco, *Jeux d'errance du chevalier médiéval. Aspects ludiques de la fonction guerrière dans la littérature du Moyen Age flamboyant*, Brill's Studies in Intellectual History 9 (Leiden, 1988).

34 See his notice in *Dictionnaire des lettres françaises. Le Moyen Âge*, pp. 1085–6.

35 Cf. B. de Lannoy and G. Dansaert, *Jean de Lannoy le Bâtisseur* (Paris-Brussels, n.d.); R. de Smedt, 'Jan heer van Lannoy, stadhouder en diplomat, De Orde van het Gulden Vlies te Mechelen in 1491. International symposium, Mechelen, 7 September 1991', dir. R. de Smedt, *Handelingen van de Koninklijke Kring voor Oudheidkunde, Letteren en Kunst van Mechelen*, 95 (1991), 55–84.

36 Cf. his notice in M.-Th. Caron, ed., *Les Vœux du Faisan, noblesse en fête, esprit de croisade. Le manuscrit français 11594 de la Bibliothèque nationale de France*, Burgundica 7 (Turnhout, 2003), p. 239.

37 *Les Vœux du Faisan*, pp. 136, 141, 142.

38 See the introduction to *Les Vœux du Faisan*, by M.-Th. Caron.

39 Cf. the letters of two ducal officers who were present: Jean de Molesme, in *Mélanges historiques. Documents historiques inédits ...* , ed. [J. J.] Champollion Figeac, Collection de documents inédits sur l'histoire de France, 4 (Paris, 1848), 2e partie: Textes des documents, no. 28, pp. 457–62; J. de Plaine, in Paviot, *Les Ducs de Bourgogne, la croisade et l'Orient*, pièce justificative VI, pp. 306–8. Even Olivier de la Marche, in the official report, had to mention the excessive expenses.

40 See H. Weigel and H. Grüneisen, eds, *Deutsche Reichstagsakten unter Kaiser Friedrich III., fasc. 5.1: 1453–1454*, Deutsche Reichstagsakten, XIX-1 (Göttingen, 1969).

41 Cf. my *Les Ducs de Bourgogne*, pièce justificative XII, pp. 321–7.

42 Müller, *Kreuzzugspläne und Kreuzzugspolitik*, pp. 59–126; Paviot, *La Politique navale des ducs de Bourgogne*, pp. 126–34, and *Les Ducs de Bourgogne, la croisade et l'Orient*, pp. 135–76.

43 M. Sommé, *Isabelle de Portugal, duchesse de Bourgogne. Une femme au pouvoir au XVᵉ siècle* (Lille, 1998), pp. 468–72.

44 F. H. Lippens, O. F. M., *S. Jean de Capistran en mission aux Etats bourguignons, 1442–1443. Essai de reconstitution de ses voyages et négociations à l'aide de documents inédits* (Florence-Quaracchi, 1942) (extracted from *Archivum franciscanum historicum* 35 [1942]).

45 Chastellain, *Œuvres*, ed. Kervyn de Lettenhove, 3, pp. 112, 116.

46 *Opera omnia*, ed. F. Harold (Rome, 1688), No. XLIV, pp. 273–4.

47 *Opera omnia*, ed. Harold, No. LXV, pp. 330–1.

48 G. de Beaucourt, ed., 'Lettre de saint Jean de Capistran au duc de Bourgogne. 19 mars 1454', *Annuaire-Bulletin de la société de l'histoire de France*, vol. 2 second part (1864), pp. 160–6.

49 Joannis Długosz, *Opera omnia*, ed. A. Przezdziecki, 14: *Historiae Poloniae Libri XII*, vol. V: *Liber XII. (XIII)* (Cracow, 1878), p. 98: 'Cassa autem et inanis fuit Ducis Burgundiae tam ampulosa legatio, solam verborum speciositatem continens, sed virtute carens, et ab omni effectu et executione longius distans.'

50 One can read a version in Mathieu d'Escouchy, *Chronique*, ed. G. Du Fresne de Beaucourt, Société de l'histoire de France, 2 (Paris, 1863), pp. 130–237; Olivier de la Marche, *Mémoires*, ed. Henri Beaune and J. d'Arbaumont, Société de l'histoire de France, 2 (Paris, 1884), pp. 348–94; the official version is that published by M.-Th. Caron in *Les Vœux du Faisan*. Another one that circulated in France has now been published in my *Les Ducs de Bourgogne*, pièce justificative VII, pp. 308–18. Cf. G. Doutrepont, 'Les historiens du Banquet du Faisan', in *Mélanges offerts à M. Charles Moeller*, Recueil de travaux publiés par les membres des Conférences d'histoire et de philologie de l'Université de Louvain, 40 (Louvain-Paris, 1914), 1, pp. 654–70; for the authorship, see my *Les Ducs de Bourgogne*, pp. 230–1.

51 Chastellain, *Œuvres*, 4, pp. 134–40; cf. my *Les Ducs de Bourgogne*, p. 159.

52 Cf. my *Les Ducs de Bourgogne*, pp. 207–27.

53 Cf. C. Marinesco, *Du nouveau sur Tirant lo Blanch* (Barcelona, 1953–4) (extracted from *Estudis romànics*, 4, pp. 137–203).

54 See the list in B. Schnerb, 'Le contingent franco-bourguignon à la croisade de Nicopolis', in 'Nicopolis, 1396–1996', ed. Paviot and Chauney-Bouillot, pp. 72–4.

55 Cf. H. Taparel, 'Geoffroy de Thoisy. Une figure de la croisade bourguignonne au XVe siècle', *Le Moyen Age* 94 (1988), 381–99; J. Paviot, *La Politique navale des ducs de Bourgogne, 1384–1482*, passim; *Les Ducs de Bourgogne*, passim. I intend to write his biography.

56 Cf. Chastellain, *Œuvres*, 3, pp. 353–8; Chastellain, *Chronique. Les fragments du Livre IV révélés par l'Additional Manuscript 54156 de la British Library*, ed. J.-Cl. Delclos (Geneva, 1991), pp. 76–9.

57 Cf. my *Les Ducs de Bourgogne*, p. 153.

58 Extracts from his letter have been published in N. Iorga, 'Les Aventures "asarrazines" des Français de Bourgogne au XVe siècle', in *Mélanges d'histoire générale (Cluj)*, 1 (1927), doc. VI, pp. 48–56. I shall provide a new edition of the complete document in my forthcoming article 'La croisade bourguignonne aux XIVe et XVe siècles: un idéal chevaleresque?', to be published in *Francia*.

59 See, for example, Lille, Archives départementales du Nord, B 214 (receipt of the tenth in the diocese of Thérouanne, 1441).

60 Cf. F. Remy, *Les grandes indulgences pontificales aux Pays-Bas à la fin du Moyen Age, 1300–1531. Essai sur leur histoire et leur importance financière*, Université de Louvain, Recueil de travaux publiés par les membres des Conférences d'histoire et de Philologie, 2nd series 15 (Louvain, 1928), pp. 193–200. A new study would be welcome.

61 Cf. De la Fons-Mélicocq, 'L'Histoire prouvée par les processions', in *Souvenirs de la Flandre-Wallonne. Recherches historiques et choix de documents relatifs à Douai et à la province*, 1 (Douai-Paris, 1861), pp. 40–51.

62 V. Fris, ed., *Dagboek van Gent van 1447 tot 1470*, 1 (Ghent, 1851), pp. 196–8. The crusaders were back in Ghent on 8 December.

63 A. de Mul, ed., *Kroniek van Axel en omgeving tot 1525*, in *Oudheidkundige Kring "De Vier Ambachten" Hulst Jaarboek* (1939–40), pp. 84–7, 95.

64 A. Castan, 'La Société de Jésus au XVe siècle', *Revue des sociétés savantes*, 6th series 3 (1876), 479–82; Ch. Le Fort, 'Une Société de Jésus au quinzième siècle', *Mémoires et documents publiés par la Société d'histoire et d'archéologie de Genève* 20 (1879–88), 98–118; H. Prutz, 'Pius II. Rüstungen zum Türkenkrieg und die Societas Jesu des Flandrers [sic] Gerhard des Champs 1459–1466', *Sitzungsberichte der Königlich bayerischen Akademie der Wissenschaften, Philosophisch-philologische und historische Klasse* 4 (1912); A. de Bil, 'Une "Societas Iesu" au XVe siècle', *Nouvelle Revue théologique*, 79th year, vol. 69 (1947), 949–56.

65 Cf. R. Haubst, 'Johannes von Segovia im Gespräch mit Nikolaus von Kues und Jean Germain über die göttliche Dreieinigkeit und ihre Verkündigung vor den Mohammedanern', *Münchener Theologische Zeitschrift* 2 (1951), 115–29; D. Cabanelas Rodríguez, *Juan de Segovia y el problema islamico* (Madrid, 1952), here pp. 191–224, with the edition of the correspondence, ap. IV – XI, pp. 303–49.

66 Cf. my article 'La dévotion vis-à-vis de la Terre sainte au XVe siècle: l'exemple de Philippe le Bon, duc de Bourgogne (1396–1467)', in *Autour de la première croisade. Actes du Colloque de la Society for the Study of the Crusades and the Latin East (Clermont-Ferrand, 22–25 juin 1995)*, ed. M. Balard, *Byzantina Sorbonensia* 14 (Paris, 1996), pp. 401–11, and my *Les Ducs de Bourgogne*, passim.

6 An Obscure but Powerful Pattern: Crusading, Nationalism and the Swiss Confederation in the Late Middle Ages

1 Until c. 1500 the people of today's Switzerland called themselves the confederates (*Eidgenossen*). But after 1500 the names 'Switzerland' and 'Swiss' were accepted, despite the fact that they originated as terms of mockery. In the following essay the terms confederates and Confederation are used interchangeably with 'Swiss' and 'Switzerland'. I would like to thank Professor Norman Housley for his precise translation of the original German text.

2 For an overview of the history of the Confederation in the fifteenth century, see R. Sablonier, 'The Swiss Confederation in the 15th Century', in *The New Cambridge Medieval History*, vol. 7, ed. C. Allmand (Cambridge 1998), pp. 645–70. When the term 'Confederation' is used in the following, the entire territory of the 13 members (*Orte*) is implied (Uri, Schwyz, Unterwalden, Lucerne, Zürich, Glarus, Zug, Bern, Freiburg im Üechtland, Solothurn, Basel, Schaffhausen and Appenzell), even though the last three did not enter the union until between 1501 and 1513.

3 For the state of play, at least with regard to the Military Orders, see C. T. Maier, 'Forschungsbericht zur Geschichte der geistlichen Ritterorden in der Schweiz (12.–19. Jahrhundert)', *Schweizerische Zeitschrift für Geschichte* 43 (1993), 419–28.

4 Niklaus Schradin, *Schweizer Chronik. Gedruckt in Sursee 1500. Faksimile-Neudruck* (Munich, 1927), fol. 5r. The title of the facsimile reprint is incorrect,

for Schradin speaks in general terms of the 'Kronigk diss kriegs ... '. A more accessible edition offers: 'Der Schwabenkrieg vom Jahre 1499, besungen in teutschen Reimen durch Nicolaus Schradin, Schreiber zu Luzern 1500', *Der Geschichtsfreund* 4 (1847), 3–66, with the quotation at pp. 10–14. On Schradin as author, see *Die deutsche Literatur des Mittelalters. Verfasserlexikon*, 2nd edn, ed. K. Ruh in association with G. Keil (Berlin and New York, 1977ff.), vol. 8, pp. 841–4.

5   Petermann Etterlin, *Kronica von der loblichen Eydtgnoschaft, jr harkomen und sust seltzam strittenn und geschichten*, ed. Eugen Gruber, Quellenwerk zur Entstehung der Schweizerischen Eidgenossenschaft, III Abteilung: Chroniken und Dichtungen, vol. 3 (Aarau, 1965), pp. 85f.: the Swiss 'hand ouch darnach durch erfordrung des helgen Rŏmischen richs und des Stŭls ze Rom der cristenheit zŭ trost vil gŭtz gethan wider die Türcken, als mann dann das warlich geschriben vindt, und sund ouch umm deßwillen begabet worden und gefrẙet, das sy das Crucifix zŭ ewigen zitten offentlichen in ir paner dŏrffent fŭren, daz eyn costlich, hüptsch klenot'. Etterlin draws here on older accounts in a *Landbuch* of Schwyz: ibid., p. 86, note 1. For further references to the Turks, see Etterlin, pp. 27, 85, 169f. On Etterlin and his work, see *Die deutsche Literatur des Mittelalters*, vol. 2, p. 636.

6   B. Widmer, 'Der Ursus- und Victorkult in Solothurn', in *Solothurn. Beiträge zur Entwicklung der Stadt im Mittelalter*, ed. B. Schubiger (Zürich, 1990), pp. 33–82. B. Kurmann-Schwarz, 'Das 10,000-Ritter-Fenster im Berner Münster und seine Auftraggeber. Überlegungen zu den Schrift- und Bildquellen sowie zum Kult der Heiligen in Bern', *Zeitschrift für Schweizerische Archäologie und Kunstgeschichte* 49 (1992), 39–54.

7   For events see *Handbuch der Schweizer Geschichte*, 2nd edn (Zürich, 1980), vol. 1, pp. 312–28.

8   See, for example, G. Franz, 'Die Bedeutung der Burgunderkriege für die Entwicklung des deutschen Nationalgefühls', *Jahrbuch der Stadt Freiburg* 5 (1942), 161–73.

9   See C. Sieber – Lehmann, ' "Teutsche nation" und Eidgenossenschaft. Der Zusammenhang zwischen Türken- und Burgunderkriegen', *Historische Zeitschrift* 253 (1991), 561–602.

10 For the Regensburg *Reichstag* of 1471, see H. Wolff, ed., *Deutsche Reichstagsakten, Ältere Reihe*, vols 22/2 and 3 (Göttingen, 1999–2001). It was only around the turn of the sixteenth century that the description *teutsche nation* was finally incorporated into the official designation of the empire as 'Heiliges Römisches Reich Deutscher Nation', thereby distancing itself from the crusading context.

11 C. Sieber-Lehmann, 'Der türkische Sultan Mehmed II. und Karl der Kühne, der "Türk im Occident" ', in *Europa und die osmanische Expansion im ausgehenden Mittelalter*, ed. F.-R. Erkens, Zeitschrift für historische Forschung, Beiheft 20 (Berlin, 1997), pp. 13–38.

12 See N. Housley, *Religious Warfare in Europe, 1400–1536* (Oxford, 2002), pp. 85–90.

13 A. Fluri, *Ablassbriefe zugunsten des St. Vincenzen-Münsters zu Bern*, Münsterbaubericht 1915 (Bern, 1915), p. 3.

14 K. M. Setton, *The Papacy and the Levant (1204–1571)*, 4 vols, Memoirs of the American Philosophical Society, nos 114, 127, 161, 162 (Philadelphia, 1976–84), vol. 2, p. 165.

15 See P. Schwenke and H. Degering, eds, *Die Türkenbulle Papst Calixtus III. Ein deutscher Druck von 1456 in der ersten Gutenbergtype*, Seltene Drucke der Königlichen Bibliothek zu Berlin, no. 1 (Berlin, 1911), Commentary, p. 27. On printed formulas for women in a Turkish indulgence dated 1482, see V. von Klemperer, K. Haebler and E. von Rath, eds, *Frühdrucke aus der Bücherei Viktor von Klemperer* (Dresden, 1927), nos CXXVII and CXXVIII, p. 115.

16 Caspar Wirz, ed., *Regesten zur Schweizergeschichte aus den päpstlichen Archiven 1447–1513*, 6 vols (Bern, 1911–18), vol. 2, p. 96.

17 For example, the leader of the crusaders in 1455 came from Malters: see *Die Chroniken der deutschen Städte vom 14. bis ins 16. Jahrhundert*, 36 vols (Leipzig et al., 1862–1931), vol. 3, pp. 409f., vol. 10, p. 217. For female crusaders, see Badische Historische Kommission, ed., *Regesta Episcoporum Constantiensium*, 5 vols (Innsbruck, 1895–1951), vol. 4, no. 12,577, p. 289, n.d., but after 1453: 'Magdalena Turnerin, crucesignata'.

18 R. Wackernagel, *Geschichte der Stadt Basel*, 3 vols (Basel, 1907–24), vol. 2/2, pp. 865f. Basel's success also prompted Strassburg to petition the pope for a Turkish indulgence: L. Pfleger, 'Die Stadt- und Rats-Gottesdienste im Strassburger Münster', *Archiv für elsässisches Kirchengeschichte* 12 (1937), 1–55, at p. 7.

19 For Bern see Fluri, *Ablassbriefe*, pp. 5–11. See also N. Paulus, *Geschichte des Ablasses am Ausgange des Mittelalters*, 3 parts (Paderborn, 1922–3), part 3, pp. 545–9.

20 A. Fluri, ed., *Ablass-Bulle Sixtus IV. zugunsten des St. Vincenzen-Münsters 1473. Erster im Auftrage Berns ausgeführter Druck durch Martin Flach in Basel 1476. Faksimile-Reproduktion nach dem einzig bekannten Exemplar des Kestner – Museums in Hannover* (Bern, 1913), pp. 4f. On the interpretations of preachers, see H. von Greyerz, 'Studien zur Kulturgeschichte der Stadt Bern am Ende des Mittelalters', *Archiv des Historischen Vereins des Kantons Bern* 35 (1940), pp. 173–491, at pp. 287f.

21 Badische Historische Kommission, ed., *Regesta Episcoporum Constantiensium*, vol. 4, no. 11,935, p. 225.

22 B. Fleury, 'Le Couvent des Cordeliers de Fribourg au Moyen Age', *Revue d'Histoire Ecclésiastique Suisse* 15 (1921), pp. 73f.

23 M. Sciambra, G. Valentini and I. Parrino, eds, *Il 'Liber Brevium' di Callisto III. La crociata, l'Albania e Skanderbeg* (Palermo, 1968), pp. 99, 182f. In 1458 Cescases made an appearance too at Solothurn and Freiburg im Üechtland: ibid., p. 194; L. Pastor, *Geschichte der Päpste seit dem Ausgang des Mittelalters*, 8th edn (Freiburg im Breisgau, 1926), vol. 1, pp. 736f.

24 J. Delumeau, *L'Alun de Rome, XVe–XIXe siècle*, École pratique des Hautes Études – VIe section. Centre de recherches historiques. Ports-Routes-Trafics, vol. 13 (Paris, 1962), pp. 31, 181.

25 F. Ehrensperger, *Basels Stellung im internationalen Handelsverkehr des Spätmittelalters*, Diss. Phil. I. (Basel, 1970, Zürich, 1972), p. 271. See ibid., p. 258, for the documented sale of alum to a businessman from Basel by a man from Nürnberg.

26 Schwenke and Degering, eds, *Die Türkenbulle Papst Calixtus III.*, pp. 20–4.

27 P. Ochsenbein, 'Beten "mit zertanen armen" – ein alteidgenössischer Brauch', *Schweizerisches Archiv für Volkskunde* 75 (1979), 129–72, at p. 146.

28 Valerius Anshelm, *Die Berner – Chronik*, ed. Historischer Verein des Kantons Bern, 6 vols (Bern, 1884–1901), vol. 1, p. 149.
29 Pastor, *Päpste*, vol. 1, p. 729.
30 For Basel see L. Zehnder, *Volkskundliches in der älteren schweizerischen Chronistik* (Basel, 1976), p. 194. For Schwyz, see 'Jahrzeitbuch der Kirche in Tuggen, Kanton Schwyz, hg. von Justus Landolt', *Geschichtsfreund* 25 (1870), p. 185.
31 For examples see Sieber-Lehmann, ' "Teutsche nation" und Eidgenossenschaft', pp. 587–91.
32 For refugees from Constantinople at Solothurn, see H. Morgenthaler, 'Kulturgeschichtliche Notizen aus den solothurnischen Seckelmeisterrechnungen des XV. Jahrhunderts, Teil II', *Anzeiger für schweizerische Altertumskunde*, n.s. 21 (1919), p. 59. On 15 December 1470 the town mayor and council at Basel commended the Greek refugee 'Matheus Sebastinis Lampaden von Constantinopel' to the protection and care of the council at Lucerne: Staatsarchiv Luzern, A 1 Sd. 97. There are further example of Greeks seeking asylum in V. Groebner, *Gefährliche Geschenke. Ritual, Politik und die Sprache der Korruption in der Eidgenossenschaft im späten Mittelalter und am Beginn der Neuzeit*, Konflikte und Kultur, vol. 3 (Constance, 2000), p. 72.
33 Staatsarchiv Zürich, A 221, Akten Türkei = H. Koller and others, eds, *Regesten Kaiser Friedrichs III. (1440–1493)* (Vienna, Cologne and Graz, 1982ff.), vol. 6, p. 66, no. 55. The published register shortens the content and omits the phrase *teutsche nation*. The occasion was a letter sent by Frederick III from Wiener Neustadt on 11 January 1455 to the civic and local authorities at Zürich, Bern, Lucerne, Solothurn, Schwyz, Zug, Glarus, Unterwalden, Uri and other confederates. Frederick III requests that the confederates provide 500 mounted troops and 1,000 footsoldiers 'wider die obberürten ungläubigen, die Turgkhen'. This they should 'tůn, als sich gepuret, gott dem allmĕ chtigen ze lobe, der cristenheit ze trost, dem heiligen reich und sunder unser teútschen nacion und euch selbs zů ere und nutz'.
34 Koller and others, eds, *Regesten Friedrichs III.*, vol. 6, p. 82, no. 98.
35 Staatsarchiv Freiburg im Üechtland, Geistliche Sachen 2009.
36 The notice relating to Frankfurt in 1454, with specific mention of the confederates, is located in *Deutsche Reichstagsakten, Ältere Reihe*, vol. 19/1 (Göttingen, 1969), p. 85. For the Nürnberg notice of 1467, see J. J. Müller, *Des Heiligen Römischen Reichs Teutscher Nation Reichstagstheatrum, wie selbiges unter Keyser Friedrichs V. allerhöchsten Regierung von Anno MCCCCXL bis MCC-CCXCIII gestanden* (Jena, 1713), vol. 2, p. 285. For reference to the confederates in the Nürnberg notice (10,000 men expected) of 1471, see *Deutsche Reichstagsakten, Ältere Reihe*, vol. 22/2, p. 806. On the participation of the confederates at the Regensburg *Reichstag* see ibid., vol. 22/3, Index, pp. 1021f.
37 Diebold Schilling, *Die Berner Chronik des Diebold Schilling 1468–1484*, 2 vols, ed. G. Tobler (Bern, 1897–1901), vol. 1, p. 78.
38 For the institution of the 'town-days' (*Städtetage*), which were a reaction to the emperor's crusading plans and the Turkish taxes, see G. Schmidt, *Der Städtetag in der Reichsverfassung. Eine Untersuchung zur korporativen Politik der Freien und Reichsstädte in der ersten Hälfte des 16. Jahrhunderts* (Stuttgart, 1984).

39   Staatsarchiv Basel, Missiven A 13, fol. 91: letter from Basel to Bern; the letter from Constance to Zürich is also referred to here.

40   See *Amtliche Sammlung der ältern Eidgenössischen Abschiede. Serie 1245–1798* (Lucerne et al., 1839–90), vol. 2, p. 426, with the refusal by the council of Lucerne, and A. Bachmann, *Deutsche Reichsgeschichte im Zeitalter Friedrichs III. und Max I. Mit besonderer Berücksichtigung der österreichischen Staatengeschichte*, 2 vols (Leipzig, 1884–94), vol. 2, p. 394. For Zürich as the location, and the participation of Bishop Ortlieb of Chur, see the letter cited in the next note.

41   On this see Staatsarchiv Luzern, Akten Deutschland, Schwäbischer Kreis. Schachtel 86: Hohenzollern. Letter from Jos Niklaus, count of Zollern, to the *Tagsatzung* at Lucerne, 27 October 1471. He exonerates himself before the confederates for a killing that he committed while attending a *Tagsatzung* at Constance on account of the Turks, summoned by the emperor's representatives, Bishop Ortlieb of Chur and Count Hugo von Montfort.

42   Staatsarchiv Zürich, B IV 1, Missiven (Entwurf). Lucerne, 20 November 1471.

43   Koller and others, eds, *Regesten Friedrichs III.*, vol. 6, p. 89, no. 111.

44   *Amtliche Sammlung der ältern Eidgenössischen Abschiede*, vol. 2, p. 430: decision of the *Tagsatzung* at Lucerne on 26 January 1472.

45   Müller, *Reichstagstheatrum*, vol. 2, p. 547. See also J. Janssen, ed., *Frankfurts Reichscorrespondenz nebst andern verwandten Aktenstücken von 1369–1519*, 3 vols (Freiburg im Breisgau, 1863ff.), vol. 2/1, pp. 285f. (report of 26–28 May 1473). In general see E. Isenmann, 'Reichsstadt und Reich an der Wende vom späten Mittelalter zur frühen Neuzeit', *Mittel und Wege früher Verfassungspolitik. Kleine Schriften 1*, ed. J. Engel, Spätmittelalter und Frühe Neuzeit. Tübinger Beiträge zur Geschichtsforschung 9, Kleine Schriften 1 (Stuttgart, 1979), 9–223, at p. 112, note 318.

46   Koller and others, eds, *Regesten Friedrichs III.*, vol. 6, p. 90, no. 113. Bishop Ortlieb of Chur enjoyed the special confidence of Frederick III and exerted himself constantly on the emperor's behalf. See J. G. Mayer, *Geschichte des Bistums Chur*, 2 vols (Stans, 1907–14), vol. 1, pp. 485f.

47   *Amtliche Sammlung der ältern Eidgenössischen Abschiede*, vol. 2, p. 457, dated 22 September 1473: a projected agenda for the next *Tagsatzung*: 'Item von des keisers wegen, ob man einen tag zu Ougspurg leisten wil, uff disem tag antwurt geben.' A decision by the following *Tagsatzungen* has not survived.

48   *Amtliche Sammlung der ältern Eidgenössischen Abschiede*, vol. 2, p. 460: four reports to the confederates about the meetings of Frederick III and Charles the Bold at Trier.

49   Koller and others, eds, *Regesten Friedrichs III.*, vol. 6, p. 91, no. 116. A copy of this letter can be found at Zürich Central Library, Sammelband H 161, vol. 11: 'Aufforderungen an die Eidgenossen wegen Türkenkrieg (1473–1521) und andere Aktenstücke', Bl. 378/379 (see Katalog, Zentralbibliothek Zürich, pt 2, p. 704). See also *Amtliche Sammlung der ältern Eidgenössischen Abschiede*, vol. 2, p. 469, 7 January 1474.

50   Koller and others, eds, *Regesten Friedrichs III.*, vol. 6, pp. 91f., nos 117–18: Emperor Frederick III to the confederates, Nürnberg, 18 March 1474. The confederates were to respond positively to the invitation, under pain of losing the emperor's good will and forfeiting all their rights and privileges. 'Und beleibt nit aussen, damit ewrent halben kein verhindrung darinn beschehe ... ' See also ibid., no. 52: the same to Zürich, with the postscript

'Ob ew aber die zeit auf denselben tag zuschicken zu kurtz werden wolte, so wollent dannoch nicht außbleiben, sonnder auf das fürderlichiste ir mogent ewer bottschafft mit volmechtigem gewallt daselbs hin sennden'. On this occasion neither text contains any mention of the *teutsche nation*. See also *Amtliche Sammlung der ältern Eidgenössischen Abschiede*, vol. 2, p. 486, 18 April 1474: 'Denen von Zürich wird aufgetragen, dem Kaiser zu schreiben, dass die Eidgenossen ihrer Geschäfte wegen seiner Einladung nicht Folge leisten können.'

51 *Urkundenbuch der Abtei Sankt Gallen*, 6 vols (St Gallen, 1863–1955), vol. 6, no. 5992, p. 532.

52 The decrees under discussion were communicated to the confederates: see *Amtliche Sammlung der ältern Eidgenössischen Abschiede*, vol. 2, pp. 356f.: on 4 July 1466 imperial and Swiss envoys met at Constance; both parties agreed to adhere to the terms of the 15-year peace sealed in 1461.

53 Bendicht Tschachtlan and Heinrich Dittlinger, *Berner Chronik 1424–1470*, ed. G. Studer, Quellen zur Schweizer Geschichte vol. 1 (Basel, 1877), p. 223.

54 Diebold Schilling, *Berner Chronik von 1424–1468*, ed. T. von Liebenau, W. F. Mülinen, *Archiv des historischen Vereins des Kantons Bern* 13 (1893), 431–539, at pp. 500f.

55 Schilling, *Berner Chronik 1424–1468*, pp. 537–9. For the entire European spectrum of this genre of letters allegedly written by the sultan, see R. Schwoebel, *The Shadow of the Crescent: The Renaissance Image of the Turk (1453–1517)* (Nieuwkoop, 1967), pp. 66, 204f. 'Sultan's letters' can also be found in the accounts of the Basel clerics Appenwiler and Knebel: see H. Pfeiler, *Das Türkenbild in den deutschen Chroniken des 15. Jahrhunderts*, Typewritten Dissertation (Frankfurt am Main, 1956), p. 21.

56 Diebold Schilling, *Die Amtliche Berner Chronik, vols. 1–3*, facsimile edn in 4 vols by H. Bloesch and P. Hilber (Bern, 1943), vol. 3, pp. 13f.; Diebold Schilling, *Die Berner Chronik des Diebold Schilling 1468–1484*, 2 vols, ed. G. Tobler (Bern, 1897–1901), vol. 1, p. 7.

57 For the following see the discussion in C. Sieber–Lehmann, *Spätmittelalterlicher Nationalismus. Die Burgunderkriege am Oberrhein und in der Eidgenossenschaft*, Veröffentlichungen des Max–Planck–Instituts für Geschichte no. 116 (Göttingen, 1995), pp. 150–61.

58 See the many references to the crusade preparations of the *teutsche nation* in A. Schröcker, *Die Deutsche Nation. Beobachtungen zur politischen Propaganda des ausgehenden 15. Jahrhundert*, Historische Studien, vol. 426 (Lübeck, 1974). For the Swiss Confederation see the subject index in *Amtliche Sammlung der ältern Eidgenössischen Abschiede*, vol. 2 und 3/2; regrettably *Türkengefahr* and *Türkenhülfe* were not included in the subject index for vol. 3/1.

59 See H. Wiesflecker, *Kaiser Maximilian I. Das Reich, Österreich und Europa an der Wende zur Neuzeit* (Munich, 1971–86), index under *Türken*.

60 A. P. von Segesser, *Die Beziehungen der Schweizer zu Mathias Corvinus, König von Ungarn in den Jahren 1476–1490* (Lucerne, 1860).

61 See above, at notes 4–5.

62 See P. Rousset, 'Le cardinal M. Schiner ou la nostalgie de la croisade', *Vallesia* 33 (1978), 327–38.

63 H. Stricker, *Die Selbstdarstellung des Schweizers im Drama des 16. Jahrhunderts*, Sprache und Dichtung new series vol. 7, Dissertation (Bern, 1961), p. 2527.

64   F. Niderberger, *Sagen, Märchen und Gebräuche aus Unterwalden*, 3 vols (Sarnen, 1909–10, Stans, 1914), vol. 3, pp. 100f., 111, 279, 352, 382, 400f., 462ff., 521f. Turkish standards captured at Lepanto were hung up in the church at Lucerne: A. Reinle, *Die Kunstdenkmäler des Kantons Luzern, vol. 2: Die Stadt Luzern*, Die Kunstdenkmäler der Schweiz 30 (Basel, 1953), vol. 2/1, pp. 245f. In 1602 people from Innerhoden took part in the Turkish wars: R. Fischer, *Die Kunstdenkmäler des Kantons Appenzell Innerhoden*, Die Kunstdenkmäler der Schweiz 74 (Basel, 1984), pp. 14, 213. The dictionary entry for *Türgg* throws up a series of references to the prevalence of *Turcica* in the 16th century: F. Staub, L. Tobler and others, eds, *Schweizerisches Idiotikon. Wörterbuch der schweizerdeutschen Sprache* (Frauenfeld, 1881ff.), vol. 13, pp. 1579–91.

65   Anshelm, *Die Berner-Chronik*, vol. 1, p. 134 (failures on the part of the pope to organize a crusade against the Turks), p. 257 (a Greek comes to Bern in 1484 as messenger for the 'imperial sultana'), p. 300 (anti-Turkish indulgences at Bern in 1484), vol. 2, p. 319 (the 1501 Jubilee helps the campaign against the Turks; miracles foretell a victory over the Turks; a Persian prince works towards the destruction of the Ottomans), pp. 324–45 (the papal legate Raimund Peraudi strives together with Maximilian I for a crusade against the Turks), pp. 397–9 (the legate Peraudi manages to persuade the members of the Confederation to reach an agreement with the pope for a crusade against the Turks). The admonishments and appeals from pope and emperor for a crusade against the Turks, which Anshelm records, are not treated here.

66   See Matthew 12: 24, where Jesus heals a possessed person. The Pharisees remark that 'he drives out the devil by using Beelzebub, the devil's lieutenant'.

67   Erhard Storck's text was transmitted in Johannes Knebel, *Diarium*, ed. W. Vischer and H. Boos, Basler Chroniken 2 und 3 (Leipzig, 1880–7), vol. 3, p. 253.

68   Johannes Dierauer, 'Rapperswil und sein Übergang an die Eidgenossenschaft', *Neujahrsblatt des Historischen Vereins des Kantons St. Gallen*, (1892), 3–16, at p. 14.

69   See H.-G. Fernis, 'Die politische Volksdichtung der deutschen Schweizer als Quelle für ihr völkisches und staatliches Bewusstsein vom 14.–16. Jahrhundert', *Deutsches Archiv für Landes- und Volksforschung* 2 (1938), 600–39, at p. 627. With the exception of its useful references to sources, this article is permeated with National Socialist ideology.

70   Haintz von Bechwinden, 'Gedicht wider die Schweizer und Reimchronik über den Schwabenkrieg. Zwei Flugschriften aus der Zeit Maximilians I. Hg. von Theodor Lorentzen', *Heidelberger Jahrbücher* 17 (1912), 139–218, at p. 167. For other examples see ibid., pp. 170, 172f. The confederates are standing in the way of Maximilian I's campaign against the Turks: ibid., pp. 185, 207f. 'Haintz von Bechwinden' was possibly a pseudonym of Heinrich Bebel: see K. Graf, 'Heinrich Bebel (1472–1518). Wider ein barbarisches Latein', *Humanismus im deutschen Südwesten. Biographische Profile*, ed. P. G. Schmidt (Sigmaringen, 1993), pp. 179–93. The later Swiss chroniclers did not forget these accusations: see Anshelm, *Die Berner–Chronik*, vol. 2, p. 141.

71   See the illustration in Etterlin, *Kronica*, p. 334 (reproduced in this volume, p. 92).

72 See the evidence in A. Blatter, *Schmähungen, Scheltreden, Drohungen. Ein Beitrag zur Geschichte der Volksstimmung zur Zeit der schweizerischen Reformation,* Wissenschaftliche Beilage zu den Jahresberichten des Gymnasiums, der Realschule und der Töchterschule (Basel, 1911).

73 See N. Housley, *The Later Crusades. From Lyons to Alcazar 1274–1580* (Oxford, 1992), who shows that crusading plans and ideas persisted after the end of crusades to the Holy Land.

74 One example of the way in which such collective points of reference (*Beziehungsbündeln*) can generate aggressive human behaviour is the anti-Jewish progroms: see the arguments by F. Graus in his *Pest-Geissler-Judenmorde. Das 14. Jahrhundert als Krisenzeit,* Veröffentlichungen des Max-Planck-Instituts für Geschichte 86, 2nd edn (Göttingen, 1988), esp. pp. 547f.

75 On the history of mentalities see the studies by F. Graus, 'Mentalität – Versuch einer Begriffsbestimmung und Methoden der Untersuchung', *Mentalitäten im Mittelalter. Methodische und inhaltliche Probleme,* ed. F. Graus, Vorträge und Forschungen 35 (Sigmaringen, 1987), pp. 9–48. On the difference between the history of mentalities and the earlier history of ideologies, see V. Sellin, 'Mentalität und Mentalitätsgeschichte', *Historische Zeitschrift* 241 (1985), 555–98. On the influence that 'l'histoire des mentalités' has exerted on Swiss historiography see C. Sieber-Lehmann, 'Ein neuer Blick auf allzu Vertrautes: Mentalitätengeschichte in der deutschschweizerischen Geschichtsforschung', *Schweizerische Zeitschrift für Geschichte* 41 (1991), 38–51.

76 The concept of *Habitus* (disposition), which played a crucial role in medieval theology, was transferred by Pierre Bourdieu from the History of Art into the discourse of the social sciences. From the many studies by Bourdieu on the subject of the *Habitus* as concept, see in particular his *Le sens pratique,* Collection Le sens commun (Paris, 1980).

77 On the concept of the 'Chosen People', see W. R. Hutchison and H. Lehmann, eds., *Many are Chosen. Divine Election and Western Nationalism,* Harvard Theological Studies 38 (Minneapolis, 1994).

78 See Housley, *Religious Warfare.*

79 See the 'Conclusions' in ibid., pp. 190–205.

80 See ibid., pp. 192f.

7 Giovanni da Capistrano and the Crusade of 1456

1 For two excellent analyses, both providing critical reviews of the problematic sources for the campaign, see J. Hofer, 'Der Sieger von Belgrad 1456', *Historisches Jahrbuch* 51 (1931), 163–212; F. Babinger, 'Der Quellenwert der Berichte über den Entsatz von Belgrad am 21./22. Juli 1456', *Sitzungsberichte der Bayerischen Akademie der Wissenschaften,* phil.-hist. Kl., 1957, 1–69, repr. in his *Aufsätze und Abhandlungen zur Geschichte Südosteuropas und der Levante,* 2 (Munich, 1966), pp. 263–310. The best narrative account is J. Hofer, *Johannes Kapistran. Ein Leben im Kampf um die Reform der Kirche,* revd edn, 2 vols (Heidelberg, 1964–65), 2.299–419. Much less satisfactory is J. Held, *Hunyadi: Legend and Reality* (Boulder, Co., 1985), pp. 155–69.

2   S. Andrić, *The Miracles of St John Capistran* (Budapest, 1999), p. 25.
3   Andrić, *The Miracles*, pp. 50–1.
4   *Acta Sanctorum Octobris*, 10 [hereafter *ASOct.* 10] (Brussels, 1861), p. 352.
5   Ibid.
6   'Quomodo volumus contra Turcam proprios sudores, propria nostra bona, panem filiorum nostrorum exponere, quandoquidem summus Pontifex in turribus, in grossis muris, in calce et lapidibus thesaurum S. Petri expendit, quem in defensionem sanctae fidei deberet expendere?' Ibid., p. 353.
7   Ibid.
8   On Calixtus's activity, see K. M. Setton, *The Papacy and the Levant (1204–1571). Volume II. The Fifteenth Century* (Philadelphia, 1978), pp. 161–95.
9   *ASOct.* 10, p. 356.
10   See P. Engel, *The Realm of St Stephen. A History of Medieval Hungary, 895–1526*, trans. T. Pálosfalva, ed. A. Ayton (London, 2001), pp. 288–95. It was symptomatic that Hunyadi would only attend the Buda diet of March–April 1456 with a royal letter of protection and an armed escort. Babinger, 'Der Quellenwert', p. 265.
11   *ASOct.* 10, p. 358.
12   *ASOct.* 10, p. 350.
13   Setton, *The Papacy and the Levant*, p. 187.
14   Hofer, 'Der Sieger', pp. 194–5 note 80; Babinger, 'Der Quellenwert', pp. 267, 306 note 1; Held, *Hunyadi*, p.166.
15   Cf. Hofer, *Johannes Kapistran*, 2.368, 372.
16   J. G. Kunisch, ed., *Peter Eschenloer's ... Geschichten der Stadt Breslau*, 2 vols (Breslau, 1827–28), 1.27.
17   See, e.g., letters to Calixtus III from King Ladislas V and Cardinal Carvajal dated 7 April 1456: G. Dobner, ed., *Monumenta historica Boemiae*, 6 vols (Prague, 1764–85), 2.413–15, 415–17.
18   J. Moorman, *A History of the Franciscan Order from its Origins to the Year 1517* (Oxford, 1968), pp. 452, 483–5; Hofer, *Johannes Kapistran*, 2.339–47.
19   *ASOct.* 10, p. 359, and see too Hofer, *Johannes Kapistran*, 2.355–60. Tagliacozzo claimed that Capistrano converted 11,000 people to Catholicism in three months, Giovanni da Tagliacozzo, 'Relatio de victoria Belgradensi', in J. M. Fonseca, ed., *Annales Minorum* (Quaracchi, 3rd edn 1931–), 12.750–96, at p. 752; G. B. Festa, 'Cinque lettere intorno alla vita e alla morte di S. Giovanni da Capestrano', *Bullettino della R. Deputazione Abruzzese di storia patria*, ser. 3, 2 (1911), 7–58, at p. 21. I am grateful to Valerie Scott, Librarian at the British School at Rome, for sending me a photocopy of this article.
20   Hofer, *Johannes Kapistran*, 2.299 note 3; *ASOct.* 10, p. 352.
21   Tagliacozzo, 'Relatio', p. 752; *ASOct.* 10, p. 361. Carvajal had himself been given the cross by the pope on 8 September 1455: Setton, *The Papacy and the Levant*, pp. 165–6.
22   For Capistrano's fellow preachers, see J. Szűcs, 'Die Ideologie des Bauernkrieges', in *Nation und Geschichte. Studien* (Cologne, 1981), pp. 329–78, at pp. 334 and 372 note 11.
23   Andrić, *The Miracles*, p. 26.
24   'acceperunt quamplures et praelati et barones signum vivificae crucis, de inferioribus multitudo, et in dies plures signamus.' *ASOct.* 10, p. 361.

25 *ASOct.* 10, p. 360.
26 'multum fructum allaturum et innumeros excitaturum ad crucem sacram suscipiendam et animose pergendum contra fidei christianae adversarios.' Ibid.
27 Held, *Hunyadi*, p. 156.
28 *ASOct.* 10, p. 361.
29 Held, *Hunyadi*, p. 157.
30 For maps see Babinger, 'Der Quellenwert', pp. 270, 273. Held, *Hunyadi*, p. 58, is inaccurate.
31 In the letter which he wrote to the king on 24 July, in which he failed even to mention Capistrano, Hunyadi related that apart from his troops and those of Jan Korogh, his only resource had been the 'homines crucesignati': *ASOct.* 10, p. 382.
32 Hofer, *Johannes Kapistran*, 2.399–400.
33 'Ac demum cruce signati licentia cum benedictione obtenta a beatissimo patre tamquam eorum capitaneo omnes ad propria redierunt laeti, admirantes ac stupentes super his, quae Deus ipse tam gloriose fecerat ministerio et officio beatissimi patris. Sicque cruciata soluta est.' Tagliacozzo, 'Relatio', p. 793.
34 Hofer, *Johannes Kapistran*, 2.410.
35 Since Capistrano was already sick at this point, it is tempting to agree with Erik Fügedi and Stanko Andrić that this letter was motivated more by the desire to keep the momentum going than by genuine plans: Andrić, *The Miracles*, p. 62. But this may be to underestimate Capistrano's optimism.
36 *ASOct.* 10, p. 384.
37 Ibid., pp. 384–5.
38 Nicholas of Fara, 'Vita clarissimi viri fratris Joannis de Capistrano', *ASOct.* 10, pp. 439–83, at p. 472 and see also Tagliacozzo's comments in Festa, 'Cinque lettere', pp. 28, 55. On the crusading army after 23 July, see also Andrić, *The Miracles*, p. 63.
39 Hofer, *Johannes Kapistran*, 2.371–2. This interpretation is supported by the letter which Tagliacozzo wrote on 15 September, in which he took the view that the crusade was intended to last beyond 23 July: 'O, s'el Patre fosse stato obedito, forse serrìa stata finita la Cruciata. Tucto augusto così infirmo se affatigò in questo et quasi niente curandose de la sua molesta infirmità, tucto suo studio ponea ne la defensione de la fede e confusione de' Turchi', Festa, 'Cinque lettere', p. 28.
40 Tagliacozzo wrote of 'sexaginta millia cruce signatorum ... qui omnes in Ungaria tam per ipsum beatum patrem quam per socios suos Ungaros cruce signati fuerant, licet inter eos essent nonnulli Alemanni, Poloni, Sclavi et Bosnenses': Tagliacozzo, 'Relatio', p. 765.
41 Lodrisio Crivelli, 'De expeditione Pii papae secundi in Turcas', *Rerum italicarum scriptores nova series*, 23, cols. 58–9. See also Hofer, *Johannes Kapistran*, 2.331.
42 A. Franke and G. Zschäbitz, eds, *Das Buch der Hundert Kapitel und der vierzig Statuten des sogenannten Oberrheinischen Revolutionärs* (Berlin, 1967), p. 257. For other German crusaders who fought at Belgrade, see Hofer, 'Der Sieger', pp. 177–8 and note 28 (Johann Tröster and Johann Roth); K. Elm, 'Johannes Kapistrans Predigtreise diesseits der Alpen (1451–1456)', in *Lebenslehren und*

Weltentwürfe im Übergang vom Mittelalter zur Neuzeit. Politik – Bildung – Naturkunde – Theologie, eds H. Boockmann, B. Moeller and K. Stackmann (Göttingen, 1989), pp. 500–19, at p. 514 note 61 (Johannes Paur, pastor of Pechtal, who died at Vienna while on the way home).

43   Held, *Hunyadi,* p. 243 note 44.

44   Kunisch, ed., *Peter Eschenloer's ... Geschichten der Stadt Breslau,* 1.27.

45   Babinger, 'Der Quellenwert', pp. 287–8, citing J. Baader, 'Zur Geschichte des Kreuzzuges vom Jahre 1456', *Anzeiger für Kunde der deutschen Vorzeit* NF 10 (1863), 251–4, which I have not seen.

46   Hofer, *Johannes Kapistran,* 2.412.

47   L. Thallóczy and H. Antal, eds, *Codex diplomaticus partium regno Hungariae adnexarum II,* (Budapest, 1907), 2.210–11.

48   Held, *Hunyadi,* pp. 167, 171.

49   *ASOct.* 10, p. 388: 'regem idcirco Albam venire cum Alamannorum crucigerorum manu ut, ejecto ipso (sc. László Hunyadi), protegendam illis arcem tribuat, omnia oppida, praefecturas et magistratus, qui in manu sunt Hungarorum, his exactis, Alemannis committat.' On crusader involvement in the outbreak of hostilities at Belgrade between the rival families of Hunyadi and Cilli, see also Hofer, *Johannes Kapistran,* 2.422.

50   Tagliacozzo, 'Relatio', pp. 765, 766; Festa, 'Cinque lettere', p. 24; Nicholas of Fara, 'Vita', p. 470.

51   Tagliacozzo, 'Relatio', p. 755; Nicholas of Fara, 'Vita', p. 470. On the size of Mehmed's army see Hofer, *Johannes Kapistran,* 2.389 note 128.

52   Szücs, 'Die Ideologie', p. 331, without substantiation; however, the Genoese merchant Iacopo de Promontorio, an eyewitness on the Turkish side, gave a figure of 'venti milia in più' for the crusaders. Babinger, 'Der Quellenwert', p. 308.

53   Babinger, 'Der Quellenwert', p. 267 note 5.

54   Hofer, *Johannes Kapistran,* 2.391 note 176; Held, *Hunyadi,* p. 167. Hofer suggests that Tagliacozzo's 60,000 represents an attempt at a global figure incorporating all the crusaders who arrived during the siege, which is ingenious but unconvincing.

55   Tagliacozzo, 'Relatio', pp. 763–4.

56   Ibid., pp. 768, 772.

57   Ibid., pp. 770, 776–8, 791, 793–4. Cf. the incidents narrated at pp. 763 and 790 to counter 'nonnulli veritatis inimici'.

58   'Le biographe s'étend en de véritables amplifications, cite copieusement l'Écriture sainte, s'abandonne à des explosions de lyrisme.' R. Lechat, 'Lettres de Jean de Tagliacozzo sur le siège de Belgrade et la mort de S. Jean de Capistran', *Analecta Bollandiana* 39 (1921), 139–51, at p. 142.

59   Festa, 'Cinque lettere', pp. 26, 54–5; Tagliacozzo, 'Relatio', pp. 784–5.

60   'Un peu de prudence suffit à l'historien pour élaguer les éléments suspects et rester en présence d'une moisson de renseignements précis dont il aurait tort de se priver.' Ibid., pp. 145–6, 150. Hofer and Babinger agreed on Tagliacozzo's reliability: 'Der Sieger', pp. 191–2; 'Der Quellenwert', p. 284.

61   Lechat, 'Lettres', pp. 150–1. Tagliacozzo repeatedly commented that these were events 'quae oculis vidi et manus contrectavi': Tagliacozzo, 'Relatio', pp. 751, 785, 795.

62   Hofer, *Johannes Kapistran,* 2.361 note 49, 365.

63 Elm, 'Johannes Kapistrans Predigtreise', pp. 504–5 and *passim*.

64 Ibid., pp. 508–9. See also G. Constable, 'The Language of Preaching in the Twelfth Century', *Viator* 25 (1994), 131–52, at pp. 149–50.

65 Christopher of Varese, 'Vita S. Joannis a Capistrano', *ASOct*. 10, pp. 491–541, at pp. 531–2. Capistrano had preached the cross at Nürnberg as late as mid-November 1454: Hofer, *Johannes Kapistran*, 2.321–2 note 55.

66 Babinger, 'Der Quellenwert', p. 288, and cf. Elm, 'Johannes Kapistrans Predigtreise', pp. 513–14, both citing Baader, 'Zur Geschichte des Kreuzzuges vom Jahre 1456', pp. 253–4.

67 The comparison with Peter the Hermit seems more apposite than the more familiar one with St Bernard (e.g. Hofer, *Johannes Kapistran*, 2.308) since St Bernard had made no attempt to lead the armies of the Second Crusade. Generally on charismatic leadership and crusading see G. Dickson, 'Encounters in Medieval Revivalism: Monks, Friars, and Popular Enthusiasts', *Church History* 68 (1999), 265–93, at pp. 285–7.

68 'Beato patri et non alteri obediebant, tamquam eorum capitaneo, imo tamquam vicario Iesu Christi; nec mirum, cum ad eius predicationes et monitiones excitati crucem ab eo sumpserant, secum et in carcerem et in mortem ire sibi polliciti ... Ipse enim erat omnium cruce signatorum rector, dux, iudex, capitaneus et imperator.' Tagliacozzo, 'Relatio', p. 764.

69 Ibid., p. 765. Cf. Festa, 'Cinque lettere', p. 53, 'più posseva fare lui de quisti Crucisignati che lo Re de Ungarìa'.

70 Nicholas of Fara, 'Vita', p. 472.

71 Tagliacozzo, 'Relatio', p. 769.

72 These details occur in the letter which Tagliacozzo wrote on 10 February 1461 describing Capistrano's final days, *ASOct*. 10, pp. 390–402, at pp. 390–1, and cf. Festa, 'Cinque lettere', p. 24.

73 Tagliacozzo, 'Relatio', pp. 762, 791–2, for the theme of conversion.

74 Ibid., p. 784.

75 Ibid., p. 768.

76 'informabat, ut cogitarent quomodo canes illi, jugiter nomen Domini blasphemantes, fidem Christi derident, ecclesias destruunt, altaria sacra profanant, non abhorrentes, virgines super altaribus, Deo dicatis, deflorare, sanguinem christianorum truculenta rabie effundunt, eos in servitutem redigunt, fidem suam autem, a diabolico viro Mahometo eis traditam, spurcitiis et ignominiis plenam, extollunt, magnificant et exaltant.' Christopher of Varese, 'Vita', p. 531.

77 Tagliacozzo, 'Relatio', pp. 777, 789; M. Bihl, 'Duae epistolae S. Iohannis a Capistrano, altera ad Ladislaum regem, altera de victoria Belgradensi (An. 1453 et 1456)', *Archivum franciscanum historicum* 19 (1926), 63–75, at p. 72.

78 'Quicunque etiam nobiscum assistere contra Turcos volunt, amici nostri sunt, Rassiani, schismatici, Valachi, iudaei, haeretici, et quicunque infideles nobiscum in hac tempestate esse volunt, eos amicitia complectamur. Nunc contra Turcos, contra Turcos pugnandum est.' Tagliacozzo, 'Relatio', p. 766, and cf. Festa, 'Cinque lettere', p. 55. See also Hofer, *Johannes Kapistran*, 2.394, and Andrić, *The Miracles*, p. 26, who may be right to see it as 'a temporary change of heart'.

79 Tagliacozzo, 'Relatio', p. 761.

220 *Notes*

80 'Ecce, filii mei, nunc tempus acceptabile, ecce nunc dies salutis. Ecce, nunc aperta est ianua paradisi, ecce tempus coronae, ecce nunc tempus redemptionis peccatorum.' Ibid., pp. 783–4 and see also Festa, 'Cinque lettere', p. 26.

81 Ibid., p. 766 and see also Festa, 'Cinque lettere', p. 26.

82 Ibid., p. 765.

83 Ibid., pp. 765–6.

84 On Nicopolis, see N. Housley, 'Le maréchal Boucicaut à Nicopolis', *Annales de Bourgogne* 68 (1996), 85–99, repr. in N. Housley, *Crusading and Warfare in Medieval and Renaissance Europe* (Aldershot, 2001), study XVI.

85 'Was sich im Lager von Belgrad abspielte, muss im Lichte jener religiösen Bewegung gewürdigt werden, die Kapistran überall auslöste, wo er auftrat. Sein Lager bei Belgrad war nicht so sehr ein Kriegslager; es glich eher jenen religiösen Versammlungen, wie sie sich die letzten sechs Jahre überall um ihn bildeten, wohin er auf seiner Missionsfahrt kam.' Hofer, 'Der Sieger', pp. 205–6; and cf. his *Johannes Kapistran*, 2.392.

86 Tagliacozzo, 'Relatio', pp. 754, 764; and see also Festa, 'Cinque lettere', p. 22.

87 Tagliacozzo, 'Relatio', pp. 754, 759, 761, 766, 769, 772, 783. Capistrano and his fellow Observants were suffused with the desire for martyrdom: ibid., pp. 752, 753, 755, 757–8, 760, 769, 772, 779, 783, 784–5, 795.

88 'O quam felices qui in hac pugna Christi morientur, quia statim ab Angelis cum Sanctis Martyribus, qui pro fide mortui sunt, coronabuntur.' Christopher of Varese, 'Vita', p. 532.

89 Nicholas of Fara, 'Vita', p. 471.

90 Festa, 'Cinque lettere', p. 28.

91 The exception is Tagliacozzo's first letter, written on 28 July 1456, Festa, 'Cinque lettere', pp. 49–56, which contains no reference to the 'Nomen Jesu': but note its prominence in the letter that Capistrano wrote to the pope on 23 July, in Fonseca, ed., *Annales Minorum*, 12.796–8, proving that it was not a later invention.

92 'post exhortationem publice factam ad defensionem fidei christianae et plenariam remissionem omnium peccatorum et ad martyrium, non aliud quam Nomen Iesu invocandum et acclamandum, tam in aqua quam in terra praecepit.' Tagliacozzo, 'Relatio', p. 761.

93 Tagliacozzo, 'Relatio', pp. 766, 772.

94 Tagliacozzo, 'Relatio', p. 781 and cf. p. 788. For Nicholas of Fara it was the 'mellifluum, potentissimumque Nomen Jesu: 'Vita', p. 471.

95 E.g., Tagliacozzo, 'Relatio', p. 795: 'Habes, igitur, Pater suavissime, unde dulcissimum Nomen Iesu et virtutem sanctissimae crucis, ut semper fecisti, possis amplius exaltare.'

96 Ibid., p. 754.

97 Tagliacozzo, 'Relatio', pp. 750, 754, and cf. 778: 'virtus sanctissimi Nominis Iesu et sanctissimae Crucis.' In his 1457 letter Tagliacozzo commented that 'Così fo liberata la Christianità da' Turchi per industria et sollicitudine et oratione del beato Iohanni de Capistrano, socto el nome de Yhesù, et la virtù de la sanctissima croce', Festa, 'Cinque lettere', p. 27.

98 *Dizionario biografico degli Italiani*, 55 (Rome, 2000), pp. 744–58, at p. 746.

99 Tagliacozzo, 'Relatio', p. 789.

100 'quomodo totus populus christiane religionis sufficiens esse posset ad reddendum graciarum acciones et dignas laudes ipsi domino nostro Ihesu Christo, qui pro sua causa nostraque proteccione solus pugnavit et expugnavit atque destruxit exercitum magni Turchi cum sua confusione et dedecore memorabili, ut in eternum pro duracione presentis seculi talis Christi Ihesu victoria gloriosa de ore omnium christianorum imperpetuum nunquam cesset.' Bihl, 'Duae epistolae', p. 74.

101 Nicholas of Fara, 'Vita', p. 470.

102 Tagliacozzo, 'Relatio', p. 751 and see also Festa, 'Cinque lettere', p. 21.

103 Tagliacozzo, 'Relatio', p. 754.

104 Ibid., p. 755.

105 Ibid., p. 756.

106 Ibid., p. 760.

107 Ibid., p. 776. The same technique had been used to drive back the Turks in 1440. Babinger, 'Der Quellenwert', p. 276.

108 Tagliacozzo, 'Relatio', p. 779.

109 Ibid., pp. 784–5, 786.

110 *ASOct.* 10, p. 382.

111 'Iam incipiunt cruce signati ad locum praesignatum convenire, jam pauperes excitantur; divites et nobiles domi sedent.' Tagliacozzo, 'Relatio', p. 759. See also Festa, 'Cinque lettere', p. 54 ('Crucisignati povirelli').

112 'populares, rustici, pauperes, sacerdotes, clerici saeculares, studentes, monachi, fratres diversae religionis, mendicantes, personae tertii ordinis beati Francisci, eremitae.' Tagliacozzo, 'Relatio', p. 767. Cf his list at p. 782.

113 Ibid., p. 791; Festa, 'Cinque lettere', p. 55; Nicholas of Fara, 'Vita', p. 472. For the First Crusade, see R. Hill, ed., *Gesta Francorum et aliorum Hierosolimitanorum* (1962; repr. Oxford, 1972), p. 96.

114 A. Borosy, 'The *Militia Portalis* in Hungary before 1526', in *From Hunyadi to Rákóczi. War and Society in Late Medieval and Early Modern Hungary*, ed. J. M. Bak and B. K. Király (New York, 1982), pp. 63–80. Tagliacozzo reported a levy of 12 fighters for every 100 households in 1456, Festa, 'Cinque lettere', p. 50.

115 Tagliacozzo, 'Relatio', p. 767; Festa, 'Cinque lettere', pp. 54–5 ('sensa cavalli' twice).

116 Tagliacozzo, 'Relatio', pp. 758, 770, 778; Festa, 'Cinque lettere', pp. 24–5.

117 N. Housley, 'Crusading as Social Revolt: the Hungarian Peasant Uprising of 1514', *Journal of Ecclesiastical History* 49 (1998), 1–28, repr. in N. Housley, *Crusading and Warfare in Medieval and Renaissance Europe* (Aldershot, 2001), study XVII.

118 Tagliacozzo, 'Relatio', p. 762.

119 This is well attested and, given Hunyadi's pessimistic assessment of the situation, wholly understandable: Hofer, 'Der Sieger', p. 199; Babinger, 'Der Quellenwert', p. 275. These facts are ignored by Held, *Hunyadi*, pp. 161–3.

120 'de Iohanni Bianco governatore no curavano.' Festa, 'Cinque lettere', p. 53.

121 'hetten jn die creitzer, sie lyessen in nicht ein augenplik leben, wan er gern gesehen hett, das sie alle erschlagen weren worden.' Babinger, 'Der Quellenwert', p. 288. Text also in N. Iorga, ed., *Notes et extraits pour servir à l'histoire des croisades au XVe siècle, quatrième série (1453–1476)* (Bucharest, 1915), p. 132.

122 'victoria, quam Dominus hesterna die dederat eis, non fuerat per operam aut
industriam alicuius baronis regni Ungariae, sed per virtutem solum sanctissimi Nominis Iesu Christi et suae sanctissimae crucis et per merita ac labores
sudoresque beatissimi patris nostri fratris Ioannis de Capistrano.'
Tagliacozzo, 'Relatio', p. 793. Tagliacozzo was not present but emphasized
that he heard about it from Jerome of Padua, who witnessed it all. There is
strong confirmation in an independent Breslau source: Kunisch, ed., *Peter
Eschenloer's ... Geschichten der Stadt Breslau*, 1.31.

123 Hofer, *Johannes Kapistran*, 1: 324, and cf. Andrić, *The Miracles*, p. 16.

124 Thallóczy and Antal, *Codex diplomaticus*, 2.465–7.

125 Tagliacozzo, 'Relatio', p. 766 and cf. p. 784, 'o pauperes filii mei, supplete
defectum christianorum'.

126 'Nolite timere, pusillus grex, nolite contremiscere. Dabit quidem Deus nobis
optatam victoriam de inimicis suis, quam praecurrentia astra designant
omnino futuram.' Nicholas of Fara, 'Vita', p. 470.

127 'Non timeas, magnifice Domine! Potens est Deus cum paucis et inermibus
Turcorum potentiam superare, castrum nostrum defendere et inimicos suos
confundere.' Tagliacozzo, 'Relatio', p. 771. Cf Tagliacozzo's reflections on the
events of 22 July: ibid., p. 782.

128 See in particular Capistrano's first letter to the pope, *ASOct.* 10, p. 382. It is
hard to believe that in such a public document he would attribute to
Hunyadi a view which the captain general had not expressed.

129 Tagliacozzo, 'Relatio', p. 783 (quoting 1 Macc. 3: 17–22, a favourite passage
of crusading enthusiasts).

130 Cf. on this issue Szűcs, 'Die Ideologie', pp. 332–6, though he pushes the evidence further than it warrants.

131 Iorga, ed., *Notes et extraits*, p. 142, from Leipzig Universitätsbibliothek MS
1092, fol. 13r–v. There has been much confusion about this MS: see Hofer,
'Der Sieger', pp. 209–10; Babinger, 'Der Quellenwert', pp. 271–2 note 3, 302
note 1; Hofer, *Johannes Kapistran*, 2.387 note 161.

132 Tagliacozzo, 'Relatio', p. 795, where the providential explanation is given.

133 'illa magna navis, tam artificiose parata, et in qua tota humana spes posita
erat, potius quam in naviculis pauperum.' Tagliacozzo, 'Relatio', p. 763.

134 'ut ex hoc innueretur, ab illo eos cruce signatos collectos esse, qui Ordinis
Minorum erat sectator egregius, aut innueretur illam cruciatam solum pauperum et non divitum esse; vel hoc faciebant, ut conformarent se cum vex-
illo patris eorum, vel ut horum sanctorum patrociniis sub eorum vexillis
pugnantes iuvari mererentur.' Tagliacozzo, 'Relatio', pp. 764–5.

135 G. Barta, 'Der ungarische Bauernkrieg vom Jahre 1514', in *Aus der Geschichte
der ostmitteleuropäischen Bauernbewegungen im 16.–17. Jahrhundert*, ed.
G. Heckenast (Budapest, 1977), pp. 63–9, at p. 63.

136 Tagliacozzo, 'Relatio', pp. 751–2; Festa, 'Cinque lettere', p. 21.

137 Above, at note 24, though the comment also reveals Capistrano's awareness
of the discrepancy in response, and he was perhaps trying to be upbeat in
writing to the pope.

138 Tagliacozzo, 'Relatio', p. 767.

139 M. Rady, *Nobility, Land and Service in Medieval Hungary* (Basingstoke, 2000),
pp. 144–57.

140 Nicholas of Fara comes the closest to a 'national' theme with the phrase 'omnes pro Christo, pro propria, proque communi omnium salute ad propellendos hostes ... animabat': 'Vita', p. 471.

141 'O pater beatissime Iohannes de Capistrano! nonne tuo ministerio, tua industria, tua opera, tuo iussu, tuaque oratione haec omnia facta sunt?' Tagliacozzo, 'Relatio', pp. 776–7.

142 Above, at note 28.

143 R. Schwoebel, *The Shadow of the Crescent: The Renaissance Image of the Turk (1453–1517)* (Nieuwkoop, 1967), pp. 48, 56 note 86.

144 Schwoebel, *The Shadow*, pp. 45, 55 note 77; Hofer, *Johannes Kapistran*, 2.373 and note 104.

145 N. Housley, 'Explaining Defeat: Andrew of Regensburg and the Hussite Crusades', in *Dei Gesta per Francos: Études sur les croisades dédiées à Jean Richard*, eds M. Balard, B. Z. Kedar and J. Riley–Smith (Aldershot, 2001), pp. 87–95.

146 Setton, *The Papacy and the Levant*, p. 188, and pp. 184–9 for naval operations generally.

147 R. Black, *Benedetto Accolti and the Florentine Renaissance* (Cambridge, 1985), pp. 237–40.

148 Housley, 'Crusading as Social Revolt', pp. 7–8.

149 J. Hankins, 'Renaissance Crusaders: Humanist Crusade Literature in the Age of Mehmed II', *Dumbarton Oaks Papers* 49 (1995), 111–207, at p. 120; M. J. Heath, *Crusading Commonplaces: La Noue, Lucinge and Rhetoric against the Turks* (Geneva, 1986), pp. 45–80.

150 'Gotfridus et alii qui secum in Asia militarunt parva saepe manu innumerabiles hostium copias deleverunt, ac ipsos Turcos tanquam pecudes mactaverunt. Sed arbitramini fortasse meliores hodie Turcos esse, victa Graecia quam olim fuerunt. At quales sint pugna Thaurinensis ostendit, anno ab hinc tertio gesta ... Erant Christiani milites qui oppidum tuebantur, pauci cruce signati, non nobiles aut divites, non bellis assueti, non armis tecti, sed rudes, incompositi, agrestes. Et hii tamen Turcos vicere, non tam ferrum quam fidem hostibus opponentes. Ab his tumidus ille Turcorum Imperator insuperabilis antea creditus, et terror gentium appellatus, in acie victus, ab obsidione deiectus, castris exutus, turpem arripere fugam compulsus est.' Aeneas Silvius Piccolomini, *Opera omnia* (Basle, 1571), p. 909.

151 Andrić, *The Miracles*, pp.157–8. The best reproduction of the fresco seems to be I. Hlobil, 'Bernardinské Symboly Jména Ježíš v Českých Zemích Šířené Janem Kapistránem', *Umění* 44 (1996), 223–34, at p. 228.

152 At Bernardino's canonization Pope Nicholas V jocularly remarked to Capistrano 'Who will take care of your canonization?': Andrić, *The Miracles*, p. 88.

153 Tagliacozzo, 'Relatio', p. 794.

154 'Haec enim felicissima gloriosissimaque victoria, de Turcis, auctore divo Joanne, et nullo alio, dicant quid velint.' Nicholas of Fara, 'Vita', p. 472.

155 Andrić, *The Miracles*, p. 29.

156 Ibid., pp. 87–8; Hofer, *Johannes Kapistran*, 2.423.

157 Andrić, *The Miracles*, p. 154.

158 Ibid., p. 163.

159 Ibid., pp. 163–6.
160 *ASOct.* 10, p. 425.
161 G. Dickson, 'La Genèse de la croisade des enfants (1212)', *Bibliothèque de l'École des Chartes* 153 (1995), 54–102; M. Barber, 'The Crusade of the Shepherds in 1251', in *Proceedings of the Tenth Annual Meeting of the Western Society for French History*, ed. J. F. Sweets (Lawrence, Kansas, 1984), pp. 1–23; G. Dickson, 'The Advent of the *Pastores* (1251)', *Revue belge de philologie et d'histoire* 66 (1988), 249–67; S. Schein, *Fideles Crucis. The Papacy, the West, and the Recovery of the Holy Land 1274–1314* (Oxford, 1991), pp. 233–8; M. Barber, 'The Pastoureaux of 1320', *Journal of Ecclesiastical History* 32 (1981), 227–67.
162 Above, at note 78.
163 By contrast, some curious beliefs were voiced during the crusade of 1514: Housley, 'Crusading as Social Revolt', pp. 16–17.
164 Tagliacozzo, 'Relatio', pp. 764–6.
165 S. Runciman, *A History of the Crusades. Volume I. The First Crusade and the Foundation of the Kingdom of Jerusalem* (Cambridge, 1951), pp. 131–2; J. Riley–Smith, *The First Crusade and the Idea of Crusading* (London, 1986), pp. 49–52.
166 'Ecce, qualis hec mutatio! Heu, quanta confusio ... ', Szűcs, 'Die Ideologie', pp. 334, 372 note 10. Cf. Iorga, ed., *Notes et extraits*, p. 142: 'Heu, quanta confusio, quod inter tot milia unicus non debet reperiri cliens! Taceo de magnis.'

8   Hungary and Crusading in the Fifteenth Century

1 On this aspect, see my 'Delinquent Lords and Forsaken Serfs: Thoughts on War and Society during the Crisis of Feudalism', in *Society in Change: Studies in Honor of Béla K. Király*, ed. S. B. Vardy and A. H. Vardy (New York, 1983), pp. 291–304. It may be interesting to note that the word *kuruc* became the name for all later rebels against the Habsburg rulers of Hungary, down to the recent past, when it was applied to intransigent 'national' politicians.
2 The exact date has not been established. See J. M. Bak, P. Engel and J. R. Sweeney, eds, *Decreta Regni Mediaevalis Hungariae: The Laws of the Medieval Kingdom of Hungary* (henceforth: *DRMH*), vol. 2 (1301–1457) (Salt Lake City, 1992), pp. 21–8. See also J. Held, 'Military reform in early fifteenth–century Hungary', *East European Quarterly* 11 (1977), 129–39.
3 See A. Borosy, 'The *militia portalis* in Hungary before 1526', in J. M. Bak and B. K. Király, eds, *From Hunyadi to Rákóczi: War and Society in Late Medieval and Early Modern Hungary* (New York, 1982), pp. 63–80.
4 *DRMH* 2: 26–7.
5 See Gy. Bónis, 'Ständisches Finanzwesen in Ungarn im frühen 16. Jahrhundert', *Nouvelles Études Historiques* (Budapest, 1965), 83–103.
6 On this in detail, see F. Szakály, 'The Hungarian–Croatian Border Defense System and its Collapse', in Bak and Király, eds, *From Hunyadi to Rákóczi*, pp. 141–58.
7 On these see F. Szakály, 'Phases of Turco–Hungarian Warfare before the Battle of Mohács (1365–1526)', *Acta Orientalia Academiae Scientiarum Hungaricae* 33 (1979), 66–111.

8 A. Kovách, 'Der "Mongolenbrief" Bélas IV. und Papst Innozenz IV.', in *Überlieferung und Auftrag: Festschrift für Michael de Ferdinandy zum 60. Geburtstag*, ed. J. G. Farkas (Wiesbaden, 1972), pp. 495–506.
9 A. Theiner, ed., *Vetera Monumenta historica Hungariam sacram illustrantia*, 2 (Rome, 1860), p. 289.
10 S. Katona, *Historia critica regum Hungariae*, 6 (13) (Pest, 1790), p. 26.
11 See J. M. Bak, *Königtum und Stände in Ungarn im 14.–16. Jh.* (Wiesbaden, 1973), pp. 141–3.
12 Aeneas Silvius Piccolomini, *Opera quae extant*, 1 (Basle 1551), p. 556, quoted by L. Terbe, 'Egy európai szállóige életrajza: Magyarország a kereszténység védőbástyája' [Biography of a European proverb: Hungary as the bastion of Christendom], *Egyetemes Philologiai Közlöny/Archivum Philologicum* 60 (1936), 297–351, here 302.
13 Piccolomini, *Opera*, 1: 926; quoted by Terbe, 'Egy európai szállóige életrajza', p. 303.
14 Theiner, *Vetera Monumenta*, 2: 240; see also Pope Pius II to Frederick III in 1459, *Ibid*, 2: 324.
15 See J. V. Fine, *The Late Medieval Balkans: A Critical Survey from the Late Twelfth Century to the Ottoman Conquest* (Ann Arbor, Michigan, 1987), pp. 143–9.
16 King Matthias exempted them from paying the tithe to the Catholic bishops, 'so that, following the example of these refugees, other people living under Turkish rule would be more willing to come here'. See the law of 15 July 1481, paragraph 4; *DRMH*, 3 (Los Angeles, 1996), p. 37.
17 See, for example, P. Engel, *The Realm of St Stephen: A History of Medieval Hungary 895–1526* (London, 2001) pp. 157–9. He pointed out that modern historiography clearly inherited the attitude of the gentry of the late Middle Ages in its judgment of these rulers and their policies.
18 So much so that the fifteenth–century law book, the famous *Tripartitum opus iuris consuetudinarii inclyti regni Hungariae* by Stephen Werbőczy (Vienna, 1517) spelled out that donations, and thus nobility, are earned primarily by *peculium militare* (I: 4).
19 E. Mályusz, *Kaiser Sigismund in Ungarn 1387–1437*, trans. A. Szmodits (Budapest, 1990), p. 123.
20 On Hunyadi in general, see J. Held, *Hunyadi: Legend and Reality* (New York, 1985).
21 P. Engel, 'János Hunyadi: The Decisive Years of His Career, 1440–1444', in Bak and Király, eds, *From Hunyadi to Rákóczi*, pp. 103–23; in what follows, I shall rely on this article and on Engel's summary in *The Realm of St Stephen*, pp. 286–7.
22 Engel, 'Hunyadi', p. 111.
23 Ibid., p. 112.
24 G. Fejér, *Genus, incunabula et virtus Joannis Corvini de Hunyad* (Buda, 1844), p. 153.
25 Joannes Długosz, *Opera omnia*, 13, ed. A. Przedziecki (Cracow, 1877) p. 701, quoted by Engel, 'Hunyadi'.
26 See Norman Housley, this volume, chapter 7.
27 Apparently, the magnates who had ruled the country in the absence of the young king (Ladislas Posthumus returned to Hungary just a few months before the siege) asked the Franciscan to come and preach the crusade, for this was the only way to mobilize the masses and thus reduce the obligations on the nobility.

28   See Norman Housley, this volume, chapter 7.

29   From the extensive literature (mostly in Hungarian) let me refer only to Jenő Szücs, *Nation und Geschichte: Studien* (Budapest, 1981), esp. pp. 101–29.

30   See G. Rázsó, 'The Mercenary Army of King Matthias Corvinus', in Bak and Király, eds, *From Hunyadi to Rákóczi*, pp. 125–40. The king had to face a major rebellion led by his closest associates, such as John Vitéz of Zredna and the poet-bishop Janus Pannonius, apparently because of this change in his politics; see Engel, *The Realm of St Stephen*, pp. 304–5.

31   The leading historian of the inter-war years, Gyula Szekfü, in his influential national history, dismissed these moralizing motives and emphasized the 'right' of the Corvinian to be just as expansionist and power-oriented as any other Renaissance prince of his age; B. Hóman-Gy. Szekfü, *Magyar Történet* (Hungarian history) ed. 2 (Budapest 1936, repr. 2000), 2: 466–7.

32   E. Mályusz, 'Matthias Corvinus', in *Menschen die Geschichte machten: viertausend Jahre Weltgeschichte in Zeit- und Lebensbildern*, 2, ed. P. R. Rohden and G. Ostrogorsky (Vienna, 1931), p. 190, my translation.

33   Rázsó, 'The Mercenary Army', p. 136. Rázsó pointed out that the king's decision to move in the direction of his weaker enemies was unrealistic, and that the campaigns in Moravia and Silesia, though keeping the mercenary army busy, ended up costing as much as, or more than, they brought into the treasury. But he admitted that the king had little choice: the two other hypothetical choices, to give up or to pursue active campaigns without additional resources, could not have been seriously considered.

34   See K. Nehring, *Matthias Corvinus, Kaiser Friedrich III. und das Reich*, 2nd revd edn (Munich 1989).

35   The most recent attempt at drawing a balance of the Corvinian's reign is J. K. Hoensch, *König Matthias Corvinus: Diplomat, Feldherr und Mäzen* (Graz, etc., 1998), esp. pp. 261–3. He does not accept the argument for necessary expansion, suggesting that a better management of the country's resources, combined with the occasional help of the papal curia and other Christian powers, would have sufficed to halt Ottoman advance into the Danubian principalities and towards the Adriatic. But in general he does not place much emphasis on the 'west or south' alternatives.

36   I. Nagy and A. Nyári, eds, *Magyar diplomácziai emlékek Mátyás király korából* (Hungarian Records of Diplomacy from the Age of King Matthias), Monumenta Hungariae historica (Budapest 1877), pp. 9–19, dated 14 April and 19 March respectively.

37   *Columen singulare* and *fortissimus Christi pugil*; in Pope Paul II to Matthias 26 May 1465 and undated 1465, in V. Fraknói, ed., *Mathiae Corvini Hungariae regis epistolae ad Romanos pontifices datae et ab eis acceptae*, Monumenta Vaticana historiam regni Hungariae illustrantia Ser. 1, vol. 6 (repr. Budapest, 2000), pp. 46, 50.

38   Matthias to Pope Paul II, 2 February 1476, Fraknói, ed., *Mathiae Corvini epistolae*, p. 109.

39   Pope Paul II to Matthias, 26 May 1465, Fraknói, *Mathiae Corvini epistolae*, p. 46.

40   Based on the papal account book, 'Pauli Cruciata' (though there was no crusade), quoted by Franknói in 'Prolegomena' to *Mathiae Corvini epistolae*, p. x, note 3.

41 See J. M. Bak, 'Monarchie im Wellental: materielle Grundlagen des ungarischen Königtums im fünfzehnten Jahrhundert', in *Das spätmittelalter-liche Königtum in europäischem Vergleich*, ed. R. Schneider (Sigmaringen, 1987), pp. 347–84, at pp. 356–8.

42 Matthias to Pope Paul II, 2 October 1465, Fraknói, *Mathiae Corvini Epistolae*, pp. 61–2.

43 Engel, *The Realm of St Stephen*, pp. 302–5.

44 Printed as Appendix no. 16 in Bak, *Königtum*, pp. 158–9. The Scythian rhet-oric was widely used during the tumultuous diets of the first decades of the sixteenth century.

45 See Bak, 'Delinquent Lords and Forsaken Serfs'; N. Housley, 'Crusading as Social Revolt: The Hungarian Peasant Uprising of 1514', *Journal of Ecclesiastical History* 49 (1998), 1–28.

46 Not even the best-informed and qualified historian of the period, András Kubinyi. See his 'Historische Skizze Ungarns in der Jagiellonenzeit', in Kubinyi, *König und Volk im spätmittelalterlichen Ungarn* (Herne, 1998), pp. 323–66; see also Engel, *The Realm of St Stephen*, pp. 369–71. The tradi-tional moralizing argument about the 'egotism' of the politically relevant strata is circular: if they had truly been following their self-interest and 'instinct of self-preservation', then they would have acted differently.

47 Giovanni Antonio Burgio to the papal secretary Jacopo Sadoleto, 13 April 1525; A. Ipolyi, ed., *Relationes oratorum pontificiorum 1524–1526*, Monumenta Vaticana historiam regni Hungariae illustrantia, ser. 2, vol. 1 (repr. Budapest 2001), p. 163, my translation.

48 All this does not, of course, imply that the kingdom's economic and military conditions would, in the long run, have permitted its successful resistance to the much more powerful and, at this time still expanding, Ottoman Empire, even if no political and strategic mistakes had been made. This point is now stressed by all competent historians (see n. 45 above).

9 Poland and the Crusade in the Reign of King Jan Olbracht

1 *Missale Cracoviense* (Mainz, 1484); Kraków, Biblioteka Jagiellońska, incunab-ula no. 2859, fols 126v–127v.

2 A. Fisher, *The Crimean Tartars* (Stanford, 1978), pp. 11–17.

3 I. Czamańska, *Mołdawia i Wołoszczyzna wobec Polski, Węgier i Turcji w XV i XVI wieku* (Poznań, 1996), pp. 153–63.

4 Today the cities of Kiliya and Bilhorod Dnistrovskyy in Ukraine; Białogród was also known as Moncastro or Cetatea Albă.

5 Quoted in N. Beldiceneau, 'La conquête des cités marchandes de Kilia et de Cetetea Albă par Bajezid II', *Sudost Forschungen* 23 (1964), 36–90.

6 S. Lloyd, 'The crusading movement, 1096–1274', in *Oxford Illustrated History of the Crusades*, ed. J. Riley-Smith (Oxford, 1995), pp. 34–65, at p. 36.

7 Miechowita, *Chronica Polonorum* (Kraków, 2nd edn 1521), p. 356. The two edi-tions of the *Chronica Polonorum* are in effect two separate texts, the original 1519 edition having undergone substantial changes at the hands of the royal censor who prepared the second edition of 1521. Only three copies of the original 1519

edition survive; with the exception of those passages which appear only in the 1519 text, all references here will be to the more common 1521 edition. For an account of the censorship, see F. Bortel, 'Zakaz Miechowity', *Przewodnik Naukowy i Literacki* (Lwów, 1884), pp. 438–51 and 637–51.

8   Bernard Wapowski, *Kroniki Bernarda Wapowskiego*, ed. J. Szujski (Kraków, 1874), pp. 17, 19.
9   Wapowski, *Kroniki*, p. 15.
10 J. Smołucha, *Papiestwo a Polska w latach 1484–1526: kontakty dyplomatyczne na tle zagrożenia tureckiego* (Kraków, 1999), p. 34. Jan Olbracht allowed a force of 2,000 men, led by Jan Karnkowski, to cross the border and help Stefan to expel Ottoman forces; these troops participated in the defeat of the Turks at Lake Katlaburg in November 1485.
11 Smołucha, *Papiestwo a Polska*, p. 41; K. Setton, *The Papacy and the Levant, 1201–1571*, 2 (Philadelphia, 1978), p. 402.
12 For an account of the election, see Miechowita, *Chronica Polonorum*, 2nd edn, pp. 347–8.
13 Miechowita, *Chronica Polonorum*, 2nd edn, p. 352.
14 These events, and their implications for the Central European crusade, are analysed by K. Baczkowski, 'Europa wobec problemu tureckiego w latach 1493–95', *Studia Historyczne* 3 (1997), 313–40.
15 For a summary of Polish and Romanian historiography of the summit, see Smołucha, *Papiestwo a Polska*, pp. 62–4.
16 The summit was convened by King Władisław, probably in an attempt to bolster his domestic position with a display of dynastic solidarity and strength. See L. Finkel, 'Zjazd Jagiellonów w Lewoczy r.1494', *Kwartalnik Historyczny* 28 (1914), 315–50.
17 Miechowita, *Chronica Polonorum* (Kraków, 1st edn 1519), p. 348. This comment was removed by the censor in the second edition of 1521.
18 K. Górka, 'Działalność dyplomacji polskiej w latach 1466–92', in *Historia Dyplomacji Polskiej*, ed. M. Biskup, 1 (Warsaw, 1982), pp. 439–500, at p. 539.
19 Smołucha, *Papiestwo a Polska*, p. 64.
20 A. Lewicki, ed., *Codex Epistolaris Saeculi Decimi Quinti* 3 (Kraków, 1894), no. 417, pp. 433–4, no. 421, pp. 435–7, no. 425, p. 441.
21 *Codex Epistolaris* 3, no. 415, pp. 427–9, no. 416, pp. 429–33.
22 The most recent published study of Cardinal Fryderyk's career is H. Rybus, *Kardynał-Królewicz Fryderyk Jagiellończyk jako biskup krakowski i arcybiskup gnieźnieński* (Warsaw, 1935).
23 B. Ulanowski, ed., *Acta capitulorum nec non iudiciorum ecclesiasticorum*, Monumenta Medii Aevi Historica Res Gestas Polonias Illustrantia 13 (Kraków, 1894), no. 2441, p. 550. no. 2487, p. 558, no. 2566, p. 571.
24 *Acta capitulorum*, no. 2441, p. 550.
25 J. Smołucha, 'Kilka uwag na temat wyprawy czarnomorskiej Jana Olbrachta w 1497 r.', *Studia Historyczne* 3 (1997), 413–42, at p. 417; F. Papée, *Jan Olbracht* (Kraków, 1936), p. 138.
26 Smołucha, 'Kilka uwag', pp. 415–16.
27 For the fullest accounts of the campaign, see Miechowita, *Chronica Polonorum*, 1st edn, pp. 349–50; Wapowski, *Kroniki*, pp.19–32; Czamańska, *Mołdawia i Wołoszczyzna*, pp.169–70; Smołucha, *Papiestwo a Polska*, pp. 59–69.
28 Miechowita, *Chronica Polonorum*, 1st edn, pp. 349–50.

29 Kórnik, Biblioteka Kórnicka (henceforth BK), MS 208, fol. 83r.
30 Czamańska, *Mołdawia i Wołoszczyzna*, pp. 169–72 summarizes the historiography of the campaign.
31 Miechowita, *Chronica Polonorum*, 2nd edn, pp. 350; Wapowski, *Kroniki*, p. 25.
32 Although Miechowita's chronicle was published in 1519, it was based on a diary of contemporary events which he had kept over twenty years: H. Barycz, 'Życie i twórczość Macieja z Miechowa', in H. Barycz, ed., *Maciej z Miechowa 1457–1523: historyk, geograf, lekarz, organizator naukowy* (Wrocław-Warsaw, 1960), pp. 15–74.
33 Miechowita, *Chronica Polonorum*, 1st edn, p. 349; Jan of Komorowa, *Memoriales ordinis Fratrum Minorum Fr. Ioannes de Komorowo compilatum*, ed. X. Liske and A. Lorkiewicz, Monumenta Poloniae Historica 5 (Lwów, 1888), p. 267.
34 Miechowita, *Chronica Polonorum*, 1st edn, p. 349.
35 M. Sanudo, *I Diarii di Marino Sanudo*, ed. F. Stefani, 1 (Venice, 1879), pp. 756, 800, 845.
36 Z. Spieralski, 'Po klęsce bukowińskiej 1497 roku: pierwsze najazdy tureckie na Polskę', *Studia i materiały do historii wojskowości* 9 (1963), 45–58; Wapowski, *Kroniki*, p. 33.
37 O. Gòrka, 'Nieznany żywot Bajezida II', *Kwartalnik Historyczny* 52 (1938), 375–427.
38 Miechowita, *Chronica Polonorum*, 2nd edn, p. 353.
39 Jan of Komorowo, *Memoriales*, pp. 273–4.
40 Smołucha, *Papiestwo a Polska*, p. 70; Wapowski, *Kroniki*, p. 35; Miechowita, *Chronica Polonorum*, 2nd edn, p. 353.
41 Jan of Komorowo, *Memoriales*, p. 275.
42 The text of the treaty (13 July 1498) is given in J. Garbacik, ed., *Materiały do dziejów dyplomacji polskiej z lat 1486–1516 (Kodeks Zagrebski)* (Wrocław, 1986), no. 19, pp. 49–55.
43 K. Baczkowski, 'Działaność polsko-węgierskiej dyplomacji w Rzeszy Niemieckiej w latach 1498–1500', *Studia Historyczne* 20 (1977), 517–40.
44 *Materiały do dziejów*, no. 18, p. 47.
45 *Codex Epistolaris* 3, no. 430, pp. 451–2.
46 Callimachus, *Ad Innocentium VIII de Bello Turcis Inferendo Oratio*, ed. T. Kowalewski (Warsaw 1964), pp. 58–65 (henceforth *De Bello Turcis Inferendo*).
47 Spieralski, 'Po klęsce', p. 55.
48 Papée, *Jan Olbracht*, pp. 172–3.
49 Baczkowski, 'Działalność polsko-węgierskiej dyplomacji', p. 523.
50 *Materiały do dziejów*, no. 24, p. 64.
51 *Materiały do dziejów*, no. 27, p. 81.
52 Vatican City, Archivio Segreto Vaticano (henceforth ASV), Archivio Consistorialis, Acta Miscellanea 6, fol. 106r.
53 Setton, *The Papacy and the Levant* 2, pp. 516–24.
54 Smołucha, *Papiestwo a polska*, p. 79.
55 K. Baczkowski, 'Próby włączenia państw Jagiellońskich do koalicji antytureckiej przez Papieża Aleksandra VI na przełomie XV/XVI wieku', *Nasza Przeszłość* 81 (Kraków, 1994), pp. 5–49, at p. 27.
56 The text of the bull is given in J. Burchard, *Liber Notarium*, ed. E. Celani, 2 (Città di Castello, 1907–13), *Rerum Italicarum Scriptores*, pp. 220–4. See also L. Pastor, *History of the Popes*, vol. 6 (London, 1956), p. 90.

57   The first bull is published in *Codex Epistolaris* 3, no. 458, pp. 478–82. The second is found in ASV, Arm. 32, vol. 21, fols. 131v–134v.
58   Miechowita, *Chronica Polonorum*, 2nd edn, p. 353. On May 30, Golfus received seventy gold pieces from the Camera Apostolica to cover the costs of his journey: ASV, Camera Apostolica, Diversa Cameralia, vol. 53, fol. 116r.
59   Warsaw, Archiwum Główne Akt Dawnych, Metryka Koronna (henceforth AGAD, MK), vol. 17, fols 218r–220r.
60   Jan of Komorowo, *Memoriales*, pp. 285–6.
61   Miechowita, *Chronica Polonorum*, 2nd edn, p. 348. Miechowita recalled Capistrano's prophecy, that the Turk would ride his horses around Kraków unless the populace turned from their sins.
62   Sanudo, *I Diarii* 2, pp. 118, 883, 1163–4, 1550.
63   BK, MS 207, fols 43v–44r.
64   For the letters pertaining to this dispute, see BK, MS 207, fols 47r–49r.
65   Baczkowski, 'Proby włączenia', pp. 39, 45. The truce was concluded in July.
66   Sanudo, *I Diarii* 2, pp. 1536–7.
67   Sanudo, *I Diarii* 2, pp. 1163–4.
68   F. Papée, *Aleksander Jagiellończyk* (Kraków, 2nd edn 1999), pp. 35–45.
69   *Codex Epistolaris* 3, no. 455, p. 472.
70   The tract, traditionally and erroneously attributed to Callimachus, is published in *Acta Tomiciana*, ed. T. Działyński, 1 (Kórnik, 1852), app. 4, pp. 15–16, and discussed by Baczkowski, 'Próby włączenia państw', p. 30.
71   AGAD, MK 17, fol. 299r.
72   F. Papée, ed., *Akta Aleksandra* (Kraków, 1927), no. 1, pp. 1–2.
73   *Akta Aleksandra*, no. 13, p. 13.
74   H. Rybus, *Kardynał-Królewicz Fryderyk Jagiellończyk* (Warsaw, 1935), pp. 160–1.
75   Isvagli had been appointed legate at the consistory of 5 October 1500: ASV, Archivio Consistorialis, Acta. Misc. 3, fol. 11v.
76   *Akta Aleksandra*, no. 35, pp. 32–4.
77   *Akta Aleksandra*, no. 41, pp. 39–40. King Aleksander later wrote to Rome in 1501, roundly defending his brother against Golfus's allegations: BK, MS 207, fols 48v–49r.
78   For example, J. Garbacik, 'Problem turecki w polityce państw europejskich na przełomie XV i XVI wieku', in *VIII Powszechny zjazd historyków polskich: historia Polski od połowy XV do połowy XVIII wieku* (Warsaw, 1960), pp. 36–60.
79   Callimachus, a member of Pomponius Leta's Roman Academy, fled to Poland from Rome in 1468, entering the service of King Kazimierz IV as diplomat and tutor: see J. Garbacik, *Kallimach jako dyplomata i polityk* (Kraków, 1948); R. J. Palermo, 'The Roman Academy, the Catacombs and the Conspiracy of 1468', *Archivum Historiae Pontificae* 18 (1960), 117–55.
80   Callimachus, *De Bello Turcis Inferendo*.
81   Miechowita, *Chronica Polonorum*, 2nd edn, p. 352.
82   W. Lunt, *Financial Relations of the Papacy with England, 1327–1534* (Cambridge, Mass., 1962), pp. 152–6.
83   BK, MS 207, fols 44r–45v, 46v–47r.
84   The letter is now lost, but is referred to by M. Sanudo, *I Diarii* 3, p. 655.
85   A. Theiner, ed., *Vetera monumenta Poloniae et Lithuaniae gentiumque finitimarum historiam illustrantia*, 2 (Rome, 1861), no. 297, pp. 269–76.

86 D. Piwowarczyk, *Obyczaj rycerseki w Polsce późnośredniowiecznej* (Warsaw, 1998), pp. 10–11.
87 J. Wyrozumski, *Kazimierz Wielki* (Wrocław, 1982), pp. 71–99; N. Housley, *The Later Crusades 1274–1580: From Lyons to Alcazar* (Oxford, 1992), pp. 346–7.
88 Piwowarczyk, *Obyczaj rycerski*, pp. 31–4.
89 B. Stachoń, *Polityka polska wobec Turcji i akcji antytureckiej w wieku XV do utraty Kilii i Białogrodu (1484)* (Lwów, 1930), pp. 95–105.
90 For an account of Polish–Hungarian relations in the time of Matthias Corvinus, see J. Górski, 'Dyplomacja polska czasów Kazimierza Jagiellończyka, część 2: lata konfliktów, 1466–92', in M. Biskup and K. Górski, eds, *Kazimierz Jagiellończyk* (Warsaw, 1983), pp. 230–84.
91 Housley, *The Later Crusades*, pp. 355, 362.
92 Górski, 'Dyplomacja polska'.
93 J. Ostroróg, *De Monumenta Reipublica*, ed. T. Wierzbowski (Warsaw, 1891).
94 *Materiały do dziejów*, nos 8–12, pp. 17–25.
95 N. Housley, *Documents on the Later Crusades, 1274–1580* (Basingstoke, 1996), no. 53, pp. 165–8; *Vetera Monumenta*, no. 297, pp. 269–76.
96 *Vetera Monumenta*, no. 297, p. 272.
97 Ostroróg, *De Monumenta*, p. 9.
98 BK, MS 207, fol. 43v.
99 BK, MS 207, fol. 44v.
100 Jan of Komorowo, *Memoriales*, p. 285.
101 Housley, *The Later Crusades*, p. 421.
102 Smołucha, *Papiestwo a Polska*, pp. 101–210; H.D. Wojtyska, 'Początki kultu i procesy kanonizacyjne Św. Kazimierza', *Analecta Cracoviensia* 16 (1984), 187–231.
103 W. Dworzaczek W., 'Jan Łaski', *Polski Słownik Biograficzny* 18 (Warsaw, 1978), pp. 229–37.
104 Miechowita, *Chronica Polonorum*, 2nd edn, p. 352.

10 The Hospitallers at Rhodes and the Ottoman Turks

1 Cf. A. Luttrell, 'The Hospitallers of Rhodes confront the Turks: 1306–1421', in *Christians, Jews and other Worlds. Patterns of Conflict and Accommodation*, ed. P. F. Gallagher (Lanham, MD, 1988), p. 82; idem, 'The Military and Naval Organization of the Hospitallers at Rhodes: 1310–1444', in *Das Kriegswesen der Ritterorden im Mittelalter: Ordines militares*, ed. Z. H. Novak (Turin, 1991), pp. 133–53. There are a number of general accounts of the Hospitallers at Rhodes. See A. Luttrell, 'The Hospitallers at Rhodes, 1306–1421', in *A History of the Crusades, Volume III, The Fourteenth and Fifteenth Centuries*, gen. ed. K. M. Setton (Madison, 1975), pp. 278–313; E. Rossi, 'The Hospitallers at Rhodes, 1421–1523', in ibid., pp. 314–39 ; E. Rossi, *Storia della Marina dell'Ordine di Gerusalemme di Rodi e di Malta* (Rome, 1926); J.-C. Poutiers, *Rhodes et ses chevaliers. 1306–1523* (Beirut, 1989); N. Vatin, *L'Ordre de Saint-Jean-de-Jérusalem, l'Empire ottoman et la Méditerranée orientale entre les deux sièges de Rhodes (1480–1522)* (Paris, 1994); idem, *Rhodes et l'ordre de Saint-Jean-de-Jérusalem* (Paris, 2000). Mention should be made of the numerous

studies of A. Luttrell, many of which are available in the collections which
have been published by Variorum Reprints: *The Hospitallers in Cyprus, Rhodes,
Greece and the West, 1291–1440* (London, 1978); *Latins, Greece, the Hospitallers
and the Crusade, 1291–1440* (London, 1982); *The Hospitallers of Rhodes and their
Mediterranean World* (London, 1992); *The Hospitaller State on Rhodes and its
Western Provinces, 1306–1462* (Aldershot, 1999). For a synthesis on the crusade
in the thirteenth to sixteenth centuries, see N. Housley, *The Later Crusades,
1274–1580. From Lyons to Alcazar* (Oxford, 1992).

2 On these issues (the conquest of Rhodes, the unpopularity of the Order and its
propaganda), see J. Riley-Smith, *The Knights of St John in Jerusalem and Cyprus. c.
1050–1310* (London, 1967), pp. 200 ff., 218 ff.; S. Menache, 'The Hospitallers
during Clement V's Pontificate: the Spoiled Sons of the Papacy?', in *The
Military Orders. Vol. 2, Welfare and Warfare*, ed. H. Nicholson (Aldershot, 1998),
pp.153–62; A. Luttrell, 'Gli Ospitalieri e l'eredità dei Templari', in *I Templari:
Mito e storia. Atti del Convegno Internazionale di Studi alla Magione Templare du
Poggibonsi (Siena 29–31 maggio 1987)*, ed. G. Minnucci and F. Sardi (Siena,
1989), pp. 67–86; idem, 'Papauté et Hôpital: l'enquête de 1373', in *L'enquête
pontificale de 1373 sur l'Ordre des Hospitaliers de Saint-Jean-de-Jérusalem, Volume
I, L'enquête dans le prieuré de France*, ed. A.-M. Legras (Paris, 1987), pp. 3–42; H.
Nicholson, *Templars, Hospitallers and Teutonic Knights. Images of the Military
Orders, 1128–1291* (Leicester, 1995); M. Dupuy, 'An Island Called Rhodes and
the "Way" to Jerusalem: Change and Continuity in Hospitaller *Exordia* in the
Later Middle Ages', in *The Military Orders*, ed. Nicholson, pp. 343–8; A. Calvet,
Les légendes de l'Hôpital de Saint-Jean-de-Jérusalem (Paris, 2000).

3 On this, see, in addition to the works cited in note 1 above, Z. Tsirpanlis,
'Filikes scheseis tôn ippotôn tês Rodou me tous Tourkous kata ton 15on ai.', in
idem, *Ê Rodos kai oi noties Sporades sta chronia tôn Iôannitôn ippotôn (14os-16os
ai.)* (Rhodes, 1991), pp. 46–63 ('Friendly relations of the knights of Rhodes with
the Turks during the 15th century' in *Rhodes and the southern Sporades in the
years of the Knights of St John (14th–16th century)*); R. Valentini, 'L'Egeo dopo la
caduta di Costantinopoli nelle relazioni dei Gran Maestri di Rodi', in *Bullettino
dell'Istituto Storico Italiano per il Medio Evo e Archivio Muratoriano* 51 (1936),
137–68; E. Zacharadiou, *Trade and Crusade. Venetian Crete and the Emirates of
Menteshe and Aydin (1300–1415)* (Venice, 1983); A. Luttrell, 'The Earliest
Documents on the Hospitaller *Corso* at Rhodes: 1413 and 1416', in
Mediterranean Historical Review 10 (1995), 177–88.

4 For what follows see Vatin, *L'Ordre*.

5 There is a large bibliography on Djem. In addition to several chapters in Vatin,
L'Ordre, one should mention L. Thuasne, *Djem-Sultan* (Paris, 1892); J. Lefort,
*Documents grecs dans les archives de Topkapi Sarayi. Contribution à l'histoire de
Cem Sultan* (Ankara, 1981); N. Vatin, *Sultan Djem. Un prince ottoman dans
l'Europe du XVe siècle* (Ankara, 1997); idem, 'L'affaire Djem (1481–1495)', in
Le banquet du faisan, 1454: L'Occident face au défi de l'Empire ottoman, ed.
M.-T. Caron and D. Clauzel (Arras, 1997), pp. 85–96.

6 For an Ottoman view of the siege of Rhodes in 1522, see N. Vatin, 'La conquête
de Rhodes', in *Soliman le Magnifique et son temps*, ed. G. Veinstein (Paris, 1992),
pp. 435–54.

7   See Vatin, *L'Ordre*, pp. 149–50. It appears that Mehmed II actually had designs on Egypt.

8   On Caoursin and his work, see Vatin, *Sultan Djem*, pp. 89 ff.

9   See G. Grasso, *Documenti riguardanti la costituzione di una lega contro il Turco nel 1481* (Genoa, 1880) (extracted from *Giornale Ligustico*). The Genoese were unable to implement this project alone and they abandoned it once they believed Bayezid II had secured his grip on the throne.

10 On these earthquakes, see N. Vatin, 'Les tremblements de terre à Rhodes en 1481 et leur historien, Guillaume Caoursin', in *Natural Disasters in the Ottoman Empire*, ed. E. Zachariadou (Rethymnon, 1999), pp. 153–84.

11 On this matter, see the Archives of the Order of Malta (AOM), Royal Malta Library 76-66 v°; G. Bosio, *Dell'Istoria della sacra Religione et illustrissima Militia di San Giovanni Gierosolimitano* (Rome, 1594–1602), II, pp. 350 ff.

12 Caoursin, *Opera* (Ulm, 1496), c 2 v°; reproduced and translated into French in Vatin, 'Les tremblements de terre', pp. 183 ff.

13 Caoursin, *Opera*, c 4 r°.

14 See Thuasne, *Djem-Sultan*, pp. 68–70, and his appendix I, pp. 391–8. The letter from the grand master to the pope dated 31 July 1482 was published in S. Paoli, *Codice diplomatico del Sacro Militare Ordine Gerosolimitano oggi di Malta* (Lucca, 1737), II, pp. 411–13 (cf. p. 412).

15 On what follows see Vatin, *L'Ordre*, pp. 255 ff.

16 AOM 78-152 r°–153 r°.

17 AOM 79-14 r°.

18 On this operation, see N. Vatin, 'Le siège de Mytilène (1501)', in *Turcica* 21–3 (1992), 437–59.

19 The grand master associated the Venetian captain-general Benedetto da Cha' da Pesaro with his reflection.

20 AOM 79-44 r°–v°.

21 Vatin, *L'Ordre*, p. 266.

22 Letter to the pope dated 18 August 1502, AOM 79-84 r°–v°.

23 See Vatin, *L'Ordre*, pp. 273 ff.

24 See Vatin, *L'Ordre*, pp. 311–15 ff.

25 See J.-L. Bacqué-Grammont, *Les Ottomans, les Séfévides et leurs voisins* (Leiden, 1987), pp. 140–5; E. Rossi, 'Le Relazioni tra la Persia e l'ordine di San Giovanni a Rodi e Malta', *Rivista degli studi orientali* 13 (1932); Vatin, *L'Ordre*, pp. 314–16. On Leo X's crusade projects see K. M. Setton, *The Papacy and the Levant (1204–1571), Volume III, The Sixteenth Century to the Reign of Julius III* (Philadelphia, 1984), pp. 142–97.

26 See Vatin, *L'Ordre*, pp. 316 ff.

27 Letter to the doge of Venice dated 1 September 1510, in Sanudo, *Diarii* XI, ed. R. Fulin (Venice, 1884), cols. 570 ff.

28 Vatin, *L'Ordre*, pp. 319–23.

29 On this point, see A. Luttrell, 'Rhodes and Jérusalem, 1291–1411', in *Byzantinische Forschungen* 12 (1987), 189–207. Dupuy maintains ('An Island Called Rhodes', pp. 343 and 346) that even in the fifteenth century, the Hospitallers saw Rhodes as a staging post on the way back to the Holy Land. On the survival of the ideal of recovering the holy places, the seizure of Constantinople as a preliminary to it, and the operation of Christian

leagues with other objectives than that of Jerusalem, see Housley, *Later Crusades*, pp. 45–8.

30 AOM 76- 137 v°–138 v°; letters dated 27 September and 20 November 1482 published by Paoli, *Codice diplomatico*, II, pp. 415–16 and 416–17. The first pointed out that he was engaged in conflict with Venice and the Holy See, while the second swore that if the other Christian princes intervened, then so would he.

31 Caoursin, *Mémoire ... sur le très célèbre pacte conclu par les Rhodiens avec le roi des Turcs, Bajazet*, in his *Opera* (Ulm, 1496), c 5 r°, translated in Vatin, *Sultan Djem*, p. 305.

32 See Thuasne, *Djem-Sultan*, p. 397.

33 See Vatin, *L'Ordre*, pp. 163 ff.

34 Ibid., pp. 156 ff.

35 Ibid., pp. 232–6.

36 Ibid., pp. 241 ff.

37 On the following, see Vatin, 'Le siège de Mitylène', and *L'Ordre*, pp. 256 ff.

38 Cf. Luttrell, 'The Military and Naval Organization', p. 147: 'In reality, the Hospital could manage little more than the defence of its own islands, some limited resistance to the Mamluks and Turks, and occasional participation in Latin crusading expeditions.' This conclusion applies even more strongly to the period that we are dealing with here.

39 Caoursin, *Mémoire ... sur le très célèbre pacte*, in his *Opera*, e 7 v°, trans. Vatin, *Sultan Djem*, pp. 310–11.

40 This argument was perfectly plausible, since the pope authorized the grand master to make peace and trade with the 'Turks' and the 'Moors' 'given that there was no other way to sustain the population of Rhodes, because of the destruction caused by the earthquakes': Paoli, *Codice diplomatico*, II, p. 405 (letter from the cardinal-chamberlain, 2 July 1482).

41 See Vatin, *Sultan Djem*, p. 94.

42 *Reiecto omni tributo ac annuo munere et annua ambaxiata quibus oratores nullo pacto possint assentire*: AOM 76–112 v°.

43 Caoursin, *Mémoire ... sur le très célèbre pacte*, in his *Opera*, e 7 v°, trans. Vatin, *Sultan Djem*, p. 311.

44 Caoursin, *Discours ... sur l'envoi du roi Zizime en Gaule*, in his *Opera*, f 5 v°, trans. Vatin, *Sultan Djem*, p. 330.

45 Ibid., p. 329.

46 See Vatin, *L'Ordre*, pp. 193–7. In 1487 the grand master tried without success to obtain from the sultan a letter confirming that it was at his request that an Ottoman fleet had been disarmed: Lefort, *Documents grecs*, docs 15 and 17, pp. 79 ff., 87 ff.

47 Vatin, *L'Ordre*, p. 233.

48 Ibid., pp. 248–54.

49 On the Rhodian *corso* between 1481 and 1522, see ibid., pp. 88–93, 117–25, 184–7, 294–306.

50 Ibid., pp. 329–33.

51 An agreement with the Ottomans dated 1410 appears to have prohibited the corsairs of Rhodes access to the Dardanelles and the Sea of Marmara: Luttrell, 'The Earliest Documents'. There is a summary of our knowledge of the waters that were protected from piracy before 1481 in Vatin, *Rhodes et l'ordre de Saint-Jean*, p. 39.

52   See Vatin, *L'Ordre*, pp. 137–43.

53   Occasionally, merchants exerted pressure on the Council to adopt a peaceful stance towards the Order's Muslim neighbours: Vatin, *L'Ordre*, p. 289.

54   L. Alessandro, 'Lettere inedite di Fra Sabba da Castiglione', in *Archivio Storico Lombardo*, 2nd ser. 13 (1886), 91–112, at p. 100.

55   Svatopluk Soucek, 'A Czech Nobleman's Pilgrimage to the Holy Land', in *Journal of Turkish Studies* 8 (1984), 233–40, at pp. 238 ff.

56   Fra Francesco Suriano, *Treatise on the Holy Land*, trans. T. Bellorini and E. Hoade (Jerusalem, 1949), p. 238.

57   Ibid., p. 45.

58   M. Fontenay, 'Corsaires de la foi ou rentiers du sol? Les Chevaliers de Malte dans le *corso* méditerranéen au XVIIe siècle', *Revue d'Histoire Moderne et Contemporaine* 35 (1988), 361–84.

59   Vatin, *L'Ordre*, pp. 53 ff. At the start of the fifteenth century, the Order had attempted to negotiate with the Mamluk state to assume a more prominent role in the protection of pilgrims at their destinations. See Luttrell, 'Rhodes and Jerusalem, 1191–1411'.

60   Nicholson, *Templars, Hospitallers and Teutonic Knights*, pp. 120 ff.

61   Luttrell, 'The Hospitallers of Rhodes confront the Turks', p. 97.

62   Vatin, *L'Ordre*, p. 171.

63   See Luttrell, 'The Hospitallers confront the Turks', p. 102.

64   Their existence is attested by a document in the Order's archives dated 1513: A. Luttrell, 'The Later History of the Maussoleion and its Utilization in the Hospitaller Castle at Bodrum', in *The Maussoleion at Halikarnassos, vol. II, The Written Sources and their Archaeological Background* (Hajbjerg, 1986), pp. 115–214, at pp. 164, 165, 189.

65   See Vatin, *L'Ordre*, p. 21.

66   See Luttrell, 'The Hospitallers confront the Turks', p. 103.

67   AOM 393-155 r°–v°. Prominent amongst the arguments that the grand master presented to the pope in a letter dated 3 January 1483 to justify making peace with the sultan was 'the liberty of the fortress of St Peter in Turkey', 'where by ancient custom captives who manage to escape from the tyrant's yoke come in search of refuge in full security': Paoli, *Codice diplomatico*, II, p. 431.

68   Naturally enough, the Hospitallers' presence at Rhodes was useful to the Christians in the West for other reasons, above all because Rhodes offered a flourishing market and an outpost both for commerce and for spying along a substantial stretch of the Anatolian littoral. But developing these points further would entail digressing from this volume's theme.

69   A. Luttrell, 'The Hospitallers of Rhodes: Prospectives, Problems, Possibilities', in *Die geistlichen Ritterorden Europas*, ed. J. Fleckenstein and M. Hellmann (Sigmaringen, 1980), pp. 243–66, at p. 252.

70   Sanudo, *Diarii* III, ed. R. Fulin (Venice, 1880), col. 1438 (letter of the Venetian orator at Rome dated 15 February 1501).

11   Reconquista and Crusade in Fifteenth-Century Spain

1   Useful surveys and discussions of the nature of the *Reconquista* are to be found in P. Linehan, *History and the Historians of Medieval Spain* (Oxford, 1993), pp. 1–21, and J. F. O'Callaghan, *Reconquest and Crusade in Medieval*

Spain (Philadelphia, 2003), pp. 3–22. See also N. Housley, *The Later Crusades, 1274–1580: from Lyons to Alcazar* (Oxford, 1992), pp. 267–304.

2   D.W. Lomax, *The Reconquest of Spain* (London, 1978), pp. 35–93, 112–66; O'Callaghan, *Reconquest and Crusade*, pp. 23–123.

3   J. Salarrullana and E. Ibarra, eds, *Documentos correspondientes al reinado de Sancho Ramírez*, 2 vols (Zaragoza, 1904–13), vol. 1, pp. 187–9, cited in O'Callaghan, *Reconquest and Crusade*, p. 8.

4   *Primera crónica general*, ed. A. Zamora Vicente (Madrid, 1946), vol. 2, pp. 772–3, cited in O'Callaghan, *Reconquest and Crusade*, p. 7.

5   Alexander II, *Epistolae, Patrologia Latina*, 146: 1386–7, cited in O'Callaghan, *Reconquest and Crusade*, p. 25.

6   O'Callaghan, *Reconquest and Crusade*, p. 26.

7   Ibid., pp. 26–32.

8   J. Goñi Gaztambide, *Historia de la bula de la cruzada en España* (Vitoria, 1958), p. 336.

9   For a magisterial survey of the diplomatic and military history of this period, see P. E. Russell, *The English Intervention in Spain and Portugal in the Time of Edward III and Richard II* (Oxford, 1955).

10   Goñi Gaztambide, *Historia de la bula*, pp. 336–41.

11   M. A. Ladero Quesada, *Las guerras de Granada en el siglo XV* (Barcelona, 2002), pp. 23–7.

12   Goñi Gaztambide, *Historia de la bula*, pp. 342–7.

13   Alonso de Cartagena, *De preeminentia*, Madrid, Biblioteca Nacional, MS 9262, fols 8-25r; L. F. Gallardo, *Alonso de Cartagena. Una biografía política en la Castilla del siglo XV* (Valladolid, 2002), pp. 138–58, especially p. 156.

14   Goñi Gaztambide, *Historia de la bula*, pp. 351–4.

15   Alfonso de Palencia, *Gesta hispaniensia ex annalibus suorum dierum collecta*, ed. and Spanish trans. B. Tate and J. Lawrance, 1 (Madrid, 1998), pp. 109–13.

16   J. Le Goff, *La naissance du Purgatoire* (Paris, 1981), pp. 319–479, especially pp. 472–7.

17   Cited in Goñi Gaztambide, *Historia de la bula*, p. 361.

18   Mosén Diego de Valera, *Memorial de diversas hazañas, Biblioteca de Autores Españoles*, 70, p. 15.

19   Goñi Gaztambide, *Historia de la bula*, pp. 358–68.

20   Ibid., pp. 371–8.

21   Cited in ibid., pp. 380–1.

22   Ibid., pp. 381–92; M. A. Ladero Quesada, *Castilla y la conquista del reino de Granada*, 2nd edn (Granada, 1988), pp. 203–4.

23   Ladero, *Castilla y la conquista*, pp. 207–13.

24   A. Ryder, *Alfonso the Magnanimous, King of Aragon, Naples, and Sicily, 1396–1458* (Oxford, 1990), pp. 290–5, 409–17.

25   Goñi Gaztambide, *Historia de la bula*, pp. 404–36; J. M. Nieto Soria, *Iglesia y génesis del estado moderno en Castilla (1369–1480)* (Madrid, 1993), pp. 328–35.

26   Cited in Goñi Gaztambide, *Historia de la bula*, pp. 341–2.

27   Ladero, *Castilla y la conquista*, pp. 145–6; E. Benito Ruano, 'Un cruzado inglés en la guerra de Granada' and 'Extranjeros en la guerra de Granada', in Benito, *Gente del siglo XV* (Madrid, 1998), pp. 149–204; C. Varela, *Ingleses en España y Portugal (1480–1515). Aristócratas, mercaderes e impostores* (Lisbon, 1998),

pp. 107–30; J. Edwards, *The Spain of the Catholic Monarchs, 1474–1520* (Oxford, 2000), pp. 122–7.

28 J. D. Rodríguez Velasco, *El debate sobre la caballería en el siglo XV. La tratadística caballeresca castellana en el marco europeo* (Salamanca, 1996).

29 E. Benito Ruano, *Los infantes de Aragón*, 2nd edn (Madrid, 2002), p. 49.

30 P. Rodríguez de Lena, *Libro del Passo Honroso defendido por el excelente caballero Suero de Quiñones*, ed. A. Labandera Fernández (Madrid, 1977).

31 Benito Ruano, *Los infantes de Aragón*, pp. 50–2.

32 Palencia, *Gesta hispaniensia*, ed. Tate and Lawrance, vols 1 and 2, passim.

33 Hernando del Pulgar, *Claros varones de Castilla*, ed. R. B. Tate (Madrid, 1985), p. 99.

34 A. Fernández de Córdova Miralles, *La Corte de Isabel I. Ritos y ceremonias de una reina (1474–1504)* (Madrid, 2002), pp. 344–55.

35 Fernández de Córdova, *La Corte*, p. 83; F. Javier Sánchez Cantón, *Libros, tapices y cuadros que coleccionó Isabel la Católica* (Madrid, 1950), pp. 23–4; I. Michael, ' "From her shall read the perfect ways of honour": Isabel of Castile and Chivalric Romance', in *The Age of the Catholic Monarchs, 1474–1516. Literary Studies in Memory of Keith Whinnom*, ed. A. Deyermond and I. Macpherson (Liverpool, 1989), pp. 103–12.

36 A. MacKay, 'The Ballad and the Frontier in Late Medieval Spain', *Bulletin of Hispanic Studies* 53 (1976), pp. 15–33; R. Wright, *Spanish Ballads*, 3rd edn and trans. (Warminster, 1992), pp. 100–23; Ladero, *Las guerras de Granada*, pp. 75–81; P. M. Cátedra, *La historiografía en verso en la época de los Reyes Católicos. Juan Barba y su 'Consolatoria de Castilla'* (Salamanca, 1989).

37 J. García Oro, 'La reforma de las órdenes religiosas en los siglos XV y XVI', in *Historia de la Iglesia en España*, vol. 3 pt 1, *La Iglesia en la España de los siglos XV y XVI*, ed. J. L. González Novalín (Madrid, 1980), pp. 253–63; Edwards, *Spain of the Catholic Monarchs*, pp. 216–17.

38 J. Edwards, 'Bishop Juan Arias Dávila of Segovia: "Judaizer" or reformer?' in Edwards, *Religion and Society in Spain, c. 1492* (Aldershot, 1996), study no. X.

39 J. García Oro, *Cisneros, el cardenal de España* (Barcelona, 2002), pp. 185–209; E. Rummel, *Jiménez de Cisneros, on the Threshold of Spain's Golden Age* (Tempe, Arizona, 1999), pp. 35–42.

40 Pedro Mártir de Anglería, *Epistolario*, ed. and trans. J. López de Toro (Madrid, 1953), p. 171.

41 For resistance to military service after 1492, see J. Edwards, 'The morality of taxation: the burden of war on Córdoba and Jerez de la Frontera, 1480–1515', *Meridies. Revista de Historia Medieval* 2 (1997), pp. 109–20 and 'A society organized for war? Córdoba in the time of Ferdinand and Isabella', in *Jews, Muslims and Christians in and around the Crown of Aragon. Essays in Honour of Professor Elena Lourie*, ed. H. J. Hames (Leiden, 2004), pp. 75–96.

Index

The following abbreviations are used:
a = archbishop [of]
b = bishop [of]
c = count [of]
d = duke [of]
e = emperor
k = king [of]
OT = [in] Old Testament
p = pope
q = queen [of]
s = sultan

All individuals except rulers are listed under their last name, unless they lived before c. 1300. When variant names are used the first to occur is listed and the alternative is cross-referenced. Written works are listed under authors when known. Entries are given letter by letter.